Contents

The French Revolution and the People

David Andress

Hambledon and London
London and New York

Hambledon and London

102 Gloucester Avenue
London, NW1 8HX

175 Fifth Avenue
New York
NY 10010

First Published 2004

ISBN 978-1-85285-540-6

Copyright © David Andress 2004

A description of this book is available from the
British Library and from the Library of Congress.

Typeset by Carnegie Publishing, Lancaster,
and printed in Great Britain by Biddles Ltd.

Distributed in the United States and Canada
exclusively by Palgrave Macmillan,
a division of St Martin's Press.

Illustrations

Acknowledgements

Thanks go firstly to Tony Morris, for encouraging me to take up this project, and to Gwynne Lewis for bringing me to his attention. Thanks also to Martin Sheppard for his sharp editorial eye. Alan Forrest has been a constant source of support and encouragement throughout my writing career, and once again provided some very useful feedback on a draft of this text. Colin Jones, to whom I owe similar debts, was also kind enough to be what I can only call supportively scathing about some of the assumptions I had allowed to creep into earlier drafts.

I should also like to thank colleagues at Portsmouth for helping to provide the atmosphere conducive to productive work. Brad Beaven in particular has been a constant source of reviving conversation and good fellowship. I must also pay tribute to the late Professor Robbie Gray, who passed away while this project was under way. A fine man and a fine scholar, he had been supportive of many aspects of my work since I came to Portsmouth in 1994, and he continues to be sorely missed by all who knew him.

My wife Jessica will I hope forgive me for not dedicating this book to her – she has had two already, richly deserved, and it is someone else's turn. I dedicate it firstly to my parents, Hylda and Robert. They raised me right, living in the love of the common people (the words of a song that made me cry once, when I was very small, if they remember ...) They also never asked any questions about why I wanted to study history, or to become an historian. They were just always there.

I dedicate it also to my daughter, Emily, who arrived to light our lives when I was deep in the study of the grim realities of eighteenth-century mortality. An emergency caesarian section was an important reminder that, the argument of this book notwithstanding, we have good reason to give heartfelt thanks for at least some kinds of progress. And finally to my newest daughter, Natalie, whose entirely natural arrival, on 15 July 2003, was just in time to reach these pages.

To what extent was the French Revolution a mass movement which resulted in significant societal and political changes btw 1789 + 1793?
- Causation + consequences of a change in regime during 1789 - 1793
- Compare + contrast roles played by 2 different grps or individuals during revolution
+ appraise the main changes to society + politics in France during this period

Introduction

This is a book about the common people of France, how they lived in the closing decades of the eighteenth century, and how they experienced the series of events from 1789 to which we give the label 'French Revolution'. It is about how ordinary working folk in town and countryside helped to create a revolutionary upheaval, how they continued to struggle for their own goals amidst the massive processes of change that had been unleashed, and how such people became both participants in, and victims of, the divisions, tensions and outright conflicts of revolutionary France.

In 1789 the French people engaged in the first mass-based social revolution in European history. There had been great episodes of civil strife across Europe before – the Dutch Revolt of the sixteenth century, the English Civil War and French Frondes of the 1640s and 1650s – but nothing like the French Revolution. Previous conflicts emerged either from the grievances of relatively well-defined elites, or were cloaked under the banners of religion. In France from 1789 there was an attempt to turn society upside-down, with an impetus that came from the real social grievances of every town and village in the kingdom. Just as the Protestant Reformation had inaugurated an era of religious wars that lasted over a century, so the French Revolution ushered in an age of social upheaval. Never again would ruling classes and elites be able confidently to dismiss the common people, of France or any other nation, as mere subjects. After this revolution the demand that everyone should be a citizen was never to go away.

To most historians looking back from the latter part of the twentieth century, that innovation was amongst the revolutionaries' greatest achievements. In immediate political terms, however, the French Revolution was a failure. A decade of conflict, both external and internecine, ended with a lapse into military dictatorship that prolonged the external war through another fifteen years, before returning the throne to the brother of the man who had held it in 1789. Internal and external struggles across that whole generation cost Europe well over a million casualties. At the time, it was the military expansionism of republican and imperial France which sowed most alarm, but it was the engagement of the common people in revolutionary politics, and especially in the sanguinary politics of the Terror, that caused the Revolution in the longer term to be viewed by many as one of the most troubling episodes of European history, at least prior to the far worse excesses of the twentieth century.

The stigmatisation of the French Revolution, and especially of the involvement in it of the common people – peasants, artisans, domestic servants, or wage-labourers – has endured throughout most of the past two hundred years. Dramatic fictional portrayals, such as Charles Dickens's *A Tale of Two Cities* and Baroness Orczy's *The Scarlet Pimpernel*, have branded the guillotine and its red-bonneted, grimy-faced disciples into public memory. The great politician and polemicist Edmund Burke, as early as 1790, wrote of 'cruel ruffians and assassins' assailing the palace of Versailles in October 1789, confronting the royal family with 'all the unutterable abominations of the furies of hell'. Eminent nineteenth-century historians queued up to reinforce these impressions. In England, Thomas Carlyle spoke of 'Victorious Anarchy' at work, while in France, after the further social trauma of the Paris Commune of 1871, Hippolyte Taine began a whole genre of anti-revolutionary rhetoric. This used a language of 'bandits', 'vagabonds', 'vagrants, tramps … thieves … the refuse of the street', and overall, 'the dregs of society' rising up to assault order and tranquillity.[1] Their leaders were 'amnestied bandits and other gallows birds', representing a rank and file with 'the instinct of savages' and 'a natural appetite for license, laziness, and ferocity'.[2]

Those who stood out against this trend tended to do so, during the nineteenth century, by idealising popular action into that of 'the People' viewed at a comfortably abstract distance, and during the twentieth century by adopting a Marxist vocabulary and perspective that in its own way was just as idealising. This focused on the supposedly progressive stance of certain groups, and the importance of perceptibly modern social classes such as wage-earners and property-owning peasants, rather than artisans, sharecroppers or migrant labourers.[3] What such researches were able to demonstrate quite conclusively, nevertheless, is that the popular actors of 1789 and after were not in any sense 'bandits' or 'vagabonds', but more usually a cross-section of a diverse and politically informed common people.[4]

Despite such necessary clarification, studies of this type also tended to disguise or at least downplay other facts. Amongst these was the unsavoury truth that the actions of such people, hardworking family folk though many might be, were very often eagerly and aggressively violent. When Simon Schama came to write *Citizens*, his 'Chronicle' of the French Revolution, which remains probably the greatest work on the subject written for a wide public in the late twentieth century, he chose to confront what he called the 'painful problem' of such unedifying events, which he saw as often being squeamishly shied away from by sheltered academics. While Schama's aim in returning the public gaze to such uncomfortable sights may have been laudable, it led him to some problematic conclusions. For Schama, 'In some depressingly unavoidable sense, violence *was* the Revolution itself'. Such violence was meted out, moreover, by popular crowds whose spine-chilling pronouncements make sensational copy – like the woman who wanted to cut off Queen Marie-Antoinette's head and '*fricasser* her liver' in October 1789 – but whose lives remain, in his writing, a mystery.[5]

Peasants and artisans do not even get a mention in Schama's index, while the entry for Marie-Antoinette covers almost half a page. This hardly seems fair, since the violence of the people is blamed for almost everything that went wrong in the 1790s – even if only brought to bear, in Schama's view, by a generation of leaders with a 'morbid preoccupation' with massacre and death, willing to dig out the 'angry matter' of popular hostility and direct it at an increasingly large number of enemies of the people.[6] Such violence, especially when it took the form of crowd attacks on individuals, lynchings, decapitations and other gruesome excesses, is easily portrayed as mere bestiality. Let us, however, place Marie-Antoinette and the working people of France in a different perspective. In 1785 the queen spent 258,002 livres on clothing and accessories.[7] After supposedly major economies in the royal household, she spent 190,721 livres in 1788. Needless to say, when she could spend this on her dresses, she wanted for nothing else.

A male Parisian labourer in these years earned around 30 sous per day, or 1.5 livres, adding up to around 300 livres annually if he was able to find work on every working day, which was far from certain. Assuming for the moment he was single, he nonetheless had to spend half this income just on bread; and in the economic crisis of 1789, this figure rose to nearer 80 per cent. A good third of the normal price of that bread was made up of duties and tolls, which were raised on goods entering the city. The amount such a labourer had left over, after rent, for 'clothing and accessories', and anything else, amounted to some 9 livres.[8] A female worker, in the laundry or needle trades, for example, earned considerably less – women's work was always inferior by contemporary definition.

The queen, meanwhile, was fond of dressing up as a peasant girl, amusing herself with acting out images of rural idyll, and indeed had a whole mock village constructed for that purpose at the Petit Trianon near Versailles (it still stands, being built of rather better materials than most cottages). A real French peasant girl, working as a farm servant in the later years of the eighteenth century, was fortunate to earn more than 30 livres in a year. Of course, she was lodged at her employer's expense, but so then was

Marie-Antoinette – all of her extravagances being met from the overstretched public purse. By 1789 those extravagances had already been publicly notorious for almost two decades. When many of the overburdened inhabitants of France were in fear of starvation – and especially of what they imagined was a deliberately plotted starvation – and the legend of Marie-Antoinette's 'Let them eat cake' was in circulation, is it really surprising that some of them contemplated a bloody revenge for her overprivileged scorn?[9]

Violence plays a great part in what is discussed in this book, but it took a multitude of forms. There was the indisputable horror of those victims singled out for popular 'justice', many of whom were guilty of no more than falling under vague suspicion through their actions or their very identities. Some of the deaths meted out to them were certainly repellent. Brutal and repellent methods of putting people to death were, however, a staple of the state's own conception of justice. Also to be considered is the 'structural violence' of an absolutist monarchy and a profoundly hierarchical society. The majority of the population were not merely poor but oppressed, overburdened with taxes, tithes and other dues payable to the social elite – mostly for no other reason than that they always had been (and sometimes for fictitious reasons invented merely to squeeze them harder). The Revolution, amongst many other things, was a long and bitter struggle, in the face of much elite resistance, to be rid of the worst of these burdens.

Social and political change throughout history is often violent, and nowhere more so than when it comes together in a revolutionary cataclysm. But lack of change is frequently violent too, either in the coercive means used to prevent change, or in the perpetuation of more general injustice and inequality. How much violence, for example, was done to the lives of peasants who saw a vast proportion of their crops handed over to the elite, while their own children, weakened by poor diet, had barely a two-thirds chance of surviving infancy? How violent were the relations between urban craftsmen and their aristocratic customers, when the latter could depute their lackeys to see off humble creditors from their doors? How violent was the economic crisis of the 1780s that struck overcrowded populations dependent on cottage-industry manufactures, leaving some with no option but to prostitute their own daughters? Oppression is not a school of virtue. The expectation that it might be reflects only a blinkered and unhistorical judgment on the lives of past actors. There is no doubt that the violence of the French Revolution was unusual, but it was also understandable as a product of its context. There can also be no doubt that many even of the poorest in France were capable of articulating their desires and aspirations in ways that encompassed, but also rose above, mere physical protest.

The common people of France lived in a violent, unjust and sometimes positively cruel world, and were all, to greater or lesser degrees, shaped by that experience. It is necessary in any study of their involvement in revolution to look at the violence thus engendered, but also to look through that violence, to its causes, contexts and aims. What is perhaps most remarkable about the events that followed the collapse of state authority in 1788–89 is that, in such a context, there was a marked absence of despair. Instead, communities and individuals took the new authorities to task, asserted their needs and desires, and attempted to build new structures of social and political relations. This led many into conflicts with what survived of the old order, and into further conflicts with new authorities and their new political visions.

Once people began to rebel, they were subject to forceful repression, forms of martial law, and summary military justice – often with the full sanction of both Old Regime and revolutionary leaderships, which were never reconciled to independent popular action, especially from the countryside. After the first months of the Revolution, politically oriented violence had often become part of the organised actions of the new state and local authorities. By that time, groups that were either explicitly counter-revolutionary, in seeking a return to unalloyed royal and aristocratic power, or anti-revolutionary, in resisting many policies of the new regime, were beginning their own violent struggles. In the general anti-revolutionary camp can be counted a significant proportion of the population as a whole, some of whom become involved in guerrilla fighting and more overt civil war. There was a constant conflict between revolution and counter-revolution, obliging the population to take sides: either positively, in mobilising for conflict for or against revolutionary institutions and innovations; or negatively, in seeking to shun engagements that were, in the eyes of the revolutionary state, compulsory for every good citizen. In such an ongoing conflict, there was for many no response that could guarantee they would not be rounded up, overrun, pillaged, conscripted or harassed. Many retreated into embittered passivity as this political landscape unfolded before them, but many others continued to strive, in the face of elite scorn, to make their voices heard.

The great and bitter irony of the Revolution is that so much of the political dictation handed down by the state and its agents was done, quite self-consciously, in the name of 'the People'. This emerged from the complexities of social and cultural evolution over the past century. France in the eighteenth century was in many respects a clearly aristocratic society, with positions of power within the state reserved almost exclusively for those of noble status. At the same time, such status was itself the goal of social aspiration, and easily obtained (at least in its outward forms) by those who had accumulated substantial wealth. The upper echelons of French society were thus a patchwork of those who had risen through legal, professional or mercantile enterprise, and those whose position was owed more directly to their blue-blooded ancestry (and who both heartily despised the newcomers, and sought to intermarry with the wealthiest of them). Beneath this wealthy elite and their families, which numbered at most some 300,000, there resided a broader swathe of non-noble propertied and professional families: a middle class in all but name, since the language of class in this sense had yet to be invented. Perhaps two to three million strong, this broad social stratum included merchants, industrialists, provincial notaries, village court judges and other legal officials – by far the largest group amongst them. They and the nobility had a near monopoly on access to secondary and higher education, and therefore to 'culture' in its elite sense. Almost all employed servants, or at least a servant, and looked down on all the other sectors of the population that were condemned, in various ways, to earn a living through physical toil.[10]

Over the course of the second half of the eighteenth century, much of this elite came to associate themselves with the values of les lumières, what we now call 'the Enlightenment'.[11] One of the many elements of this that was of particular importance by 1789 was the concept of the 'public', and of 'public opinion'. This opinion became increasingly courted by policymakers, since it was felt to represent a single tribunal that could rightfully judge political conduct. Educated readers were increasingly addressed as a public with a right to know about what had previously been the king's secret affairs, even though in practice the royal authorities had no inclination to listen to anyone who did not support their views. This was not least because public opinion, being the view of the whole public, could not be embodied by any single piece of writing or by one critical voice.[12]

By the later 1780s, the French professional, propertied and educated elites had become accustomed to thinking of themselves as the public, and in a more political register as the nation, believing that their voices spoke for the entire people. For many, the new focus on nation and people was the star that would guide them towards a new settlement. They clung to that belief resolutely throughout all that followed, claiming the right to dictate to the general population, and dismissing any contrary signs from the common people themselves as the misled products of ignorance, criminal deviance, or the actions of those who were not really part of the people at all.

This book does not claim to venture into radically new ground in portraying the lives of the rural and urban working masses of France in the 1780s and 1790s. It does, however, aim to provide a synthesis. Major works of scholarship have been devoted to some of these people, identified as Parisians, as artisans or peasants, or as 'crowds', 'sans-culottes', or the rebels of various counter-revolutionary risings. More recently, attention has been given to the experiences of the female half of the population.[13] Efforts at a general treatment of the common people as a whole have, however, largely been confined either to anecdotal versions of 'everyday life' or to slim overviews.[14] Given the vast weight of accumulated scholarship, it seems worth attempting to replace these with something more substantial. The first three chapters of this study offer an overview of the lives of working people in the 1780s, including in Chapter 3 a discussion of the paths into social marginality and revolt that followed from the precarious nature of those lives. The remainder of the book follows a chronological narrative, in which brief coverage of the political contexts (in Chapters 4 and 8) is interspersed with more detailed examination of popular attitudes and activities during the Revolution. The final chapter both addresses some of the features of French political life in the later 1790s, and offers some concluding thoughts and observations.

What follows cannot fairly be described as an uplifting tale, but it is one which should have an abiding interest. It challenges us to see violent social change and political confrontation from the perspective of the broad population, where the forces that bring people into conflict with the state, and with each other, cannot just be subsumed into metaphors of eruptions from 'below' or presented as a grotesque cavalcade of harpies. Every person who was drawn into the violence of the Revolution had their own attitudes, motives and grievances. Many of them did wicked things, many others lived in dread; some did both. Nevertheless, if one thought may be said to have been generally shared as their nation descended into revolution, it was that the old order of things had become intolerable.

The journal of the English traveller and agronomist Arthur Young records an encounter with a peasant woman as he walked up a hill in Lorraine on 12 July 1789. She told him of her poverty, and the various authorities and overlords to whom the family had to pay taxes and dues. He reported her words on the current situation, and his own observation:

> It was said, at present, *that something was to be done by some great folks for such poor ones, but she did not know who nor how,* but God send us better, *for the taxes and the feudal rights are crushing us.* This woman, at no great distance, might have been taken for sixty or seventy, her figure was so bent, and her face so furrowed and hardened by labour, – but she said she was only twenty-eight.[15]

The image this presents is shocking to a modern sensibility, as indeed it was clearly striking to Young. It is worth remembering, however, that far worse poverty and structural oppression was endured by the peasants of many countries across Europe in this period. Eastern Germany, Poland, the Balkans, and even some Mediterranean lands, saw real serfdom, with levels of restriction and brutal control that were rare exceptions in France.[16] It was not, in the end, the sheer weight of accumulated oppression that brought the French to revolution. The underlying irony of the position was that they were free enough to imagine more freedom, but oppressed enough to be willing to risk revolt, when the edifice of the state seemed to totter.

As so often in human history, reaching a state of justice proved a more vexing quest than could have been imagined at the start. When structural violence provoked violent events, that original provocation was easily forgotten, not just by later observers but by the participants in such events themselves. There can be no simple question of whether the ends justified the means, because many of the most objectionable means sprang from conflicts entirely peripheral to the original concerns of the majority, and a great deal of violence was committed against just such 'poor ones' in the name of their own liberation. In the end, there was liberation, of a sort, though at a terrible price. Whether that price was worth paying will be for the reader to judge.[17]

1

Peasants

In the eighteenth century millions of French people, like millions more elsewhere, lived and loved and suffered in a rural obscurity that was once thought to be almost impenetrable. The French peasantry, all twenty million and more of them, were almost always seen as an undifferentiated and static mass. The *paysan* was a staple figure of elite and urban caricature, dressed in a smock and clogs, brandishing an obscure farming implement, and mired, literally and figuratively, in the soil. Although the eighteenth century saw extensive elite discussions on the 'improvement' of agriculture, these rarely paid any attention to discerning what the rural population actually felt, thought or wanted. The peasants' duty of obedience to all of their supposed superiors was taken for granted, and their triple burden of dues owed to state, church and feudal lord, or *seigneur*, seemed a fixed point in the social order. In 1789 these people would mount two insurrections that would shatter such perceptions. The first was a paper insurrection, in the *cahiers de doléances* that poured out their communities' grievances at the king's request. The second was a real uprising, as the signs and instruments of social and political oppression were treated to the full force of stored up indignation and anger in the summer of that fateful year.[1]

There was, in fact, no such thing as a typical peasant in the 1780s, let alone an undifferentiated mass of peasantry. Agriculture was practised in a huge variety of environments, from the marshes of the Landes to the high slopes of the Pyrenees, from the open-field farms of the Paris basin to the remote and hedge-bounded smallholdings of the western *bocage*, from the mists of the far north to the sun-baked shores of the Mediterranean. Those who lived from agriculture sometimes dwelt in isolated farmhouses, sometimes in hamlets, or a whole variety of villages; even, in the south east, in quite substantial small towns. Their households might include servants, unmarried siblings and elderly relatives, might be a couple and their children alone, or might even be several cohabiting families in the large isolated farmsteads of the upland Auvergne.[2] All dealt with complex lives and harsh conditions, often in ways that could be starkly at odds with the view from above.

The vision of the peasantry as a mass is somewhat paradoxical in itself, since it is often observed by historians, as it was sometimes by contemporaries, that eighteenth-century France was a state with a bewilderingly complex and particularistic network of local conditions and arrangements. Boundaries of church and state districts, court jurisdictions, direct and indirect tax systems, law codes, customs and privileges ran in complete disregard of each other, to the extent that they are almost impossible to map. For example, the region known to its inhabitants as the Corbières, a rectangle about sixty kilometres by forty between Carcassonne and Perpignan, was divided between parts of three administrative *généralités*. Two Catholic dioceses covered most of the region, but two others encompassed outlying areas. Most higher judicial functions were covered by one *sénéchaussée* court, but this jurisdiction also excluded parts of the Corbières, which fell under several other courts. Tax-gathering came under yet another division of regional offices. Some outlying communities fell almost entirely under a range of authorities that had no other presence, civil, judicial or ecclesiastical, in the region. To complicate matters yet further, across this small area ten different measures of volume were in use for agricultural produce, and a remarkable fifty variations on the meaning of the term *sétérée* for area existed – the largest version being over three times the size of the smallest.[3] Any province of France could procure the same kinds of examples: maps of Anjou, or of Basse-Auvergne, show boundaries riddled with holes, enclaves of other jurisdictions, outlying associated areas – enough to drive a cartographer mad.

This apparent chaos, for the peasant majority, actually held some significant advantages. Their primary concern was not with the complexity of the wider administrative map but with the single community in which they lived. There it was usually quite clear what the structures that surrounded them were, and what tensions might exist between them. Peasant communities in the eighteenth century were adept at manipulating the various systems and structures that attempted to control their lives. Even if they could not break out from the heavy burdens imposed on them, they could use every crack and crevice of this chaotic system to resist them.

Peasants were also far from being always isolated or ignorant of the world around them. The interactions of everyday life ensured that most communities remained tied to, and to some extent concerned with, the affairs of the outside world. Many rural communities by the 1780s had become tied into the expanding field of industrial production, as commercially oriented textile spinning and weaving occupied large number of households across swathes of northern and southern France. Less industrial forms of handicraft manufacture were commonplace, generating market relations outside the individual village, even if only in the local region. Workers from some of the most isolated regions of France, such as the Auvergne and the Limousin, migrated regularly to work in the large cities, especially Paris, whence they returned with new perspectives on urban life to share with their fellows. Others migrated for seasonal agricultural work, or with herds of livestock, either to far pastures, or for sales in urban markets. On a smaller scale, weekly markets drew rural inhabitants into local urban centres regularly, as did less frequent but larger fairs. Here the exchange of news was eagerly sought, frequently facilitated by alcohol. Even within villages news found its way, via travelling pedlars, or passed in relay from village to village in the to and fro of daily life.[4]

One of the additional factors of apparent fragmentation, later used by radical revolutionaries to lambast peasant backwardness, was the fact that so many of the French did not actually speak French in their everyday lives. The southern third of the country spoke dialects of Occitan, effectively so different from 'northern' French as to be another tongue altogether – and they did not even speak one version of this, but at least six major regional varieties, each with their further local peculiarities. Within the 'French-speaking' centre and north there were again some nine identifiable regional variations. At each of the six corners of the French 'hexagon' different languages entirely were spoken: Flemish to the north, German in Alsace, Italian in Corsica, Catalan and Basque at either end of the Pyrenees, and the Celtic Breton tongue in the west of that peninsula. Such diversity should, on the face of it, have made for ignorance and parochialism. The fact that a peasant's 'native tongue' was not French did not mean, however, that he (or she) was wholly ignorant of the language, and every village had, if nothing else, its priest who could read and write, and translate for the locals' benefit when necessary.[5]

Before we conclude that the average peasant community was a vibrant and outgoing place, however, we need to record some of the grimmer and most basic aspects of individual and household life at this time. The first and last enemy, faced almost daily in some fashion or other, was death itself. It hovered over the beds in which peasant mothers gave birth: that act itself was a significant cause of female deaths. A third or more of all women would experience the trauma of stillbirth, which was the fate of up to one in twenty of all births. The fear of death, and of damnation, was such that midwives were empowered to baptise sickly infants, and held a parish office, chosen by the women of the village under the supervision of the local priest. In the perilous moments of birth, an emerging hand or foot could be baptised, if there was a fear the baby might die in the womb, and parents themselves were permitted to do this, if they found themselves alone. The spread of knowledge about 'scientific' midwifery practices was encouraged by the state from the 1770s, and this undoubtedly helped to save some infants, but many continued to succumb to complications brought on by the consequences of poor diet, overwork and illness in the mother.[6]

To be born alive was but the first obstacle – at least a fifth of all children died within their first year, rising to as much as a third in more impoverished districts. Fewer than half of those born would reach their fifteenth year. The reasons were both complex and simple. A multitude of diseases battened on a population lacking more than a basic knowledge of hygiene (though even that was a noteworthy advance over earlier centuries), and which could not have afforded the services of a medical profession that in any case remained helpless in the face of almost all disease. Around half of all infant deaths were attributable to birth defects or maternal diseases. Where twins were born, it was rare for either to survive.

In one sense, death remained the great leveller. No social class was immune from tragedy, as the history of the eighteenth-century French royal family shows. Louis XV inherited the throne at the age of five in 1715 from his great-grandfather, having lost his grandfather, father and elder brother to illness within the preceding few years. He fathered ten (legitimate) children, seven of whom survived infancy, but would pass on the throne in 1774 to his grandson Louis XVI, having lost his son and an elder grandson in the interim. The royal family was blighted once more in the summer of 1789 by the death of their eldest son, aged eight. They had lost a daughter at eleven months old in 1787, and two other children in infancy, leaving an elder daughter and four-year-old son and heir – who would himself succumb to disease in 1795. Smallpox had accounted for a number of these deaths, and inoculation worked wonders against that particular killer in the later decades of the century, but the almost miraculous nature of the protection it afforded merely highlighted how many more sources of sudden or lingering death remained.

Nevertheless, if wealth and power was no shield from death, poverty was still a key factor in the dangers of childhood. The worst time for infant mortality amongst the peasantry was the season running into the harvest, August to October, the dreaded *soudure*, when 40 per cent of deaths occurred as breastfeeding mothers had to toil in the fields, and families lived on the last, rapidly spoiling remnants of the previous year's crop. In a bad year, when the previous harvest had been small, this period could begin as early as April, provoking a real fear of starvation. French agriculture never collapsed into a state of famine in the later eighteenth century, as it had to catastrophic effect several times in the reign of Louis XIV, but the fear that it might was ever-present.[7]

MAP 1. Pre-revolutionary France.

Most peasant families could afford no more than a one- or two-room, dirt-floored house, which they might well have to share with any livestock they owned. Dark and ill-ventilated – if they had a rear room, often only the chimney let light into it – such houses bred disease. In cases where they were walled in mud and dung, this was almost literally true. The diet of the villager was poor in protein and vitamins, rarely containing meat, or even green vegetables. In the most extreme cases, as travellers reported from the high Pyrenees, villagers lived almost exclusively on a thin porridge of milk and barley or oats.[8] This was at first sight odd, since these communities lived largely from sheep-rearing, but their animals were too valuable to be consumed for food. To be more precise, such were the burdens on many amongst the peasantry that they could not afford to rear animals for their own consumption.

This was the case even in more fertile and prosperous regions. Here we can examine an example in detail. On 1 August 1779, Pierre and Mathieu Reynes, father and son, stood before the royal notary in the town of Villefranche de Lauragais, thirty kilometres south east of Toulouse, and agreed to lease 'the farm called La Grave and the lands in dependence' for one year, commencing the next All Saints' Day, 1 November.[9] They were leasing it from Jacques Maurel, agent of 'the high and powerful seigneur', the marquis d'Hautpoul. The lands comprised about twenty-five hectares, including both fields and pastures, and a small vineyard. La Grave was thus a good-sized farm in an area of mixed farming, offering at first sight the chance of a secure living and a balanced diet for its tenants. However, we need to examine the consequences of the lease in more detail. It was in the form known as 'half-fruits', a sharecropping contract, and spelt out in depth exactly what this meant.

In the first place, the tenants would pay a substantial rent in kind: thirty-six chickens at Christmas, the same on St John the Baptist's Day (24 June), and thirty-six capons on All Saints' Day, when the lease would expire. They were to provide six hundred eggs throughout the year. They were also expected to buy and raise pigs, geese, ducks and turkeys, of which Maurel would take the half of his choice when ready for sale. Any other livestock on the farm were to be divided similarly. The tenants were obliged to maintain the lands and property in good condition, providing the tools and equipment necessary for this themselves, and it was noted separately that they would pay for ploughs already ordered by Maurel from the local blacksmith. They would also ensure a supply of hay and straw for animal feed, and pay half the cost from their own pockets if more was required than could be grown.

As for the main arable fields, these were worked in the three-field system:

one third for wheat, one third fallow, and one third for 'maize, beans, or other vegetables and grains'. This division was enforced by the contract, which also noted that if the tenants failed to exploit all of the land in this way Maurel would be free to lease the unused portions to another tenant. Given the general nature of farming and land use in the region, it is likely that overall only some six to seven hectares were available for wheat each year, yielding some one hundred *sétiers* (a measure which varied widely across the country, but which can most easily be thought of as a substantial sackful). Of these, the tenants had to provide seed-grain initially, probably some twenty *sétiers*. They were then obliged by their lease to give twenty to Maurel 'in advance', pay the costs of cutting and threshing, which would probably amount to ten *sétiers*, and then give the formal 'half-fruits' to Maurel from what was left. Overall, Pierre and Mathieu Reynes would have a profit on the year of some fifteen *sétiers*, a mere 15 per cent of the total yield. To provide bread for an average family of five took around twenty *sétiers* per year, at a bare minimum. There was no guarantee of the lease being renewed after one year, whereas the tenants were bound at several points in the contract to act as good husbandmen, placed under a series of restrictions, and made subject to the law if they breached these. Neither Pierre nor Mathieu was literate enough to sign the written contract (although neither, it appears, was Maurel).

These two men were far from being at the bottom of peasant society: they were leasing a good-sized farm unit, and it may indeed have been only part of the lands they worked. Yet the owner, through his agent, was able to extort from them a huge proportion of the produce, while they met almost all the costs of upkeep, and provided all the means necessary for farming. To this we should add a range of other burdens: of taxation, and of dues to feudal seigneurs, and also of the tithes of the church, which alone could be anything from 8 to 15 per cent of the crop. The half of the livestock that they were allowed to keep by their lease probably had to be sold to meet their other obligations. The simple, direct conclusion to be drawn from this is that the peasantry of France had to bear a near-crushing burden of demands from their social superiors. The fact that agriculture continued to support a population growing at a healthy rate – expanding production in the later eighteenth century by around 1 per cent a year – is testament to their ceaseless toil, and to the ingenuity of their search for additional resources.[10]

In a nation where fewer than 15 per cent of the population made its living entirely outside agriculture, the land inevitably remained the mainstay of employment. At the same time many, if not most, of the rural population also undertook non-agricultural work just to make ends meet. Although some 40 to 45 per cent of land was owned by peasants, this ownership usually meant possession of a tiny patch of land – for example, in the region around Orléans, some 80 per cent of peasants owned less than four hectares, barely enough for basic subsistence, while further south-west around Limoges, almost 60 per cent cultivated less than two hectares, leaving them in need of waged work to survive. Inhabitants of this region, known as Limousins, were renowned for their migrations in search of labouring work, often as stonemasons. They shared this trait with the relatively densely-populated but isolated upland province of Basse-Auvergne, around the town of Clermont-Ferrand, which men left each year as seasonal migrants, both as labourers and in a wide variety of trades – stonemasons, hawkers and peddlars, chimney-sweeps, livestock traders, military pioneers, sawyers, sailors, coppersmiths, ropemakers. At the same time, the villages and towns of the region were centres of linen, lace and other textile manufacture, along with papermaking, woodworking, cutlery and leatherworking.[11]

The way of life of the Limousins and Auvergnats had evolved over a relatively long period. In other regions newer industries had become staples of peasant existence by the later decades of the century. Textile manufacture for international markets had grown steadily in importance, to the point where it often provided the bulk of peasant income in some regions. The town of Cholet in southern Anjou, for example, with a population of some 6000, was the centre of a textile industry that involved perhaps as many as 40,000 workers in outlying communities, from whom goods were fed through the town's market to the ports of Bordeaux and Nantes for export to the colonial Americas. To the north, in the villages of parts of Flanders, there was a long tradition of woollen manufacture, but this had expanded by the 1780s to the extent that it was only the textile industry that enabled the population to sustain itself – numbers had grown far beyond the resources of the village fields, and much food was purchased at urban markets. In such cases, although families clung to their agricultural roots, they did not hesitate to sell parcels of land in order to purchase materials if funds had run low. They would seek to buy replacement land when funds became available, but they showed no sentimental attachment to ancestral plots. Some studies suggest that, by the 1780s, as many as 75 per cent of inhabitants here were resigned to complete landlessness, a condition shared by between 20 and 40 per cent of households in many other regions.[12]

Patterns of land use and landholding could vary dramatically even within a region. The Paris Basin, for example, a circle around the city up to a hundred kilometres in radius, was noted as a *pays de grande culture*, a zone of large farms growing almost nothing but the high-quality grain demanded by urban bread-consumers. Such farms were frequently owned by absentee landlords who rented them ('farmed them out', in the technical sense) to *fermiers*, who then worked them with the hired landless labourers who made up the great majority of the population – a population thus largely condemned to buy its food from markets or from the larger farmers. Nevertheless, this pattern was interspersed with several other forms of agriculture in the same overall region. Areas within a day's travel of Paris were largely given over to intensive cultivation of fresh produce for the city's markets by smallholding *maraîchers* or market-gardeners. Similar patterns could be found on the fertile floors of some of the river valleys, where water transport allowed the quick movement of goods. Being close to the city also produced a substantial trade in wet-nursing, with thousands of urban infants of every class despatched to villages through a network of agents each year. The sides of valleys were frequently given over to the cultivation of vines, often in small holdings, which created a substantial class of vine-growers who, although technically landholding, were condemned as much as the landless to buying their food from others. Between these zones and the *grande culture* areas, pockets of relatively infertile soil, hilly, or partially forested lands created an intermingling of almost every other size of holding, and a wide range of agricultural practices.[13]

Thus it was that a community in the Vexin, a zone just under halfway from Paris to Rouen along the Seine, was marked by large holdings, a clear divide between prosperous *fermiers* and others, and a trade in the extra-regional movement of grain, while a few miles away to the north, in the Beauvaisis or the Pays de Bray, peasants cultivated farms perhaps a third or a quarter of the size, and grew rye or oats for their own consumption, along with the production of cheese, hemp or flax, and sometimes the rearing of pigs and cattle for sale. Pockets of textile production also punctuated such zones, especially nearer the large towns. Such regions might be socially less polarised than the Vexin, or its larger southern cousin the Beauce, but their inhabitants were often no more secure from want than the landless labourer. A labourer was at least mobile in times of need – a fact ironically recognised by the *fermiers* in some districts, who tried to link labourers to small parcels of land in order to tie them down and make them further dependent on purely local employment opportunities.

In the Cévennes hills north of Nîmes, at the opposite end of France, the population had developed complex networks of agriculture and proto-industry to support itself. Groves of mulberry trees produced leaves gathered by the ton to feed farmed silkworms. Thousands of families worked to rear these grubs, and to unwind the silk from their cocoons – a job usually given to young women, who worked with their hands in the basins of scalding water needed to soften the silk. The water was heated with another proto-industrial product, the local coal, grubbed from shallow pits in the hillsides by dozens of small peasant producers with traditional rights to mine small seams. Coal was also hauled in carts to the nearby towns and cities, and on their return journeys the carts brought the grain from the lowlands that fed the Cevenol population.[14]

The silk also went to the towns, where further communities were occupied with its spinning and weaving – there were some 2000 spinning-machines in the 1770s in and around Alès, the chief town of the Cévennes, contributing to a weaving industry around Nîmes maintaining over 5000 looms. A minority of this production took place in the towns themselves, most being based in the outlying villages, undertaken by households which also maintained at least a nominal attachment to the land. This was a wise move in the 1780s, as increasing international competition hit the silk industry hard. Viticulture was also a staple industry of the Cévennes. Although the wine itself was of poor quality, the growers compensated by turning it into distilled spirits, which travelled and kept better, and which had some reputation as a local speciality. Official observers noted the reluctance of proto-industrial workers to sever their final ties to the land by moving to the towns, recording the peasants' sense that land remained a standby, and the ultimate guarantee of stability, in their fragile economic calculations.

In this context, the landlessness of the Flanders peasant was a marker of just how great the pressure was in that overpopulated region. Moreover, such overpopulation itself may have been a consequence of the strains on the peasantry. Around Saint-Etienne south west of Lyon one observer, the future revolutionary minister Roland, suggested at the end of the 1770s that a deliberate cycle of relatively early marriage and rapid reproduction was being fostered by the combination of underlying poverty and the availability of work in both the silk-weaving and metallurgical industries. The pittance paid to a swarm of young auxiliaries might become the last bastion against starvation. If this image is itself bleak, we can at least acknowledge that, far from being the hopelessly mired mass of caricature, by the end of the eighteenth century most French peasants were clearly juggling a wide range of economic possibilities, making ends meet through a variety of resources in an 'economy of makeshifts' that required ingenuity, flexibility and assertion.[15]

Peasants built their lives around the elements of stability that could be gleaned from an unstable environment. The nuclear family, although the basis of most households, was as yet difficult ground on which to build continuities. Unwilling, or unable, to marry until they were in a position (often through inheritance) to set up on their own, rural inhabitants rarely began families before their late twenties. The average age for a man to marry in the 1780s was between twenty-six and twenty-eight, for a woman a year or two younger. These figures were at an all-time high, reflecting strong population pressure on the land as the total population rose from some 25 million towards 28 million in the decades between 1760 and 1789 – although, as noted, some 'industrialised' areas may already have been reversing this trend. Somewhere over 10 per cent remained unmarried, not counting the small number who took religious vows. It was virtually un-thinkable for a single person to form a household – utterly unthinkable for a single woman – so this cohort was pushed inexorably through their lifetime towards dependency on relatives or pauperism, the latter ever more likely as they grew older.

If they were very lucky, the married couple might have thirty years together, but figures suggest that only a third of marriages lasted anything like that long. In some regions, the figures seem to have been even worse – in Lorraine, only some 20 per cent of peasant marriages endured until the menopause, which itself came early, around forty.[16] Children came quickly to most couples in this Catholic society – indeed a significant percentage in less than nine months from the date of the marriage. This may reflect the fact that, in many regions, the ceremony of betrothal, which could be up to several months before the formal wedding, was seen as more significant than the final ceremony. This was clearly not always the case – on 11 February 1782 in Blénod-lès-Toul, in Lorraine, the vine-grower Germain Liégois, aged thirty-one, and Marie Aubry, aged twenty-six, and daughter of a vine-grower herself, agreed a contract of marriage and went through a betrothal ceremony. They were married the very next day, but their first daughter was born only four months later. The decade or more that separated puberty and marriage presented a real challenge to Catholic morality, and the church campaigned ceaselessly against fornication, and the drinking and dancing that encouraged it.

Even though it is probable that most peasants married individuals for whom they felt some affection, there is no doubt that choice of partners was limited in small communities. Evidence from southern Anjou on the lower Loire suggests that two-thirds of marriages were contracted within the same community, the vast majority of others with members of neigh-bouring communities. Socially there was a diffuse but predictable spread of intermarriage in this region between different occupational and status groups. Three-quarters of those who farmed larger plots, and were thus relatively economically secure, married into families of similar status, the remainder marrying widely amongst families of millers, agricultural artisans and smaller farmers. Peasants working small farms, in more precarious circumstances, formed a less consistent grouping, and married amongst themselves on only a quarter of occasions. They otherwise married most often into families of agricultural labourers, and after that to larger farmers, if they were lucky, or to vine-growers and general artisans. Agricultural artisans – blacksmiths, coopers, carpenters and so on – were at a pivotal point in the networks of the rural community, but were as likely to marry into labouring families as to large farmers, and more likely, in fact, to marry into the small-scale commercial bourgeoisie of the region. One noteworthy feature of this region's proto-industrial development was that essentially landless textile workers, although living in the rural environment, only rarely married into purely agricultural families by the later eighteenth century, looking more towards other artisans or the ranks of the bourgeoisie for their partners, while marrying amongst themselves on nearly 60 per cent of occasions.[17]

Once a couple had married, children tended to arrive every couple of years. If one was stillborn, or died very young, another child was often conceived immediately, reflecting the role of breastfeeding in delaying conception. A woman probably had a dozen years, perhaps fifteen, before the onset of menopause. If she lived that long, she might therefore give birth around seven or eight times, but lose half these children before adolescence. Her own chance of seeing her children reach that age was no better than two in three, and parents probably had only an even chance of seeing their first grandchild. For households to survive, remarriage was frequently essential and often rapid, widows and widowers sometimes pairing up within a year or eighteen months, as soon as church rules and local mourning customs allowed. The looming presence of the stepmother in European folktales reflects a social reality, albeit with a misogynist twist. Although widowers with children were swifter to remarry than widows, stepfathers were nonetheless almost as common, given that disease preyed on men and women indiscriminately, and accident or injury in agricultural labour were everyday realities alongside the risks of childbirth – life expectancy overall for the two sexes was almost equal.

With a step-parent in the home, the clash between household and family, in a wider sense, became visible. There were wide regional variations in customary laws on inheritance, from near total freedom of parents to bequeath as they saw fit, to effective primogeniture, to enforced equal inheritance for all children. In contested circumstances, other members of the wider families on both sides would seek to defend the rights of their 'blood' in the children, and dispossess step-parents and children. Marriage, whatever the choice of partner, remained a transaction between two families whenever the smallest amount of property was involved. Legal contracts formed part of the arrangements, and these would often detail the provision for heirs, and for reversions of property if a spouse died without issue.

Germain Liégois was unusual in having inherited from his father eight years before the marriage. His contract assured to his wife Marie half-ownership of a house, and three vineyards and a garden, with a total value of 600 livres. He signed the contract with a cross, but despite his illiteracy Liégois was relatively prosperous. Notarial records from the village of Tourville-la-Campagne in Normandy suggest the sort of goods brought to peasants' marriages as dowries by the bride. These varied little in kind across the century, and most often began with a bed and a bolster, six to a dozen sheets, and similar numbers of tablecloths and napkins. Up to a dozen shirts might be thrown in, and several coats, plus assorted *menu linge*, or underwear. A chest or coffer was often also given, and sometimes a small amount of money – in one case from 1764 'thirty livres, five with which to have furniture'.[18] In the first half of the century, however, sums had frequently been larger: several hundred livres, especially for the weddings of prosperous *laboureurs*, men who owned their own plough-teams, along with a hectare or more of land (which was in itself a token amount, of course, enough for vegetables or a paddock. The husbands would doubtless have had more substantial landholdings themselves). By the 1760s the largest piece of land given in dowry was a quarter of a hectare, not much bigger than a domestic garden.

If the act of marriage was never really a private affair, the life of the couple itself normally lacked privacy too. Not only did they usually have to sleep in the same room as other members of the household, but the emotional and sexual basis of their relationship, like everyone else's in the community, was a matter of public discussion. The gathering of village women at the well and washpump was frequently the tribunal of moral judgement on the housekeeping and business abilities of a couple, and on their more intimate relations. The unmarried young men of the community also exercised their own kind of rough justice – lampooning husbands suspected of being henpecked or cuckolded. Suspected adulterers might come in for rougher treatment, with the scattering of rotting refuse around their house as just one possibility. Marriages of widows or widowers to younger single people were frequently lampooned in longstanding traditions of *tapage*, noisy singing and banging of pots outside the couple's windows. Such marriages, like any irregularity in marital conduct, threatened the delicate supply of potential partners for the as yet unmarried, and were thus subject to a degree of real hostility.[19]

Within the household, long-term patterns of relations between parents and children varied widely across France. In Flanders, parents might sell some of their property to set a child up in a new dwelling. As we saw, near Toulouse Pierre and Mathieu Reynes were in partnership as father and son. It was often the case that a child was not in a position to start a family until the parent was already unfit to continue work, in which case a property might be signed over to the heir, often with a specific written condition that the parent must be cared for throughout their lifetime – life at sub-sistence level could be deeply unsentimental. In the high Pyrenees, great store was set on the continuity of the household, a tradition dating back into the middle ages, when the term for house, *domus*, also described a family, as in its use for an aristocratic 'house' or lineage, such as the House of Habsburg. Here a single heir inherited all. This included cases where the eldest child was female – in such cases a husband was expected to 'marry into' the house, taking its name, while the woman retained legal rights as the real head of the household. Younger siblings had few choices. If they were lucky, they might marry the heir of another house. If less lucky, they might scrape together enough resources to set up on a parcel of land with another non-inheritor as spouse. If they chose to remain in the original household, they condemned themselves to a dependent state. Unmarried siblings were put under the authority of the head, who could forbid them to marry while they remained in the house, and who put them to work on menial tasks. Some observers compared the condition of these individuals to slavery.

Despite these variations, it is fair to say that the household provided more security than the nuclear couple itself, and the speed with which most widowed peasants remarried reflects their concern to reconstitute this centre in their lives, with the division of labour it implied. Childrearing and the preparation of meals were quite clearly seen as the domain of the female, along with laundry – more of a seasonal than a regular activity, however, as many items would be washed no more than a few times a year. Specifically male activities varied with the type of farming. In the most extreme examples, this could involve months spent away with flocks on mountain pastures, or similar periods of time absent each year as migrant labour. Generally, there was a tendency for men to occupy them-selves outside the immediate environs of the home, on the general fieldwork of farming, mending hedges, fences or ditches, tending to horses or cattle, fulfilling labour obligations to the seigneur or roadmending during the obligatory state *corvée*, buying and selling crops and stock, negotiating leases, or dealing with the business of tithes and taxes. When women worked outdoors, it was more likely to be closer to home, in a vegetable patch, with smaller livestock, or in pursuit of more immediate home needs, such as the gathering of firewood. Women would also take responsibility for selling domestic produce, such as vegetables or eggs, and possibly also thread or cloth, at local or urban markets.

These distinctions were never hard and fast. It is unlikely that many men ever joined the women of the village at the washpump, or that many women were allowed to undertake ploughing, but they may have done. When, for example, firewood had to be gathered from woodlands whose ownership was disputed, which could easily lead to conflict with the feudal lord or state officials, or with other communities, this was no 'mere women's work'. Certainly male and female members of the household, young and old, would be called upon whenever necessary to complete tasks essential for survival. The labour of the whole household was part of the ritual of the harvest, because that was the only way to complete the arduous labour before the crops began to rot in the ground. Children, of course, both male and female, would be put to work on whatever tasks it was felt they could manage as soon as they were able – their first domestic chores were likely to start as soon as they could understand instructions, and certainly by the age of seven they were expected to be contributing to the household economy.

Such household economies frequently included waged labour alongside the family, and the delicate balance between the need for extra labour, and finding the money to pay for it, afflicted many peasant farms. The sums involved were not great but represented another squeeze on cash incomes. A general male farm-servant in Normandy was paid around 60 livres per year, or around 100 sous per month. This figure changed little across the century, whereas salaries for shepherds in the same region seem to have risen from around 50 livres towards 80 or more in later decades. On the other hand, cowherds were paid a pittance – well under 20 livres, at which price they must have been fed and lodged, or else they would have starved. Female farm-servants in the 1770s were earning between 20 and 36 livres per year, plus an allowance of cloth, and, in one case, the guaranteed upkeep of her clogs. Such figures can be contrasted with daily wage rates for short-term labour. An ordinary day-labourer might earn 9 sous and his dinner, a thatcher 12 sous, a ploughman 13 sous, a reaper up to 15 sous, and a carpenter around the same. For a six-day week these translate to sums between two and three-quarter and four and a half livres.[20] Thus a male farm-servant made barely a third of what a craftsman could earn in a month, while the latter sum was equivalent to the entire annual wage of a servant girl. Seen from another angle, such servants were the unmarried offspring of other peasant households: even if only earning a pittance by working elsewhere, they were relieving their own families of their upkeep.

Nevertheless, finding sums in cash to pay servants was always difficult, and many had to settle for living in credit to their masters, or decamping to the seasonal fairs in the hope of finding another who might pay something in advance. Sources of cash income were few and far between. We have seen how much of the grain crop was commonly taken in rents and dues, and vegetables for sale at market could add only a little to income. Stock-rearing for urban markets was one common option. In the early 1780s in Normandy, one might get as much as 60 or 70 livres for a single cow, and 30 to 45 livres for a sow. Lambs might fetch 7 to 8 livres and older sheep 10 to 15. In such circumstances, it is not surprising that in Anjou, where farmers could often afford to rear only one or two cattle for sale, the beasts might be transported to market in a cart, to avoid the risks of a journey on foot.[21] The other side of this coin, of course, is that the death through disease or accident of a peasant's beast was a financial catastrophe, and might even lead to the sale of a portion of their lands to finance replacements – if, of course, the peasant was fortunate enough to own any. It is no wonder that proto-industry had established such a hold in so many regions of France – throughout the long economic upturn that marked the decades up to the 1770s, cash payment for all the weaving and spinning the household could produce must have seemed like manna from heaven.

In many forms of proto-industry, and in farming at times like the harvest, all the various sources of labour amongst the household and community flowed into each other. There is every sign that peasant villages were places of constant sociability, with a rough and ready solidarity, based on the knowledge that help given would usually need to be returned one day, but also on real human warmth. One unfortunate young woman who gave birth to an illegitimate son in Montigny, a village of peasant-weavers in Flanders, was tended by all her female neighbours. The women sat by her bedside, did her chores and tried to give her constructive advice about her plight, while a succession of them nursed the infant, all between their own tasks in their homes and in the fields. All this, alas, was not enough to lift her from her melancholy, and she drowned herself after stifling the child at six days old.[22] Such tragedies were exceptional, but the sympathy expressed is noteworthy, given the censorious reputation of small communities.

The same sentiments in the context of male relations were more likely to be cemented through group drinking, and to lead to physical violence against those who challenged the village's rights or threatened an individual member. When groups from different communities met at fairs or markets (prime sites for recreational alcohol consumption) old hostilities could flare, the names of the villages becoming rallying-cries for brawls or cries for assistance, which often led to the same thing. In some regions of France, male violence and group solidarity merged into the practice of vendetta – this was the case both in Provence and at the opposite corner of France in

Brittany. Here the solidarity involved might embrace the whole community, or become the more dangerous situation of factions within the same community or district. Murderous revenge for real or imagined wrongs was far from unknown, and authorities had little opportunity, or inclination, to investigate these closely in clannish communities far from urban justice.[23] Such deeds were usually done with the knife, but in some areas of France the gun had become a symbol of manhood – in the valleys north of Montpellier, for example, where firearms were easily procured via the arms trading privileges of Avignon and Roussillon, and where bullet wounds became the most common cause of unlawful death.[24]

If men and women expressed their solidarities in different ways, they all nonetheless recognised that such actions were essential. This pursuit of stability through solidarity was reflected, not without tensions, in the formal existence of the community. Unless it was an exceptionally small hamlet, it normally formed a parish of the Catholic Church, and its inhabitants were thus the 'flock' of the local priest. Historically, but with declining significance, the community might form the jurisdiction of a court belonging to a seigneur, and generally continued to be linked together more significantly under the yoke of such a lord's financial rights and dues. More directly, however, the village formed what was known as a 'community of inhabitants'. As such, it was entitled, and frequently required, to regulate its own collective affairs. What this meant varied from region to region. Some of the most extreme examples can again be found in the high Pyrenean valleys, where village communities were run by assemblies of heads of households, and banded together into wider confederations of communities to resist outside intrusion, including seigneurial claims. Such was the vigorous defence of these areas' independence that by the end of the eighteenth century most had long since won either formal or tacit freedom from seigneurial impositions, and also paid little in the way of state taxes.

Across much of southern France, where communities tended to be larger and more concentrated than elsewhere, there was a lively tradition of municipal democracy, accepting that an assembly of heads of households was as near to democracy as this society could get. Widows, as heads of households, were permitted to take part, but had generally fewer rights than male heads. All across France, even where such traditions did not have deep roots, villagers were actively encouraged by the state in the late eighteenth century to meet regularly, and to elect officials to conduct the business of the community. This business was frequently a question of managing the village's relationship to the demands of the state itself. Communities were taxed collectively across much of France for the *taille*, the main direct tax on property. Thus the community or its officials had the unpleasant task of deciding how much each individual should pay, but little formal sanction against them – the state simply made the officials make up any shortfall from their own pockets. Similarly, there was a regular lottery for service in the militia, France's military reserve, which was widely detested, as was the compulsory service that the state demanded of peasants for road-building and maintenance, the *corvée*. Less unpopular, but still awkward, was the need to find funds to maintain and repair the fabric of the church, and other communal institutions, such as water troughs, wells and laundry houses. Special local taxes might be raised for such needs. More routinely, the community managed the use of any common land and woodland it possessed, and decided the date of harvests – which would require the work of all the villagers, perhaps arranging outside hired labour as well.[25]

The community of inhabitants frequently came into its own in defending its collective interests. If in the Pyrenees this meant seeing off all comers from the vantage-point of extreme isolation, in other regions of France it often meant entering into litigation with neighbouring communities. Rights to commons were frequently both vague, to some eyes, and extremely specific, to others. Ancient boundary stones might mark different communities' pastures, and these might be moved, or the symbols on them be recut on different rocks. Flocks or herds might 'stray', firewood might be gathered where villagers felt it had no right to be. Open conflict could easily break out over such issues, the cohort of young single men in the community often feeling obliged to defend their rights with fists and sticks, or worse. Such conflicts often ended up in the courts, sometimes in law suits that dragged on for decades, if not generations. But no community dared be seen to back down; their resources were too few, and too precarious, not to be defended.

The officials chosen by the community were known in northern France as *syndics*, and in the south more usually as *consuls*. In many areas, the number of such officials was linked to the size of the community. Elsewhere a single syndic was chosen. This official, somewhere between a mayor and a town clerk, represented the community's interests in relations with outsiders, the local seigneur, the church and the state. Increasingly through the eighteenth century, the state, through its regional official, the intendant, and his deputies, the *sub-délégués*, supervised the work of syndics, laid down regulations for their role and imposed further responsibilities on them. They were thus, in some senses, agents of the state in the village, but continued to act for the villagers. The role could be perceived as a burden, making the holder potentially unpopular with those whose tax assessments he had to manage. In some regions the state's officials took up the practice of nominating the syndics themselves, while this was sometimes elsewhere the privilege of the seigneur. In other places it remained a genuinely elective office, and might also be an expression of the phenomenon of the men called 'cocks of the village' – the big fish in their very small ponds. Across France in this period there was a growing tendency for control of village life to fall into the hands of the more prosperous minority, and for the more 'democratic' aspects of community management to fall into abeyance, with the active collusion of state officials.[26] This, however, was not a universal trend.

The varying patterns in the election of syndics between the 1760s and 1780s in five very different communities near the River Oise, north of Paris, illustrate the complexities of village political relations.[27] The largest village was Cormeilles-en-Vexin, made up of over two hundred households by the late 1780s. It elected over thirty men to the role of syndic in this period. Their identities reflected a community with a diverse economy: fourteen were substantial farmers, eight were artisans, three were day labourers, two were innkeepers and one was a vine-grower. Only once, in the crisis years of 1788–89, was a syndic re-elected. This man, Jean Louis Toussaint Caffin, had held the related office of *syndic perpetuel* since 1782 and represented the village at the assembly that produced the local *cahiers de doléances*. He was a *fermier de seigneurie*, one who leased lands from the local lord to sublet or work them with hired labour, and also a flour merchant. As a prosperous and substantial figure, he may have seemed to the villagers to be their best resort in a time of crisis. Although the syndics of Cormeilles were socially diverse, most of them were relatively well off compared to their fellow villagers – two-thirds of the village paid less than 10 livres in *taille*, whereas only seven of the syndics paid this little, and half paid over 50 livres. One syndic, possibly Caffin himself, paid the enormous sum of 2000 livres, a third of the entire village's assessment.

At the opposite end of the scale to Cormeilles was Mézières, a village which never had more than a dozen households over this period. Over half of these paid less than 10 livres in *taille*, but the remainder paid over 50. The village was socially polarised between landless labourers and prosperous farmers. Two of the latter, André and François Leger, were syndics twenty-one times between them in this period, usually alternating in office. François Leger, like Caffin in Cormeilles, was also a *fermier de seigneurie*, and personally paid some two-thirds of the village's *taille* assessment. André paid around 10 per cent. As employers, they could probably command the votes of the other villagers, however unwillingly, when they wished it.

Although these two villages differed dramatically in size and social structure, the evidence suggests that they were both controlled by their more prosperous inhabitants. This, however, was not always the case. In Butry, a vine-growing village on the slopes above the Oise, none of the some fifty households paid more than 50 livres in *taille*. Those chosen as syndics were close to the village average in terms of wealth and occupation – four-fifths were vine-growers, as were two-thirds of the villagers, and only a fifth of the syndics paid more than 20 livres in *taille*. Re-election was rare, and in this village the syndic's role seems to have been a burden widely shared amongst average members of the community. Likewise in Méry-sur-Oise, where vine-growing and farming were mixed, the pattern of syndic election more or less matched that of the village as a whole. Amongst some hundred households, 70 to 80 per cent paid less than 10 livres *taille*, and less than 10 per cent paid over 20 livres. Only 20 per cent of syndics paid this much, and nearly half of them were vine-growers, like a third of the villagers overall; 10 per cent were day labourers, like a fifth of the villagers. Sometimes the syndics only barely passed the tax threshold for office laid down by the state.

In Butry and Méry we can see relatively homogeneous communities managing their affairs collectively. In one final example, Fosseuse, the pattern was more complex. Like Mézières, this was a polarised community, though somewhat larger, with over forty households. The local miller and flour merchant, who was also a large agricultural leaseholder, paid up to 80 per cent of the village's *taille* assessment in some years. There were many landless labourers in the village, and 90 per cent of the households paid less than 10 livres. Only once, however, in 1768, did the 'cock of the village' manage to get elected as syndic. Almost all the syndics chosen over this period paid less than 10 livres *taille*, and three of them were actually illiterate, something not found in any of the other villages. Several men were re-elected for a number of terms, including Charles Tuquet, a day-labourer who paid less than 3 livres *taille*, and Etienne Boyer, who left no record of his occupation but paid less than 5 livres, and served as syndic from 1773 to 1777, and again in 1787. Clearly there was no single straightforward relationship between economic and political power in these villages, all within a few miles of each other.

Nevertheless, what these villagers shared, alongside the vast majority of French peasants, was the triple burden of state, church and seigneur. The power of the state, as touched on above, was mostly experienced as a direct imposition, although we shall see that state institutions could occasionally be put to work for the community. The relationship of the rural community to the church, however, was both a more intimate and a more complex one.[28] Villagers lived in a world that still bore the stamp of the supernatural. The powers of the priest's blessing, of religious rituals, and of the consecrated host, were held to be an essential counterweight to the awful uncertainties of climate and chance. Crops and livestock were blessed regularly, the host might be brought to the scene of a fire in an effort to stop it spreading, and church bells were rung to ward off thunderstorms before the harvest. The bells themselves were consecrated objects, often cast on site by itinerant specialists, to the accompaniment of prayers, incense and holy water. Ceremonially 'baptised', they gave out a sound which theologians agreed was itself a form of prayer.[29]

The village priest, often a key member of the community, fulfilled many roles.[30] He confessed and absolved, christened and married, and bore the last sacraments to the dying. He was also a conduit for state information, and the priest in the pulpit had been expected since the seventeenth century to communicate and explain state decrees to his flock. He also worked in close collaboration with village gatherings on communal business, as possibly the only formally educated member of most villages, and certainly one of a literate minority. Such business itself was frequently conducted in or near the church, with Sunday after mass the traditional time for meetings. In many regions of the west, where a *bocage* landscape was characterised by woodlands, impenetrable hedgerows and parishes made up of small hamlets and isolated farmsteads, the church might be one of the few centres of communal life, and the clergy here were central to the perception of community.[31] Where villagers lived more closely together, such as in the south east, alternative centres challenged this role. The tavern or *cabaret* in such rural townships was often seen by clergy as posing a direct threat to the influence of the church. It was the natural gathering place of all those least likely to respect clerical authority, and its sale of alcohol could be a direct provocation to anticlerical outbursts, especially where the clergy set themselves directly against the tavern, for example by seeking to restrict opening hours through appeals to civil authorities.

Such issues of social discipline, which the clergy of course saw as moral concerns, were not the only areas of tension with the rural population. Actions linked to what were increasingly seen as superstitious practices, including those mentioned above, were fought against by many clergy throughout the century, influenced in part by new scientific thought, but more profoundly by the serious-minded theological Catholicism which many of them professed. Nevertheless, the peasantry clung to the apparent effectiveness of their own views, and to other agents who abetted them. The eighteenth-century countryside was criss-crossed by travelling *devins* and *guerisseurs*, soothsayers and healers, who offered spells and prophecy, love potions and cures for sick beasts. Whether these were the honourable survivors of pagan traditions or mere charlatans may be disputed, but the peasantry certainly resorted to them with undimmed eagerness. A report from the south-western town of Agen in 1791 noted that country priests in living memory could be heard summoning 'sorcerers and sorceresses' to leave the church before mass, and 'one often saw people leaving, believing themselves sorcerers or, what is more likely, to impress that belief more easily on these good people'.[32] The reporter may be exaggerating for effect in this case, but it is clear that worship at local shrines, supposedly to saints or the Virgin, frequently involved pagan overtones, such as the offering of gifts to the saint. Many areas equally abounded in legendary beasts and bogeymen, werewolves and vampires.

Before we condemn these beliefs as scornfully as the enlightened elite did, we might recall that twenty-first century culture remains obsessed with 'alternative' remedies, the paraphernalia of the 'New Age', and the same tales of horror that captivated the peasants of the eighteenth century on long dark evenings. Moreover, the contemporary elites who ridiculed such beliefs were themselves helplessly credulous in the face of more supposedly materialist explanations and miracle-cures, such as the 'animal magnetism' of Anton Mesmer.[33] The church's own concern with demonic witchcraft in earlier centuries had helped to reinforce many of the peasants' beliefs, and the more austere and inward-looking Catholicism of a new generation found few takers amongst the rural community. Anguished concern for the health of one's soul was infinitely less useful to a hard-pressed cultivator than practices hallowed by the generations, which might, so it was believed and hoped, be of practical material benefit. Nevertheless, if some peasant beliefs seemed to hark back to a pre-Christian world, and other practices of sociability hinted at rising anticlerical scorn, little could dim the clear underlying sense that the clergy were a privileged link to the afterlife, in a world where death was ever-present. As the Revolution was to prove, actions which threatened the availability of that link would be contested violently.

The clergy also had a complex economic relationship to the village. The church collected a tithe on the produce of the land, which in theory was for the upkeep of religious buildings, the priests' living expenses, and for charity towards the poor. Such tithes, like so much else in Old Regime France, had become complicated by long usage. Rights to collect the tithe in many villages were now owned by either lay landowners and seigneurs, or by religious institutions distant from the particular parish. Thus the tithe in itself, rather than being a clear payment for services rendered by the clergy, had often become just another part of the package of onerous dues claimed from the peasant by the wider system. The parish priest, meanwhile, charged fees for his services, notably for weddings, baptisms and funerals. To further complicate matters, it was quite possible for clerics and religious institutions – bishops, cathedral chapters, monasteries and abbeys – to be both landowners and seigneurs, and thus to claim rents and feudal dues from large numbers of peasants. In return for this, the church maintained extensive networks of charity, but these were not always enough to assuage resentment at clerical pursuit of their economic interests. Historically, however, such resentment had been relatively muted, and state taxation had been the great bugbear of the peasantry, occasioning massive revolts through the seventeenth century. By the last decades of the eighteenth century, in contrast, growing resentment was being provoked by the third dimension of the peasants' burden, the seigneurial regime. To understand this, we must explore how that regime had evolved, and was evolving.

Seigneurialism had begun as medieval feudalism. In the middle ages, much of the peasant population had been literally 'unfree' – serfs, bound by law to the lands they worked, under the rule of a lord whose rights over them were near absolute. Over the centuries, such seigneurs' 'ownership' of the peasants had gradually shifted towards a financial relationship. As the wider social structure altered, serfdom as a condition became harder to maintain, and lords themselves had more need of money, or of produce that could be sold for cash, than they did of servitude. Feudal rights were amended to mean rights to payment from those who worked the land – an annual rent, a share of the harvest, a fee if land changed hands or was inherited. Seigneurs also retained extensive rights over common lands in many areas – it was assumed in law that such lands were ultimately theirs, and they could plant woodlands, or harvest timber, regulate others' use of the land, and even divide and enclose it, if they chose, regardless of the use to which the community was accustomed to put it.[34]

Rights to game remained in seigneurs' hands, forbidding peasants from killing pests such as rabbits and pigeons, which were bred for lordly tables, and prohibiting the hunting of any game by those without privilege. The right to ride over peasants' crops without compensation in pursuit of deer or boar was also a privilege of the lord. Seigneurialism likewise entailed all the honorific privileges of lordship – a special pew in the local church, prayers offered and incense burned for their well-being, the right to a weathercock on the manor house, and to various other ritual gestures of submission. The rights of lordship further extended to the dispensing of justice, and tens of thousands of seigneurial courts guarded their tiny jurisdictions jealously. Royal justice had intervened by the eighteenth century to take away many significant judicial functions, but seigneurs, their agents, and the judges they appointed, still frequently made and enforced the laws which regulated their own relationship with the peasants.[35]

At the heart of the 'feudal regime' as it operated by the 1780s were several key elements: the clear relationship of superior and inferior legal and social status and the significance of financial benefits to the seigneur. Although the implications of these elements were very different, they had both led by this time to seigneurial rights becoming a marketable commodity, with profound implications for the peasantry. In the eighteenth century, just as land could change hands, so too could the feudal rights over it, and thus the rights over its inhabitants. Rights were purchased for the income that derived from them, and for the social status they conferred – nobility was the goal of almost all social mobility, and possession of a *seigneurie* or fief was a near-essential step towards it.

The gradual accumulation of landed property, and the eventual addition of a noble title, was a classic route upwards, still widely pursued in the late eighteenth century. Thousands of bourgeois families with professional or mercantile backgrounds were investing in lands and titles all through the 1780s, just as generations before had done. Meanwhile, great aristocrats continued to derive a substantial portion of their wealth from feudal exactions. In 1777 François-Louis de Bourbon-Conty, a relation of the king, sold the *comté* of Alais to Charles-Eugène-Gabriel La Croix Castries for 770,000 livres.[36] This enormous sum must have seemed a reasonable investment, for Castries was in no need of new titles to boost his prestige. He was a member of the inner circle of the royal court, and served as minister of the navy in the American War, being raised to the title of marshal of France by the king in 1783. The purchase gave Castries seigneurial rights over much of the Cévennes, including some fifty parishes, as well as substantial land-holdings and various other rights and privileges – tolls on local bridges, a watermill, fees on the sale of meat, and a 10 per cent levy on all new mines, which constituted a considerable element of the local economy. What is perhaps more noteworthy is the extent to which these rights were farmed out for commercial exploitation. Although Castries was punctilious in his feudal rights, visiting all fifty parishes to receive homage, he left the sordid details of money-making to non-nobles. Direct and indirect seigneurial dues of all kinds were let out, and sometimes then sublet and even sub-sublet, to local merchants and other individuals with money to invest and a profit to pursue. This included not just claims over crops, tolls and dues, but even the rights to charge for judicial functions.

Such systems of sub-letting could become even more complex, as is shown by the example of the Hautpoul family. We encountered the marquis d'Hautpoul earlier, as a landowner leasing through his agent, Jacques Maurel. The family held many lands reaching from Toulouse towards the eastern Pyrenees, some of which were leased out on a long-term basis. They were also seigneurs over an interlocking complex of lands. Rights to some of these were farmed out, while at the same time the Hautpouls held other seigneurial rights themselves that they had leased as vassals from other seigneurs. Thus a bourgeois, Pierre Cros, paid 6800 livres to lease three seigneuries from Paul de Fleury, a member of the family by marriage, while the family itself held the seigneurial rights over the community of Coustaussa from the bishop of Alet. In either case, harsh obligations fell on the peasant communities. In Coustaussa such was the range and force of seigneurial rights that less than 3 livres per year could be extracted by the state in taxation from each inhabitant. The province of Languedoc, within which all this activity fell, was unusual in the degree to which this farming of rights went on, but it clearly indicates the vigour with which such rights were pursued as a source of income, right up to the eve of the Revolution.[37]

Some of the consequences of this were remarked on as early as 1756 by the marquis de Mirabeau, who was both a member of the old nobility and a writer on agricultural reform. In a semi-satirical, semi-nostalgic tone he recalled the days when seigneurs actually lived on their estates, where at least 'if they annoyed their inhabitants, [they] annoyed them in person ... and they consumed the fruits of their so-called extortions right on the spot, without permitting anyone else to annoy the people'. He went on to observe that 'when nobody knows the seigneur of his domain any more, everyone will rob him – and that is as it should be'. It will be clear from the examples above that seigneurs of such extensive lands as Castries and the Hautpouls could not possibly fulfil this resident function – the former was a government minister, and the head of the latter family, known as 'Hautpoul the Magnificent', served in the household of the king's sister-in-law. Mirabeau further noted the prevalence of the trade in seigneurial rights, and the increasing lack of respect that peasant communities felt for 'new' seigneurs, including a willingness to challenge their rights in the courts, which was hitherto unheard of, according to him. Much of this was due, he suggested, to the social character of the new lords, who lacked the rapport with the rural population created by centuries of heritage. As he pointedly remarked, 'peasants have a fine ear and a good memory, and they will always say that their seigneur is no better than they are and that, if he is wealthier, he knew better how to lay his hands on money; as for the rest, let him eat two dinners'.[38]

Mirabeau's views clearly hark back to a 'golden age' which doubtless never existed, but there is no doubt that the prevalence of absentee seigneurs, who left their lands in the hands of profit-seeking agents, and the parallel arrival of 'bourgeois' with newly purchased fiefs, who preferred profit maximisation to feudal obligation, was a problem for those who lived under this yoke. It is also apparent that even old-style resident seigneurs were encountering problems with 'their' peasants by the 1780s, often because of attempts to increase feudal dues. Despite Mirabeau's words, seigneurialism was a powerful and active force in the lives of many villagers. In a number of regions, it was the seigneur who actually convened the village meetings that were elsewhere an expression of communal autonomy – this was the case in much of Lorraine, for example, and in the Corbières, where the seigneur also chose the village's officials from an elected short list.

If the state and its officials took an active role in regulating village organisation, this was not always without problems for the elite. In Burgundy, for example, tensions between villagers and seigneurs were rising in the later eighteenth century, as villagers increasingly used the instruments of royal justice to challenge feudal exactions.[39] Peasant communities, possibly encouraged by urban lawyers, found the will and the funds to launch lawsuits contesting the legitimacy of a wide range of dues, such as the requirement for communities to pay towards the upkeep of seigneurial fortifications, or to use the collective bread ovens. They also contested the seigneur's traditional right to claim extra dues upon the marriage of a daughter, and the more common attempt by seigneurs to claim the exclusive right to one-third of previously communal woodlands. It was in the state's interest to support peasant attempts to lighten these burdens, because it returned revenue to the 'unprivileged', and hence taxable, portion of the population. Less cynically, it also freed funds for productive agricultural investment. Almost without exception, however, the peasants lost their cases. The fact that they returned to the courts time and again across the 1770s and 1780s, despite repeated failures and the costs involved, indicates how strongly they were prepared to resist.[40]

If tensions in Burgundy were rising on the eve of the Revolution, and seigneurs were being put on the defensive, in the Corbières and elsewhere the seigneurial regime was fighting back. One reason was the recession in the textile industry, which had also hit the Cévennes. Wealthy merchants who had diversified into land and seigneurial property now attempted to increase their returns from these investments as commerce faltered. Joseph d'Airolles, the son of a textile magnate, gave up the business almost entirely from the 1770s and became an ardent maximiser of feudal revenues. Despite owning only one-tenth of the seigneurial rights to the community of Villefloure, for example, d'Airolles was prepared to pay for a prosecution for alleged illegal sheep-grazing there against the inhabitants that dragged on from 1760 to 1784. On one occasion he personally apprehended a man who was using a cart to collect firewood illicitly, and had his horses confiscated by the local court. Older aristocrats and religious foundations with seigneurial rights also suffered from a general economic slump. This led some to put their lands and rights up for sale to bourgeois customers who would exploit

them more thoroughly, while others began to pursue revenue more ruthlessly. In the community of Villerouge-Termenès, the agent of the archbishop
began a law suit against the villagers in 1785 that was to drag on into the
Revolution, concerning whether or not feudal dues and tithes were payable
on the relatively new food crop, the potato.[41] Although, as in Burgundy,
the overlapping spaces between royal and seigneurial justice left communities
some room for challenge and manoeuvre, the seigneurs almost always won
in the end. Such victories, however, were increasingly won at some cost in
time and money, and with a further price paid in growing reports of
'insubordination' and a spirit of antiseigneurial resistance, especially amongst
the younger generation.[42]

Although the great weight of the seigneurial system bore down on the
peasantry, they never ceased to fight against it. Indeed the very extent of
conflict is a token of the peasantry's vigour in pursuing their own interests
against the 'higher' social echelons. The seigneurial 'offensive' or 'feudal
reaction' seen by many observers in the second half of the century was an
effort by many seigneurs to recodify and clarify their rights, which may
have disadvantaged many communities. It can also be seen, however, as
testimony to the growing contestation of those rights by the communities
themselves.[43] It is a further irony of the long-term development of French
agriculture that a healthy peasant resistance to imposed changes and burdens
in many areas, maintaining collective farming practices and traditional
common rights, inhibited the kind of revolutionary improvement in pro-
ductivity that advocates of 'English' methods sought throughout the century.
If, as we shall see, the land of France was coming under greater pressure
in the 1780s, this was partly at least because peasants insisted on their right
to continue using that land as they saw fit, and not as large landowners or
managing tenants wanted it used.[44]

As a largely subsistence-based rural population, the peasantry remained
nonetheless subject to that greatest of tyrannies, the weather. With the
manufacturing sector mired in a period of faltering growth, and heavy
population pressure on resources, France began in 1785 to experience a run
of climatic problems, perhaps linked to a series of major volcanic eruptions
in Iceland in 1783–85 that had sent high-level ash-clouds to distort weather
patterns. There was a fair harvest in 1785, but a very dry summer which
caused problems with the raising of forage crops for livestock. The harvest
of 1786 was bad in western France, and a second dry summer led to a
failure of the hay harvest, forcing many peasants to dispose of livestock
they could not feed through the winter. By 1787, when the harvest was
uniformly poor, wider political confrontation was already moving the kingdom towards revolutionary change, in which the sufferings and resentments

of the peasantry would play a crucial role. Before resuming that story, we need to bring into focus that small minority, living amongst the great sea of the peasantry, whose relative geographical concentration would give them a crucial role in revolutionary political events – the inhabitants of the towns.

2

Artisans

To pass from the rural to the urban environment in this era was truly to enter a different world. It often meant quite literally passing through a gate in a fortified wall, leaving behind fields and cottages, and moving into a maze of narrow streets, overhung by four-, five- or six-storey buildings, where people, their lives and their work, were piled upon one another. The urban environment was one in which the presence of people, and their noises, smells and waste, had erased much of nature. It is true that in most towns livestock were brought to market, and possibly even reared in yards within the walls; but it is also true that, in the districts where the poorest lived, not even the sun could penetrate the warren of passages between tall buildings that had obliterated any sense of a natural landscape.

Although the population of France was overwhelmingly rural, the urban population was widespread – the territory of France held far more towns than any other European state, as many as seventy-eight with a population over 10,000 by the end of the eighteenth century (compared to only thirty in England), and over 280 with more than 5000 inhabitants. Paris was the largest city in Europe after London, with at least 600,000 inhabitants (some estimates suggest it was nearing 700,000 by 1789). Lyon, Bordeaux and Marseille lagged far behind this figure, at around 100,000, but each was an impressive regional metropolis nonetheless. Although many towns were relatively stagnant in size, others boomed through the century – Bordeaux doubled in size on the profits of the Atlantic slave trade, which also benefited other ports such as Nantes and La Rochelle. Marseille also swelled on the back of an extensive Mediterranean shipping network. Textile towns in the north and south, from Lille and Rouen to Nîmes, also saw their populations as much as double.

The smallest towns were little more than enlarged villages, dominated at their heart by a church, often with an open market square in front of it, surrounded by the homes of the wealthier inhabitants. A few backstreets accommodated the poorer townsfolk and their places of work. Such workplaces might also be incorporated into higher-status buildings. A central feature of urban architecture in the eighteenth century was the mixing of social groups within many buildings. The aristocratic elite in the larger cities could afford to maintain private town houses, or *hôtels*, often enclosed within a walled courtyard, but almost all other urban residents lived in rented apartments. The classic format of such an apartment block saw the ground floor rented out as retail and workshop space, relatively high-ceilinged and well-appointed living-quarters on the next two floors, and another two, three or even four floors of progressively smaller and cheaper accommodation above. Servants were often lodged in the attics of buildings where their masters lived on the first or second floor.[1]

In Paris in the 1780s a prestigious first-floor apartment of anywhere up to six or eight rooms might be let out for 700 livres a year, while a set of two small rooms higher up could be had for 100–150 livres, and a single fifth- or sixth-floor room for as little as 40 livres. Nightly lodgings were priced at 1 or 2 sous, and often meant being crammed in fifteen or twenty to a room. As is often the case with property rental, the lower-status rooms could in fact be more profitable per square metre. As urban populations rose, builders met the demand for accommodation by working upwards. Sometimes, as in central Paris, this was made impossible by a lack of solid foundations, and housing stock was increased by filling in courtyards and open spaces with new buildings backing onto the old, sometimes linked by only the tiniest alleyways or passages to the original streets. Such infill was not necessarily solid construction. One three-storey building on the rue Haute in Rennes in 1777 included five ground-floor shops and workshops, linked to rooms above, containing seven households. No less than thirty households, however, lived in wooden shacks of one or two storeys that filled the rear courtyard. Of these thirty, nineteen were so poor as to be ineligible to pay the royal poll tax, or *capitation*.[2]

Some cities managed to increase both in size and density. Bordeaux developed a sprawling range of suburbs through the eighteenth century, and constructed public squares and a range of magnificent public buildings, while also maintaining a dense hub of medieval streets. Such was demand that high-density housing still commanded profitable rents, even when there were suburban alternatives. Lyon, by contrast, was on a more con-strained site. The centre of the city was wedged between the rivers Rhône and Saône, and steep hills limited the possibilities for outward expansion. Nevertheless, while the centre became a warren of interlocked buildings, connected by covered passageways that survive to this day, Lyon also spread to new quarters on the surrounding hills – not least because its silk weavers needed light to work by. Such urban sprawl also began to produce social segregation. Paris had already shown signs of this in the seventeenth century, as the medieval heart was shunned by the rich and the noble in favour of newly developed zones to the west. Cardinal Richelieu built what is today the Palais-Royal at the heart of one such new district, and although the Champs-Elysées was still an open space at the end of the eighteenth century, the westward drift of wealth had already marked out the Faubourgs Saint-Honoré and Saint-Germain as prestige addresses.

As the rich reached out towards the countryside even in their town houses, they left the working classes behind in the artificial landscape of the city centre. Here even the mud underfoot bore little relation to the soil, being largely a compound of horse manure and the refuse of thousands of households without any other means of sanitation – and in the major towns a population of crossing-sweepers scraped a living clearing paths for those whose footwear merited such concern. Such streets were nonetheless home to real 'urban villages'. The neighbourhood community took as keen an interest in the lives and affairs of its members as did any peasant village, and was as likely to conduct its business and its disputes in public, before the common gaze. The street was a real centre of collective existence. People met and gossiped on doorsteps, spread their wares for sale before their shops, and even worked at their crafts in the open air, where they might see what they were doing without the expense of candles. In many cases, the role of the street as a link from one place to another became secondary to its role as the hub of local existence, much to the anguish of authorities who wished to speed up the movement of goods and people.[3]

Urban life was public in many other senses. Few amongst the working population were able to afford a fully self-contained household, where all the services of domestic life were carried out within the home. For many, cooked food only came from the *traiteurs*, sellers of hot food, who for a small sum would also allow local people to cook their own food in their ovens. Laundry could not be done in the home, and in Paris as many as two thousand washerwomen were employed on the banks of the Seine, and on barges on the river itself, keeping the city's linen clean. Water for other uses either had to be collected by householders or servants from local wells or fountains, or purchased from the water-carriers who trudged back and forth from the river, carrying a thirty-litre load in their yoked pair of pails and delivering to all floors. The constant passage of such deliveries, and all the other movements of this outdoor, disjointed way of life, made the bare wooden staircases and passages of urban buildings throb with activity.

While all the trials and tribulations of childhood, marriage and household formation amongst the peasantry equally applied to urban dwellers, their lives were in some senses even more on display than those of the countryside. Mere proximity, and the fact that most people lived in thin-walled and shoddily sub-divided apartment blocks, made the most private disagreement public. City-dwellers in particular were beginning to adopt some habits that made the necessity for such visibility a virtue. The second half of the eighteenth century saw consumer goods begin to appear in the inventories of the urban household. The single religious print of previous generations was replaced on the walls by popular engravings, or by the more colourful products of the ceramics industry, which turned out countless illustrated plates. Books, too, became more commonplace, as did furniture that was more than just utilitarian storage.[4]

Clothing expanded its range of styles and colours, sturdy wool giving way to the new cotton fabrics with all manner of patterns and weaves. For ordinary urbanites, and especially Parisians, a main source of such garments was the second-hand trade, which dealt in the cast-offs of a well-established elite consumer culture. Historians a generation ago, who first noted this, spoke of the wearing of second-hand clothes in this way as if it were a symbolic humiliation, but it is far more likely that men and women, particularly of the younger generations, welcomed the chance to display themselves in a range of finery that would have been far beyond their means if bought new. It also helped to mark them out from the peasantry, still clad in fusty brown, and such a distinction was valued by an urban culture which looked down on the countryside. Such scorn was highly ironic, since a majority of residents in the expanding major cities were at best one generation, or even only a few years or months, away from a rural or small-town origin, and many kept up active family contacts with those left behind.

Town and country were never in any sense sealed off from one another by gates and walls, but in other important ways they were fundamentally different. Entering a town meant not only leaving the natural environment for a largely artificial one, but also entering the cultural and legal space controlled by the town – for, like so many other bodies in Old Regime France, towns had their privileges, their own rules and rights. At the centre of many of these complexes of rights were the skilled tradesmen, and their families, who made up the established core of the urban population. The higher classes, such as merchants and nobles, floated above the 'real' daily life of the town, although often exercising considerable formal power through the purchase of municipal privileges, the urban equivalent of the *seigneurie*, which made them part of the town's official existence vis-à-vis other towns and the state. Lower groups, such as domestic servants and unskilled labourers, tended to either become isolated and marginal, trapped in furnished lodgings and pining for home, or formed their own relatively enclosed sub communities – this was the case, for example, with the Limousins and Auvergnats who came to Paris. It was the artisan classes who gave urban life much of its particular character. One very direct way in which they did this was through their own privileged corporations of trades, more commonly called in English 'guilds'. Under the guild system, groups of artisans in a particular town – hatters, carpenters, joiners, shoe-makers, tailors, goldsmiths, bakers, saddlers, weavers, and so on – were granted a formal collective identity by the state, allowed to set rules for the practice of their trade, to appoint officers to monitor and enforce those rules, to govern entry to the trade, and to police the workers they employed.[5]

Full members of corporations were 'master craftsmen'. These masters were able to work freely at their trade in their particular town, and had the protection of the guild against unfair or unlicensed competition and unruly workers. Masters were also able to take on apprentices to work for them. Apprenticeship was the traditional way both to learn the practicalities of a trade and to qualify for formal membership of it. Adolescent boys were taken into a master's workshop through a contract between the master and the boy's parents. The term of apprenticeship generally varied between two and five years. The apprentice would usually be housed and fed by the master, who agreed to teach him all the 'secrets' and 'mysteries' of his craft, in return for his labour and a payment by the parents. Once a boy had completed an apprenticeship satisfactorily, and received the appropriate certificate from the guild, he was in theory able to become a guild master.

Guild masterships were not, however, given away freely to everyone who qualified. They were privileged offices and as such had a value. Their numbers were restricted by the statutes of the corporation, and further limited by a requirement to pay a considerable fee to register. For low-status trades such as tanners and potters, this might be 300 livres, rising to over 1000 for masons, carpenters and goldsmiths, and over 2500 for the drapers, the most prestigious of the historic *Six Corps* of Paris. Blood relatives of existing masters were often allowed around some of these restrictions, but others might have to wait many years before the opportunity to acquire a mastership presented itself. As this was a longstanding fact of artisan life, it had incorporated itself into the structure of the individual's career. After completing an apprenticeship most artisans became, for at least several years, 'journeymen', or in French *compagnons*. The two different terms illustrate two sides of this position. Journeymen frequently travelled widely, sometime completing a literal *Tour de France*, working in many different towns, acquiring a wide range of skills and knowledge of different products and methods. They worked as the 'companions' of masters, in a loose sense, as they were very much subordinate to them officially, and they also es-tablished networks of 'companionship' amongst themselves. Cutting across the network of guilds, each of which represented one trade in one place, were several networks of unofficial journeymen's organisations, each of which embraced members of many trades in many towns. These provided lodging and sociability for newly arrived members, and often acted as 'labour exchanges' to place them with local masters.

The mobility of artisans was one thing that marked out their milieu from the rural background. Rural migrant labourers might move long distances, but they tended to follow set regional patterns, as we have seen. Journeymen did not always move from one end of France to the other, but some did, and their routes varied widely. In Tours, in the Loire valley, three and a half thousand journeymen of various trades worked during the 1780s. A map of their birthplaces shows a sharp peak in the region around Tours itself, but also a long gentle slope out to almost every corner of France. Previous work had also spread them widely: over 10 per cent of those with identifiable previous workplaces had worked in Paris, almost as many in Orléans, and in Nantes at the mouth of the Loire. The other towns of the Loire valley had accommodated smaller contingents, and around 5 per cent had worked further south in Bordeaux. Smaller numbers had worked in localities spread across almost half of the country.

In theory, this mobile artisan world ran to its own order and logic – including clear stages of career progression, legally defined status, and collective organisations with economic and social functions. Needless to say, it did not actually work so smoothly. The world of the trades boiled and bubbled with conflict, within and between different groupings, so that a snapshot of any city's artisans at a moment in the 1770s or 1780s would reveal unexpected coalitions and oppositions up and down the 'career-ladder', and differences in economic circumstances that bore little relation to the notion of such a 'ladder'. To begin to explore this, we must note some things that artisan life was not. It was not, first, a stable world of uniformly small workshops and long-term, paternalistic social relations. Although the relationship of apprenticeship clearly was intended to take this form, not all masters had apprentices, and not all apprentices worked out their term.

For many masters it made more sense to work alone unless there was a large job to be done, in which case one or more journeymen could be hired, either by the day or for a specified period, or even for piecework. Where apprentices were employed, they would spend more time as general dogsbodies and the butt of journeymen's practical jokes than learning from the work of the master – often because a master prosperous enough to afford apprentices and journeymen did little of the work himself. The vagaries of individual fortunes could also drive holes through the model of formal subordination. A master who could afford to employ three or four journeymen for a contract might find later that he had to hire himself out as labour to another master, and work alongside such journeymen, only to regain prosperity later when new clients or contracts came along.

Nor were artisans all independent traders providing individually hand-finished goods for personal customers. Even in the tailoring and shoemaking trades, workshops were as likely to be fulfilling a wholesale contract as supplying individuals. Clothing and shoes were bulk exports from France in the eighteenth century, to the Caribbean and American colonial markets, and throughout the Mediterranean. The majority of artisanal work was done, not for consumers, but for other artisans. Thus a carriage-maker who supplied a carriage to a customer would have dealt with joiners, wheelwrights, upholsterers, saddlers, locksmiths, ornamental painters, glaziers and others to produce the finished article. Within a business like the making of furniture, a cabinet-maker or joiner conducted more deals with inlayers, stonecutters, marble-polishers, lacquerers, locksmiths and other woodworkers than he did with customers. Indeed, even finished articles might be sold wholesale to the growing number of luxury emporia in the largest cities of France.

Moreover, not all artisans were members of corporations and subject to their rules. The jurisdiction of such corporations was limited geographically to their own town, but even within that town there might be enclaves free of such regulation. In Paris, the eastern suburb called the Faubourg St-Antoine had enjoyed since 1657 a royal privilege giving complete freedom from guild regulation.[6] Five other smaller enclaves within the city had similar privileges, mostly due to their ownership by a seigneur or a religious house. There were similar areas in other large towns – Saint-Sever in Rouen, and the district known as Vaise in Lyon, for example. In Bordeaux there were two very different 'free' zones: around fifty hectares inside the city under the authority of the cathedral chapter of Saint-André, and an area of several square miles in the north-western suburbs controlled by the chapter of Saint-Seurin. In such zones individual artisans could work free from the interference of corporate regulation, though they could run into legal trouble if they attempted to do business with others inside the regulated zone. Even within regulated areas, there were illicit workers known as *chambrelans,* because they worked hidden in their own rooms (*chambres*), not in a visible workshop.

Artisans who worked in smaller towns might have no dealings with the corporate world, simply because their community was too small to have been granted its own guilds. Furthermore, and strikingly, it was possible for many trades to operate without a guild structure, even in larger cities. In Bordeaux, most notably, there were some fifty incorporated trades encompassing over 1800 registered masters in the late eighteenth century, but also over thirty municipally recognised trades without guild structures, covering possibly as many as three thousand 'free' masters.[7] These included cooperage, a huge industry due to the confluence of Atlantic shipping with the wine trade, and a wide range of services connected to the port, such as porterage and boating. Nevertheless, such work still tended towards regulation and corporatist practices – on the docks of Paris, for example, stevedores who dealt in different cargoes were nominated to their posts by different regulatory bodies, as were the porters of the various *Halles*, or marketplaces. The number of men authorised to shovel coal on the docks was limited by law to twenty-eight, while to become a porter for the customs service required a payment of 800 livres and a recommendation. This was, of course, largely unskilled labour, but its regulation reflected its place in the world of privilege that governed so many official attitudes to work practices.

One of the central features bestowed by guild membership was corporate identity. By being part of a corporation, the master artisan participated in a society where such membership was a definition of social identity. Just as peasants only really acquired a place in society when they could act collectively as a community, through legal forms, so it was that only in a corporation were artisans officially part of society. If an artisan was interested in his social status, in acquiring respect and standing within his community, establishment as a guild master was an almost essential step: wherever it was possible, it was definitely desirable. Similarly, though many artisans survived outside the guild system, few were likely to prosper there. The guilds clung jealously to their rights and privileges, and defended them vigorously. They could take offenders to court, and even act more directly, since they had police powers over the conduct of their trade within their area. Materials could be impounded, masters fined, and workers reported to the state police authorities for discipline. It was clearly better to be on the inside of this system than outside.

Master artisans in France's larger cities built up networks of relationships across generations that could weave the core of a city's trades into a powerful bloc – sons of well-established masters were apprenticed to masters of similar status in their own or other trades, and subsequently married daughters of other masters, thus becoming masters in their turn through relationships on both sides, using both institutional and familial resources to consolidate the opportunities for advancement and security. To be apprenticed to a master in one's city of birth was already to be a member of a fortunate minority – only about a third of apprentices in Lyon in 1786 could claim this link between work and origins, and most of this group could thereby have looked forward to integration into the city's guilds. The other two-thirds of 'incomer' apprentices had to fight for advancement with the journeymen who flocked to the city, and probably move on themselves at some point.

Despite the manifold advantages of guild status, many masters found that their economic needs came into conflict with their guild responsibilities. Here again the everyday practices of artisans added another layer of complexity to the simple theoretical image of their world. As the guilds sought to establish a concrete social identity for their members, they also sought to stabilise the work that they did. Stability and subordination were key values for Old Regime society, and the aspiration of the guilds was to establish a system in which apprentices and journeymen acknowledged their dependence on masters, obeyed their authority, and followed clear, guild-controlled procedures for work. This included the day-to-day practice of labour and its payment, and the longer-term issues of job mobility, both within a particular guild's jurisdiction and around the country. The legal rhetoric of the guilds suggested that masters and journeymen had a common interest in preserving a stable, well-ordered system; but from an economic perspective a variety of conflicting interests prevailed. Such interests formed a shifting web that cut across the master-journeyman line, and often threw up divisions amongst masters themselves.

In the first place, the way in which work came to masters was irregular and problematic. For most artisans, contracts were not the result of a customer walking into an open shop off the street. Rather, in their world of subcontracting and interconnected manufacturing practices, artisans worked with people they knew, and found work by keeping in touch. For a master, it was as important to be found in the local bars, where other artisans could be met, forthcoming work heard about and discussed, contracts bid for and deals done, as it was to actually be at work. Indeed, in some senses, maintaining an image of sociability, approachability and open-handedness was work. Connected to this is the fact that many artisan jobs were short-term, and needed to be completed in a hurry. The classic example is the production of mourning-wear, which threw a city's tailors and seamstresses into a frenzy when a prominent person died, but which, if a day or two late, was useless. Artisans needed to be flexible, and able to respond to quick changes in demand, or to sudden opportunities – if a contractor went bankrupt, died, or was injured in an accident, work was there for the taking. Few would hesitate to make a move in such circumstances, even if it meant cutting across official hierarchies and demarcations.

The journeymen themselves also frequently organised counter-hierarchies and alternative practices for regulating work. Either through their associations, or through purely local arrangements at the inns where many itinerant journeymen lodged, it was common for 'last in, first out' policies to be enforced, and for recent arrivals to be obliged to shift jobs, or even leave town, in favour of more settled and senior journeymen. This was the quid pro quo for the way in which journeymen's organisations helped to find work, and provided sociability, for such itinerants. It helped to ensure that, while mobility was possible, long-resident journeymen, perhaps with family responsibilities, were most likely to stay in regular work. It also enabled both journeymen and masters to negotiate a delicate relationship between an inadequate supply of settled local labour, known and reliable, but which might expect to be well paid, and a potential abundance of mobile labour, of distinctly unknown quality, employable more cheaply. Such ongoing negotiation was fraught with conflict, however, as one case demonstrates.

In November 1782 Pierre Vandercruysse, a master tailor in Rouen, complained to his guild that five of his six journeymen had walked out. The guild authorities lodged a complaint with the police, who found pieces of cloth taken from the workplace in the rooms at the inn where the journeymen were lodging. Brought up before the local royal court, the journeymen admitted walking out, but claimed that in so doing they were following instructions from the senior journeyman responsible for the rules of the inn, which were well known to the guilds. These practices were illegal, as rulings in 1763, 1766, 1777 and only two months before in September 1782 had shown. But of course such a sequence of repeated rulings also shows that the practices were continuing, and must have had at least the tacit support of some masters. Indeed, when in 1777 it had been ruled that journeymen had to go through a guild placement bureau to find work, some masters, including Vandercruysse himself, had lodged an unsuccessful appeal against this. It is also noteworthy that, between 1778 and 1780, Vandercruysse had recruited his journeymen from the inn where the five who walked out lodged, then had tried recruiting from two other places, before resuming relations with that inn in 1782. Furthermore, the court case hinged not on the cloth found in the men's rooms, for no theft charges were pressed, but on the issue of guild regulations. Vandercruysse's action may have had any one of a number of aims: to pressure the guild to enforce controls more tightly, or to change the balance of power in his relation with the inn by harming the reputations of those who lodged there, or to hinder the work of the other masters for whom the five men had left to work. It may even have been a tactic to provoke a wider dispute between journeymen and the guild to bring down the official placement bureau.[8]

All this stood in stark contrast to the guild ideal. In everyday practice everything in the artisan world was negotiable, and the formal rules of guilds about materials, prices, wage rates and rights were honoured only when it suited the parties concerned. Guilds laid down strict rules to prevent journeymen leaving a master's employ other than by mutual agreement (or dismissal), but at the same time the most common reason for journeymen to abandon work was that they had received a better offer from another master, who was in more urgent need of workers.[9] While the guilds' fixed ideas of rank and status were challenged by such economic imperatives, they also clashed with both masters' and journeymen's values of honour.

In some ways, honour was itself closely linked to economic, or at least material, issues. Journeymen, both individually and collectively, frequently resorted to a language of affronts to their honour when they felt that they were being offered low wage rates or problematic working conditions. They asserted that the wage they received was the price of their labour, which they had the right to negotiate themselves, or to demand customary levels, depending on which argument suited the moment. Since this 'price' was part of a free contract, journeymen did not view themselves as formally subordinated to masters, so to attempt to treat them as if they were was an insult. Arrangements for the work of journeymen frequently included the tacit or explicit recognition of this status. Journeymen who lodged on a master's premises were especially touchy about being taken for domestic servants, and expected the actual servants to wait on them, serve meals, tidy their rooms and make their beds, and generally treat them as superiors. This was even more the case in journeymen's relations with apprentices, who were formally subordinated to the master. Journeymen could refuse to work unless apprentices showed them suitable deference, which included tasks such as unlocking and preparing the workshop before waking them in the morning, and might include any of the domestic duties of a servant.

At the same time, disgruntled journeymen knew exactly how precious a commodity the honour of their masters was. Honour in this sense has sometimes been called 'social honour', 'reputation', or 'credit', and that last term hints at its importance in this context. Artisans lived and died by credit. For the average master, cash transactions were few and far between – even if he were selling to consumers, many of them would not pay immediately, especially not if they were aristocrats, who had long perfected techniques for living beyond their means. Artisans trading between themselves lived even further from a final cash reckoning. They survived on their credit – on the belief of other people that they were good for the money eventually, or at least good for an indefinitely continued and fluctuating relationship of deferral of reckoning. Such other people included the innkeepers who sold them drink, the bakers who sold them bread, their landlords, and their journeymen themselves, who probably had to use their master's reputation to guarantee credit for their own everyday needs.

Creditors also included all their business contacts, who might equally be a master's debtors at the same time.

Credit was lubricated by such payments as might be possible – it would not be extended indefinitely for food and drink, for example, and journeymen also expected to be paid at reasonable intervals – but its main facilitator was reputation. And reputation was a topic of continual discussion. As artisans networked for business opportunities, so they also networked to maintain their reputations, and wherever possible to disparage others. They would hotly deny any charge of defamation, of course, but this was a world in which everyone took a risk in doing business, and where rumour and gossip were picked over carefully. Thus one of the most effective tactics for discomfiting a master, if you were an employee or a rival, was to spread rumours of business or personal problems.

Disputes that dwelt on the language of honour cut across others that dwelt on the language of liberty, which for many journeymen was an expression of similar ideals. In August 1783 in Bordeaux, the shipbuilders' corporation posted a deliberation requiring shipwrights to possess certificates of good conduct from their masters. This resulted in a strike amongst carpenters and caulkers, in which officials of the corporation were repeatedly insulted and denounced as thieves, as well as being exposed to physical threats. The guild officials explained in court as they applied for sanctions against the strikers that 'the workers wanted to be free; that they [said that they] would never be made to submit themselves to holding tickets of leave'.[10] A language of equality, or rather of equality of honour, was also present in such confrontations – both masters and journeymen could become enraged if not addressed by their counterparts with the formal *vous*. Masters were expected to respect journeymen's customary holidays, allow them to take part in *compagnonnage* ceremonies, and even to contribute funds to collective celebrations. The presence of masters, with their wives and daughters, on such occasions was a further mark of respect, as was the giving of *étrennes*, new year gifts, and *pâtés de veille*, seasonal feasts. Under strained circumstances these relationships, of course, could turn nasty, and masters' female relatives were a favourite target of abuse, usually only verbal, by angry journeymen. In its own way, this was a displacement of anger it was not always possible, or politic, to display to masters' faces – respect for the master inside his own workshop was ingrained into the journeymen's culture, even if that sometimes meant inviting him to step outside to a local bar to receive a tirade of abuse.

Disputes between masters and journeymen were only one dimension of the contests that could divide the artisan milieu. The guilds themselves were highly litigious bodies, and displayed an obsessional interest in defending the boundaries of their privileges. Defining precisely who was permitted to work in what place with which materials took up a large amount of court time in Old Regime France, especially as appeals, counter-appeals and fresh cases launched to overturn previous verdicts could cascade across decades. Underlying this inter-guild conflict was a set of contradictory legal and economic facts about work in France. The system of apprenticeship and mastership supposed that there were specific 'secrets' of each individual trade, and that only insiders to that trade fully understood them. This was the notion of a 'trade' defined in law through the whole corporate system. Yet it was an elaborate fiction. With the exception of a few traders like jewellers, goldsmiths and glaziers, most artisans worked with one of a few basic materials – wood, leather, cloth, iron and other common metals. Within each of these fields there were only so many possible ways of treating materials. What a locksmith could do, a blacksmith probably could, if he put his mind to it. Likewise, a saddler could probably make shoes, and a carpenter, limited by definition to construction work, could build furniture. Even more outrageously, a seamstress could, if not prevented by law and custom, turn her hand to making men's clothes, thus imperilling the careers of tailors throughout the land. Unlicensed, free-for-all competition was the terror of the economic Old Regime, and the whole guild system functioned to keep it at bay. Of course, at the same time, individual masters and workers took the work that they could find, and frequently the work that they thought they could get away with, but to the minds of the guilds' leaders this just proved the degeneracy of humanity if not subjected to strict rules.

Ironically, at the same time as guilds strove to defend their corporate privileges, they also frequently fought out bitter political battles in their own ranks.[11] The masters of a particular guild were generally divided, by custom and practice, and sometimes by guild statute, into three groups. The two largest groups were the *jeunes* and the *modernes*, which might be described respectively as 'young' and 'established' masters. The *jeunes* generally had little voice in corporate affairs, but would in time graduate to the ranks of the *modernes*, from which candidates would be chosen to swell the ranks of the third group, the *anciens*. This group was made up of those who had held office in the guild, as elected *jurés*, *syndics* or *consuls*. Naturally, guilds were not simple democracies and their electoral systems were often in the pockets of the *anciens*, who thus exercised a strict control over who could join their ranks. More importantly, for day-to-day practices, control over who held guild office meant control over the policing and taxation functions of the guilds. Like so many other corporate bodies across France, the guilds paid for their privileges by collectively contributing to the king's coffers, and how this burden was passed on to individual members was in the hands of the guild's officials. Likewise, it was in their hands to apply regulations on the quality of materials and workmanship, the recruitment of apprentices and journeymen, and the competition for work. Any and all of these could be used to victimise some masters and turn a blind eye to the sharp practice of others.

Just as the the guild's façade concealed wide variation and conflict, so there was wide variation amongst the associations formed by journeymen. Not all were illicit. There was a long tradition of local religious confraternities in France, groups of men whose association fulfilled both a socialising and a charitable function, and many of these were formed by journeymen. Dedicated to the patron saint of the locality or the trade, these groups' religious origin gave a certain legitimacy to what could also be a drinking club and focus for work-related disputes.[12] However, the institution of the confraternity was in steep decline by the end of the eighteenth century, as such overtly religious behaviour seemed to go out of fashion in the urban milieu, and many of the confraternities that continued to function amongst journeymen had shifted their nature more firmly to a social and economic basis. In Marseille in 1787, for example, journeymen hatmakers gathered under the umbrella of the 'Luminary of St-Catherine'. A court ruling against them noted that this was a 'venerable pious institution', but that its religious functions had become merely an 'excuse' to allow journeymen to hold meetings on religious premises and to store funds there, supposedly for religious services.

In its condemnation of the association the court alleged that journeymen arriving in the city were forced to pay into these common funds, and that, when sufficient monies had been collected, the journeymen took it upon themselves to 'band together and riot'. Although it also noted that such actions had the aim of forcing masters to concede the journeymen's desired pay rates, the court seemed to suggest that the opportunity for debauch was the primary goal of the association. It also noted the existence of written statutes for the groups, which 'carried licence so far' as to lay down how many hats a worker should make in a day. As the court concluded, 'everything about such acts is illicit, clandestine, and contrary to every law and regulation, old or new. We must completely destroy these unruly and abusive associations'.[13]

The Marseille hatters' association had clearly evolved in the direction of what is known generally as compagnonnage. Nineteenth-century nostalgic accounts of compagnonnage groups often portrayed them as ancient, quasi-masonic networks of lodges, with quite specific and complex hierarchies and rivalries. They were almost certainly rather looser, vaguer groupings than this. Membership in compagnonnage groups seems to have been most prevalent in the building, furnishing and clothing trades, areas where, as we noted, work might easily overlap official guild demarcations, and where job opportunities were also rapidly shifting. Compagnonnage was most prevalent in the cities which marked out some of the most common routes of the artisan's *Tour de France*: a rough square from Orléans and Troyes in north-central France, down through Burgundy via Dijon and Mâcon, into the Rhône valley, Lyon and Marseille, then west along the coast through Nîmes and Montpellier, inland to Toulouse and to the Atlantic at Bayonne, up through Bordeaux to La Rochelle and Nantes, and finally inland along the Loire via Angers and Tours to complete the figure. Geographically and economically, compagnonnage provided journeymen with resources to compete in a fluid and frequently harsh market.

At the heart of compagnonnage was the inn where itinerant journeymen lodged. As we have already seen, such inns could by themselves act as centres for recruitment and collective journeyman organisation. Via the rituals and identities imparted by compagnonnage, inns in different cities were linked together into networks for the shelter, socialisation and employment of journeymen far from home. The inn lodged the workers, its hostess was known as the compagnons' *mère*, and two compagnonnage officers kept them in order. The 'roller' performed the dual function of keeping a roll of members and also 'rolling' them from one job to another, balancing demand and equity for new arrivals. The 'captain' or 'first in the town' was a president who guarded the rules of the association and managed its rituals. Members of the compagnonnages wore garlands of ribbons on special occasions, with the colour designating their trade, ritually greeted one another, and ceremonially bade farewell to members who departed for other towns – this, like many of their rituals, usually involved considerable consumption of alcohol. Perhaps for this reason, violent brawling was also common – the 1787 ruling against the Marseille hatters noted that 'they pit association against association and engage in the most ferocious fighting'. Journeymen who fell victim to injuries or the law as a result of such incidents could expect the support of their comrades, up to and including a ceremonial funeral.

Compagnonnage blended an adherence to the idea of ritual, secrecy and solidarity with paradoxical elements of instability, inconsistency and even improvisation. The term *devoir*, 'duty', was the most common label applied to compagnonnage members by themselves and others in the eighteenth century – they were *compagnons du devoir* or *devoirants*. Such members applied many labels to non-members, amongst the most common being *gavots*, a term of abuse implying rusticity, originating in southern France, where it was used to describe peasant migrants from Haute Provence and Spain. However, it was also the proudly held name of an alternative, rival compagnonnage, especially strong in Lyon and the Rhône valley. *Gavots* and *devoirants* might occupy different inns in the same neighbourhood – in Lyon the locksmiths of the two rites lodged separately on the rue Ecorcheboeuf, as did *gavot* joiners, while *devoirant* joiners had a fourth inn on the neighbouring rue Ferrandière. Fighting between the two groups could nonetheless be significant, and the stakes of such fights, in addition to prestige and collective virility, might include the right of the compagnonnage to control access to work in the town. This right was sometimes contested even more formally, through agreed trials of craft skill, which often also included substantial wagers, spent on feasting by the winners.

Such contests seem to display a compagnonnage tradition that was institutionalised, permanent and profound, but a court case in Troyes in 1782 revealed another side to journeyman organisation. After one journeyman leather-dresser was persuaded by his master to complain to the police that he had been 'forced' to pay 30 livres for initiation into the *devoir*, it emerged through the courts that the weekend of drinking this involved had been part of an effort by three other journeymen leather-dressers to restart the *devoir* in their trade in Troyes.[14] By the end of the weekend they had gathered in some seven others, initiating five of them in an upstairs room at their inn with a baptism of wine and an oath never to reveal the secrets of their ceremonies. However, a fight broke out when some wished to return to work on the Tuesday morning while others wanted to continue drinking, and the group split up. The three initiators of the ceremonies were still owed 54 livres by those they had enrolled, and owed 30 livres themselves to the inn-hostess who had initially agreed to be their *mère*. This woman, Marie Brey, subsequently renounced this role, noting especially that she had not been given the papers of the *devoir* to keep, as was proper. These papers were in the hands of another inn-hostess, Marie Maître, who had served as *mère* until 1776, when she renounced the role after one of the periodic prohibitions of the compagnonnages. The *devoir* still owed her 60 livres, and it was when she threw out a group of *devoirant* tenants in 1782 that they moved to Brey's inn – and Brey, it emerged, had worked for Maître until setting up on her own at her marriage. The papers of the *devoir*, when examined, proved to be a chest with a picture of Saint Jacques on the lid, referred to by the journeymen and their *mères* as a 'master Jacques'. It contained nothing but some playing-cards and the empty cover of a notebook.

When accounts were written of the compagnonnages in the nineteenth century, the name 'children of Master Jacques' would be given to the *devoir*, and attributed an origin in the architect of Solomon's Temple. Likewise the *gavots* would be called 'children of Solomon'. Quite clearly, however, such tales were fanciful genealogies for rites which were in many cases simply a jumble of local arrangements, personal associations and the haphazard borrowing of religious imagery. Journeymen who were firmly organised into rival camps in one city might find themselves working and socialising alongside each other elsewhere – either because the compagnonnages' influence did not reach a certain place, or because it had faded, or even because these two groups, or others, had blurred into each other. Parisian journeymen had no compagnonnages, and were known to scorn the rites when encountered elsewhere, as games fit only for apprentices and rustics. Moreover, even in their heartlands, the two main groupings were not dominant – accounts of their meetings and ceremonies rarely speak of more than a few dozen members in cities where particular trades were known to have hundreds of journeymen. On the rare occasions that compagnonnage numbers reach the low hundreds, it is for special events such as particularly significant funerals – though in Marseille in 1787 it was reported that two hundred tanners and hatters had gathered in the course of their disturbances. A similar number of journeymen joiners were noted at compagnonnage ceremonies in Bordeaux in 1788, but there were 126 employers in that trade at that point, so it is certain that there were many more journeymen.

Before moving on from the world of artisan work, there is one other crucial element that must be considered: the work of women. Guild life was, for the most part, geared to male priorities. Journeymen's associations and the concept of the *Tour de France* were entirely male-oriented, and the legal status that masters and journeymen contested was normally available only to men – women were not 'legal persons', and were thus unable to enter contracts or enforce their rights in public life. This, however, is a generalisation that, like most others about eighteenth-century France, must be qualified. Women's work permeated the artisan world, and their need to work is suggested mutely by the thousands of such women's infants put out to rural wet-nurses from the great cities every year – the artisans' workday was twelve or fifteen hours, if not longer, and a working woman had no time to breastfeed. The upper classes had also declined to breastfeed, until the moralistic strictures of Rousseau brought it back into fashion for some from the 1760s, but for working women there was never a real choice.

The majority of master-artisan enterprises, although headed nominally by the husband, relied to a greater or lesser extent on the work and resources of the wife. Marriage itself might be a key aspect in the acquisition of mastership, bringing the funds for fees and premises. Many other female artisans worked on their own account, even if married to a master or journeyman – often, in the latter case, forced to live a precarious life apart if the master insisted on his journeyman 'living in', the wife being left in a furnished room, to snatch odd moments with her husband whenever possible. The multifarious trades involved in dressmaking, general seam-stressing and linen-working, down to the less 'skilled' fields of laundering and repair work, were undertaken by women, as was the selling of goods at many urban markets – the market-women of Paris, the *poissardes*, were stalwarts of the urban scene, with the historic right to present personal greetings to the king at the New Year and upon royal births. Women in trades such as these were acknowledged by the legal system, which had created the special status of *marchande publique*, or 'female public merchant', to give them rights to trade and to protect their economic interests despite their sex.

In the major textile town of Rouen, the opportunities this gave are shown by the female-led guild of ribbonmakers.[15] This was the most vigorous of a group of guilds in the city that incorporated women, the others also being associated with clothing and textiles, except for the guild of grain merchants. Such female and mixed-sex guilds, however, numbered only seven out of 112 guilds in the city. Two-thirds of the ribbonmakers' membership of 160 were female, of whom half were married, one-sixth widowed and one-third unmarried. Evidence suggests that some husbands of these women worked in their wives' businesses, just as wives did for husbands elsewhere. Female guild officers did all the things that male ones did elsewhere – dealing with regulations and the payment of taxes, controlling entry to the trade and literally patrolling workshops and the streets in the police function against rogue traders. Like many another guild, the ribbonmakers were engaged in a constant fight to protect their economic 'turf', and had in fact expanded it by incorporating lacemakers, fringers and general textile decorators into their organisation in previous decades. They clashed, as did many of the city's textile guilds, with the attempts of the merchant mercers to sell all kinds of both finished goods and raw materials, and with other groups such as the *tissutiers*, weavers of bands of silk who tried to edge into making even narrower bands: ribbons, in other words. Cordmakers clashed with the ribbonmakers' rights to produce lacings, while the ribbonmakers them-selves sought to encroach on the *passementiers*' rights to make braided decorative edging. Female masters here, granted the legal status of honorary men, did everything their male contemporaries did to protect and extend their corporate rights within the legal and social intricacies of the guild world.[16]

Elsewhere women can be seen inserting themselves into areas where guild and other legal restrictions were less significant. In Brittany, for example, while some skilled trades involved in construction had formed guilds, the general business of contracting for construction remained free, and women here played an active (if minority) part.[17] In some cases this meant acting as financial guarantors for male relatives or associates, and was little more than an investment opportunity for the well off, but in others a number of women bid for building contracts either in equal partnership with men, or entirely on their own. Virtually all, however, had had to enter the business through family connections, there being no clear route into the industry for a single and unconnected female, and indeed no route at all through the formal acquisition of skill: no female apprentices were taken on. Nevertheless, female-led businesses made up between 10 per cent and a third of such enterprises in the region, and were clearly more than a mere fringe group. One reason for this may be that in Brittany, unlike most of France, inheritance customs enforced a sharing of property between both daughters and sons, and there was thus both more opportunity for women to acquire capital, and more incentive for men to seek an engagement with the holders of such resources. Women also worked freely in the building trades in unskilled and semi-skilled roles, from cart-driving to hod-carrying, and although their sex meant that they were routinely denied the same levels of pay as men, they were not expected to do any less work.

A similar pattern of engagement by women at both the less skilled and the more informal levels of production can be seen across France. One reason for the expansion of 'putting-out' work into the countryside was the opportunity for the employment of the low paid, of whom women were the central group. It is also to be suspected that many more women worked in the interiors of artisan workshops than are accounted for by official figures – again, either they were illicit workers, or unmarried daughters whose knowledge of craft skills, as opposed to more 'marriageable' qualities, was not something to be boasted of. Amongst the independent workers of the urban 'free zones' and the hidden *chambrelans*, women again played their parts. Their relative concealment from the official record has everything to do with their sex, and nothing to do with their work.

Overall, the uncertainties and instabilities of life amongst the trades of France may have made the structures of artisan organisation less consistent and less universal than those organisations would have liked to believe, but artisans themselves were clearly at the heart of urban social existence. Especially in the larger cities, with their multi-storey tenements, master artisans often took responsibility as 'managing tenants' for the regulation of life within their own building. This might involve knowing the affairs of several dozen households, and frequently being legally responsible for good order in the building and its environs. Such artisan figures were also often prominent in broader neighbourhood life. One common office was that of parish church councillor, or *marguiller*, which involved financial management of church buildings and funds, and negotiating relationships with the clergy. In previous generations this had sometimes been a prickly task, as for example in the 1720s and 1730s, when disputes between Jesuit and Jansenist interpretations of Catholic doctrine had split the Parisian church, amongst others, and seen some clergy imprisoned, and others at war with the views of their parishioners.[18]

In a more general sense, town life integrated public and collective activities with daily existence. In any but the smallest town, the gathering of crowds for markets, fairs and processions fostered the exchange of information, and sometimes the collective expression of public anger – events which included all elements of the working population. In Paris especially, a lively public culture of debate, in the squares and pleasure-grounds of the city as well as its bars and cafés, had given a potential political edge to almost every gathering of the general population.[19] If the lower ranks of the artisan world were scorned by commentators for their riotous debauchery at cut-price taverns outside the city's customs barriers, others amongst the skilled workers might circulate in the same spaces as the social and cultural elites.[20] The master glazier Jacques-Louis Ménétra, who wrote a semi-literate *Journal of My Life* in the late 1790s, claimed to have strolled on several occasions in 1770 with the philosopher Rousseau, and played draughts with him once at the Café de la Régence.[21] Whether or not this particular anecdote is true, there is no doubt that men of both types, and women too, flocked to the Tuileries gardens and the galleries of the Palais-Royal for entertainment, diversion and profit.

Through the later decades of the century, the kind of sensitive and wary response that any careful artisan gave to commercial information was increasingly extended by the Parisian population to news of the actions of the state. Watched over by suspicious, but frequently powerless, police agents, the urban working classes shared in a pattern of critical commentary on royal government and the affairs of the court which dated at least from the Jansenist controversies of the 1720s. Further such controversies in the 1750s, and deeply unpopular taxation and judicial policies in the 1760s and 1770s, bred a groundswell of negative sentiment. The state was sufficiently strong until the mid 1780s to whisk away individuals with particularly seditious views into the fortress of the Bastille, as it had done for centuries, but it had no mechanisms sufficiently robust to suppress an ongoing daily engagement with critical political opinions that was entrenching itself amongst the general population of the capital.[22]

During the 1780s, with the Revolution hidden in the future, such problems of everyday engagement with the wider social and political sphere seemed to be overshadowed by changes in the nature of artisan collective life itself. The economy of the Old Regime which mandated the existence of guilds had been struck a death-blow in 1774, when the royal minister Turgot, a believer in the free market ideals of physiocracy, abolished the guild system outright. Under this new system, anyone was to be free to ply a trade, subject only to the payment of an annual business tax. This situation had not endured long, little over a year in fact, before the perceived social disorder and insubordination of the journeyman classes it brought about caused a reversal of policy – along with Turgot's fall from office.[23] The guilds were not, however, reinstated as they had been before. Although outwardly similar, the post-1776 guild system had done away with many of the particular heritages, traditions and peculiarities of the individual guilds and their rules. In Paris, the new system also condensed down over a hundred guilds into forty-four 'new' ones. The engineers of this new system were the police and financial bureaucrats of the state. For them the guilds were an instrument for the management of economic relations and a conduit (as they had always been) for taxation and royal policy initiatives.[24]

The new guild system did away with any formal requirements of skill for accession to mastership – this was now purely a matter of the payment of appropriately large fees. It also created a level of guild member below the master, the *agrégé*. For a smaller fee, *agrégés* were allowed to practise their trade legally but were excluded from the training of apprentices. Of course, now that formally sanctioned skill was not a requirement to trade, apprenticeship itself became a more precarious issue, and the numbers of *agrégés* expanded much faster than the number of masters in the following decade, as they decided they did not need apprentices or any of the other status-perks of full mastership in order to prosper. Moreover, in a decisive challenge to older visions, women of means were now free to invest in all guild positions just as men could – and they were to start to do so, in small but significant numbers, across all trades. Ironically, although policing of this new system now passed much more directly to the state, it did nothing to alleviate the problem (from the guilds' point of view) of hidden and 'false' workers, or of the free zones such as the Faubourg Saint-Antoine.

The position of journeymen (and women) under the new system demonstrated its other side. If the approach to the guilds seen from above was one of liberalisation and a rationalisation of administrative frameworks, seen from below, the 1770s and 1780s marked a sharp intensification of authoritarian policing in the world of work. Although the examples throughout this chapter have shown that, into the 1780s, relations and tensions in the world of work could still be fluid and multi-levelled, the impetus was towards a closing down of avenues of worker resistance. If it was now easier, for those with the funds, to enter the ranks of the employers, the law, and its interpretation by the summary jurisdiction of police courts, took a steadily harsher line on the rights of those compelled to continue as workers. If journeymen were not formally reduced to the status of the domestic servants they despised, they were nevertheless progressively stripped of their old legal claims to stand alongside the masters as another corporate group with their own prerogatives.

From September 1781, new legislation compelled journeymen to register their employment with guild bureaus, and a wide range of supposedly 'disciplinary' practices were imposed through guilds across the country.[25] Although the intention was to foster subordination, in many cases it had precisely the opposite effect. Locksmiths in Rouen, for example, were supposed to be entered by their masters in registers which were to include a physical description, and to carry a countersigned receipt when moving from one job to another. An inspection in August 1783 revealed that many journeymen were unregistered, many others had given false names or origins, and in general the system was being abused by journeymen, 'certain of impunity' thanks to the connivance of masters who wanted their work, not their submission.[26] Shoemakers in Troyes seem to have done much the same. Other guilds tried harder. The tailors and bakers of Troyes fought to get journeymen to carry the *livret* or 'work passport' required by law, to enrol themselves with the guilds, and to give the proper notice before quitting a job. In October 1782, the master artisans of Toulouse complained that journeymen 'affected to openly oppose' the execution of the 1781 laws, in the face of a particularly harsh implementation supported by the local judicial authorities. The hatters of Lyon tightened their regulations against journeyman 'insubordination' again in 1784, trying once more to forbid all the apparatus of compagnonnage. In Paris itself, a joint police and guild patrol of sculptors' and stonemasons' workshops visited seventeen sites on 5 October 1785, finding 159 unregistered journeymen, but only seven whose papers were in order.[27]

Despite the continuing ambiguities and collusions between master and journeyman that many of these examples suggest, artisan employment in law and state practice was increasingly often seen narrowly as a master-servant relationship where, once an engagement was made, the obligation to work to order far outweighed any claim to specify the conditions of that work. This authoritarian tone, the ironic counterpoint to economic liberalism, was carried forward strongly into the coming decade. It also reflected a second major dimension of social and economic change that was taking place in the last decades of the eighteenth century. France, like

Britain, was embarked on the as yet uncertain first stages of industrialisation. Like Britain, this involved the expansion of the role of the individual entrepreneur and the general individualisation of economic relationships, at the same time as more and more people came to be employed doing the same work for the same masters. The growth of rural proto-industry was a key part of this development. While this had its own dynamics, the ability to exploit widespread networks of unorganised and relatively isolated workers also added to the power of merchants who actively sought to break the bounds of artisan control in more urban milieus. This was especially the case in cities such as Lyon and Nîmes, where silk-weaving had an artisan core workforce that sought to safeguard its autonomy against an entrepreneurial merchant elite. The latter wanted to combine the relative docility and low prices of their rural workers with the concentration and skills of the urban core, with whom they already dealt as wholesale suppliers and resellers of finished goods. It is no coincidence that both these cities had particularly agitated histories in the revolutionary decade to come, as their pre-existing high level of social tension served to inflate conflict under a number of political labels.

The underlying structural tensions of the manufacturing sector were a more serious problem for the French in the coming decade than most could have anticipated. What is now apparent, even if relatively overlooked at the time by elite observers, is that the artisan classes were poised for engagement with the looming social and political crisis. Forming the backbone of the urban population, schooled in institutional organisation and dispute, attuned to languages of both credit and liberty, and alert to public news, gossip and scandal, they would be at the forefront of developments that would bring down the old order, and then pose further challenges to the new. However, as we shall see, the social imagination of the late eighteenth century was already charged with alarm and suspicion about a variety of subordinate and marginal groups, in ways that were persistently to cloud the prospects for acknowledgement of popular political engagement throughout the coming decade.

3

The Margins

The Old Regime was a society that craved order. Discipline, hierarchy and subordination were its avowed goals, and the alternative was feared to be chaos. Yet, as we have already seen, within the world of the artisans disorder was endemic, and occasionally became violent. In the countryside, peasant insurrections were not unknown, and the more subtle forms of challenge and disobedience were widespread. Order was the goal of this society precisely because it was such a rare and precious commodity. Nowhere was this more evident than in the attempted control of the criminals, vagrants and other marginal figures that seemed to elite observers to pose a perpetual threat to order, life and property.

Like other late-eighteenth-century absolutist states – notably Prussia, Austria and to a lesser extent Russia – the French monarchy had developed increasingly strong notions of 'police', of a 'policed people', and a 'well-ordered police state'. This, however, meant much more than modern conceptions of policing. The word might best be seen as meaning 'social administration', embracing the pursuit of law and order but also many other functions. The controls that the guilds exercised (in theory at least) over their workers came under the umbrella of 'police', as did the regulation, for example, of the wet-nursing trade – the police of Paris registered the wide network of rural women who accepted infants from the urban population, and supervised the work of the agents who connected up nurses and clients. Such 'administration', however, was of a most authoritarian kind. For example, the Parisian police *inspecteurs* who were charged with the repression of criminality ran a network of secret agents recruited from within the 'criminal classes' themselves, and were feared throughout the city for their capacity to snatch suspects from the streets and throw them into the cells of the Bastille.[1]

The level of surveillance accorded to Paris was exceptional, for in the capital the office of lieutenant-general of police was a senior government post. In provincial cities the equivalent positions, created at the end of the seventeenth century with the aspiration to a general surveillance, had either lost functions to other judicial bodies or been absorbed into the general running of the municipality, and there were few or no special funds or personnel for police beyond the traditional part-time city watch. One of the few groups that did operate in many larger towns went under the archaic name of 'archers', and were charged with the control of vagrancy, detaining individual beggars and bringing them to whatever institutions existed locally for accommodating them – usually religious foundations, though sometimes municipalities also took charge of charitable poorhouses.[2]

Out in the countryside, policing was an even less well-equipped affair. The national network of mounted police, the *maréchaussée*, was spread thinly in brigades of three to five men that had to cover hundreds of square miles. Its total strength by the 1770s was just under 4000 men, an increase of around a third after recent reforms, but not all were always available for service or properly equipped.[3] Nonetheless, it was the only armed force available to authorities short of calling on a military garrison – this was done when necessary, but even the Old Regime recognised the disadvantages of turning troops on the population too often. Although the *maréchaussée* was ineffectual against large-scale disorder, it worked well as a general 'highway patrol', and was responsible for rounding up thousands of marginal and suspicious characters each year – a report in 1790 concluded that some 230,000 people had been detained in government workhouses since 1768.

To fall into poverty was itself sufficient to arouse the concern of the authorities. Widows, orphans, the sick, the crippled and the old were understood as the necessary recipients of charity, the poor who could not be blamed for their fate. It was individuals such as these that the established networks of charity, administered by the multifarious organs of the Catholic Church, existed primarily to support. One should note immediately that such relief was never intended to do more than preserve the poor at the barest level of subsistence. Nonetheless, every parish priest had as part of his duties the administration of funds, either from previous endowments or current donors, for the relief of such poverty, and cathedral chapters, abbeys and other establishments likewise frequently made such provision. In times of general hardship, gifts, especially of foodstuffs, could be extended to whole sectors of the population and even entire communities.

The poor, in a general sense, were understood to be a part of the social fabric, and alms-giving was a religious obligation. The church, through its nursing orders of nuns, also administered what passed for public medical care. Epidemic disease, from smallpox to scarlet fever, battened on the population in waves, and outbreaks of typhoid fever were almost annual occurrences in some regions. Malaria threatened wherever there were water-ways and stagnant pools, even coming to Paris annually as 'autumnal fever'. Over a hundred different fevers were identified by contemporary doctors, who were also emphatic in noting the cause of their spread both in poverty and poor hygiene. Such illnesses routinely carried off the young and the old, and were in that sense merely part of the tragic tapestry of live for the poor. In some cases, however, even in the later eighteenth century, they could create real social dislocation. Typhus and enteric fever struck central Brittany so hard between the 1760s and 1780s that the local population may have fallen by as much as 4.5 per cent. Disease on this scale, taking working adults as well as young and old, could devastate whole communities.[4]

Disease was an agent of impoverishment as much as of mortality. Ironically, the industries which were helping to support so much of the population in both town and country could also ruin their health. Weavers and lacemakers, who often had to scrimp on lighting, commonly suffered from *la vue mangée* – their sight 'eaten' by their work. Pneumonia struck down many flax workers, as did crippling arthritis, as they worked in damp conditions to protect the thread. Lung diseases of all kinds, and especially tuberculosis, afflicted migrant workers who tramped long distances, especially in winter, and also the young girls who did so much of the menial labour in the silk industry. Paper-making also entailed damage to the lungs, as did working with glass and hot metal. Shoemakers and tailors alike suffered throughout their bodies for their hunched postures and close work. To grow old in such a trade was frequently an achievement in itself, although also one likely to leave you crippled. It was little wonder that the resources of charity were continually overstretched.

There were as many as two thousand hospitals in France, although the smallest might be no more than a room or two and a couple of nuns based in a market-town. Some were major public institutions, such as the Hôtel-Dieu in Paris, and attempted to provide real medical care, although ironically the title *hôpital* was more often reserved for hospices for the indigent and incurable, and all major towns had their *hôpital général* for this purpose – that of Paris embracing a number of facilities, including the hospital-prisons of La Salpêtrière and Bicêtre. At their worst, these could be little better than squalid dumping-grounds for those who had nowhere else to die, and they certainly bred disease, but they were shelter and a sign that social obligation had some meaning.[5]

It was also largely through a charitable mission, and also to further more directly individuals' access to salvation, that the church provided education for the population. The majority even of the upper classes learnt their letters from clergymen who taught either as private tutors or more often in the schools run by elite teaching orders such as the Oratorians. This service was extended to the lower classes, especially in urban areas: Paris, for example, was dotted with small chapters of the Brothers of the Christian Schools, who lived a monastic lifestyle while teaching basic literacy and numeracy on a parish basis. It was thanks to orders such as these that it was unusual for an artisan to be illiterate by the 1780s, and even a majority of urban women were basically literate. Rural provision was much sparser, though some parishes maintained basic schools, and even elsewhere a parish priest might give a few lessons to altar-boys or other protégés. Real literacy was still a minority achievement, falling below 30 per cent in the most dispersed areas of habitation.

Beyond its educational mission, which might be seen as inadvertently contributing to a more critical and informed public through wider literacy, the conscious endeavours of the church with regard to poverty lacked any reforming effort. Charity existed not to improve the general lot of the poor but to relieve what was seen as unavoidable suffering, and to enable donors to be charitable – for the good of their souls, and incidentally to support the social order by emphasising its reciprocity. Charity had no answer to poverty that lacked a visible cause in age, health or deformity, and in such cases the doctrines of contemporary policing reigned supreme. An artisan or a labourer out of work, or a peasant who had somehow lost his land, were, it was frequently assumed, necessarily bad characters. During much of the century, it was widely believed that France's rising population was actually declining, and this, along with general ignorance about the functioning of complex labour markets, meant that unemployment was seen largely as a consequence, not a cause, of idleness.

It was an article of faith for the educated observer that work was always to be had in the fields, while the urban landscape provided many examples of men getting by without turning to beggary. The streets of major towns and cities all had their share of *portefaix* and *commissionnaires* – street porters and errand-runners, who for a few pennies would carry baggage, deliver letters or perform any other small menial service. Some of these were associated, formally or semi-formally, with institutions such as the law courts, the markets, and even the prisons – hence the survival in modern English of 'commissionaire' for a uniformed doorman. In eighteenth-century France such doormen were usually called *suisses*, or 'Swiss', reflecting a continuing tradition of employing ex-soldiers from that region in this often intimidatory role. As well as offering jobs for adults of this calibre, street life also provided employment for younger men and boys as crossing-sweepers and bootblacks – known by the telling name of *décrotteurs*, since manure was the greatest risk to footwear. Unskilled and relatively rootless labour of this kind, while remaining an expected resort of the 'honest' poor, also hovered on the edge of social distrust. People in these positions were the most likely to be 'undomiciled', a category of Old Regime jurisprudence that designated someone without a long-term fixed abode, often determined by whether they owned any furniture. To be *dans ses meubles* was to be fixed in the social framework; to be reliant on furnished lodgings was not. The risk of instability the latter created in the minds of the police meant that such figures were likely to be detained or expelled from the locality on the mere suspicion of criminality. They were also those most feared by the general community, and the solidarity of such communities, both rural and urban, was often reflected in their collective hostility to the unknown poor.

Unemployment frequently led to migration, especially from rural areas, and this in turn triggered another set of official alarms. All movement from one place to another was suspicious. Tinkers and peddlers brushed against the law constantly, and had to justify themselves by constant and conspicuous display of their wares. Seasonal migrants or journeymen were well advised to obtain 'passports' from their local authorities before setting off on long journeys to offset the risk of being turned back as vagrants. Such documents were so common that many authorities had pre-printed forms into which identifying details could be inserted. To be mobile and masterless placed an individual on a short and steep slope in official eyes (and those of the surrounding population). The general term for such individuals was *gens sans aveu*, 'people without an avowal'; in other words, those for whom no one respectable would vouch. To be defined in this fashion meant at the very least expulsion from the locality for the slightest brush with authority, and might indeed lead directly to incarceration. From vagrancy to vaga-bondage was a short downward step, and then a shorter one still led to the condition that was the abiding fear of society: brigandage.[6]

Brigands were the armed and organised manifestation of what could lurk outside the boundaries of the ordered society. Any episode of riot or major disturbance would sooner or later be attributed to shadowy gangs of bri-gands, an ill-defined and always hidden underworld, which at the same time was supposedly often in the pay of political factions intent on opposing some particular government scheme or order. It appears that neither the authorities nor the general population of the eighteenth century troubled themselves about the logical flaws in such a scenario: brigandage was as-sumed to exist, thus disorder was caused by brigands. It also suited all parties to such disorder to pretend that it was undefined, and uncatchable, outsiders who could take the blame, rather than discovering that members of their supposedly ordered communities had broken the bounds of social control.

Government action against poverty and marginality had for many decades focused heavily on actual or potential brigands. From the mid 1720s, the authorities attempted to enforce the enclosure of beggars within the existing

general hospitals for the indigent. Instructions sent out to the police authorities responsible for managing this process assumed that most beggars
would be adult, almost all would need to be rounded up by the police, and
a good third of them would be dangerous or bad characters who would
merit trial and formal imprisonment. A study of western Normandy in the
period 1724–33 indicates that, by contrast, most who entered the general
hospitals did so voluntarily, and at least a quarter were children under ten,
while only a further quarter were adults between twenty and fifty-nine.
Begging was much more the province of the 'traditional' recipients of charity
than the authorities were prepared to admit, and it also appears that such
recipients were not receiving that charity from its supposed sources within
communities. Many such communities were eager to denounce 'dangerous'
beggars for arrest – beggars who turned out, upon investigation, to be
orphan children and other 'useless mouths'.[7]

By the last quarter of the eighteenth century, rising levels of poverty were
a grave problem in France but amongst the least understood of all the
country's troubles. A prevailing belief amongst the elites in the fruitfulness
of French agriculture concealed the fact that many sectors of the rural
population were being driven to the edge of their resources. We have already
seen, in a general sense, that peasants found it hard to make ends meet,
but across France the pre-revolutionary generation was being squeezed
from its lands. In Lorraine, where population was growing exceptionally
rapidly, there was a decline of some 20 per cent in the number of secure
landholding *laboureurs* compared to the decades before 1750, while numbers
of wage-dependent *manoeuvriers* rose by a similar proportion. Even in areas
of slower population growth, such as the open-field grain-growing region
of the Vexin, north west of Paris, there was a similar long-term pattern.
From 1685 to 1789, in a sample of forty villages, the number of large
prosperous farmers remained static at just under 300, while the number of
smaller but still independent landholders declined from some 250 to around
100. The number of wage-dependent labourers rose from just over 700 to
some 1000, those described as farm-servants more than doubled to some
350, and those working in rural industry rose from under 300 to almost
500. Similar instances occurred across the country, and the underlying
reasons are highlighted by figures from the mountainous Auvergne. There
the population rose by almost a third between 1740 and 1789, creating a
seller's market for land and resources and a buyer's market for labour.
Wages on average rose by only some 25 to 50 per cent over the century,
while rents rose by around 140 per cent, with food prices close behind.
Costs of rents and other necessities pushed many smallholders and tenant
farmers into debt, followed by dispossession. Such situations underlay the

increasing change in this region, and many others, to rural industry and seasonal migration. Similar figures prevailed for Paris, where wage rises were even lower – barely 17 per cent since the first half of the century.[8]

Educated observers began to wax eloquent about the risks of vagabondage from mid century, as the visible consequences of these hidden processes started to emerge. Guillaume Le Trosne, a magistrate in Orléans, wrote in 1763 that 'vagabonds are essentially the enemies of work ... It is assuredly not work that is lacking but the good will to work.' He advocated branding on the face and life sentences with hard labour for vagabonds, and noted the intimidation that such figures exercised in the countryside. This view echoed that of Jean-François Joly de Fleury, intendant of Burgundy, who wrote in 1759 that 'mendicity is the school of thieves and assassins. Beggars have neither religion nor morals, thus one must not be surprised that they commit all sorts of crimes and wanton acts.' He further observed that the charity such figures received from rural communities was 'extorted ... through the fear of arson'.[9] As a consequence of such attitudes, new initiatives were put in place by 1768. The *maréchaussée* was given renewed orders to arrest vagabonds, defined officially as 'those who for six months in succession have carried on neither a profession nor a trade, and who, having no position or property on which to subsist, will be unable to be avowed or to have their respectable character and conduct attested to by persons of dignity and trust'.[10] The set penalty for such individuals was three years at hard labour in the traditional location for hardened felons, the royal galleys – although by this time chaining men to oars had become obsolete and had given way in practice to imprisonment within a naval base.

A network of new, state-controlled institutions was also established to confine the indigent. These *dépôts de mendicité* were placed in each of the country's thirty-two administrative *généralités*, and by the end of 1773 had received some 71,000 inmates, of whom some 58,000 were police detainees. Of all these, however, only 968 individuals received the sentence to the galleys laid down for confirmed vagabonds. Even at the height of this new wave of repression, the authorities could find only a small proportion of individuals who met their criteria for the worst category of offender. Nevertheless, attitudes to the existence of such vagabonds persisted, and throughout the years running up to the Revolution the police continued their policy of large-scale detention of the socially marginal and 'dangerous'.

One group widely suspected, somewhat paradoxically, of deviant intentions was that of domestic servants. Menservants in particular were regularly denounced in texts on policing as a debauched and corrupted group. Yet they of course were the members of the lower classes resident within the homes of the rich and powerful. It seems from the various manuals on servant-keeping published in the Old Regime that servants were supposed to exist in a state of almost childlike dependence on their masters, whose duty it was to provide Christian moral guidance and discipline, for which the servants should be duly grateful and obedient. Doubtless the impossibility for most of living up to such an unrealistic goal helped to define the servant as a dubious figure.[11]

Servants were outsiders. Most came from a rural background, but worked in towns, and as many as 95 per cent of servants were not native to their place of employment. They made up a significant and visible cohort – perhaps as many as one-sixth of the whole population of Paris, and between 5 and 10 per cent of that of other towns. While female servants rarely migrated more than twenty or thirty miles, menservants might travel the length of the country. Paris was a great clearing-house for domestic service, and a valet or lackey born in Provence or Brittany might end up in Rouen or Bordeaux by way of the capital and possibly several other cities. Male servants also had very high job mobility. There is every indication that, especially at the more menial end of service, they were prepared to change jobs as often as every few months, perhaps seeking slightly higher wages, slightly better conditions, more amenable fellows or masters, or even just the new suit of clothes in the form of their master's livery. Male servants tended to settle into two groups. The first was those who saw service as a career in which it was possible to acquire status, as a steward of a major household for example, and perhaps then to retire after twenty or thirty years into a comfortable bourgeois lifestyle. For the second group, the great majority, service was a stop-gap, a source of board and lodging on arrival in a new city, or a way of earning a little capital to branch out on their own in trade. Social aspiration, in both cases, was a key factor, and had become a literary cliché by the 1780s, Beaumarchais's (and Mozart's) Figaro being the prime example.

Female servants had a much more consistent profile. The great majority were between fifteen and thirty, and they tended to stay in service for around a decade. Their ambition was to marry, and the reason most were in service was because they had no other way of raising a dowry – they were orphans, or younger siblings of impoverished households, or may have left home for any of the reasons that families break up. Several hundred livres were needed to make up a respectable marriage portion and attract the journeyman artisan or small farmer whom such women aspired to wed. By hoarding their meagre earnings, wearing their mistress's cast offs, and shunning all frivolous expenditure, such a sum might just be saved.

Given that both male and female servants largely viewed service as a means to an end, a conflict of viewpoints with their masters was inevitable.

This is especially the case as servants saw it as their right to skim off what profit they could from the opportunities open to them. This might involve mere perks, such as a cook selling rabbit-skins or trimmings from joints of meat, or embrace outright theft, especially when relations with a master or mistress deteriorated and a servant was contemplating abandoning his or her post with wages in arrears. Servants were commonly not paid until the end of a contracted period of service, and threats to withhold back-pay could be held over the head of one who proved recalcitrant. A sense of crude justice led many to make up the deficit with items of linen or cutlery purloined from the household. Others, of course, were just plain dishonest and took what they could get.

There were risks involved in such practices. Technically domestic theft was an aggravated offence, implying as it did a breach of trust from within a household, and the penalty was death. This may be one reason why servants in fact made up a relatively low proportion of those convicted for theft in the eighteenth century (only about half what one would expect, considering their numbers in the population). Masters and mistresses cannot have wished to see their cook or maid go to the gallows for a trivial matter – either through sentiment, or because it washed the household's dirty linen in public in a graphic manner. Many wealthier masters also viewed the 'take' of the servants as a price worth paying to keep sordid money matters out of their own hands.

While living in a frequently tense relationship with their masters, servants were also seen as a marginal and distrusted group by the rest of the population. Native town-dwellers seem to have heartily despised domestic service and to have sought to avoid it at all costs. In Marseille, for example, whereas male children and adolescents in artisan families were expected to pay their earnings into the family budget, females were commonly permitted to save theirs towards their dowries, so as to avoid recourse to service. Everyday contempt for servants was expressed by a wide spectrum of writers. The official viewpoint was given by a late eighteenth-century manual of police:

> Hatred of work, the desire to enjoy the pleasures of the cities, a taste for laziness, the habit of vice ... the hope of getting rich, and lastly, the most shocking egotism are the motives which cause domestic work to be cherished ... One may thus correctly conclude that the class of servants is composed exclusively of the scum of the countryside.[12]

From a writer of the Enlightenment, Louis-Sébastien Mercier, came a hardly less damning indictment:

> Today, servants who go from house to house, indifferent to the masters whom

they serve, can meet an employer they just left without feeling any sort of emotion. They assemble only to exchange the secrets they have unearthed: they are spies, and being well paid, well dressed, and well fed, but despised, they resent us, and have become our greatest enemies.[13]

Given such views, it is ironic that, right up to the end of the Old Regime, aristocratic masters and mistresses saw nothing unusual in appearing naked before their servants as they dressed or bathed. On the other hand, all masters and mistresses felt free to punish recalcitrant servants physically, and servants who were severely battered occasionally had recourse to the courts for redress. Servants sometimes also fought back, which brought further cases to court, but this was exceptional. These elements attest, in a backhand way, to an underlying intimacy which still existed between many masters and servants, and especially between mistresses and maids in smaller households. Although it is likely that the elite who controlled large house-holds saw servants more as objects, some conflicts which erupted into physical fights ended with expressions of amity and renewed affection on both sides. While gifts to servants in masters' wills were perhaps merely customary, some servants, of the few for whom service was a lifetime career, made bequests to their masters and mistresses.

On the wider urban scene, servants were both envied and despised. They could ape the manners and dress of their masters, and live secure from want, so long as they offered a degrading, but always suspect, submission. Male servants, especially the many general flunkeys and lackeys, tended to respond to the perceived slights of other social groups with a public ag-gression which made them even more feared. This aggression was heightened because it was a central role of the servant to shield the master from the general population. An entourage of servants kept the rabble away and might be deputed to see off importunate creditors from the artisan classes, by force if need be. Stout doormen and conspicuously idle lackeys guarded the aristocrat's portals specifically to intimidate callers who were not of superior rank. Ironically, such servants' lives were probably made harder in the last years of the Old Regime by new habits of sentimental domesticity that spread amongst the elite. The wealthy came to value their family life and the quiet orderly running of their household more highly than public display, so servants tended to be pushed 'below stairs' to the position they were to occupy in the nineteenth century, being required to behave with more constraint, at least in their masters' presence. They also found them-selves working much harder to keep up to new standards of domestic cleanliness and order, as previously despised bourgeois values such as these became fashionable.

Much of this new work necessarily descended on female servants, who throughout the century remained not just a marginal but also a highly-vulnerable group, exploited in more than the merely economic sense. Like most women at this time, their character was all they had, and dismissal could be fatal to their prospects. All that meant for some, however, was that they were easy prey for their masters. Sexual abuse of female servants was a cliché of literature but also a real and abiding threat, and one which appears sometimes from the historical record as almost epidemic. By the later eighteenth century, moreover, the charitable legal assumption of earlier times that a woman who accused her master of rape should be believed was being overturned by more cynical views. Charges were sometimes countered with the protestation that she had been only too willing, or was using the charge to extort money and cover the consequences of debauchery with others. It was, of course, the consequences, unmarried pregnancy, which generally brought such cases to judicial attention.

An unmarried woman who found herself pregnant was bound by law to declare the fact to the authorities, a move designed to curb infanticide, but one which also allowed her to make a claim about paternity, and to record her story of the circumstances of the act. Some women chose to evade this requirement, successfully concealing their pregnancy under layers of skirts: pitiful infant corpses found on rubbish-heaps or in holes scraped hurriedly in the ground were sometimes the result. Women who had given birth alone and in terror were hunted down by the authorities, and their claims that the child had been stillborn were given little credence. Death was the official penalty for such a crime, although less harsh sentences were often passed in the more 'enlightened' decades of the later eighteenth century.

In the face of such a fate, many women chose to make their plight public. Such déclarations de grossesse are a litany of victimhood – and if they may sometimes have been in part a rhetorical strategy, there is no reason to suppose they were not often the truth. Female servants were the single largest category making such declarations, since they frequently found themselves isolated and vulnerable to assault. Female domestics had to stay up late at night, perhaps cleaning, or baking bread alone in the kitchens, or rise early in the mornings to sweep and light fires. They rarely had quarters of their own in which to sleep, bedding down in kitchens or antechambers in all but the very newest houses. They might need to visit secluded areas, such as stables or wine cellars, and in any of these places they might be assaulted. This was not just by their masters, who formed a declining, but still significant, proportion of reported culprits through the century (despite the fashion for respectability), but also by fellow servants, and by the tradesmen, visitors and guests who frequented a busy household. Evidence from Bordeaux and Aix-en-Provence suggests that women in their later twenties were more likely to claim seduction by fellow servants or workers, while three-quarters of those who were seduced by their masters or other higher-class figures were under twenty-five – perhaps reflecting a difference between a group actively courting betrothal and a younger cohort vulnerable to the passing attentions of bourgeois or noble. At least a quarter of this latter group recorded that they had been promised substantial gifts in return for their favours, and some may have even seen this as a short-cut to financial security. Many declarations, however, explicitly stated that force was used against them.

Brutal, violent rape was an everyday possibility for such women, but so too were all the other steps used by the seducer to achieve the appearance of consensual sex, of which the most common, the easiest, yet cruellest, was the promise of marriage itself. The repetition of a few simple words overcame so many women's hesitations, or calmed their fears when they had, in fact, been left with no real choice. Many of them stressed later that they yielded to advances precisely because they felt it would secure a betrothal and tie the man to them. Others allowed men who had initially forced themselves upon them to continue to abuse them for weeks or months in the hope that marriage would follow. It was, for the victims, their only hope by that stage. Perhaps already pregnant, their honour lost, only marriage could save them from being cast out from respectable society. Some women even went so far as to live with their abusers, risking social ostracism for this concubinage, and often finding themselves on the streets when their condition rendered them less desirable.

The only consolation for such women was that it was easy to get rid of an unwanted child – at least, in practical terms. Every town of any size maintained institutions for foundlings, run usually by the church, though sometimes by municipal authorities themselves.[14] A mother could hand in her child, or leave it on the steps of a church. Some institutions even had revolving postboxes where babies could be passed inside the building without the mother showing her face. Such infants were often left with tokens – a bead, a scrap of coloured cloth, anything distinctive – to act as a pledge of future recognition, and of a hoped for reunion, but such plaintive relics most often lay forgotten in drawers and cupboards. We may note as an aside that foundling homes saw a rising proportion of legitimate children deposited with them in the later decades of the century, which the authorities attributed to a 'criminal indifference' on the part of parents, but which was more likely a response to poverty.[15] Death rates in these places often exceeded 90 per cent. Ironically, female foundlings who survived the terrible conditions were often placed in service, and sometimes found themselves repeating their own history in a new generation. A few brave souls shunned the foundling homes and managed to retain contact with their children by placing them, as many working mothers did, with rural wet-nurses, but acknowledging possession of a bastard required enormous moral courage.[16]

The mothers who did abandon their infants could either forget their child, and move away in the effort to erase their past, or try to remain and rebuild a shattered life. But for those whose name had been bandied about by their seducer, or even simply those whose pregnancy had become known in their neighbourhood, there was sometimes no way back. Prostitution was often not the permanent and irrevocable 'fall' that it was condemned as. Women did sometimes see selling sex as a temporary stage in their life, or even a mere sideline to other work, such as laundering and needlework. Nevertheless, turning to prostitution made such a woman into a creature who risked condemnation by all ranks of society. She also ran a significant risk of death from venereal disease, and from the gruesome and compulsory treatments that could be applied for it if she ran foul of the authorities – carriers of disease were regularly confined to provincial *dépôts de mendicité* and institutions such as the Parisian Salpêtrière, technically a hospital, but in practice a women's prison.[17]

Prostitution has attracted perhaps more hypocrisy than any other social institution. If there were no clients, there would be no prostitution. But in the Old Regime, as before and since, it was the women who were condemned.[18] The prostitute, as portrayed by contemporary moral and medical thought, was an immoral being. By abandoning the explicitly feminine virtue of sexual purity, she had demonstrated that she was devoid of decency and prey to carnality. Speculation, some of it serious, some of it lurid, wondered about her physical and mental differences from normal women, while she was placed by the police into a category of permanent outlawry. In Paris prostitutes were exploited by the police and their network of spies – both as sources of information on the wider underworld they inhabited and for their sexual services. They were also, like beggars, regarded as a surplus and disposable social category, and before the collapse of France's colonial ambitions in America in mid century, were liable to be rounded up and shipped to Louisiana or Canada for forced settlement.[19]

Nevertheless, in Paris especially but also in every large town, prostitution continued to be a flourishing business. A well-developed service industry in the capital, with several tens of thousands of workers, it catered to every social class. Singers, dancers and actresses from the Opéra and other theatres were regarded by their audiences as *de facto* prostitutes, available to those who could afford to give generous favours. At the highest level of society, grand courtesans plied their trade amongst the aristocracy, accommodated in luxurious apartments in the Palais-Royal and other fashionable haunts. The last great mistress of the old king, Louis XV, Madame du Barry, was said to have been a common prostitute raised up by a court faction for her uncommon beauty and debauchery, and introduced into the king's favour to gain them influence. Such tales at once outraged and titillated an ever-widening reading public, supplied with obscene books by networks of clandestine printers, smugglers and publishers beyond the borders of France.[20]

Most prostitution lacked any such glamour, and young women who defiantly described themselves to the police as seamstresses or linen-workers paraded in the Tuileries gardens, the Palais-Royal and other Parisian open spaces, as they did in similar places in Bordeaux, Lyon and elsewhere, waiting to *accrocher*, or 'hook', a likely customer. Many were perhaps indeed the part-timers known as *grisettes*, but part-time often led swiftly to full-time prostitution. Others lingered in taverns, and women who served in such establishments were also regarded as *de facto* prostitutes, barred by law from seeking damages if they became pregnant. Catherine Jacob, only nineteen and already incarcerated as a diseased *vénérienne* in Montpellier in 1788, had run through a succession of unsuccessful employments as a servant with no fewer than six religious houses and a carpenter before ending up working for a bar owner, and presumably making the unfortunate move into the sex trade.

Other prostitutes worked out of brothels, which might be a refined form of exploitation or offer some protection from random assault, depending on the keeper. Some brothel-owners, even female ones, tried to lure young women into prostitution by taking them on as servants. It was said that the coaches arriving in Paris from the provinces were met by procurers, on the hunt for naive peasant-girls in search of work who could be lured into brothels on false pretences. They might then be offered up as virgins to especially discerning clients. Some men would pay extra for an unwilling victim. Perhaps more alarming yet is the record from Toulouse of an attack on the *dépôt* holding several venereally infected prostitutes by the girls' own families, seeking not to rescue them from a life of vice but to return them to it. In the problematic economic climate of the 1780s such resorts were common, as a report from a charitable order in Lyon made clear in bemoaning 'the cessation of manufactures which gives rise to an infinity of young girls unfortunately abandoning themselves, in the majority of cases in order to find in their crimes an aid to the subsistence of their families'.[21]

Not all women who entered the sex trade were mere victims. One cannot help feeling a grudging admiration for the resourcefulness of Marie Geneviève Guy, an eighteen-year-old servant of the comtesse d'Escherny who declared to the Parisian police on 8 April 1790 that she was pregnant as a result of seduction by a saddler named Schmit, who having promised to marry her had now decamped to Strasbourg. Four months later, on 19 August, the comte d'Escherny made a complaint against one 'Madeleine Guy', former servant to his wife, who was claiming that he had impregnated her, and had persuaded another girl to make a similar claim. He had tried to give her money, after she first claimed to have been seduced by a tailor, but she had then sought to blackmail him with a series of ever higher demands. Now, as he refused to pay her anything, she had begun to appear at his house, attempting to raise up a mob against him and denouncing him as an aristocratic seducer of innocent girls. She had even burst into the building, making hysterical threats, which had put his wife into convulsions. The comte claimed that Guy was living in a *ménage à trois* with another woman and a man named Saint-Amand, and that both women were making a living *en commerce public* – by selling themselves. The whole scheme, he said, had been cooked up by Guy and Saint-Amand. Despite the few discrepancies of detail, it is clear that Mlle Guy was one young lady who would stop at nothing to secure her future, 'respectable' avenues having become blocked.[22]

Nevertheless, in the frequently applied but somewhat limited vocabulary of eighteenth-century public argument, to call a woman a whore or a slut – *putain, pute, salope, garce* – was the definitive insult, just as for a man the twin charges of thievery and beggary were the ultimate condemnation – *voleur, gueux, fripon*. Sexual modesty for a woman was the equivalent of honest work and independence for a man; to appear to lose either was to become an outcast. In the wider structures and assumptions of society, sexuality and property also ran in parallel, and the authorities fought vigorously against challenges to the established order in either field. It was quite common in the urban milieu, for example, for poorer couples to cohabit prior to marriage, and this brief concubinage, like premarital conception, was generally viewed with a blind eye by society. Even longer-term liaisons could be tolerated if they did not draw attention to themselves. The police felt obliged to swoop, however, when in 1778 a group of young men and women in the Saint-Leu district of Paris elevated their unmarried unions into a system that also challenged the authority of religion, claiming that sacraments and church attendance were unnecessary. The men and women were segregated in different institutions 'designed for the correction of immorality', and the more obstinate of the women ended up being exiled far from the city, despite their continued protests 'that there was no need for baptism or marriage and that they were united to their men and the fathers of their children by their own free inspiration'.[23]

Utopian free love had no place in the well-ordered police state. Neither did homosexuality, and a police register from the early 1780s records the arrest of several hundred Parisian men of every social class by an inspector specially charged with this task. Some were caught *in flagrante delicto*, others were more commonly discovered in known haunts of pederasts, sometimes with clothing or hairstyles that quite clearly marked them out to the police, and presumably to each other, as members of an alternative subculture. Interrogations hinted at a range of activities from direct cash prostitution to parties, aristocratic seduction and more straightforward emotional relationships.[24]

Sexual irregularity in a more general sense was widely seen as the handmaiden of crime. The arrest reports of thieves throughout the century are a litany of raids on taverns and lodging houses, where the suspect was found 'in bed with his whore', or 'in the arms of his concubine'. The notation 'thief and concubine' was the most common label applied to female prisoners in the Parisian prisons. Such women were recognised by the police as essential parts of the network of crime, helping to conceal ill-gotten gains or selling on stolen goods, passing messages and aiding the evasion of the authorities. They might even help their lovers plot escape from prison, as did Jeanne Carrier, repeatedly imprisoned in the late 1740s for her criminal associations, including smuggling women's clothing to one imprisoned lover to aid his escape. Some women were noted as the lovers, possibly simultaneously, of a string of criminals, while others seem to have devoted themselves to only one. Or at least only one at a time – the life expectancy of an active thief was not very long, and a girl had to make a living.[25]

Criminality was a broad and diffuse phenomenon in the eighteenth century. Professional brigandage marked its outer edge, and criminal gangs gave currency to the many legends and myths that banditry engendered. In the four years before his execution in 1721, the Parisian gang-leader Cartouche established a reputation as a cross between Dick Turpin and Robin Hood that seems not entirely unmerited – his massive gang of some two hundred members specialised in looting the houses of the rich; and if he did not make an explicit point of redistributing wealth, he was said never to have refused a man in need. In the 1740s similar things were said of Rafiat, though his gang's habit of braining people in the street was less savoury. In mid century, the smuggler Mandrin was a nationwide legend for daring, bravado and defiance in the face of the authorities. Such figures continued to spawn tales of their exploits into the 1780s. One Poulaillier headed a gang that camped in the Bois de Vincennes, near Paris, in 1784. As a contemporary diarist recorded:

> Each day some new story was told of this ingenious brigand who ... took a malicious pleasure in introducing himself each time he left a place. He had

a reputation for humanity ... He not only did not permit any kind of killing, but also was very open-handed, zealously helping the indigent. It was claimed that once in a tavern he paid the bill for a brigade of the *maréchaussée* that had drunk there with him, not failing to identify himself, as was his custom, when making off.[26]

Such professional criminals may have viewed generosity to the poor as a good investment – like guerrilla fighters, they lived amongst the people like fish in the sea. The mythical open-handed bandit is a figure, however, that crosses cultures, and reflects the natural desire of many to see authority flouted and the high brought low by one who is good at heart. In any case, other robber gangs were notoriously brutal, and most criminals were much more small-scale and opportunist. Perhaps the majority of all crime was in fact prompted by short-term desperation. The theft of small amounts of food, clothing or money was by far the commonest offence recorded in city and countryside, augmented in the latter case by the frequent theft of firewood, sometimes by people from nearby towns. Most of those brought before the courts were captured, if not for their actual first offence, generally after only a short period of criminal activity. Clumsy efforts at pickpocketing in an urban crowd, being spotted with a suspicious bundle of linen and no good explanation, attempting to flee with food from a market stall, these were the commonest routes to the prison, the whipping post or the gallows.

One study of the courts based in the towns of Libourne and Bazas, in the hinterland of Bordeaux, suggests that some 17 per cent of apprehended thieves were vagabonds, under 6 per cent servants, 27 per cent peasants and almost 33 per cent artisans. These proportions perhaps reflect the fact that most crime reported to the courts occurred in the towns of the region: between 25 and 35 per cent in Libourne and Bazas themselves, with the highest totals otherwise in the locations nearest to these centres. Further into the countryside, crime was either less common or simply unreported, and perhaps dealt with more informally. It is noteworthy that in the twenty years prior to the Revolution the number of incidents of theft that reached these courts never rose above twelve in any one year, and in 1780–82 dipped to between two and four. The number of thieves charged was often higher, peaking in 1786 with thirty-five individuals charged in relation to only seven incidents. Goods stolen were most commonly cash, in 23 per cent of cases, and then a variety of common items: food and produce 18 per cent, household goods and clothing 14 per cent, wood 10 per cent. Horses, mules and other livestock accounted for some 17 per cent, and a range of other valuables for the remainder. In the vast majority of cases, the overall value of goods stolen was small, reflecting the fact that some 45 per cent of victims were artisans, peasants or servants, and over 33 per cent traders or professionals. Theft did not involve the poor plundering the rich, but rather all classes suffering the occasional consequences of a mix of opportunism and desperation. In only a few incidents, such as some episodes of horse theft, do anything approaching professional criminals seem to have been involved.[27]

In comparison to the already low reported levels of theft, criminal violence appears almost negligible – only 1.5 per cent of offenders from one study of mid century Paris. Such figures are almost certainly misleading. For example, in Libourne and Bazas over the course of the eighteenth century, some 271 crimes against property were lodged with the courts, of which sixty-six resulted in verdicts. Over the same period, 345 cases of assault were lodged. Of these, only twelve were pursued by the royal prosecutors, with seven cases reaching verdicts. Of the remaining 333 cases lodged by private plaintiffs, a mere sixteen were brought to full trial. Over the same period private plaintiffs lodged a further 204 complaints about purely verbal insults, none of which came to full trial. It appears that the act of lodging the complaint with the court served in itself as an act of self-justification, and also as a spur to an arbitrated settlement. Within Paris, the neighbourhood *commissaires*, junior magistrates of the Châtelet criminal court, frequently recorded declarations about disputes, fights and insults which seem to have served a similar purpose.[28] What such records also demonstrate is that this society, which seemed to live in such fear of violent thieves and brigands, was itself home to everyday violence of many kinds.

All societies are violent, when examined closely. Present-day Western Europe and North America, with their teeming urban environment and culture of material possessions, experience levels of crime far in excess of almost all earlier societies, and also devote far greater resources to the largely unsuccessful effort to suppress this activity. Other areas such as South Africa and Russia today live with levels of criminal violence that would have represented a vision of hell to eighteenth-century French people. More fundamentally, modern societies continue to exhibit extremely high levels of interpersonal violence, especially of men against women. Where our contemporary culture differs from that of the Old Regime is perhaps only in the fact that physical intimidation and violence are no longer seen as publicly acceptable behaviour.

It was fully accepted by the eighteenth century that inferiors, such as children, domestic servants and apprentices, and also wives, could be legitimately subjected to violent punishment. Evidence from the family courts of Rouen through the 1780s and into the Revolution shows that men in particular were likely to stand by and allow another man to beat his wife, even to the point of drawing blood, under the justifying banner of so-called 'moderate correction'. Women neighbours and relatives were far more likely to plead for it to stop, or to actively intervene, but men seem only to have done so when blood had been shed or when weapons were taken up and the possibility of murder arose.[29] Men's casual acceptance of their right to commit violent acts was frighteningly clear.

In the eighteenth century, however, physical pain was also a staple of the criminal justice system – from the mere extreme discomfort of a period in the pillory, to the routine administration of whippings and brandings for thieves and vagabonds. Execution itself, a weekly reality in major urban centres, frequently involved the infliction of humiliating agonies prior to death. The penalty of 'breaking on the wheel', used for aggravated crimes, was essentially being beaten to death with an iron bar, beginning with the breaking of all four limbs. Even hanging was not a sudden sharp drop, but meant five or ten minutes of slow strangulation. Men and women were also still burnt at the stake in the eighteenth century. For the most extreme crimes, such as the attempted assassination of Louis XV by a servant in 1757, the courts were prepared to sanction a lengthy process of torture, mutilation and dismemberment as fitting punishment.[30]

Individual honour, as well as the social system, rested on physical sanctions. Many of the abortive court cases and declarations to the police noted above emerged from situations where insults had become physical fights – not merely amongst the labouring or artisanal classes but involving merchants, lawyers, bailiffs, tax collectors and a host of other figures who felt that they had a position in society to defend. Unsatisfied with the outcome of an encounter, they might resort to police or courts to get their point aired publicly, but their attitudes were no doubt identical to those of many other individuals who felt that a kick or a blow in a similar incident had vindicated their claim. When wider social gradations were at stake, pure intimidation was a common currency of social exchange – this was in many ways the function of the male servant. In a famous incident from earlier in the century, the author and philosopher Voltaire was once beaten up by the servants of a member of the Rohan family, one of the highest in the nobility, after their master felt himself insulted by the lowly scribe. This was noteworthy only for the future fame of the victim, being in itself an everyday occurrence.[31]

A society resting on a basis of physical threat was vulnerable in the extreme to the appearance of weakness. Throughout most of France, the relationship of peasant to seigneur was one where all the strengths lay on the side of the latter – the weight of the law, in his own hands and that of the state, backed up his authority and that of his agents, and his right to go armed, and to arm his servants if necessary, left a largely unarmed peasantry helpless. The drive to keep the peasantry disarmed, partly to protect game but also to maintain this inequality of power, saw confiscatory sweeps by *maréchaussée* and even troops deployed through some regions in the 1770s and 1780s.

There were some places where this was less than successful, and in the area around Lozère, in eastern Languedoc, was to have dramatic consequences. In this region where the bulk of the peasantry was armed, hostility to seigneurial authority produced, where conditions were right, a pattern of 'seigneur-baiting' which became a major leisure activity for local youth.[32] In the community of Le Puech in the 1740s villagers poaching on the seigneur's game regularly abused and assaulted his servants and gamekeepers. The seigneur was old, frail, and too poor to initiate decisive legal action or recruit a more formidable set of servants, and became literally afraid to set foot outside his château. His son, on leave from the army, was on one occasion beaten up and flung in a river by a gang he attempted to disarm. With the balance of power in the community so decisively upset, the death of the old seigneur could not bring about a change, and his son continued to complain to more distant authorities about armed gangs, physical threats, attacks on his servants and property and unsuccessful attempts to restore order as late as August 1788.

In the community of Soubès authority was flouted even more brazenly. One reason was that two seigneurs shared rights in the village, and one of these, Peyrottes, was a drunkard who actively encouraged local hostility to the other seigneur, de Lugnan. Peyrottes orchestrated, or at least lent his presence to, weekly sessions of *tapage* – noisy, drunken demonstrations in which insulting songs and remarks were hurled. On one occasion, de Lugnan brought in the *maréchaussée* to arrest the ringleaders of this activity, but Peyrottes hid them in his own seigneurial prison cells. Such disorder continued throughout the 1740s and 1750s, and indeed grew worse. De Lugnan's own family did not help – his eldest daughter seems to have been a nymphomaniac, mother to three bastards by three different peasant fathers, and was imprisoned in Montpellier at the family's request in 1766. This story, which became legendary in the region, meant that de Lugnan's other daughters were frequently accosted and propositioned insultingly. All this was accompanied by similar activities to those in Le Puech, and armed villagers regularly slaughtered game in full view of the seigneur. In 1772 the two brothers Jaoul, millers by trade and inveterate poachers, first burst into the château and waved a gun at the seigneur, and later in the year attacked his son, leaving him for dead. This clear case of attempted murder was never brought to trial – the brothers drove off the seigneurial bailiffs with gunfire, and a plea to higher authority for additional forces does not seem to have been heeded. In any case, the seigneur would have been risking his own life by pursuing the matter further.

Conditions in this region, where resident seigneurs often had little wealth or real social power to back up their extensive privileges, and where gun ownership and a culture of young men forming gangs encouraged collective resistance, were unusual. They help, however, to define the extent to which the social order remained fragile across France. If particular sets of circumstances allowed it to be effectively overturned, or at least openly defied, for long periods in these small communities, other circumstances could create more widespread short-term upheaval over much larger areas. The outbreak of rioting is the clearest example of this, and the classic form of riot in the Old Regime was that over grain.

The perceived tendency for consumers, and particularly female ones, to respond by violence to shortages of grain and flour at urban markets was on the whole incorporated into the world view of the elites – in other words, they understood this behaviour as nothing new, and therefore not threatening to the social order. Such an understanding frequently required mental gymnastics. When a grain riot broke out at Rouen in 1752, the local archbishop reported to the duc de Luynes that it had been started by poor female spinners, protesting at merchants' refusal to buy their work outside the guild-regulated times and places. Women crying that 'they are trying to starve us' then grew agitated, and, joined by vagrants, set upon the nearest grain warehouse and pillaged it. Rioting then spread more generally to other storehouses in the city. De Luynes recorded this explanation as bald fact, while noting that the riots had needed a regiment of infantry to restore order, that the population had posted placards calling for the release of arrested rioters, and that a number of well-to-do people had been seen to take part in the pillaging. These particular facts did not disturb the general view that the riot must have originated amongst women and vagrants.[33]

A generation later, in late April and early May 1775, rioting over grain assumed far more menacing proportions, sweeping in waves through Paris, Versailles and the surrounding arable region. The disturbances emerged from the minister Turgot's liberation of the grain trade from police control in September 1774. This decision, part of his short-lived and sweeping programme of reforms, succeeded in aggravating a tense situation created by a poor harvest in that year, so that by the following spring prices were rising and local shortages becoming apparent. The Parisian basin was a region in which complex markets for grain had developed, including a considerable degree of long-distance and wholesale trading, where much of the grain produced locally came from large farms and was destined for urban markets. Thus the region was particularly vulnerable to suspicions that local shortages and price rises were being created artificially by merchants and farmers in pursuit of profits from more lucrative markets elsewhere – or even more directly from hoarding grain to create a *disette factice*, a 'false dearth' that drove up prices. Suspicions of this type were common currency even amongst the educated, and such rumours could drive hard-pressed populations into an anxious frenzy.[34]

The recent social history of the region also added to the tension. Here as elsewhere, individual peasant households were being driven closer to the edge of subsistence by rising population and the consolidation of farms in the hands of larger landowners. The spark for a dramatic explosion of social grievances came at the market town of Beaumont-sur-Oise on Thursday 27 April 1775. On the 22nd, a price of 26 livres for a sack of mixed wheat and rye had provoked murmuring, and when the next market, five days later, appeared well-stocked, customers expected to see a fall in price – and were reported later to have clearly threatened violence, saying that 'starving or being killed amounted to the same thing'.[35] When one trader demanded 32 livres per sack, he was seized and dunked in the local fountain, then dragged to the office of the municipal authorities, where demands were made for an order to lower prices. Adhering to the Turgot regime, the authorities, in the shape of the local senior notary, refused, but then had to watch as the crowd seized full control of the marketplace, drove out the merchants and sold off the grain for 12 livres a sack. This action went by the name of *taxation populaire* and was acclaimed by the common people as a time-honoured right in periods of crisis.

Only three men of the *maréchaussée* were in the town, and one of those was a fifty-five-year-old invalid. Neither the initial riot, nor its contagious spread, could be checked. On the next day, the neighbouring town was the site of pillage as soon as its market opened, word having been carried by individuals from Beaumont of the previous day's events. On that same day, a grain barge moored at a mill on the Oise was stripped of a shipment worth over 19,000 livres by individuals from at least seventeen villages. Although they reportedly set a price of 18 to 20 livres per sack, the owner of the grain said only some 300 livres had actually changed hands. Over the following days the disorders spread rapidly, reaching the market of Versailles on 2 May, and ripping through Paris on 3 May, when only police action to close the gates of the central markets protected them from pillage. Reports said that over a thousand individual bakers' premises were stripped. Once again, money was sometimes paid at the popularly determined 'just price', sometimes not.

Incidents fanned out across the Paris Basin, amounting eventually to some three hundred separate disorders over twenty-two days. On twelve occasions barges or carts were intercepted en route to urban markets, and there were over eighty riots that began in markets, of which almost half spread to take in systematic searches for grain stored in urban property for wholesale distribution. This was a developing economic trend in the *grande culture* grain-exporting areas, and one which in popular minds stank of secret conspiracy to keep grain away from open sale. Doors were battered down, proprietors threatened with murder or arson, and huge stocks of grain disappeared, again usually with only token payment at best. It was also in the grain-exporting areas that the most widespread form of disorder occurred, where over two hundred communities experienced expeditions of peasants to the premises of prosperous *fermiers* or *laboureurs*, stripping them of grain stored on site for later sale. As in the urban disturbances, rioters brooked no interference and did not hesitate to break into barns and store rooms, or to issue threats to those who tried to stop them. Nevertheless, in all these episodes, which frequently involved the actions of hundreds of people at a time, no one was killed or even seriously injured.

As the wave of activity rippled out, the state eventually swung into action to stop it. Large-scale military reinforcements were moved into the area, with some 25,000 troops mobilised for this purpose from the first days of May onwards. Effective martial law held the peace at markets through June, July and August, by which time the annual price cycle had begun to dip decisively, with the aid of government subsidies and official imports from abroad. The massive military presence held in check a population that still simmered with resentment and gave the events the name they acquired immediately, and have been known by ever since, the Flour War.

Of those eventually tracked down and arrested for participation in the disorder, ninety-three were women and some 455 men. Women, as the stereotypical frontline consumer and manager of the domestic budget, were in the forefront of disorders that began in marketplaces, but had tended to give way to their menfolk during the rural episodes, which often took on the overtones of an almost paramilitary community mobilisation. Most common amongst those detained, of both sexes, were those in their thirties and forties with young families, and sometimes dependent elderly relatives, to support. The bulk of the detainees represented a broad range of market-dependent consumers: the unskilled day-labourers, the semi-skilled or dependent skilled, such as journeymen artisans, the notionally independent skilled artisans, and the smallholding peasants, especially from vine-growing areas. Closer interrogation of the supposedly skilled workers sometimes revealed that they had in fact been reduced to casual labouring by a slump in demand for their services. Even those who practised a trade such as buckle-selling, butchery, stonecutting or clothes-dealing might be revealed by tax rolls as hovering on the brink of poverty. Nevertheless, the mendicant poor seem to have played no part in these round-ups – partly because the authorities were instructed to pursue only those who might have the resources to make amends to their victims, but partly also because the socially marginalised beggar genuinely had no place in the collective action of these communities.

The Flour War and its subsequent repression revealed starkly just how far the common people of France were prepared to go in defence of their communities' right to subsistence. Violent collective action was the most spectacular resource in an extensive repertoire of assertion. Peasants and artisans alike could draw on traditions of collective legal action, and there is evidence that the former group were more keen to assert themselves in this fashion as the century went on. Many artisans were seeing the avenues of legal dissent closed down through the 1770s and 1780s, just as domestic servants were constrained more and more tightly into a formal framework of dependency, while their own aspirations and experiences proved the artificiality of this limitation. Around these relatively well-defined groups, the swirling numbers of casual labourers, urban street-sellers, errandmen and other dispossessed groups were growing larger, and in ever-tighter competition for work and survival. The least of these was to prove capable of drawing on the same repertoire of popular action and assertion during the revolutionary upheavals to come.

In 1780 French observers looked on with smug self-assurance as London was racked by the Gordon Riots, several days of disorder touched off by Lord George Gordon's anticatholic agitation, which expanded to attacks on symbols of state and royal authority, the opening of the prisons and widespread looting. When the British state was forced to call in troops from surrounding areas to restore order to the capital, French writers waxed lyrical on how much better policed Paris was, with its lieutenant-general of police, its spies, its inspectors and its troops on standby. Louis-Sébastien Mercier was amongst those taking this view, while also reporting during the 1780s that the Parisian population, for one, was riven with insubordination, 'visible in the little people for several years, and above all amongst the trades'. He felt it to be a 'neglect of all discipline' that could very well bring 'the worst effects'. Nevertheless, he too noted that 'a riot which would degenerate into sedition has become morally impossible', due to the firm hand of authority.[36] Mercier's and his fellows' powers of prophecy would be proved as defective as their memories by events that began little more than a decade after the Flour War, events in which the common people's willingness to defend their own interests and put forward their own solutions to the pressing problems of France were manifest from the start.

4

From Crisis to Constitution

France by the later 1780s was a kingdom in profound turmoil. Although the many and varied groups that made up the social elite did not realise it at the time, the rising tide of social tension was about to collide with other problems that they were only too well aware of. Since mid century, France had struggled to pursue a policy of colonial expansion overseas alongside more traditional goals of diplomatic dominance in Europe, but that struggle had been largely fruitless. The empire in North America and a promising position in India were snatched away by the British in 1763, while in the same Seven Years' War, Prussia survived overwhelming odds to humble France's new alliance with Austria and Russia. It was the attempt to reverse this humiliation that led France into the American War of Independence in 1778, alongside a wide coalition of anti-British maritime powers. Gratifyingly complete victory for the colonists led, however, to no territorial gains for France, merely the accumulation of further state debts to finance six years of far-flung naval and military campaigning. A tense international situation, with revolts in Holland in 1787 leading to Prussian intervention, and looming conflicts in eastern Europe, forced France to keep spending high.[1]

The resulting debt rapidly spiralled to crippling levels – by 1788 repayments accounted for 55 per cent of all revenues received, pushing the state into a position where outgoings exceeded income by almost a third. The problems of the state were structural as well as circumstantial. Attempts by the monarchy to reform archaic and Byzantine structures of public finance went back decades, and had occasioned increasingly serious rifts between the crown and the privileged interest groups that dominated the internal affairs of the nation. The very real prospect of state bankruptcy had become dramatically apparent by 1786, when the king's finance minister warned that only drastic reform could rescue the state. For the educated and propertied classes of France, these developments were electrifying, and the literate culture of the newspaper and pamphlet press resounded with new visions of the polity that might result from an imminent collapse.[2]

As peasants and workers alike watched the economic situation deteriorate into 1787, various factions and interest groups amongst the elite were contesting for power. The preferred route out of the crisis for the king and his ministers was a rationalisation of the structures of tax gathering, justice and administration, cutting down on the exorbitant privileges of the higher echelons of society. For the elite groups who ran the systems of tax gathering, justice and administration, and who frequently had purchased the rights and dignities of their offices, the escape route was for themselves to be given more power. The situation deteriorated still further in May 1788, when the crown attempted to reform the judicial and tax-gathering systems by royal fiat, abolishing the privileged judgeships of the regional courts, or *parlements*. Elite protest developed into a wider crisis, as the public nature of the protests drew in a popular constituency, with major riots in several centres. This prolonged opposition produced only further financial chaos, with a partial state bankruptcy following in August, and capitulation to the reinstatement of the *parlements*.[3]

The only route out of the deadlock now seemed to be an Estates-General. This was the body which, had it had a continuous existence in France, might have already evolved towards being what the eighteenth-century British Parliament was, a permanent legislative body. Its role in French history had been episodic, however, and since 1614 it had not met at all, and had been little missed. Now, however, it seemed to offer all sides a way out of their impasse – a body which could claim to be the authentic representative of all the French, and which even the crown's bitterest enemies recognised as having the ability to define and implement new forms of taxation. At an earlier stage of the crisis, in November 1787, a meeting of the Estates-General had been agreed for 1792, but it was now brought forward to the spring of 1789.

The Estates-General was an elected body, and would sit, as it had always done, with representatives from the Catholic clergy, the nobility, and the remainder of the population – the 'Third Estate'. The winter of 1788–89 saw a dramatic shift in the political contours of the crisis. Privileged opposition to the crown, which had attracted such widespread support until this point, suddenly came to seem self-interested, as the judges of the Paris *parlement* tried to insist that the Third Estate should be no more than one equal voice amongst the three orders. A pamphleteering war broke out as others asserted the rights of the great majority (or at least the educated and propertied elements of it) to a stronger role in the forthcoming drama. For many amongst that educated public, it had become apparent by the early months of 1789 that a thoroughgoing elimination of the role of privileged groups in public life, and a general consolidation of the rights of propertied society, was now the only appropriate way forward. The crown agreed that the Third Estate should choose twice as many representatives as each of the other two estates, but it was still intended that the three estates should sit in separate chambers, and that each of them should have a separate vote, raising fears that the privileged clergy and nobility would block real change.

Throughout the months surrounding the election of the Estates-General, massive popular action, occasioned by both political alarms and a critical food-supply situation, pushed France closer to the brink of a total break-down. When the 1200 deputies of the Estates gathered at Versailles in early May, however, the division between nobility and 'commons' (a label the Third Estate rapidly adopted) was still at the top of their agenda.[4] Repeated refusal by the Third Estate to meet as a separate body kept the Estates stalemated through May and early June, even as outside agitation continued, and the finances of the state slipped further towards total collapse. The crown began to contemplate desperate measures. On 17 June Third Estate members voted to call themselves the 'National Assembly', amid repeated calls for all three orders to meet as one. On 20 June they swore to give France a new constitution, under the (mistaken) impression that force was about to be used against them, and on 23 June they defied direct royal orders cancelling their previous decrees, insisting on the inviolability of noble status, and telling them to meet as one of three chambers. On 27 June the crown caved in on the procedural issue, and agreed to instruct the three orders to meet as one, but also began moves to build up the military presence around Versailles and Paris. Early in the life of the Estates, the crown had been forced to relax censorship on reports of its proceedings, so news of these dramatic developments flew around the capital and the country.

This was the context for a further, epoch-making, popular intervention, in the events leading up to the fall of the Bastille, and effective royal capitulation to the Third Estate agenda. As we shall see, these events and others that shook the whole of France throughout the summer of 1789 revealed the divisions in the new nation as effectively as they put paid to the old order. Decisive moves to end the special status of the seigneurs, for example, agreed on the night of 4–5 August, alienated a significant portion of the elite, while also leaving the peasantry deeply unsatisfied. The following months saw the foundations of a new structure of national politics laid down, in which the popular voice, in theory at least, was confined to the margins. On 26 August the Assembly approved the 'Declaration of the Rights of Man and the Citizen', one of its most lasting achievements, although perhaps also one of its most hollow. Its seventeen articles set out a highly individualistic vision of a liberal polity, in which citizens' activities were constrained only by the protection of each others' freedom, and by the needs of public order. The four fundamental rights were declared to be 'liberty, property, security and resistance to oppression'.[5]

The defence of property had already clashed with what many amongst the lower orders clearly saw as resistance to oppression. Buried in the language of the document were some profound assumptions that limited individual freedom. The 'nation' and its 'general will' were rendered supreme in a whole series of pronouncements on legislation and public activity, implying that, despite the explicit focus on the individual, the state, as the embodiment of the nation, would retain the right to impose itself as it saw fit. As part of this national individualism, the Assembly also voted, on 10 September, to create a single-chamber legislature under the new constitution. This of course removed the possibility, now politically unacceptable, of a privileged class holding a special place in lawmaking, as in Britain, but it also precluded any revising function or authoritative questioning of the decisions of the single chamber, as the emergent United States Constitution envisaged through its Senate.

The Assembly's constitution-making was interrupted in the first week of October by another popular intervention. Political stalemate over a royal veto on earlier decrees was broken by a march of Parisians that forced the royal family to agree to move their residence to Paris. The Assembly voted to follow, but, once established in Paris, it made further efforts to restrict the popular voice in future politics. In the last week of October it decreed a regime based on a taxpaying qualification for voting and political participation. In order to be able to vote at all, one had to be an adult male, an established resident of the locality, not a dependent servant, and paying annual direct taxes to the value of three days' labour (a sum to be fixed by the localities according to prevailing wage rates). Fulfilling these requirements made one an 'active citizen', a dignity which may have extended to over two-thirds of the adult male population, forming a cohort over four million strong in 1790.

This group could only exercise direct power, however, at the very local level. All higher positions were filled through electoral colleges, chosen by the active citizens from those amongst them who paid tax above a higher threshold – ten days' labour. To be eligible for election to the new Legislative Assembly, a citizen had to pay over fifty livres in taxation, some three to four times more again.[6] To go along with this, the administrative geography of France was decisively rationalised. In a measure that was announced in principle in December 1789, and finalised in detail in February 1790, all of France was divided into eighty-three 'departments', of roughly equal size, which were to be the basis for every aspect of administration.[7] The departments were the core of the electoral process, where the colleges of 'electors' met and voted, not only for administrative and representative positions, but also for judges – and eventually for priests and bishops, in a radical reform that would shake the foundations of French society.

As the National Assembly solidified its goal of building a society of property-owners and taxpayers, it was never free from the threat of its original enemy, the recalcitrant royalist nobility. Grouped under the increasingly pejorative label of *aristocratie*, this faction would remain the bugbear of the new order throughout the coming decade. Although active aristocratic plotting was in part a figment of the alarmed imaginations of revolutionaries, there was enough reality in it to give those imaginations fuel. A group of nobles around the king's youngest brother, the comte d'Artois, had fled France in July 1789, forming the first wave of an emigrant, or *émigré*, aristocratic opposition. By September these first émigrés had found refuge in Turin, where they formed a committee to promote counter-revolution. Their plans tended to hinge on the twin ideas of a physical rescue of the royal family and military intervention by the powers of Europe, both of which aims proved at this point chimerical. One nobleman, the marquis de Favras, was hanged by the revolutionary authorities in February 1790 for what appears to have been an almost single-handed rescue bid, but the counter-revolutionary committee had few funds with which to attract wider support, and the monarchs of Europe, while making disapproving noises, seemed content to let France suffer. Nevertheless, the discontented seigneurs of France were a constituency that would only grow more aggrieved with time, and by the end of 1789 the religious factor had already begun its penetration of revolutionary politics, bringing a popular constituency into action against the policies of the state.[8]

Late in 1789, in a desperate quest for funds to stave off the bankruptcy that still loomed over the French state, the National Assembly decided, with little debate over the wider consequences, to take control of the resources of the Catholic Church.[9] These resources were vast, amounting to at least 6 per cent of the agricultural land surface, huge reserves of built property, and a portfolio of feudal rights of equal magnitude. The argument used was that the church's wealth existed because of the accumulation of individual donations over time, which had primarily been intended to benefit its charitable works. The state appropriated the wealth with the avowed intention of taking on the care of the poor directly, and also of funding a church refocused away from privilege and magnificence onto its primary pastoral role. The wealth of the church was drawn upon from the end of 1789 by the issuing of assignats – originally a form of bond guaranteed by the *biens nationaux*, the 'national property' taken from the church, but which would soon become a form of paper money in their own right.[10] Meanwhile, early 1790 saw the National Assembly taking charge of the church. In mid February it voted to abolish monastic orders not occupied with educational or charitable works and ordered the inventorying of their property for disposal. Popular discontent stirred by these early moves was driven further towards outright revolt by developments later that same year.

In July 1790 the Assembly produced its plans for the definitive reorganisation of the church: the Civil Constitution of the Clergy. In this scheme, the number of bishoprics was cut from 136 to just eighty-three – one for each of the departments – and a similar process of geographical rationalisation was envisaged for lower organisations. Departmental and district electors were given the role of picking new bishops and parish priests, respectively, as the Catholic clergy became salaried state officials. As such, they were all to take an oath to the Nation, Law, King and Constitution, as a condition of holding office. After several months of growing dissension, over a hundred clerics within the Assembly itself asserted on 30 October 1790 that such a reorganisation required explicit papal approval. At the end of November, the Assembly decreed the taking of the oath by the clergy as an immediate requirement, and that failure to do so would constitute resignation from office. This law was promulgated on 2 January 1791, and set off what was possibly the most thoroughly divisive single episode in the history of the Revolution. Popular fury at the inter- ference with the priestly role, coupled with an equal fury in some regions at priestly refusal to conform, shattered any hope of uniting the country behind the work of the Assembly.

Ironically, it was also at this moment, as counter-revolution acquired a popular Catholic constituency, that the political spectrum began to widen even more at the opposite end. An organised radical movement developed, especially in Paris, dedicated to pushing the Revolution's social and political changes further. In a further sharp irony, it was only weeks before such groups were accused by more 'mainstream' revolutionaries of abusing the ignorance of their own popular rank and file in the service of conspiratorial ends. The formation of clubs for political discussion marked one of the Revolution's unique features – even if the idea in part had evolved from the reading rooms and discussion groups of the Enlightenment, and in part also from second-hand knowledge of similar forms of sociability in the English-speaking world. The first clubs were marked out as descendants of the Enlightenment by sharing those earlier societies' generally elite mem- bership. The greatest club of all, which met in the Jacobin monastery on the rue Saint-Honoré, near the National Assembly, had formed initially from members of the Assembly itself, and continued to charge subscription fees that excluded anyone without substantial resources.

Despite such elitism, the Jacobin Club, as it soon became known, pion- eered the radicalisation of politics through public debate. In form it was effectively a reproduction in miniature of the Assembly itself, and its public gallery allowed the Parisian population, and a procession of provincial and overseas visitors, to share in an evolving 'left' perspective – the terms left and right to describe politics dating precisely from this period, when the aristocrats sat to the right of the president in the National Assembly, and their radical foes as far away as possible to the left. The Jacobins were officially known as the Society of Friends of the Constitution, implying that their opponents were enemies of it. The club was a site where radical orators, a small minority in the Assembly itself, could gather support for their views and rehearse their arguments, and a means for the left-leaning sections of the political class to mediate their views into policy proposals for the ears both of the Assembly and the wider population. As time went on, the moral authority of the Jacobins, although challenged by splits and schisms, continued to grow, until the club eventually became one of the principal motors of state policy.[11]

Patriots in provincial cities and towns hurried to organise themselves by its example, especially as the conflicts of the Revolution seemed to be becoming ever-more entrenched. In Bordeaux, for example, a reading group of educated patriots that had met at the Café National since 1789 grew into the 'National Club', while the commercial and legal elite of the city came to dominate a second club which took the same title as the Parisian society, and absorbed several smaller groupings in 1790–92. In Marseille there was more unanimity, and the first meeting of its club was presided over by the city's mayor on 11 April 1790. Here too the mercantile classes dominated, leading a patriotic stand against the older clique of municipal dignitaries who, as at Lyon, had mercantile origins but had become semi-aristocratic by 1789. Overall, some twenty provincial societies had already sought correspondence, or affiliation, with the Paris Jacobins by January 1790, swelling to three hundred by the end of the year, and nine hundred by the following summer.[12]

As the newly established political class of electors and officials coalesced into such new institutions, and as popular interventions in politics, from both radical and counter-revolutionary directions, grew louder, the prospect of a smooth transition to government under the new constitution faded from sight. By midsummer 1791, two years of structural reform had left the country little less turbulent than it had been in the summer of 1789, and things were about to get worse. On the night of 20–21 June 1791, Louis XVI and his family fled Paris, bound for the eastern frontiers, where lurked the largest concentration of émigré aristocrats, and the military forces of Marie-Antoinette's brother, the Austrian ruler and Holy Roman Emperor. The escape itself went almost farcically awry. The carefully plotted relay of military escorts collapsed because the king and queen insisted on travelling in the same vehicle as their children and governess: this and their luggage meant that only the largest and slowest carriage could accommodate them. Troops stationed along their dawdling path assumed that they were not coming and returned to barracks.

The king himself, disguised as a valet, was recognised – in ironic fashion, from his portrait on a revolutionary assignat – when they stopped for refreshment in the town of Sainte-Ménéhould, and the party were finally taken into custody at the town which gave its name to this episode: the Flight to Varennes. It says much for the mood of the country that the municipal authorities of these places – mere small towns – took it upon themselves to query and then detain the royal party without outside orders. The fugitives had got only two-thirds of the way from Paris to the frontier, where they hoped to find loyal followers in the military garrison of Montmédy.[13]

There was nothing amusing, however, about the manifesto in his own hand that the king had left behind. In scathing language he denounced all the acts he had been forced to agree to since coming to Paris as the coerced deeds of a prisoner, and condemned the National Assembly as itself the pawn of 'men of faction'. He itemised the functions of the royal executive from justice and foreign affairs to taxation and military discipline, and concluded that the new constitution would leave him but 'the vain shadow of royalty' in all these functions. Moreover, he saw in recent events the dominance of the 'mentality of the clubs', which meant for him a sort of factional fanaticism. Louis believed that such men and ideas could only drag the nation to calamity, unless he freed himself from the grip of Paris and negotiated a new and more robust constitutional settlement as he saw fit.[14] In its tone, and in its conclusions, this was scarcely less than a (somewhat petulant) declaration of war on the work of the Assembly; it is little wonder that its members, sitting in emergency session, did their best to ignore the existence of this document.

The leadership of the National Assembly was, in fact, desperate to keep the king as the keystone of the constitution. Only on the farthest fringes of the radical movement had anyone given serious thought to a republic, and the alternatives – abdication in favour of Louis's young son, or a new royal family altogether, given that the king's own brothers were more ardent in their counter-revolution even than Marie-Antoinette – both led in the unthinkable direction of putting power, as regent or king, in the hands of the trouble-making and dissolute duc d'Orléans. Thus, from the early hours of 21 June, when news of the escape first circulated, the very word 'escape' was purged from the official vocabulary – Louis XVI, and his entire family, had been kidnapped by counter-revolutionary plotters. The recaptured king was persuaded to acquiesce in this fantasy for the sake of peace in the kingdom, and his family's safety. The National Assembly itself weathered this crisis with remarkable equanimity, but not before the powers that governed Paris had clashed violently with radical popular protest in a 'massacre' on 17 July that would live long in the memories of those who now sought a republic and to be rid of their perjured king.[15]

The final weeks of the National Assembly's life were given over to concerted efforts to reinforce central authority against both popular radicalism and counter-revolutionary threats.[16] Even as it passed new stringent legislation against émigrés and oath-refusing priests, the Assembly learned of the Pillnitz Declaration, issued by the rulers of Austria and Prussia, in which they threatened military action to support Louis – a message that was too vague for many émigrés' tastes but reinforced the fear of foreign invasion in France. The king accepted the new constitution on 13 September, amid general rejoicing, and an apparently genuine short-term collective amnesia about the events of June and July. The National Constituent Assembly met for the last time on 30 September, handing over power to the new Legislative Assembly which moved into the same chamber in the Tuileries on the next day.[17] The Constituent Assembly had barred its members from election to its successor in May, and most of them were doubtless glad to escape what had become a vipers' nest of suspicion and hostility.

The active threat of aristocratic counter-revolution would have imperilled the affairs of the National Assembly, even without any other kind of stimulus for dissent. What was produced by September 1791, however, was a 'settlement' that would prove to be little more than a pause in the decline towards ever-wider political agitation, social strife, international conflict, and ultimately civil war. To see why the efforts of the Assembly to 'end' the Revolution were so profoundly in vain, we must examine more closely the tensions and ruptures within the body politic that helped create the Assembly itself, and which dominated its existence even as its members tried again and again to deny the people a real voice. From the teeming streets of Paris to the farthest fields and hillsides of *la France profonde*, grievances were aggravated and new dissent fomented by the quite overt attempt to exclude the common people from the reckoning of the Revolution they had made.

5

Collapse and Revolt

The critical and obstinate resistance of the social elite to government reforms that made up so much of the pre-revolutionary crisis did not take place in isolation from the wider population. Through the news networks and gossip-filled streets of the cities, this agitation permeated to every social level. As early as September 1787, central Paris saw a week of sporadic disturbances as crowds celebrated the return of the judges of Paris's *parlement*. The judges' refusal to register new taxes had seen them briefly exiled from the city by royal order, but they returned unrepentant, and artisans and others joined the legal clerks and students who were the courts' traditional auxiliaries in attacks on troops, effigy-burnings, slogan-shouting and general disorder to celebrate the victory over the king's ministers.

This anti-despotic sentiment was stirred further by other dramatic short-term problems that directly affected the lives of almost everyone in France. In 1785–86 a run of bad harvests had begun, and this culminated in 1788 in a nationwide disaster, with wet weather through the spring, and a freak hailstorm in July that ravaged crops across a swathe of north-central France. By the spring of 1789 rural grain supplies were running low and urban bread prices were soaring. These problems combined with the effects of the Eden Treaty signed with England on 26 September 1786, which cut restrictions on imports of English manufactures, in return for similar liberalisation of imports to England of French alcohol. While this may have been good for some vine-growers, the disproportionate strength and low costs of the English textile trade saw France flooded with cheap imported cloth. To industries already having structural difficulties, this seemed like deliberate government sabotage, and stoked up grievances amongst employers and workers alike. In some regions of northern France, over three-quarters of spinning and weaving workers became unemployed as the crisis bit. In the two towns of Amiens and Abbeville, 5672 cotton-looms had been working in 1785. By 1789 there were only 2004, and some 36,000 people had lost work as a result.[1] Seven of every eight knitting-looms also fell silent in the same period. In 1787 the silk harvest failed, giving similar cause for misery to many in southern and south-eastern France in an industry already in longer-term difficulty. As many as 25,000 silk workers may have been unemployed at Lyon.

The rural population was driven back on already-shrinking agricultural resources, and the high price of grain did them little good when most could not produce enough for their own needs, and when tithes, taxation and seigneurial demands took so much. The urban population began to look with anxiety outwards to the country, while the peasants looked with equal fear to the towns, and to the movements of grain that continued, authorities and speculators alike seeking to stockpile for the troubled future. From the very first rumours of economic difficulty, producers and consumers alike had begun to look for someone to blame. Their suspicious gaze increasingly fell on the social and political elite. Starving the population into submission seemed a logical step for the state and the aristocrats to take, as popular mobilisation supported rising political dissent. With troubles continuing to mount, fears grew that France faced the consequences of a famine pact of apocalyptic magnitude.

Historians have struggled for generations to characterise the titanic upheaval that was to burst on France. Opinion has swung back and forth between blaming the poor, lauding them as part of a social revolution, and even seeking to minimise the actual impact of their role, and of their views. Clearly, the upper echelons of French society were responsible for the overt political changes of this period, but such change both unleashed wider social forces and had to respond to the consequences of such movements. Every phase in the political struggles amongst the elite was shadowed and highlighted by popular engagement. Such was the complexity of the crisis into which the country had been plunged by 1788 that all actions which challenged the crown met with popular support, and the elite groups that led resistance took care to project themselves as the deserving guardians of the people. In April and May Paris rioted, first to welcome home the dissident duc d'Orléans from exile, then to protest against moves to abolish the *parlement*. Similar protest convulsed Rennes, the capital of Brittany, throughout the summer, while in Grenoble the urban population rallied to defend their *parlement* against royal troops on 7 June. This became known as the 'Day of Tiles' as the soldiers were pelted with tiles from rooftops as they marched into the town.

Rumours began in July 1788 of a general rising across the country, and in August of royal troop movements to surround the capital. Further rioting in Paris at the end of that month left several dead, as assaults on the forces of order began to become more determined. After a two week lull, an attempt on 14 September to storm the house of the commander of the Paris *Garde* was rumoured to have left fifty dead, though there is no official evidence for more than a few wounded. Winter weather, and political developments, seem to have calmed Parisian tempers after this, but the wider momentum for change continued to grow. As the winter drew on, and the crisis began to acquire the contours of a battle against the privileged orders, popular actions across the country mirrored this evolution, being given sharper focus by the ever-worsening subsistence situation.[2]

Widespread troubles began in the countryside, as the effort to supply the towns with grain began to take its toll. As early as September 1788 it was reported from Avoise, midway between Le Mans and Angers, that the threat of peasant resistance had made it impossible to find men willing to risk their lives driving grain wagons. The overall shortage of grain also led to widespread defaulting on the payment of dues in kind to seigneurs. Government orders imposed in November 1788 obliged farmers who had grain to sell it only at markets, to forestall speculation, but this also prevented them from selling directly to their poorer fellow villagers, stoking up resentment and leading to the kind of attacks on shipments feared in Avoise. As the winter arrived, it rapidly became one of exceptionally bitter cold – much of France was snowbound from November until mid January, and periods of heavy frost devastated vineyards, olive groves and orchards, destroying peasant livelihoods. In the towns unemployment continued to grow, throwing individuals and households onto the resources of local charity – up to half the workforce in Elbeuf and poorer parts of Lyon, a fifth of the population in Bayeux, and a sixth in Rouen. Paris was reported to shelter up to 80,000 unemployed, some local, but many who had fled to the city from elsewhere, and could appear to be dangerous strangers or even brigands. The figure of 30,000 brigands in the city was to be cited almost obsessively by figures of all political stripes to account for popular upheavals and threatened rebellions throughout the coming years.[3]

By late 1788 such rumour and alarmist speculation was already epidemic. The secretary to the military governor of Normandy wrote in June 1788 blaming the local intendant and the municipality of Caen for hoarding grain, and, in September the mayor of Le Mans accused the *maréchaussée* of taking bribes from speculators. In December 1788, when the judges of the *parlement* of Paris inconclusively discussed the grain-supply problem, a diarist noted that 'the plan [for a monopoly] originated at too high a level' for them to act against it.[4] The idea that there was a famine plot afoot was thus not an ignorant misapprehension of the common people but rather the common currency of elite exchange. Such remarks and beliefs easily passed to other ears, which could take them as proof of the plot, as did a similar current of scorn for the needs of the people. Through the spring and into the summer of 1789, magistrates and administrators were denounced, and in some cases lynched, for suggesting that the people should eat grass. Marie-Antoinette very probably never remarked that the poor should eat cake if they had no bread, but it was a witticism that many an elite audience would have appreciated.

Fear and alarm about the general crisis, and about the actions of the elite, led to the first stirrings of popular direct action against their superiors by the end of the winter. In the Franche-Comté, around Besançon, there had been reports of collective violence against seigneurs and their rights as early as January 1789. Similar threats of a general uprising emerged in the Dauphiné around Grenoble in February and in Provence in March. By the time that such attacks became a clear reality in the spring, the political stage had been transformed, and the grievances of the general population aired, in unprecedented fashion.

The Estates-General was formally summoned on 24 January 1789, in the depths of the subsistence crisis. Pamphlets and proclamations had circulated for months across the land, calling for the Estates, and arguing over its form and function, and the population of town and village alike rushed to participate in this thoroughly new kind of consultation. Since nothing like this had been attempted for 175 years, the state rather naively took a relaxed approach to the procedures, unaware of the potential consequences. Any male over twenty-five who paid any kind of tax was allowed to take part in the Third Estate elections, and the process spread downwards to every parish. Villages met, often under the chairmanship of their priest or local judge, and sent delegates onwards, culminating in some three hundred gatherings at the seats of higher district courts – called *bailliages* or *sénéchausées* in different regions. Townspeople were also polled, if less simply, and guilds, municipalities and other bodies were often involved in the initial stages, before they too sent their delegates to the final meetings. At these meetings, delegates were chosen to attend the Estates-General itself. More importantly in many eyes, those delegates carried with them their locality's *cahiers de doléances* – their 'registers of grievances'.[5]

The *cahiers* were a traditional accompaniment to the Estates-General, a form of preliminary agenda-setting that marked out, in its original medieval form, the essentially consultative nature of the assembly – the king asked his subjects what was wrong and thereby implicitly promised to do something about it. The electoral regulations had been clear on this point: 'His Majesty wishes that everyone, from the extremities of His realm and from the most remote dwelling places, may be assured that his desires and claims will reach Him.'[6] In the critical circumstances of 1789, however, the *cahiers* produced much more than a respectful request for attention to a limited range of issues. They were composed by every parish and urban group that met, and passed forward to the *bailliages*, where they were composited into the Third Estate *cahiers* that actually went forward to Versailles. In this

demands of the 3rd estate — reform — abolition of tax system

process of composition, the prosperous property-owning and legally trained middle classes turned the Third Estate *cahiers* into documents largely concerned with the country's constitutional and fiscal crises, demanding a thorough-going review of every aspect of administration, a complete overhaul of the taxation system, new permanent representative political institutions, and in many cases an end, in one form or another, to the structures of social and political privilege that underpinned the state. The vehemence of many of these documents may have been startling, once the obligatory deferential language has been discounted, but their content was hardly surprising, given the times. It was matched in many of its aspects by demands composed by nobles and clergy, electing their own representatives at the same time.

What was obscured in this process, however, was the extent to which the rural parishes had used the *cahiers* to vent an extraordinary range of griev-ances, and to do so with both frequent venom and occasional eloquence. The crushing burden of taxation was their principal priority, often described in specific terms of its impact on their own lives, but next after this came complaints about the equally onerous burden of seigneurial rights, and then of church tithes. *taxes = burden*

The parish *cahiers* make up a vast body of material, and have been analysed to produce many differing conclusions. The latest as-sessment of the parish *cahiers* is that they were a real effort by communities genuinely to consider what were their most problematic burdens, and to imagine a way of life in which these had been rationalised for the communal good – even if 'communal' might only mean the best for that particular parish. Nevertheless, while parishes complained of the burden and inequity of taxation, what they wanted was a simplification and a lightening of the burden. They were not simply showing mulish refusal to support the state.

One of the keys to lightening that burden was the ending of the many exemptions granted to the privileged classes. Alongside that went a profound wish to do away with the seigneurial regime, perceived as an unjust and onerous relic of a tyrannous past. The community of Saint-Vincent-Rive d'Olt, in the region of Cahors, put it thus:

> The lands of nobles and the church, should they not be submitted to taxation? Why protect them from it? Why subject the lands of poor people exclusively to it, and why thrust thus upon the Third Estate all the burden of taxation? ... Our community has so many charges to which it is subjected by a dozen seigneurs who have these rights recognised as easily as one changes a shirt.[7]

Lignères-la-Doucelle, in southern Normandy, took a more programmatic approach:

> The inhabitants request that there exist in the kingdom only two taxes, one a land tax and the other upon industry ... That salt be sold freely. That all seigneurs,

gentlemen and other privileged persons ... of whatever kind ... pay taxes at the same rate as the commoner. That seigneurial dues be declared redeemable ... That milling privileges be ended, and each be free to grind his grain where it suits him. That the *corvées* due to seigneurs be abolished ... That all seigneurial jurisdictions be abolished, or at least that they be grouped together into districts, in which each seigneur may name an officer for a limited time, in the absence of which the king will provide one.

The parish of Vitry-sur-Seine provides an example of a more complex agenda about property and privilege, in what is the fourth of some twenty separate demands in its text:

The total suppression of all privileges whatsoever. Our parish ... contains fifty bourgeois properties with the best land of the locality ... not paying any tax. Moreover these privileged men profit from the misery of the inhabitants of the parish to buy up the land and houses which come on the market by offering a price which no parishioner can give, given that he is burdened annually with paying taxes from which the privileged are exempt. And if these privileges are not stopped in their tracks, Vitry, which is on the doorstep of Paris, will soon find itself three-quarters populated by valets of independent means who assume the honourable title of *bourgeois de Paris*, and let or buy a manor.[8]

The clear hint here that attacks on privilege were not confined to concerns about abusive seigneurs leads us towards other aspects of the *cahiers* which complicate the picture of France in the early spring of 1789. The economic disruption of the previous years, and the poverty it had exacerbated, created a situation in which the fear of beggars and brigands had begun to rise towards fever pitch. At least 10 per cent of the population was indigent by the 1780s, and this figure began to soar upwards as the crisis intensified – doubling and perhaps even quadrupling.[9]

What was in normal years a frequently resented burden of charitable support became in critical moments a criminal extortion of the more prosperous classes – or that, at least, was how many amongst those classes saw it. Communities from Cahors to Rouen, from Lille to the Auvergne, denounced beggary in their *cahiers*, called for national administrative solutions, and pleaded that they were at threat of violence and arson from gangs of marauding able-bodied paupers. Texts spoke of an 'elite of paupers that begins by begging and ends by stealing', imbued with a 'spirit of disorder, of independence, of roguery, of rapine and theft'.[10] There were widespread calls to prevent paupers moving around the country, by tighter and more punitive laws, and by restricting charitable eligibility to the parish of birth.

From beggary, some *cahiers* moved on to the labouring poor – complaining in one case, from near Cahors, that beggary was such an easy life that large landholders could not recruit labour to work their lands, and were thus themselves in danger of starvation. Another *cahier* stated categorically that 'the manual worker, naturally improvident, having nothing to induce him to save, becomes less anxious for work and soon falls into idleness'.[11] It suggested as a remedy the taxation of earned income, to force more work from the labourer. Over half the parishes of Normandy included in their *cahiers* a request for tighter controls on rural drinking establishments, sites of idle debauchery by the labouring classes. Similar messages came from as far afield as Nîmes in the south and Quimper at the tip of Brittany. The issue of gleaning – the right of poorer villagers to collect overlooked grain after the harvest – divided the countryside. For some it was simply another opportunity for the poor to get by without seeking real work, while for others it was 'the patrimony of the poor', and one of many communal rights and resources, that enabled survival at the margins, which were increasingly under threat from more intensive and rational agricultural practices. The right to gather firewood from communal and seigneurial forests was similarly divisive, and remained so throughout the 1790s.

The demands expressed in the *cahiers de doléances* cannot be reduced to a unanimous voice of protest directed towards a common end. They clearly reflected some of the many tensions inherent in a complex society hovering on the brink of seismic disruption. Nevertheless, it is hard not to share the perception of the great nineteenth-century scholar Alexis de Tocqueville:

> I have read attentively the cahiers of the Three Estates ... I observe that here a law and there a custom is sought to be changed, and I note it. Pursuing the immense task to the end, and adding together all the separate demands, I discover with terror that nothing less is demanded than the simultaneous and systematic repeal of all the laws and the abolition of all the customs prevailing in the country; and I perceive at once that one of the great revolutions the world ever saw is impending.[12]

The period of March and April which had seen the drafting of the *cahiers* and the associated electoral assemblies had also seen considerable popular unrest. From one end of France to the other, hunger and fear joined together and burst out as collective action. All of the largest towns of French Flanders – Lille, Dunkirk, Valenciennes, Armentières, Hazebrouck, Douai, Cambrai – saw at least one episode of *taxation populaire* over grain during this time. A major riot broke out and lasted two days at Orléans on 24–25 April. As early as 2 April, the intendant in Alençon wrote to his superiors that the *maréchaussée* were deeply reluctant to risk their lives intervening in such episodes, especially as they largely shared the people's suspicions of an elite plot. In the far south east rioting developed into something more systematic.

On 14 March in Manosque, some thirty miles north of Marseille, the local bishop was stoned by a crowd which accused him of encouraging hoarding. As electoral assemblies began to meet in this region some ten days later, there were minor disorders in Marseille, but serious revolt in the neighbouring city of Toulon, where workers in the naval arsenal had gone unpaid for two months. Over the following week, violence spread, or broke out spontaneously, in centres across this region – in Aix on 24 March, and spreading in an arc to the east, encompassing at least a dozen towns across an area forty to fifty miles wide.

This rioting was no mere wanton destruction. Posters put up in Marseille noted that workers had been excluded from the electoral assemblies, and called for protest: 'it is right and proper that our opinion be heard; if you have courage, show it now'.[13] In the towns of Barjols and Saint-Maximin, protestors forced the submission or replacement of local officials. At Riez, another bishop was attacked in his palace as a hoarder, and also forced to hand over the papers and titles of his feudal rights. Monasteries were treated similarly – one was sacked in Barjols – as were some châteaux. Seigneurial mills, with their irksome monopolies, were destroyed in the town of Pertuis, and across the region lawyers and agents for feudal lords had their archives confiscated and destroyed, and were forced to pay back recent fines they had enforced and to make formal renunciations of their masters' rights. In the town of La Seyne, the protestors even extorted payment from their victims for the time they had had to take away from work.

Once this week's work was done feudalism was dead in this region, as were many local taxes and the tithes of the church, at least in the eyes of the general population, who simply refused to pay. In the alpine valleys of the Dauphiné, similar events occurred in mid April. Peasants from the village of Avançon had already warned their seigneur, a judge in the Aix *parlement*, that they saw the Estates-General as having freed them from all pre-existing dues. On Sunday 19 April they seem to have gone further, driven by the prevailing shortages, and decided to demand back from him the grain they had paid him the previous year. An armed band set out from Avançon on the 20th, recruiting help from neighbouring communities under the same seigneur, and invested, invaded and searched the seigneur's residence – neither stealing nor damaging anything. As the seigneur was away, his servants were forced to promise that he would formally renounce his rights by the 26th. When the *maréchaussée* was called in, the peasants remained defiant, threatening to drive their cattle into the seigneur's crops. When cavalry were summoned the villagers simply decamped into the forest until they left. Cooler heads prevailed when formal legal action was threatened, and the deadline for the peasants' demands passed without a formal victory, but the seigneur noted that it was now physically impossible to pursue the collection of his dues.

Other villages in this area were less strident but no less emphatic, meeting to proclaim, and often to print and publish, their freedom from any dues, their demands for more even-handed treatment over leases, and other anti seigneurial agendas. Reports into the early summer suggested that such meetings continued on a regular basis, with some communities agog with plans to burn châteaux, and others, cooler-headed, passing resolutions demanding a fair rate for the redemption of dues. The attitudes on display here were common across France, if not yet directly acted upon everywhere. A stream of letters from peasant communities reached the government during the spring, protesting that their grievances had been watered down or ignored in *bailliage* assemblies, and reiterating bitter protests about seigneurialism and the other burdens of the population. A remarkable sense of defiance of authority had been nurtured even in the remotest parts of France. Events at the centre, in Paris itself, would simultaneously display the force of such popular alarm and assertion.

Parisian elections to the Estates-General did not begin until 21 April, having been delayed by bureaucratic disputes over the jurisdiction of the various bodies that would supervise them. The capital was excluded from the relatively broad franchise provisions of the rest of the country, and a minimum 6 livre poll-tax assessment was necessary to participate in the electoral meetings of the sixty new 'districts' into which the city was divided. This created a potential electorate of well over a hundred thousand, but also clearly disfranchised the working classes of the city – labourers, journeymen, independent artisans and poorer masters. Even literate pamphleteers were driven to comment on this. One noted that it was 'revoltingly unjust' that 'disdainful rejection should be the lot of those humble and useful men' in favour of wealthy property-owners, when it was the workers who 'maintain them in luxury by improving their fortune'.[14]

Nevertheless, those who felt differently were not afraid to air their views – a published petition signed by 108 propertied Parisians had observed that 'It must be recognised that there is a class of men who, by the nature of their education and the kind of work to which they are doomed by their poverty, are equally devoid of ideas and willpower, and incapable, at present, of taking part in public business'.[15] With such views on open display, and with news already reaching the capital of the excitement stirred by elections elsewhere, extra troops were posted throughout the city, and stores of arms were moved to more secure locations. The general population thronged the streets, and in a few cases managed to raise protests at their exclusion from individual districts, but these were brushed aside. Nevertheless, the actual attendance at district meetings – on average just under 200, some 11,700 in total, under 10 per cent of the qualified electorate – suggests either a surprising indifference on the part of many, or a fear of exposure to the public gaze. A barrister who took part in the elections wrote a pamphlet denouncing just such a fear, and the reasoning behind it:

> They were afraid of what is called *the populace*. They protected our assemblies with stout barriers, and manned these with armed soldiers ... Have you not betrayed the people's trust? Have you at least responded to it? Which district has passed one motion in favour of this class, deserted by its fellow-citizens? [16]

The author went on to note how his district assembly had been surrounded by a crowd awaiting news of its proceedings, and recorded his version of their words to him as he departed: 'Monsieur, are they thinking of lowering the price of bread? I have eaten none for two days ... it's so dear! ... They make us pay fifteen sous for it now! ... Ah monsieur, don't forget us, we will pray for you ...' The plaintive tone claimed here was echoed more stridently in a printed petition claiming to be from the 'one hundred and fifty thousand Parisian workers and artisans' who were excluded from electoral participation: 'Are we not men, Frenchmen, citizens? ... We can scarcely recognise, among 400 electors [chosen by the districts to form a central assembly], four or five who know our needs, our way of life and our misfortunes, and can take a reasonable interest in them.'

With bread approaching double its normal market-price, and consuming over 80 per cent of a labourer's average earnings (if he could find work), this perception of a disregard for the workers' problems had explosive consequences. In the Faubourg Saint-Antoine, the artisan district to the east of the city, the wealthy wallpaper manufacturer Réveillon was heard to say in his district assembly that, if bread prices could be lowered, it would be possible to lower the workers' wages, and make goods cheaper to buy, thus stimulating the economy. This extremely imprudent observation, echoed in a neighbouring district by Henriot, a saltpetre works owner, was translated to outside ears as a straightforward call for wages to be cut. Réveillon was in practice a model employer, albeit a strict one, and not without concern for his workers' welfare, even paying those he had had to lay off temporarily during the previous winter an allowance of 15 sous a day. His little lecture on political economy, however, had disastrous consequences. Workers in the faubourg, and across the city, learnt the distorted version of his words – possibly from a group of workers actually present at the district meeting. A journalist recorded two years later that he had seen such a group treated with scorn by the wealthy bourgeois electors, and that this humiliation had then been translated into action.

Events that followed over the next week are usually spoken of as the 'Réveillon Riots', but it is worth noting that they were no mere sudden and local explosion of violence. Réveillon had spoken on 23 April. On the 24th calm was reported by the police authorities, and Réveillon himself was elected to the central electoral assembly. On 26 April the police could still report calm, but by then discontent was smouldering across the city. The Estates-General had originally been planned to open on the 27th, but had been alarmingly postponed to 5 May. On the night of the 26th, crowds gathered in the Faubourg Saint-Marcel, another poor labouring district south of the Seine, and were heard to complain about those 'speaking ill of the people', specifically Réveillon and Henriot who had said that 'a worker could live on fifteen sous a day'.[17] By three in the afternoon on Monday 27 April a regular procession, according to some reports encouraged by workers from central districts, had formed in Saint-Marcel and moved north. At its head were hanging effigies of the two manufacturers, and a placard reading 'By order of the Third Estate, Réveillon and Henriot are condemned to be hanged and burned in the public square'. The reported shouts of the protestors were even more alarming: 'Death to the rich! Death to the aristocrats! Death to the hoarders!'

The electors, meeting in the archbishop's palace on the Ile de la Cité, panicked as the column was reported to be approaching. Clerical deputies renounced their privileges on the spot, and three Third Estate electors met the column in the Place Maubert, on the left bank south of Notre-Dame. Their lengthy harangue produced the dispersal of the column, an event which prompted the lieutenant-general of police to dismiss it as a 'contemptible masquerade'. However, the protestors, and perhaps others from around the city, regrouped. They proceeded to the central Place de Grève, the traditional site of public executions, and performed their effigy-burning, before trying to march up the rue Saint-Antoine to Réveillon's premises. A detachment from the Gardes Françaises, the city's military garrison, blocked their progress, but only diverted them to Henriot's nearby house. He fled, while his property was ransacked, and his furniture and clothing taken to a nearby marketplace and publicly burned.

This caused the police to bring up further military reinforcements, which by the small hours of the morning had restored order. As day dawned on 28 April, however, new crowds began to gather in both the Faubourgs Saint-Antoine and Saint-Marcel. The police failed to block the river crossings, preferring to concentrate some 350 troops near Réveillon's works. The Saint-Marcel crowd was therefore able to advance towards Saint-Antoine, joined in its progress by dock workers and other labourers from the banks of the Seine. This crowd swept aside the main body of Gardes Françaises, who retreated leaving some fifty troops barricaded inside the Réveillon works. Five to ten thousand demonstrators now thronged outside the barricades, joined by unnumbered spectators. It was a stand-off, but one that was to be broken in extraordinary fashion.

In the middle of the day, a procession of carriages filled with the flower of the nobility approached the Faubourg Saint-Antoine, *en route* to watch horse-racing at Vincennes. The coachmen forced a path through the thronged streets, but aristocrats who refused to join the crowd in shouting 'Long live the Third Estate!' were roundly abused. The duc d'Orléans, a cousin of the king and a noted trouble-making liberal, scattered money to the crowds after hearing their complaints of hunger. Many subsequently accused him of instigating this and other disturbances to come. This theory was given extra credence by what happened when his wife's carriage headed back from Vincennes later in the day, along with others. For some reason, the duchess's conveyance turned up the rue de Montreuil, reaching a point at which its way was blocked by the barricades around the Réveillon works. The Gardes Françaises opened a path for the carriage, which was immediately followed by a crowd whose temper had been reignited by the renewed passage of the aristocrats. Réveillon and his household fled, and the combined factory and residence was put to the sack. As at Henriot's house, there seems to have been relatively little individual looting, and an almost formal burning of the offender's possessions – in this case in three huge bonfires in the grounds. Both domestic and factory contents were destroyed.

Military reserves were immediately summoned. The cavalry that arrived first were dragged from their horses, and the infantry that followed opened fire, at first with blanks. The crowds, hemmed in the narrow streets, fled into the neighbouring buildings and pelted the troops from above with roof slates, furniture and stones. They cried out 'Liberty! Murderers! We won't give way! Long live the Third Estate! Long live the King!' [18] In the face of this, live ammunition was authorised and troops were given instructions to shoot to kill. This overwhelming force steadily regained control, finally entering Réveillon's premises around eight in the evening, killing the rioters found within, mostly the imprudent few incapable of escape due to their consumption of Réveillon's wine – the limits of this behaviour suggested by the 2000 bottles left intact in the cellars.

This dramatic confrontation left twelve soldiers dead and some eighty wounded. As many as three hundred protestors may have died, and certainly well over three hundred were wounded. In the face of such horrific events scarring the days before the opening of the Estates-General, the authorities did almost nothing. Rather than attempt a formal investigation of the course of events, they simply hanged a few looters caught red-handed. The press and public rumour were happy to blame a wide variety of culprits – from the ubiquitous 'brigands', to the aristocracy bidding to defend privilege by presenting change as anarchy, to the duc d'Orléans, and even to shadowy figures amongst the clergy, who had been seen as agents of famine and disorder since the Flour War. Notably, few bothered to consider whether the crowds might have been expressing legitimate fears and grievances on their own behalf.

The 'Réveillon Riots' were to pale into insignificance beside events to come later in the summer, but it is worth pausing to note again how unprecedented this event was – an effective insurrection of thousands of workers, targeting men who had appeared to threaten their subsistence, facing down armed force, and almost ritually destroying the property of their targets. Doubtless both Réveillon and Henriot were lucky to escape with their lives, but if they had been caught and killed, it would have been a popular execution, not a frenzy of bloodlust. Ordinary people, in the capital as in Toulon or the valleys of the Alps, were taking action to defend themselves in disregard of the normal forces of authority.

It is fair to say that the authority of the state, as expressed in the will of the king and embodied in previously existing institutions, collapsed in France after the drafting of the *cahiers de doléances*. Into the spring of 1789, as the Estates-General gathered at Versailles in May and soon found itself in political deadlock, rumours continued to circulate which placed the blame for food shortages at the door of the highest in the land. The high nobility and the king's ministers were accused of plotting against each other and against the good of the people. By June and July the clergy and the *parlements* were drawn into such alleged plots, and apocryphal appeals from the Third Estate deputies at Versailles, calling for an uprising to protect them, were in circulation.

Areas of the far north and Picardy saw renewed grain rioting from the end of April into May. Large organised parties of peasants invaded and searched abbeys and monasteries, stripping them of their stores of grain, in some areas as a direct requisition, in others offering what they claimed was a fair price. Seigneurs and even some prosperous Third Estate farmers received similar treatment, and protest evolved into forced renunciations of feudal rights by June. Meanwhile, rural areas close to Paris, where crops were frequently ravaged by the roaming game from royal forests and other aristocratic hunting reserves, saw a forceful backlash. A local *sub-délégué* claimed that famine had cast 'a sort of despair into the soul of the peasant', but this despair led to yet more determined collective action. Communities set out to destroy game, beginning with the prince de Conti's reserves from 1788 into early 1789, and spreading via other elite playgrounds to ravage the queen's own private reserves at Saint-Cloud in June. Firewood as well as game was stripped out, and once again church properties came under assault – a minister reported on 11 June that rich farmers near the abbey of Saint-Denis now owned large wagons that they had bought for 'ludicrously low prices' from other locals, and which, as he put it, 'once belonged to the abbey'.[19]

May, June and early July saw episodic violence – or, as we should perhaps think of it, popular insurrection – flare across France. Rouen experienced a major grain riot on 28 May, and early June saw similar episodes in Brittany, and in Champagne whole districts were reported to be turning out to hunt down seigneurial game. Around Lyon, reports in early July indicated that the peasantry was refusing to pay the tithe, and that the urban population had demanded the suspension of duties on goods brought into the city after a rumour that this had been granted by the king. The bishop of Uzès, near Nîmes, had begged in June for royal orders to the peasantry confirming the need to pay tithes. In Languedoc, seigneurs and local officials reported sinister crowds repeatedly gathering from May. Violence was reportedly widespread in the same month in the area around Poitiers, and at least one parish near Le Mans declared that they would pay no more rents. On 3 and 4 May, tax offices in Limoux, south of Carcassonne, had been destroyed. Threats were made elsewhere to do likewise, and the evasion or outright refusal to pay taxes and tolls on goods was becoming epidemic. Reports from Rennes and Nantes of threatening crowds of peasants emerged in early July, and the sub-délégué of Ploermel in central Brittany made clear the nature of some threats on 4 July:

> Tempers are so high that the threats I hear make me and all other sensible folk greatly fear the riots and disturbances which will surely follow the tithe-gathering this year ... All the peasants around here and in my area generally are preparing to refuse their quota of sheaves to the tithe-collectors and say quite openly that there will be no collection without bloodshed on the senseless grounds that as the request for the abolition of these tithes was included in the cahier of this [district], such an abolition has now come into effect.[20]

These beliefs had nonetheless burgeoned in the aftermath of the Estates-General elections. The lieutenant-general of the bailliage of Saumur put it succinctly, if smugly, during the process itself:

> What is really tiresome is that these assemblies ... have generally believed themselves invested with some sovereign authority and that when they came to an end, the peasants went home with the idea that henceforward they were free from tithes, hunting prohibitions and the payment of feudal dues.[21]

This was echoed by a parlementaire from Aix:

The lower classes of the people are convinced that when the Estates-General sat to bring about the regeneration of the kingdom we would see a period of total and absolute change, not only in present procedures, but also in conditions and income.

Such views, as another commentator noted from Provence, were often interpreted as the will of the king himself, who was rumoured to wish 'every man to be equal', and thus 'these poor misguided people believe they are exercising their rights and obeying the king'. Senseless, misguided and generally tiresome these actions may have been for the higher orders, but by mid July 1789 they were adding up to a momentum of change that would be, in a word, revolutionary.

As will already be clear, the peasants and workers of France were not motivated by any revolutionary ideology, nor were they acting with the approval of that other significant group, the professional and propertied middle classes. The bundle of hopes and fears that made up the general popular response to recent events by mid 1789 was amorphous, albeit focused strongly on aristocratic villainy, and unguided by anything more than vague aspirations to liberty and justice, as understood within the communitarian frameworks of the common people. Nevertheless, these motivations were far from negligible, and the movement towards some kind of climactic confrontation was accelerating, spurred on its course by very real hunger and desperation.

Such movement had enveloped large sectors of the French population, and in some cases was turning them against each other as much as against the state. As state authority appeared to collapse, in many areas the middle classes sought to take over its mission of social order. This had happened as early as April 1788 in Troyes, where voluntary patrols organised by the municipality had begun to police the streets. Between February and July 1789 other towns followed suit under a number of guises: Bar-sur-Aube, Sens and Amiens followed the lead of Troyes with volunteer patrols; Etampes, Caen and Orléans revived ancient municipal rights to form companies of 'musketeers' or 'free archers'; and in Marseille and Limoux a more innovative approach saw new bourgeois militias conjured into existence. From June this process went a stage further, as some rural regions began to conduct officially sanctioned arming of village communities, fearing brigandage against their ripening harvests – this happened in the north in the regions of Douai and Lille, and in nearby Hainault, and in the south in both Gascony and Languedoc. In all these cases, and others, armed men now stood by to resist brigandage, but also to defend themselves if necessary against the state. As the deadlock at the Estates-General evolved towards more open confrontation from late June, with the proclamation of the

'National Assembly' by the Third Estate deputies, the state indeed began to contemplate the use of military force against its population.

On the face of it, such action should have been a decisive option for the state in the summer of 1789, but for a variety of reasons it proved deeply problematic and ultimately disastrous. Since the early spring, many military units had been dispersed in penny-packets around the cities and market towns of France, guarding against disturbance, but also separated from the influence of senior officers and subject to the blandishments of the civilian population in favour of the Third Estate. The army was a force of young men, half under twenty-five, the vast majority of whom had joined up at some point in the previous decade of growing social polarisation. At least 60 per cent came from the artisan and urban classes, more likely to see their service as a job rather than the quasi-feudal relationship of loyalty that a stereotypical peasant recruit was thought to have. They were poorly paid, with a daily rate around a third of what even an unskilled labourer could earn. Though soldiers were of course paid for every day, they still had to buy their own shoes and shirts, and any food above the meagre basic ration, which itself was deducted from their pay. They were equally poorly housed, often sleeping several to a bed in barracks, and also subject to a recently introduced regime of punishments and discipline that many regarded as a humiliating Prussian import. From a total strength of some 150,000, around 3000 deserted each year. In the patriotic fervour of 1789, appeals to these men from civilians could break through the traditional mutual scorn that held soldiers to be little better than armed beggars and looters, and civilians to be feather-bedded ingrates. The French army therefore was not a safe instrument for authority to direct against its own people.[22]

Even within Paris, disaffection was apparent, and the Gardes Françaises that had suppressed the Réveillon Riots in April had by late June become less reliable. On 24 June two companies refused instructions to prepare for public order duties, and on the 28th a larger body threw down their arms when issued with ammunition in anticipation of disorder, moving to the open space of the Palais-Royal gardens to fraternise with crowds supporting the Third Estate. A complex *affaire* unravelled over the next ten days, in which fourteen ringleaders were arrested. Crowds protested, obtaining the men's release, and other troops declined to resist. Ultimately the authorities had to reduce the fourteen's punishment to a symbolic level to appease their supporters.

While all this heightened the fervour of those supporting the 'nation', middle-class patriots remained hesitant about its popular implications. A diarist recorded that peace-loving citizens 'felt a certain uneasiness ... apprehending fatal consequences to an insubordination which was spreading to so many members of society'.[23] Nevertheless, by the end of the first week in July, such peace-loving citizens were also aware that a large force, substantially made up of Swiss and German troops less amenable to fraternisation, was being concentrated in the environs of Paris. These troops were already being used against the population: on 6 July, the duc d'Orléans himself, despite his subversive reputation, had needed the support of soldiers to clear the gardens of the Palais-Royal, after the failure of a personal attempt to pacify a crowd that had been listening to violently radical speeches. This incident was brought to a peaceful conclusion by the presence of the troops, after the duke's personal exhortation to restraint on their part. A confrontation which touched closer to the lives of many Parisians developed two days later, as the still-soaring price of bread led crowds to besiege customs posts around the city, demanding the suspension of entry duties on foodstuffs. German cavalry of the Royal Allemand regiment were used to guard the customs men and to enforce payments. These same horsemen – often actually natives of Alsace – were to play a key role in events which erupted days later, which would mark the irreversible onset of a revolutionary process.

As feelings in Paris and elsewhere ran ever higher in the first week of July 1789, so the stakes in the national political game had been raised. On 6 July the National Assembly had created a 'Constitution Committee', and on 9 July renamed itself the 'National Constituent Assembly', re-emphasising its determination to remould the institutions of France. It had also, on the 8th, formally requested the king to withdraw his military reinforcements from Paris. On 11 July it seemed as if all these measures had been spurned. In what was effectively a *coup d'état* from above, the king appointed a new set of ministers with a clearly reactionary complexion. This necessarily involved the dismissal of a minister who had been hailed as a popular saviour upon his appointment the previous August – Jacques Necker, the Swiss-born financier who had previously steered France through the American War of Independence, and who in 1788 had replaced, to general rejoicing, the Brienne ministry which had been forced to declare France effectively bankrupt.

Although Necker had actually launched no new initiatives, expecting the Estates-General to provide solutions to France's problems, he was seen by public opinion, and especially by Parisian popular opinion, as having fended off the threat of a famine pact in the winter of 1788–89. Although prices could not be prevented from soaring, his resort to traditional policing of the grain trade had at least got supplies to the capital, and the assumption was that, however bad things were, they would be worse without Necker. His dismissal seemed to signal that the nefarious aristocratic forces that were assumed to be ready to profit from famine had retaken control of government policy. It was this element, allied to a general alarm at the combination of political and military manoeuvres, which led Paris to erupt.

Necker had been sacked, by letter, on the Saturday evening. The news leaked at Versailles the same evening and reached the ears of Parisians by the following morning, Sunday 12 July. On this day of rest, the crowds at the Palais-Royal and other pleasure spots were naturally at their height, and grew even larger as word spread. In the Palais-Royal gardens, speakers saw the situation in stark terms, putting forward 'proposals ... aimed at repelling force by force, at defending our homes against the fury of a threatening army of mercenaries'.[24] The air was one of looming catastrophe, and of what amounted to national mourning for the fallen Necker. The theatres of Paris were invaded by crowds – some 3000 strong at the Opera – forcing the abandonment of their afternoon performances, and large groups gathered all along the boulevards. Famously, a waxworks was made to yield up its images of Necker and the 'patriot' duc d'Orléans, and these became the emblems of a parade of some five to six thousand that marched anticlockwise along the boulevards from the Temple in the north east to the Place Vendôme in the west. This parade was actually escorted (albeit perhaps unwillingly) by a detachment of the paramilitary *Garde de Paris*. The crowds then moved from the Place Vendôme to swell an already large body of people around the Place Louis XV (the modern Place de la Concorde) and the adjacent Tuileries gardens. Royal troops here attempted to control the crowd, and a confused mêlée ensued, in which individuals on both sides fired an unknown number of shots and groups of horsemen charged bodies of civilians. Although it was later widely claimed that an old man was killed by the cavalry, there is no evidence for this.

This clash would nonetheless be immortalised in accounts of the Revolution's origins for several reasons. One was that prime culprits were the already unpopular Royal Allemand cavalry and their leader, the prince de Lambesc, who had been stationed on the Place Louis XV; another was that the clash happened in the heart of polite Paris, in the open space most given over to genteel strolling, not the loud, brash and sometimes bawdy space of the Palais-Royal or the boulevards. Since observers had already characterised the crowds on the boulevards as 'beggars and wretches', it was convenient for writers at the time to set a key moment of the Revolution's origins somewhere where the participants could be said to be more representative of the nation.[25] It was also, of course, all the more shocking that lawyers, merchants, clerks and other bourgeois had been subjected to violence normally reserved for 'the people'.

Nevertheless, the people of Paris, in all senses of the term, were taking part in insurrection, and indeed had begun to do so in some instances before news of Necker's dismissal. The customs barriers, symbols now of famine plot, and already threatened on 8 July, were attacked again on the night of 11 July. At one, the Barrière Blanche, Royal Allemand detachments found themselves in a stand-off with crowds that lasted through the 12th, until at about 8 p.m. a small skirmish developed into fighting, in which one man, an Alsatian shoemaker, was shot in the stomach and killed. This incident was swallowed up in the forest of rumour which sprang up around the Tuileries scuffles, rumours which led the Gardes Françaises to change sides decisively and emerge from their barracks as evening drew in, joining crowds in forcing the outnumbered cavalry to abandon central Paris.

The night of the 12th to the 13th passed in a confusion of alarm, with gunsmiths' shops being plundered. One clear movement of that night was to continue and enlarge the attack on the customs barriers. Crowds invested and torched no fewer than forty of the fifty-four barriers, and in a number of places also attacked the stone wall which linked them into a continuous chain. As in the Réveillon Riots, large bonfires were sometimes made of the fixtures and fittings, as well as the records and documents of the customs offices. Witnesses described the assailants as poorly dressed, or in more hostile terms as rabble – though the royalist author who made this comment also had to note that the rabble was escorted by a group of Gardes Françaises as it did its work.[26] The arson was quite calmly carried out – in at least two cases, customs posts were reprieved from burning explicitly because of the risk to neighbouring buildings.

The crowds, seeing themselves as acting to forestall a famine plot, moved on the morning of 13 July to the great monastery of Saint-Lazare. When they forced open the doors, they were able to take away fifty-three cartloads of grain, which were sold publicly at the main markets. The crowd, made up of all social classes, also removed some 25,000 litres of wine in casks, eight barrels of beer and 600 bottles of wine, which were not seen again. Defending the nation was thirsty work, and such wholesale pillage was clearly viewed as legitimate. Twenty-three mainly poor or indigent people were subsequently arrested, however, and charged with looting the monastery of non-essential items. Respect for property remained high on the insurrectionaries' agenda, as long as that property did not stand in their way, and as long as isolated individuals could be picked out as the thieves. Fine judgments about the crowds' motives are further complicated by the fact that, after releasing a number of minor criminals detained within the Saint-Lazare buildings, and doing the same at La Force prison – which was found abandoned, the military commander having changed into plain clothes and fled – the crowds avoided the two prisons of Bicêtre and the

Châtelet, where more serious offenders were thought to be held. A prison mutiny in the Châtelet on the morning of the 13th was suppressed by gunfire from a Gardes Françaises patrol, with onlookers helping to restore order, leaving four dead or dying prisoners and twenty wounded.

The morning of the 13th also saw the summoning, by drum, cannon and alarm-bell, of the sixty electoral districts into emergency session. This followed a previous decision of the Parisian electoral assembly, on 11 July, to proceed to the formation of a bourgeois militia – again, we may note, before the news of Necker's fall. Having adjourned themselves until the 13th, the news and events of the 12th had brought many electors, and many more spectators, to the Hôtel de Ville (Paris's city hall), where the districts had been ordained to meet at 5 a.m. on the 13th. From very early on that day, alarms went out across the city. District assemblies met in their local churches, and by the middle of the day the formation of a city militia was under way – by the afternoon of the 13th decreed at 48,000 in strength. There followed a hectic search of the city for arms for such a body, discontent and suspicion growing as various sites proved barren, and delegations returned empty-handed after being refused access to the royal stockpiles at the Invalides. The guns that had been found in private hands were loaded with powder confiscated from a boatload found on the river. By the Monday evening, Parisian militiamen and Gardes Françaises were jointly patrolling the city.

A night even more chaotic than the 12th ensued, as patrols from individual districts roamed far beyond their boundaries, challenging random passers by, and each other, and as the undoubtedly criminal elements of the city's population sought to profit from the confusion – some of these were caught red-handed and summarily hanged for theft by militia patrols, who themselves seemed little better than brigands to some terrified observers. The author Restif de la Bretonne recorded several traumatic encounters that night as he made his way home across the city, with men he called variously 'brigands', 'bandits', 'ruffians' and 'formidable rabble', all claiming to be militia patrols.[27] The flood of volunteers for militia service had swept up many men of the labouring classes, whose possession of weapons terrified the middle-class administrators of the city when they drew breath at the end of the crisis. For now, however, every armed man on the Parisian side was welcomed as the city was continually swept by new rumours of advancing royal troops.

This is the atmosphere from which emerged the conflicts of 14 July. The morning of the 14th was marked by incidents which suggested that royal authority had ceased resistance to the Parisians. At the Invalides, the commandant was obliged by overwhelming force, and the sentiments of his own garrison of military pensioners, to hand over the 30,000 muskets stockpiled there. This happened while several thousand troops camped on the Champ de Mars nearby did nothing – their officers had decided that to order them to march would merely be to invite mutiny. A far more tense situation developed at the other end of Paris, where the medieval fortress of the Bastille loomed over the Faubourg Saint-Antoine, guarding a stockpile of gunpowder essential to make the Parisians' arms effective. The commandant here had formidable walls to shelter behind, and had been reinforced by a small detachment of reliable Swiss troops. A large crowd, mainly composed of militiamen from the faubourg, but with many onlookers of both sexes, gathered outside the fortress through the morning, and tense negotiations, brokered by representatives from the assembly at the Hôtel de Ville, went on until the early afternoon. They were broken up at that point as confusion between the crowd and different elements of the castle's garrison led to an attempt to break in, followed by a lethal fusillade from the defenders and the onset of a real siege.

Later in the afternoon the arrival of small detachments of Gardes Françaises and some of the cannon captured at the Invalides turned the balance of the day. Once the artillery had been positioned to threaten the main gates of the fortress, the garrison, after further negotiations, surrendered shortly after 5 p.m. Somewhere in the region of a hundred Parisians had been killed in the fighting, but only one member of the garrison. Several more, however, were killed by vengeful crowds, and de Launay, the governor of the Bastille, was hacked to death by a crowd on the steps of the Hôtel de Ville. He had been brought there by municipal troops in an effort to protect him, but it was also there, on the Place de Grève, that the day's other famous victim perished. Jacques de Flesselles was the Provost of Merchants, the Old Regime mayor of Paris. He was thought to have prevaricated when the crowd sought arms on the 13th, and was shot dead as he left the Hôtel de Ville to vindicate himself. His head and de Launay's were paraded on pikes.

Much ink was spilt in the following weeks by those who sought to bracket off the intemperate popular vengeance suggested by these killings from the glorious popular salvation represented by the fall of the Bastille. Leading journalists reported that de Launay, for example, had incited his own murder by insulting the crowd and threatening it with reprisal. Such approaches, however, say more about the fastidiousness of the elite's sensibilities than they do about the inevitable brutalities of an armed confrontation.[28] The working people of Paris who had actually been subject to the everyday authoritarianism of the royal state, and who believed implicitly in the threat of military assault on the city, had few qualms about seeing off that threat, and dispatching men they saw as complicit in it. Nevertheless, that eager response was not without its own problems.

The turbulent complexity of the mass mobilisation within Paris is captured incisively by the experience of Collenot d'Angremont, an official of the Saint-Roch district, around the Palais-Royal. He later recounted what happened to him in the victorious city on the night of 15 July:

> I had orders [from the district] to inspect the exterior of Paris, the Arsenal, the Bastille etc., etc. To carry this out at night I was on horseback: on the Quai de la Feraille, my horse was stabbed twice with a pike ... they took from me my sword, a pistol and my hat. Returning ... I passed down the Rue Croix des Petits Champs, where a large number of Guards took aim at me, incited by many women yelling out of their windows, 'He's a traitor, kill him' ... Arriving behind [the church of] St-Roch, I was beaten with musket-butts and knocked from my horse ... in that state I was carried to the church by two honest citizens whose names I did not know ...[29]

Even if we accept that all of d'Angremont's various assailants were acting in good faith against the feared aristocrats, clearly the liberation of Paris from the 'plot' of 11 July did not immediately produce a new order, but rather what many observers would see as comprehensive disorder that would need to be rapidly tamed. Nevertheless, whatever had been the king's intentions in dismissing Necker, they were now moot. On 15 July he announced to the National Assembly that troops were being withdrawn from Paris, on the 16th Necker was recalled to office, and on the 17th the king visited Paris and accepted a cockade in the new revolutionary colours of red, white and blue, symbolising to Parisians' eyes the effective surrender of royal to revolutionary legitimacy. Even as the political scene at the centre was changing irrevocably, events across the nation were both echoing this transformation and provoking further disquiet.

Communities in every corner of France had been avid since May for news of developments at Versailles, news which often reached them very late, and in the form of personal letters from Third Estate deputies – it was common by June and July 1789 for large crowds to gather to hear these read out in urban centres, and also for addresses signed by hundreds, sometimes thousands, of people to be dispatched in return, demanding or beseeching progress. Deputies sometimes solicited such addresses as part of the political struggle with the court and nobility, but they frequently also lamented the news of violence which reached them from the provinces, appealing for calm and the orderly distribution of reliable news, not inflammatory rumour.

It was the reliable news of Necker's dismissal that stimulated events elsewhere almost as dramatic as those in Paris. This information reached

1. The life of the peasantry as seen by the *Encyclopédie*. Most agriculture was carried out without the aid of the many kinds of machinery seen here.

2. Artisanal workshops: the *Encyclopédie*'s attempt to depict the 'mysteries' of the mirror-making and tin-smithing trades.

3. Popular anger erupts in Paris: the Réveillon riots of April 1789.

4. 14 July 1789, the taking of the Bastille. French Guards, oppressors of the people in April, turn their cannon on the fortified symbol of royal power.

5. The Jacobin Club, a satirical print: observe the figure at the secretary's table.

6. The execution of Louis XVI, 21 January 1793. Like most such images, this exaggerates the size of the machinery of death: the frame stood only about six feet high.

7. Revolt in the Vendée: a revolutionary 'liberty tree' falls victim to Catholic-royalist wrath.

8. Federalist Lyon fallen to the Republic: the representative Collot-d'Herbois (on horseback), directs fire at protesting crowds.

the provinces generally between 15 and 19 July, and the response in some areas was immediate – powder magazines, arsenals and stores of public funds were seized; grain shipments to the capital were suspended; military garrisons were either subjugated or 'converted' to declarations of loyalty to the nation; the ongoing process of militia formation and municipal takeover by revolutionary committees accelerated still further; neighbouring towns consulted over defensive alliances and stern warnings were dispatched in writing to the capital that aristocratic plotting would not succeed, and that the agents of despotism were traitors and scoundrels who would be hunted down.

While this was going on in some areas, other towns remained in a state of tension which did not ease until the further news from Paris of the events of 14 July and its sequels arrived, and there then followed a further and more thoroughgoing wave of conversions and takeovers. Nevertheless, the essentially alarmed and defensive reaction to the initial news was not really calmed by what followed. Just as it had been assumed throughout the previous year that a famine pact and aristocratic plot were under way, and that great resources were available to the enemies of the nation, no one now believed that a semi-symbolic victory at the centre removed the underlying general threat. From the middle of July onwards, France became akin to an armed camp, but one without any central coordination or authority, and one where the enemies were mostly feared to be internal.

Even as political alarms convulsed the country, the social and economic crisis continued to deepen. Partly prompted by the revolutionary situation, but also by desperation, urban grain riots were endemic through the second half of July, reaching the level in some areas of pitched battles with military convoy escorts, and in others of the murder of individual merchants. As in Paris, demands escalated against the network of tolls and excise duties, with threats to burn buildings on top of simple refusal to pay. There was still no sign of resolution to any of the dimensions of the revolutionary crisis, and alarm continued to spread, moving now from the urban centres to further antagonise the peasantry.

MAP 2. France in 1793: Administrative departments.

6

Revolution and Reordering

The urban revolutions in Paris and elsewhere had a dramatic rural echo through late July and early August 1789 in a phenomenon that has come down through history as the Great Fear.[1] Currents of alarmed rumour swept the country, and provoked towns and villages to arm themselves against brigands that the aristocratic enemies of the people were said to have let loose against the ripening harvest. The transmission of alarms was extremely rapid, and, with the countryside in many areas literally up in arms, confusion and apprehension held brief reign. But it is important to qualify the nature and form of these responses. It was common for the fear of brigandage to reach what hindsight sees as exaggerated proportions, and the nature of rumour tended further to that end in a time of great tension. Brigandage, for all its mythical qualities, was an entrenched element in French people's understanding of the social landscape. So too was a conspiratorial style of explanation: revolutionaries in the National Assembly confidently asserted that the apparently simultaneous explosion of alarm over such a wide area had to be the work of a coordinated aristocratic and clerical plot, while aristocrats who fled France during that summer were later recorded by the English traveller Arthur Young as being equally confident that revolutionary emissaries had launched a planned antiseigneurial agitation, drawing on funds supplied by the duc d'Orléans.

Approximately two-thirds of France experienced the Great Fear, in currents flowing from around half a dozen original, and often insignificant, incidents. Large areas were untouched: Brittany, two-thirds of Normandy, much of the south-western coastal region and two-thirds of the Mediterranean coasts, Alsace, Lorraine and eastern Champagne, and the far north – a region particularly troubled over the previous year. A current of fear spread south east from Nantes after that city was alarmed at reports of troops approaching the city, and sent out its own militia cavalry to scout – these were then taken by villagers for enemies, a perception heightened by fear that the city might seek to requisition the harvest during the prevailing subsistence crisis. Rumour, and a neighbourly concern to alert other communities, then diffused the alert, as it did in the Oise valley near Paris, where a dispute between a farmer and some itinerant harvest labourers, who reportedly threatened to ruin his harvest if he did not increase the wages he was offering, became an alarm over marauding bandits that swept the valley.

Similar disputes, squabbles, and occasional incidents of unauthorised harvesting may have started several other currents of fear across central France. In southern Champagne a current that began on 24 July with reports of gangs of brigands seen sheltering in woodland was revealed to have been sparked by a straying herd of cows. Of course, the dust raised by such a herd, and the noise they made moving through undergrowth, was indistinguishable at a distance from approaching horsemen or lurking brigands. Likewise, muttered threats to return in force made by small groups of alms seekers who received a harsh welcome could be easily discounted, but not if one was already primed to expect such large gangs to exist. It would be wrong to speak of these events as an 'irrational' response, even if they were frequently conducted in an atmosphere of panic fear. When all news was of a general crisis, and with reports sometimes arriving from several different directions of alleged brigands at large, a failure to stand on alert would have been equally irrational. Peasant communities and townsfolk across France did not start shooting randomly at each other or descending on neighbouring communities to commit mayhem. They generally stood fast, or even rallied to their neighbours, against a perceived external threat. As that threat steadily failed to materialise, a calmer, but still tense, situation returned.

If the Great Fear has been easy for historians to write off as a delusion, what cannot be denied are its consequences, which helped to create unprecedented social change. Fear-driven communities formed themselves into 'revolutionary' self-governing bodies. When they took action, it was visibly against their seigneurs and the symbols and realities of feudal authority and exaction. This was counterpointed by sharper outbreaks of significant insurrection, adding to those already seen in the north and south east. The northern districts of Hainault and Flanders were struck again in July by violent peasant resistance to the annual leasing of tithe collection rights. Serious antiseigneurial violence broke out in the Franche-Comté, on 19 July, and continued until the end of the month. An attack on one château here, at Quincey, seems to have touched off a powder magazine, destroying the building and its assailants in an explosion that was immediately attributed to deliberate seigneurial revenge. News of this treachery spread across eastern France, triggering more uprisings.

Far from this news, in the Norman *bocage* south of Caen, peasants began to visit seigneurial châteaux in force around the 21st, seizing and destroying feudal titles and papers in around two dozen localities over the following two weeks. On 26 July, a rural and urban uprising broke out in Mâcon and its surrounding district, north of Lyon. Bitterness against local elites here had been exacerbated by a divisive campaign over the elections to the Estates-General. Attacks on grain convoys escalated to full-scale antiseigneural revolt, with over twenty châteaux invaded, along with numerous religious foundations. Here, unlike in Normandy, pillage was common and some buildings were torched. Even before news of such incidents reached Lyon, riots against municipal tolls in the city, and generally tense social relations, had led the local elite to form a *corps de volontaires* to supplement the royal garrison – which itself, unlike in Paris, was welcomed, and reinforced, as a protection against social disorder. Popular demonstrations were denounced as 'the first foundations of anarchy'. By the end of July 1789 some of these volunteers were being sent out 'to hunt down the château-burners' in the surrounding region.[2] As the currents of the Great Fear lapped near the city, the extensive landholdings of the Lyonnais bourgeoisie were defended by these troops, even to the extent of further hostilities with the population of the Lyon faubourgs as volunteers returned from their punitive expeditions with prisoners.

Alsace, the easternmost region of France, was also struck by insurrection. Leaders of the urban bourgeoisie seized power in the main city, Strasbourg, only to learn that in some cases their own rural properties were under threat from peasant forces. It was in the east – both Alsace and Franche-Comté – that some of the harshest measures of feudalism, including the last areas of real serfdom in France, survived, which may perhaps account for this region's particular strife. Outside the regions which experienced widespread action, more isolated antiseigneurial episodes broke out in some forty localities from western Brittany to the eastern Pyrenees, with clusters to the east of Paris and in the Rhône valley, and a wider scattering across the south west.

Such risings were only ever the work of brigands in the minds of outside observers, or of the outraged seigneurs who wrote in protest to the National Assembly through the summer. What seemed to them to be inexplicable outbreaks of insubordination, which could only have been generated by criminal outsiders, were often in fact orchestrated and preplanned by peasant communities. Not only did elected agents such as village syndics frequently come to the fore, peasants sometimes obliged local notables such as priests, lawyers or seigneurial agents to march with them, affirming by their presence that this was a communal response, and sometimes even acting as mouth-piece for communal demands. Reluctant participants among the peasantry were cajoled in some areas, openly threatened in others, to get them to put their weight behind a collective demonstration. Numbers involved in such actions were usually over a hundred, reaching three or four hundred quite frequently, and reportedly climbing as high as six thousand for one assault on a château in the Franche-Comté.

These effectively paramilitary operations were largely the preserve of men – in the thinking of the time, the absence of women added legitimacy to the actors' self-proclaimed cause. In some areas, documents circulated purporting to give royal permission (or even orders) for the destruction of feudal obligations, and the rumoured existence of these outstripped any traceable real presence – one would be hard put to tell if any villages actually believed themselves thus commanded, or were merely willing to seize on this as a pretext. Certainly, when royal proclamations denounced such texts as forgeries, there was no sign of any peasants owning up to a mistake. The relative violence and vindictiveness of peasant expeditions depended very much on local conditions, and while some châteaux were ransacked and destroyed, in other cases peasants were punctilious in only rectifying their specific grievances. In the Dauphiné, where discontents expressed earlier in the year were reignited in July, the abbey of Sylve-Bénie was visited on three successive days by groups from different villages, each of whom stripped out from the abbey's registers only those pages that dealt with their dues – leaving behind, finally, only the binding.[3]

A counterpoint to the predominantly rural and peasant character of these actions was a series of machine-breaking episodes. The wrath of unemployed and marginalised workers, liberated from social constraint by political turmoil, turned on the most immediate material targets. Between late July and early September workers around Saint-Etienne, near Lyon, attacked everything from a steam-pumped coal mine to a mechanised tableware workshop. As early as 14 July itself, a crowd of textile workers in Rouen attacked and destroyed hundreds of spinning, carding and weaving machines in the industrial suburb of Saint-Sever. Such unrest flared repeatedly throughout the following month, spreading to neighbouring towns. It was also widespread in the woollen industries of Picardy, especially around Abbeville. This activity targeted structures and innovations that were thought to strip workers of employment, and would continue periodically in the following years.

In the atmosphere of the Great Fear, such proto-industrial unrest seemed a drop in the ocean of peasant anger. Just as news from Paris arrived in the provinces only fitfully and sometimes in distorted form, so news from the rest of France was frequently distorted in its travels to the capital. By the beginning of August, the deputies of the National Assembly were learning of a situation which appeared to be at once a general insurrection of the rural population and a general threat of aristocratic brigandage. Still fearful themselves of assault by the latter, the deputies came together for a session on 4 August, where some planned to denounce feudal privilege and call for the end of seigneurialism. In this way, they presumably hoped to both pacify the peasantry and cripple the powerbase of the aristocrats. As the session evolved, they achieved both more and less than this. By the morning of 5 August, the Assembly had committed itself to abolishing all privilege and distinction within public life – no more titles of nobility, no more municipal or provincial privileges, no more honorific distinctions of any kind, and no more feudal regime. For the country at large, this was a moment with as much revolutionary weight as 14 July, if not more.

News of this move flowed out across the country, helping to quell uprisings that were, in many cases, already dying down (they had achieved, after all, exactly what they had set out to do). From the peasantry's point of view, it seemed a massive victory, a new dawn of social esteem and financial liberty. As far as the legislators were concerned, however, the peasants' actions had been brigandage, notwithstanding their motives, and there was no question of allowing them to go unpunished. A National Assembly decree on 10 August 1789 reaffirmed this stance, and allowed for the immediate use of military force against disorder. Royal orders went out the next day confirming that insurgents could be tried under summary military justice, while the continued detention of numbers of individuals across France showed that there was no spirit of amnesty abroad.

On 11 August the Assembly codified what it had meant by its declarations of the 4th. The first article of the decree observed that 'the National Assembly abolishes the feudal system entirely'.[4] The following articles, however, made it clear that this meant two different things. The honorific rights of seigneurialism were destroyed, which included the exclusive keeping and hunting of game, with its attendant crop damage, and the feudal rights that bore directly on individuals, such as serfdom. Onerous and tiresome rights of toll collection and monopoly rights to mills, bread ovens and wine presses were also to be stripped away. Rights over justice were to be transferred in time to new local courts. In contrast, rights that were effectively an income on land, such as the main feudal dues, quit-rents and fees, were ruled to be a form of legitimate private property. To escape these, peasants would have to buy themselves out (at a rate not yet settled, but a figure of twenty or thirty times the annual payment had already appeared in some discussions).

This was still a victory for the peasant perspective – the ending of the special and oppressive status of the seigneur was the most that many villages had hoped for in their *cahiers*; total and immediate removal of the entire feudal burden seemed a pipedream. There had been a revolution in the meantime, however, and the insurrectionary activity, accompanied even in peaceful areas by refusal to pay demanded dues, demonstrated that peasants believed that they had removed the feudal burden from themselves. If village leaders knew in their hearts that the legal position was never going to be as simple as that, they would equally well have seen how much could be achieved by collective resistance and, like any good farmer, they planned for the future but lived for today. So long as continued resistance failed to bring the heavens down on their heads, in the form of massive armed repression, they would continue in their rejection of the increasingly in-dignant demands for payment of dues that began as the harvest of 1789 was gathered in.

If rural politics fell into a pattern of determined but quiet confrontation for much of the remainder of 1789, the urban population of Paris was set on a path of more overt collision with authority, one that launched the Revolution forward into further conflicts. Paris was governed after the fall of the Bastille by a new political establishment that while 'revolutionary' was also of the highest social calibre. At its head as mayor was Jean-Sylvain Bailly, one of the most eminent astronomers of the late eighteenth century and a leading figure in intellectual life before 1789. Alongside the civil administration, whose ranks were filled with men who had already held legal and administrative roles before July, was a military headquarters for the Parisian National Guard – the official name for the new citizens' militia. While the rank and file of this militia included many from the working classes, the headquarters had been placed under the charge of the marquis de Lafayette – a liberal political hero and officer of the American Revol-utionary War, but also a member of the high nobility. Lafayette turned his attentions to militarising the National Guard, creating a staff of militarily experienced, and hence largely noble, senior officers, and encouraging a movement to exclude less respectable individuals from the ranks.[5] This process took some months, and the National Guard would never be a simple passive military machine, but by the end of August radical satirists were already observing the difference between *patriotes* and *patrouillotes* (patrollists) in their relations with the people.[6]

Groups of working people taking direct and bloody political action had clashed with the authorities only a week after the fall of the Bastille, when a crowd hunted down and lynched Joseph Foulon and his son-in-law Louis Bertier de Sauvigny, accusing them of plotting to interfere with the harvest. Both had been Old Regime administrators – the latter intendant of Paris since 1776 – and were also implicated in the organisation of military oper-ations around the capital earlier in the month. Foulon was further reviled for having said, allegedly, that the hungry should eat straw. Taken from official custody, they were shot, stabbed and hanged before their heads were paraded in triumph – Foulon's with his mouth stuffed with grass. Bertier, who died second, had been taunted with this, to cries of 'Kiss Daddy!' Within the National Assembly Barnave, later to become a popularly reviled moderate, was caught up enough in the moment to query whether the blood spilt had been particularly pure, but the general mood was one of revulsion: one speaker called such episodes 'revolting scenes'; another noted that 'resistance to oppression is legitimate and honours a nation; licence debases it'.[7]

Such popular licence, however, continued to pursue its own aims, and in the first days of August further protests over food broke out – the deputy mayor of Saint-Denis, to the north of the city, was murdered and decapitated by a crowd on suspicion of promoting a grain-shortage. On 7 August any and all public gatherings except official district sessions were condemned as seditious by the municipal authorities, although only a day later they lowered bread prices by decree, giving in to the material pressure of popular hunger. Calm followed for a couple of weeks, but by the last week of August drought conditions were hindering the water-borne and water-powered delivery and milling of the new harvest, and both prices and tempers again rose. Despite this, controls on the grain trade were again withdrawn on 29 August. Around this time, the authorities took action against the unemployed who had gathered in Paris over the preceding months, and who had been kept occupied in charitable 'public workshops' (mostly ditch-digging and quarrying). There were some 22,000 of these men, and their concentration and rootlessness made them suspect as potential brigands. After a series of clashes over wages, and alarming rumours – that, for example, they were preparing artillery emplacements on Montmartre to bombard the city – military force was used to send most of these men on their way back to their native provinces, in the time-honoured fashion of dealing with the shiftless.

While most working people probably held the same fears about such characters as the authorities, further conflicts within the city's population reflected a clear official hostility to any lower-class self-organisation. A variety of working groups sought to use the new political situation of the summer to break out of their subordinate position and campaign for better pay and conditions. These included journeyman apothecaries, bakers, shoemakers, tailors and wigmakers (a large group, given the demands of eighteenth-century fashion for daily changing and resetting of hairpieces for both men and women). Not only were such demands for regulated change refused by the authorities, but public meetings of such groups were banned, even being broken up by force on occasion. Wigmakers, who were suffering economically as the aristocratic elite began to shun Paris, and indeed to emigrate entirely, eventually succeeded in getting municipal mediation for a new system of distributing work, but only after 4000 had met on the Champs-Elysées and threatened major disorder.[8]

Domestic servants were suffering a similar decline in their earnings, especially as Paris was the central labour exchange for this class, and as many depended on short-term and casual hirings that were in increasingly short supply. Servants' complaints ran more deeply than the merely economic – they continued to be branded by the new order as unfit to exercise political rights, due to their dependent status, and could neither vote in local assemblies nor enrol in the National Guard. Although a threat to hold a public demonstration 40,000 strong never came off, protests by both groups and individuals continued to trouble the public scene.

From the end of August, popular activity generated further alarm across a number of contrasting, but convergent, fronts. On one side, groups thousands strong, organised by district and trade, held a series of processions across the city to the Sainte-Geneviève church on the Left Bank, ostensibly to give thanks to the city's patron saint for their deliverance in July. An educated observer wrote that there was 'something horrifying in the arrangement, composition and immensity' of such marches – a telling adjective, given the supposedly celebratory nature of these rites.[9] Secondly, overt political agitation continued in the Parisian open spaces, and any worker who wished to attend could hear radicals denounce the king and the aristocratic party for delays in producing a new constitutional settlement – at least one march that set out from the Palais-Royal to make their feelings known at Versailles was broken up by the National Guard at the end of August. The city authorities denounced such gatherings as sites where 'the factious, through their half-knowledge and their criminal enthusiasms, might impose [their views] on the credulous and ill-informed class of the people'.[10]

The third dimension of concern was yet another worsening in the food supply, so that bakers' shops required military guards from early September. Fights began to break out in their queues, and voices were heard denouncing all this as another vile famine plot. There was little or no separation in popular minds between concern over bread and the wider political situation. The provision of bread to the capital had always been a matter of political responsibility, lauded by the state as part of the king's paternal concern for his subjects. The politics of famine plot, ingrained at every level of society, were the suspicious reverse of this deferential coin – if the provisioning function was no longer being fulfilled, there had to be a political reason. Earlier in 1789, opinion had focused on blaming nefarious but unidentified aristocrats for the shortages. Now the fault was placed right at the top.

By mid September, popular alarm had begun to provoke regular large demonstrations. In the space of three days, 16 to 18 September, grain deliveries were twice intercepted by crowds of women and brought to the doors of local authorities for distribution, and the Hôtel de Ville itself was twice besieged by angry women demanding firmer municipal action. This dimension of mass demonstration meshed with concerns over the continuing political stalemate at Versailles, and especially over a conservative attempt to give the king a veto on future legislation. Even as violent demonstrations against the city authorities continued, and as individuals were arrested throughout September for outbursts blaming Bailly or Lafayette for their troubles, an underlying sentiment was also spreading that bringing the king to Paris could solve both the economic and the political troubles at once.

The catalyst that brought these factors together in violent action was a banquet at Versailles on 2 October, where royal bodyguards and officers of the newly arrived Flanders Regiment made 'counter-revolutionary' pronouncements of loyalty to the royal family, particularly the queen, and allegedly trampled on the revolutionary tricolour cockade. The radical press carried outraged news of this the next day, and word spread through public meeting-places. On the morning of 5 October, crowds of women in the central markets and the Faubourg Saint-Antoine took the lead in a widespread agitation, including commandeering church bells to sound the alarm and summon the local National Guards to arms.[11] Growing crowds converged by mid morning on the Hôtel de Ville, which was invested by groups still mostly female, and searched – some cries were heard to find and punish the municipal leaders, but no actual violence was done, and others claimed to be seeking arms. Some 3,500,000 livres in cash was left untouched in the city treasurer's offices, and after sounding the alarm bell from the pinnacle of the hall, the crowds regrouped in the Place de Grève outside.

According to witnesses, the main demands expressed by the crowds were still for bread, and murderous threats were being made against the absent Lafayette and Bailly. At this point, Stanislas Maillard, a clerk who had made a name for himself at the taking of the Bastille, arrived at the head of a body of troops, and by his own account was persuaded by the women to lead them on a march to Versailles, there to petition the king for redress. In the early afternoon, this march set off, taking with it some cannon from the nearby Châtelet, and swelling to some six to seven thousand as bystanders were harangued into joining them *en route*. They arrived in the early evening, swarming into the meeting room of the National Assembly, daunting the more timid deputies with their begrimed appearance and selection of weapons, and securing reassuring replies from a number of speakers to the demands that Maillard put forward for bread, and the punishment of the

2 October 'traitors'. Six women were put forward as a deputation to meet the king (one memorably swooned in his presence), and the session was closed.

The women had left behind them in Paris a scene of confusion. Thousands of National Guards, summoned to arms by the various alarms, crowded the Place de Grève, and, as the afternoon wore on, began to call on Lafayette to lead them to Versailles. After much temporisation, he agreed to do so, and in the hours before midnight an armed force well in excess of twenty thousand reached Versailles. The night that passed was wet and miserable, and the crowds became increasingly angry at the lack of visible signs of progress. Some of them forced their way into part of the château close to the queen's apartments, and clashed with the royal bodyguard. A seventeen-year-old journeyman was shot dead from a window, and two bodyguards were killed and decapitated in the ensuing violence. Some accounts have the queen only one closed door away from the vengeful mob – though what would have happened if a crowd had been confronted with the legendary and reviled 'Austrian bitch' in person, clutching her nightclothes around her, is a moot point. The royal family were snatched away to safety in another part of the building as National Guard battalions which had retained discipline prevented a wholesale invasion of the château. A deal was hastily brokered between Lafayette and the king and queen – the latter would return to Paris with the crowds and take up residence in the Tuileries palace at the heart of the city.

This journey was accomplished on the same day, and took the form of a popular triumph: the Parisians lauded their own activity, and also the king, whose personal goodwill had not yet decisively been questioned, once removed from the corrupting surroundings of the court. Within days, the National Assembly voted to transfer to Paris, and took emergency measures to disburse funds to relieve the bread crisis. The Assembly also voted in a new martial law statute on 21 October, coincident with a fresh outbreak of bread-rioting in central Paris that saw a baker lynched on the Place de Grève. Within twenty-four hours, two men were executed for their role in the events of the day – one for complicity in the murder, the other for seditious agitation in the Faubourg Saint-Antoine. This swift punishment marked a new turn in the authorities' relationship with the Parisian people.

Political authority was now concentrated in Paris, and all but the most isolated radicals in national and municipal politics recognised that unconstrained popular involvement in political agitation was a threat not just to political stability but to their own lives. This perception was made more acute by the continuing underlying belief that anarchy was a weapon of the aristocratic counter-revolution, and that popular excess might, and might be designed to, lead to a massacre of patriots and a military and aristocratic take-over. An alternative, slightly less convoluted hypothesis had it that the duc d'Orléans was fomenting extreme opinions in order to make himself king over the rubble of a popular uprising. The solid cohort of respectable revolutionaries took stern measures against either eventuality, cracking down on seditious remarks in the radical press, bolstering the discipline of the National Guard with new, more socially exclusive, regulations, and giving a solid legal base to the power of the Paris central authorities, hitherto uncodified products of the July Revolution.

Continued provincial unrest provided more justification for such manoeuvres. To the east of Paris in the textile city of Troyes alarms about famine-plotting had merged with Luddite fears of machinery to cause major rioting in early September. As well as murdering the town's mayor, crowds torched the homes of local officials and destroyed several machines that had been brought in as prototypes for the modernisation of the local industry. In Rouen martial law had to be invoked at the end of October to control machine-breaking riots which put paid to some 700 spinning jennies, on top of those eliminated in the summer. A defiant opposition to the subordination and unemployment that machinery seemed to threaten ran through the whole revolutionary decade and successfully inhibited efforts to follow the 'English' model of industrialisation.[12]

Events such as these were the context in which the National Assembly worked through the remainder of 1789 to consolidate its new model of a propertied and individualistic national political order. Although there was a wave of strident and principled objection from some more democratically minded Assembly deputies and journalists, the measures concerning active citizenship and rights of election passed with remarkably little popular opposition or disquiet. Even the intellectual objectors were in a fairly small minority, as the necessary connection between a stake in society through property (and taxation, of course, fell largely on property) and a stake in politics through voting seemed self-evident to most. One factor which may have quelled incipient wider concern was the decision taken shortly afterwards to confirm each and every village, parish or community as a fully-fledged commune, or municipality, in the new order, with its own share of local autonomy and its own elected mayor. Since taxation was more widely distributed over the rural majority anyway, and with village relations so often based on the clientage of the poorer to the richer, the active citizen franchise was quite wide enough to keep the peasantry happy, embracing 90 per cent or more of householders in some areas. In the urban centres, most of the 30 to 50 per cent of men disenfranchised were more concerned with feeding themselves and their families through another winter than with finding themselves now 'passive', or sometimes more politely 'non-active', citizens.

None of this is to suggest that 'the poor' were beneath politics, but it beggars belief to think that millions of people, having lived through a revolutionary crisis that created great economic upheaval, and with the luxury trades that supported the workers of many towns in chronic decline, were foaming with anxiety to take their places in what seemed to be merely the administrative arrangements of the new order of the now-finished Revolution. In the one major urban centre where serious internal dispute remained there was an explosive response. The particularly severe economic condition of Lyon contributed significantly to its high level of popular turbulence. During 1790 the local philanthropic society, formed by wealthy patriots to supplant the failing resources of church charity, distributed aid to over a third of the population in many of the city's silk-weaving quarters. The fact that the rulers of the city came from a merchant oligarchy that had long been in overt conflict with the artisans here exacerbated tensions that elsewhere were more easily deflected onto patriotic celebration or anti-aristocratic action.

The Lyonnais elite that had founded its volunteer corps to protect property in 1789 kept this body in existence into 1790, only in January of that year allowing a National Guard establishment to be founded alongside it – well after such militias were firmly entrenched elsewhere. Tensions between the higher urban elite and the neighbourhood leaderships of the artisan classes erupted in February 1790. The spark was the garrisoning of the city's central fortified arsenal by the volunteers in strength, but one of the underlying issues was the manipulation of the active citizenship requirement in a blatant attempt to narrow the electorate to 'safe' proportions. Ensuing rioting saw the arsenal seized by crowds, and its weapons distributed in a general armament. Municipal leaders came under attack, and collectively caved in to the rioters' demands. The volunteers were disbanded, and the franchise lowered to admit some half of the adult male population – a high proportion for a city, probably higher than any other major urban centre. Ironically, in the subsequent elections, a relatively conservative council was returned, giving rise to dark rumours that popular disorder had yet again served the purposes of anti-revolutionary groups by frightening potential 'patriots' into voting for the forces of social order.[13]

Returning to the countryside, if there was initial satisfaction among the peasantry with the new order of things, the old order had by no means disappeared in late 1789 and early 1790. The decree abolishing the feudal regime, although receiving wide dissemination, remained unratified by the king until November, and until that point many seigneurs and their agents persisted with attempts to claim the full panoply of feudal rights.[14] Even after ratification, the decree was no real protection for peasants against such demands, as it expected them to go on paying until the formulae for redemption of dues were agreed. More oppressive still, the apparatus of seigneurial justice that ran so blatantly in the lords' favour was left to operate undisturbed until the summer of 1790. Existing cases were pursued, and even new ones begun, in defiance of the peasants' perception of what the summer's events had meant. Communal resistance was the inevitable result. Most dogged in those areas that had already risen up once in the previous year, but commonplace elsewhere, challenge and defiance of seigneurial demands remained mostly in the realm of words, but occasionally broke out into violence late in 1789. From the end of November, these troubles began to grow into a wave of new collective direct action.

The core zone of these new movements was the south west, which had remained relatively peaceful hitherto. They began in the Périgord, around the town of Sarlat. Several châteaux were raided in the course of December, with demands made by large groups of armed peasants for the repayment of collected dues – sometimes politely, with the offer of receipts, sometimes with noisy threats. As in earlier episodes, those reluctant to join in the collective resistance were also sometimes threatened – 'the first to pay his rent will be hanged', as was heard in one parish on 6 December.[15] Three alleged ringleaders from these incidents were later seized and detained in Sarlat, where they became the focus of further action. The alarm was sounded in a dozen neighbouring parishes on the night of 14 January 1790, and the next day four to five thousand peasants invaded the town, opened the prison, freed the three men, and locked up in their place a local noble they had captured. As this movement spread, it took on new symbolic forms. The church pews reserved for seigneurs and other members of the elite were made into bonfires, weathervanes (possession of which was a symbol of privilege) were torn down, and maypoles planted amongst general celebration. These would evolve over the following years into 'trees of liberty', spreading into a nationwide phenomenon with a lasting role in the symbolism of Revolution.

Movements of this kind spread across the countryside between Bordeaux and Montauban throughout the first three months of 1790, in some one hundred recorded incidents drawing personnel from over three hundred communes.[16] Armed groups of several hundred were commonly involved. While symbolic attacks and maypole plantings remained frequent, they were also accompanied by enforced repayments of dues and rents, and interdiction on further pursuits or payments on pain of death. Scarcely had this discontent died away, in the spring of 1790, when it was given new impetus by the National Assembly's first definitive rulings on the settlement of the feudal issue. Not only were these to be the cause of further unrest, they also coincided with the first large-scale manifestations of two interlinked phenomena that would wreak havoc in the years to come: active counter-revolutionary revolt and religiously inspired popular anti-revolutionary action.

Many Catholics, who had long viewed their religion as under attack by the general secularising influence of the Enlightenment, were already inclined to see the Revolution as another stage in this process. The sequestration of church assets proved decisive in provoking dissent over the longer term, but the initial flaring of alarm was linked more closely to sectarian prejudice. The key decision to grant full rights of political participation to Protestants in December 1789 was a marker here: it was in the south, where Protestant populations were most concentrated, that counter-revolution would first take on a religious tint. The spark appears to have been ignited by François Froment, a Catholic fanatic from Nîmes convinced that his father had been hounded from municipal office by Protestant business interests, and also convinced that 'religious zeal' was needed to 'stifle the revolutionary delirium'.[17]

Froment met the émigré comte d'Artois in Turin in January 1790, and came away with blithe, and unfounded, assurances of support for a plan to form Catholic companies across the south, ready to rise up and seize the cities in simultaneous insurrection. Some such bodies had already come into existence in a variety of locations, as the kind of conflicts played out in Lyon between volunteers and National Guards elsewhere took on a more sectarian tone. Through the spring of 1790 this movement spread, so that Toulouse, Nîmes, Uzès, Montauban and various smaller centres soon possessed either religiously divided National Guard establishments or parallel volunteer corps dedicated to Catholicism. Anti-Protestant propaganda saw the 'Catholic party' swept to power in municipal elections across the region, and in April an unsuccessful clerical bid within the National Assembly to have Catholicism declared the state religion was supported in the south by mass meetings and further anti-Protestant rhetoric.

Just as this movement appeared to be consolidating its success, it began to break down into uncontrolled violence. At Toulouse, rioting was sparked on 29 April by a pro-revolutionary crowd's attack on a group signing a Catholic petition, and the patriot municipality subsequently succeeded in arresting the leader of the Catholic companies, breaking the movement. On 10 May in Montauban a more dramatic clash began when some five thousand women, some of them armed, gathered to prevent the inventorying of religious property by revolutionary officials. This grew rapidly into wider threats to attack Protestant property, and what was ultimately a Catholic popular insurrection forced the Protestant National Guard to surrender after a siege of the town hall. Thousands of Protestants fled the city as a counter-revolutionary municipality detained and disarmed patriots. Attempts to rally both Catholic and Protestant support from surrounding communities met with little success, and there was little further violence. However, within days, the National Guard of Bordeaux, later joined by that of Toulouse, had begun to march on the town. The threat of siege caused the municipality to back down, reversing its detention policy as tempers cooled and sectarian relations normalised.

Such abortive and relatively bloodless episodes were thrown into sharp relief by events in June at Nîmes, home of the original conspirator Froment, who was head of his own Catholic force in the city. Here sectarian tension was extremely high, with generations of bitterness going back to the violent revolt and bloody suppression of the Protestant Camisards in the 1710s. Protestants held the commanding heights of the economy, forming a wealthy oligarchy managing the lucrative and vital silk trade. Local Catholics, who until 1789 had been able to monopolise political power, resented the perceived arrogance of this elite, and the Catholic peasants and workers who were still suffering from the collapse of the silk trade added this social grievance to their religious suspicions. Protestant peasant communities outside the city, however, looked on their co-religionists as potential protectors against Catholic bigotry, with which they were all too familiar.

Catholic voters succeeded in blocking Protestants from municipal office in Nîmes in February 1790, but in June the Protestants returned with a vigorous campaign in further elections for the new department administration. When a Protestant National Guard arrested a Catholic protestor outside an electoral meeting, rioting ensued which led to panicked firing into the crowd and a general sectarian call to arms in the town and surrounding countryside that, unlike at Montauban, was widely answered. On 14 June superior Protestant forces put the Catholics to rout, and over the next two days carried out a massacre of their leaders, other Catholics, and monks caught up in the violence. Some two hundred or more perished overall, many in the final siege of one of the city's fortified gates, but many more were massacred in flight or captivity. While this gruesome episode shattered the local counter-revolutionary movement, it also offered Catholic counter-revolutionaries across France a powerful symbol of their suffering and potential fate.

The electoral spark for the violence at Nîmes was part of the larger-scale restructuring of France that brought its own problems in its wake. A heavy burden of duties had been placed on the new departmental colleges of

electors. This is especially the case when one considers that the revolutionaries chose to make voting an arduous process of roll-calls and the individual
writing of names on ballots, and further complicated the process by forbidding individuals to announce their candidacy for office. This move was
intended to head off the formation of factions and to encourage the emergence of general merit from the private reflections of those voting. Not
only did each elector have to decide for himself who to nominate – potentially leaving the scrutineers with a vast list of names with only a few votes
each – but there was no guarantee, even when a majority could be found
for one name, that the individual would agree to serve in that post. Inevitably, attendance at assemblies tended to tail off over the several days
which they lasted, and informal deals and discussion tended to produce a
political class to fill the various posts that was very much drawn from the
ranks of the assembly itself. Those ranks, by design, were made up of the
propertied and educated, who could afford to give time to these unpaid
proceedings and to the burdens of office that followed.[18]

Only in 1790 did anything approaching half the electorate take the trouble
to vote for the membership of these assemblies, and in the following years
electoral participation tailed off to pitifully small proportions, as the rural voter
in particular came to be alienated from the whole process. While it is scarcely
surprising that the better off, and particularly the professional middle classes,
came to occupy almost all public positions, this created a social division
that was more than merely economic: a country numerically dominated by
the rural population that had already expressed its views dramatically and
directly came to be ruled, even at the local level, by townsmen.[19]

Although this was to prove an extremely problematic cultural divide, that
is not to say that there was not a will, amongst both local and national
political elites, to ameliorate the condition of the mass of the population.
As early as 3 August 1789 one moderate leader, Malouet, had spoken up in
the National Assembly for legislative action against rising unemployment
and beggary, in terms not of repression but of governmental social responsibility. In January 1790 the Assembly formed a 'Mendicity Committee' to
probe the statistical realities of poverty, and to lay down ground-rules for
tackling such problems throughout the 1790s. The scope of the problem was
immense: returns from individual towns spoke of one-ninth or one-sixth
of the population in permanent destitution, and when in the following
year the committee was able to report on a detailed survey from some
fifty-one of the new departments, over 1,900,000 indigents were counted in
a population of seventeen million: almost an eighth.[20]

The committee, and especially its guiding light, the philanthropic noble
La Rochefoucauld-Liancourt, took a highly principled stance on the nature

of poverty, its causes, effects and remedies. The committee rebelled against the old notion of the nature and purpose of charity, and spoke instead of *bienfaisance*, which can mean both 'doing good', beneficence, and 'welfare' – expressed, as early as January 1790, as a right to subsistence coming from membership in society, and which society at large had to guarantee for those unable to help themselves. This did not mean that they were soft on the stereotypical sturdy beggar, and the Old Regime system of *dépôts de mendicité* was retained with very little amendment in 1790, effectively sentencing such individuals to imprisonment – where they were joined by petty thieves and prostitutes, as overburdened local authorities frequently drew no distinction between all these forms of deviance. When in December of that year fifteen million livres were allocated for a nationwide programme of relief work for the unemployed, this was predicated on a rigid exclusion of known vagabonds and those without identifiable previous employment. Temporary relief workshops in existence, widely viewed as harbouring such creatures in droves, were to be shut down.

There were no unproblematic solutions. One scheme in Paris to give help directly to women and children, by employing them in spinning workshops, echoed some pre-revolutionary measures of relief and seemed very successful. It expanded into a system employing some 4800 at its peak in the following year, and although it shrank significantly thereafter it continued in existence until 1795. It was dogged, however, with claims that it soaked up public money while competing on subsidised terms with other less 'unfortunate' spinners, and that it was a haunt of lax discipline, and worse forms of debauchery, amongst those perceived as only one step removed from vagabondage or prostitution.[21]

Nevertheless, the new civic definition of the deserving poor was taken up spontaneously in many areas. *Comités de bienfaisance* were formed in countless centres, including the individual districts of Paris, after the fall of the Bastille. Many of these raised tens of thousands of livres in public donations and helped thousands of individuals. This took place alongside the continuing but faltering resources of church charity. The large parish of Saint-Eustache in the impoverished heart of Paris raised huge sums from the city's devout donors – 133,000 livres in 1789 alone – but continued uncertainty saw the parish accounts drained by the demands of the poor – they were 95,000 livres in deficit by 1791. Problems of overwhelming demand continually afflicted charitable and welfare structures in the years that followed. In the wider country, no clear structure of 'revolutionary' aid was developed until the last months of the Assembly's life, and the growing negative consequences of the clash between Revolution and church disrupted existing networks and compromised vital agencies of relief. Many of the charitable hospitals and *hôtels-dieu* which tended the old, sick and poor were themselves the corporate owners of considerable land and feudal rights, which entangled their affairs not only with the fate of the church but also with that of the wider seigneurial system.

The National Assembly's attitudes concerning the feudal regime worsened the entanglement, while also reinforcing the social and political plight of the rural population. In mid March 1790 the Assembly confirmed definitively many of the provisions of its decrees of August 1789, most notably that feudal dues on land would have to be redeemed and were not 'abolished'. The Assembly further sided with the seigneurs by ruling that possession of rights could be 'proved' by evidence of their prior enjoyment – rendering vain the effort of peasants to destroy titles and charters over the previous year. Peasants were also obliged to come to individual contractual settlements for the redemption of dues, rather than working, as they were so often accustomed to do, as communal units. They were further bound to redeem all relevant dues at once, rather than being able to dispose of only the most onerous ones (or exercise any other choice in the matter). On 3 May 1790 further regulations were published confirming these last points, and also specifying that the tariff for redemption was to be twenty times the annual payment for dues paid in cash, and twenty-five for those given in kind. A complex sliding scale was put forward for redeeming occasional dues (such as land transfer fees). Yet again the point was reiterated that peasants were obliged to continue to pay all unredeemed dues indefinitely, and that such debts remained enforceable at law. It was not even clear that seigneurs had to accept redemption if the peasants offered it – no overt mechanism was created to force the issue.

The clarification of these issues provoked a double wave of protest and contestation.[22] From across the country, seigneurs petitioned the Assembly for assistance in enforcing the law against recalcitrant, obdurate and at times openly hostile peasant communities and individuals. They were seconded on occasions by harassed municipal officers. The mayor of the small community of Bucy-le-Roi, in the region of Orléans, wrote in June 1790 that he was doing his best to maintain respect for the payment of harvest dues, but that much of the village, including his subordinate municipal officers, had been persuaded by a rumour that the dues had in fact been abolished and were using this as justification for failure to pay. The mayor could cite the relevant decrees which proved his point, and could even name the man he knew was responsible for starting the rumour – an illiterate ploughman and frequent rumour-monger who had become incorrigible since escaping punishment for his involvement in unrest the previous October. Nevertheless, the mayor was powerless to force his colleagues and neighbours to accept his official version of events when it was so clearly at odds with their interests.

If this mayor was a lone voice for obedience to authority, far more widespread were the communities where revolutionary authorities stood shoulder to shoulder with their constituents, and launched their own complaints about the continuation of feudal obligations. The rates cited assumed a return to the seigneurs of 4 to 5 per cent annually on their supposed 'investment' in dues. This was in itself disputable as a measure of their real worth relative to land values in different regions, but crucially it neglected the fact that peasant communities were still suffering the economic and social costs of a run of poor harvests. Petitions, sometimes plaintive, sometimes belligerent, observed that the offer of redemption on these terms was an empty gesture, since 'the poor are never in a position to accumulate a large sum of money', as a priest in the Ardèche phrased it as early as January 1790.[23] Communities in the Dauphiné made the same points with particular force, given their uprisings of the previous year, and the meeting of electors for the departmental administration of the Ardèche dispatched a formal collective protest on the issue in May, demonstrating that this was a grievance felt across the spectrum of rural inhabitants – indeed it should be remembered that feudal dues of this kind were paid largely by those who owned or rented enough land to gather their own harvests. This was not a matter of the rich versus a class of paupers but of privileged or absentee owners of feudal property versus the real backbone of the population.

The regions of the south west that were only just calming down after the wave of unrest through the winter now saw vehement denunciations of the redemption structure. Everywhere across France, whether communities protested furiously or settled into sullen silence, the mechanism of redemption was almost universally ignored in practice, just as dues themselves continued to go unpaid. Even in the remote southern region of the Corbières, which saw no major collective disturbances through the Revolution, the great majority of some 129 local communes contested their feudal dues, including sixty-nine which launched formal legal challenges to seigneurs' rights, and at least fifty-nine (overlapping with the previous group) that collectively refused to pay. In almost every commune there was some indication of individual or group resistance to payment. One village, Gardie, which had a very light seigneurial burden, managed to raise the sum necessary to buy this out – the total of 11,555 livres suggesting how impossible this task was for most more heavily burdened villages.[24]

By midsummer 1790 the countryside across France was once again simmering with discontent. Most towns, however, were in the midst of organising for a great revolutionary celebration. Ironically enough, the origins of what was named the 'Festival of Federation' lay in centralist fears about the purpose of regional federations, or meetings and pacts of loyalty and mutual assistance between neighbouring towns' National Guards. These had begun on a small scale as early as August 1789, and had spread in a random, bottom-up fashion through the succeeding winter, notably in the south east, where there was a relatively high density of medium-sized urban centres, and also where social and political tensions continued to run high. A variety of political agendas, not all entirely comforting to the National Assembly, had been voiced in such gatherings, along with an undercurrent of continuing divisive anti-rural fear and suspicion. A further irony is that, in many regions, National Guard organisations were still coming into being in the first half of 1790, and that, in the Limousin for example, this included the formation of units at the level of the individual village, frequently with nobles and ex-officers at their head. An inward-looking defensiveness, more reminiscent of the Great Fear than of the antiseigneurial agitations already under way elsewhere, seemed to characterise many such formations. Even these, however, could be found 'federating'.[25]

In March 1790 the Assembly took matters in hand and decreed that the federation movement should have an official goal, and that 14 July 1790 would be a national day of celebration of the achievements of the first year of Revolution, marked by simultaneous gatherings across the country and by a huge gathering in Paris attended by elected delegates of every community's National Guard. To make the message clear, the centrepiece of all of these ceremonies was to be the collective swearing of an oath of loyalty to the Nation and the Law – unity and order were the implicit watchwords.

One might have expected the Parisians to be suspicious of this agenda, but instead they seem to have taken the event to their hearts, and the carving out of a vast earthen amphitheatre from the military parade ground of the Champ de Mars was accomplished with the aid of tens of thousands of volunteer labourers. Prints and propaganda celebrated the participation of men and women of every class in this endeavour, although one suspects that patriotic middle-class gentlemen and ladies may have done little of the serious manual labour required. Popular enthusiasm may indeed have been consolidated by the wider programme of festivities that was planned and advertised for the days following the 14th – banquets, balls, revelry, punting jousts on the Seine, fireworks, and a vast expenditure on food and drink by the municipal authorities. Sixty thousand people are claimed to have enjoyed a ball at the central markets on 18 July, while the open spaces of the Champs-Elysées and the now-demolished Bastille were turned over to feasting and dancing.[26]

Nevertheless, even such saturnalian revelry was counterpointed by two facts. The first was that the politicians who organised the festivals persisted with their heavy-handed didactic message. Both the regional festivals in the main cities, and the Parisian gathering, centred on a spelling out of the value of the moderate revolutionary agenda, and on a reinforcement of a national unity which remained centred on the authority of Assembly and king. There were an estimated four hundred thousand people on the Champ de Mars, including tens of thousands of provincial delegates. The military formations paraded in disciplined ranks, while the crowds were packed in as passive spectators to a celebration that revolved around a Catholic mass, and the oath-taking of the political leadership and the king himself. Real popular participation would have to wait for the later revels. The second was that all was not sweetness and light even within the context of the festival. Smaller towns and rural communities that were all supposed to join in this simultaneous moment of unity often neglected it – in the Haute-Vienne department of central France, a fairly typical rural environment, half of all municipalities ignored the call to organise, and many of those that did merely held an oath-taking ceremony without additional fanfare. Partly this may have been due to lack of funds and preoccupation with more practical local issues, but partly also it reflects a widespread rural unwillingness to engage with the revolutionary townsmen's agenda. Even in Paris itself the form of the ceremony excited mutterings. The open space of the Palais-Royal was stirred by speakers reporting that the king had not played an active enough role in the festival, and that his enthusiasm for it had seemed inadequate. One rumour even ran that the king's oath had not been taken properly, and that the National Assembly had decided in emergency session to compel him to take it again.[27] Such alarms, and the underlying suspicion that they reveal, tarnished what was supposed to be the Revolution's climactic act of unity. Before another month was out, further seeds of what was to become a long drawn out agony of national dissolution and division had been sown, not least by the common people's persistent refusal to be the passive citizen-subjects that the political class wished them to be.

7

The Widening Gulf

The Festival of Federation marked the approximate mid-point in the labours of the National Assembly, as it ploughed on with its work of giving France a constitution. By June 1791, the finishing touches would be being put to this constitution, and the initial stages of elections to a new Legislative Assembly had begun. At that point, however, a crisis erupted, fuelled by the tensions that had already accumulated in the Revolution's first year, and a multitude of new ones added over the following months. This meant that the new Assembly finally met only in October 1791, after a summer in which the whole revolutionary project had teetered on the point of collapse, and in which bitter social and political division had been further entrenched.

The urban population had not faced the same major structural upheavals as the peasantry, and one might have expected their relations with authority to have run a little more smoothly. What in fact emerged by mid 1790, and developed swiftly in the year thereafter, was a complex and troubled relationship in which ordinary working people persistently sought a political role in the face of increasingly violent rejection from the holders of power. Lyon was a site of particular hostility, and in June and July 1790 violence again erupted there. The hated municipal tolls were the pretext for direct action by the population, raiding shops and stores in a classic *taxation populaire*. The National Guard forces that had seemed radical when confronting the volunteer corps earlier in the year now showed a more conservative face in defence of property: although the authorities had to back down in the face of crowd protests and suspended the tolls, the National Guard took revenge on popular districts with brutal policing. Shots fired from one such neighbourhood on 26 July provoked an invasion by 1800 troops two days later. Their mission to 'disarm' the area led to the smashing of furniture and shredding of mattresses, and even the destruction of weaving on the loom – striking directly at workers' livelihoods.[1]

After such an episode, the 'patriotic' spokesmen and pamphleteers who had done much to stoke up anger against the authorities deserted the people – proclaiming, in a now familiar pattern, that violence which threatened the social order had to be the product of counter-revolutionary agitators, brigands and foreign infiltrators. The second half of 1790 indeed saw counter-revolution begin to gather strength as more than just a fear in the minds of revolutionary patriots. The violent events of the spring and early summer in Nîmes and elsewhere had already shown that religion was a crucial factor in rallying opposition, and the first major gathering of counter-revolutionaries now amplified that significance.

The event took place at the château of Jalès, in the rural area known as the Vivarais, in the south of the new department of the Ardèche – a region of small and isolated communities on the rising land north of the towns of Provence. Here, arranged by local nobles and clerics, and with a nod of approval from the Turin counter-revolutionaries, some twenty-five thousand Catholic National Guardsmen from the surrounding areas – the rank and file being ordinary peasants and townsmen – were brought together on 18 August 1790 in an event inspired by the Federations of July. The meeting was held with proper authorisation from the local district and department, but it proceeded to demand the release of Catholics held after the events at Nîmes, and the expulsion of Protestants from the administration of the Ardèche and neighbouring Gard departments. The tone of the whole gathering was violently Catholic and royalist – calls for immediate action against supposedly 'Protestant' revolutionary authorities had to be held in check by the leadership. As the meeting broke up, a permanent committee was formed to further its members' interests, comprised of men with a clear royalist agenda.

If the actual outcome of the Jalès meeting was relatively insignificant, it was enough for the National Assembly to order prosecutions of the authors of the counter-revolutionary motions put forward. Local courts dragged their feet over this, but the issue was revived in October by the clandestine publication of a 'manifesto' alleged to come from the 'faithful Frenchmen, armed in the Vivarais for the cause of their religion and of monarchy against the usurpers of the so-called National Assembly'.[2] This document declared the Assembly to be made up of criminal traitors whom good Frenchmen would bring to justice, along with the instigators of the October Days who had imprisoned the royal family in Paris. Over the course of the next year, exhortations of this kind would become commonplace, and violent sentiments would simmer in the Vivarais before breaking out there as in many other areas, spurred on by an ever-worsening religious conflict.

As the new year of 1791 opened, the National Assembly found itself locked in conflict with the Catholic church over its Civil Constitution, and pursuing a confrontational route in this matter through the imposition of an oath of loyalty on the clergy. In this way, the national political dilemma over the church was about to be projected down to every local parish. The beginning of 1791 was an inauspicious moment to ask the rural population, in particular, to accept major changes to the role of the church in their lives. If the conflicts over the feudal regime had already shown how much at odds the National Assembly was with its rural citizens, decisions taken over taxes and tithes at precisely this point reinforced that divide. The much-sought end of fiscal privilege for the rich was accompanied by the equally desired abolition of many indirect taxes on the purchase and movement of goods, as the framework of the new structure of taxation was confirmed at the start of 1791. When all this was demanded in the *cahiers*, the population of France may have been assuming that the two things would balance out, and that the remaining burden of taxation would be lightened. Doubtless, whether through naivety or a sense of grievance with the extravagances of royal expenditure, most would have assumed that the overall tax burden would fall. It did not, however. The urban classes, who saw tolls on their consumer goods abolished later in 1791 (they had been preserved until then as an emergency source of municipal finance), did fairly well. They did even better because the bureaucracy of the state was in no position to contemplate the mammoth task of inventorying and taxing all the various forms of movable and invested wealth. The one great source of wealth that could not be hidden, and which had already been inventoried under the Old Regime, was of course land.[3]

Taxes on the majority of householders who owned or worked land actually rose after the abolition of Old Regime systems. In the Nord, around Lille, per capita taxation rose by over 12 per cent at once, and shot up by half after 1792 when wartime demands were made on the system. In the Puy-de-Dôme, the region of Clermont-Ferrand, on the other hand, little changed, and in Upper Brittany per capita taxes doubled while remaining below the levels paid in the Nord. Such doubling of official assessments was commonplace, but also almost randomly distributed across the country, thanks to the inequities of Old Regime documentation.[4] It would take until the 1830s to complete a new national land survey, and this left, for example, the peasants of the Ariège, high in the Pyrenees, paying barely a fifth of the sums demanded from those of the same wealth in the Seine-et-Marne on the doorstep of Paris.

The irony is that, even with these increases, taxes never brought in enough income to the state. Refusal to pay remained as epidemic as it had been in 1789, especially in the more isolated areas. Elected local administrators lacked any professional expertise or long-term interest in fiscal efficiency, and it became general policy to avoid coercive methods after early attempts to be more aggressive met with outrage. National Guards from Carcassonne raided neighbouring villages in the Val-de-Dagne to collect unpaid taxes several

times in 1790, and again in May 1791, provoking the village priest of Villar
to protest to the authorities that troops behaved 'as if on enemy soil' in
communities composed of 'the most sincere friends of the constitution'.[5]
He had been obliged to write himself, since the village's mayor was in
custody. More routine tax-collection continued to be auctioned off as a
profit-making enterprise to private individuals and companies, introducing
another layer of potential dishonesty, ineptness and resistance. Estimates
suggest that some 45 per cent of projected revenue may have been collected,
by various methods, in the first year of the new system; this rapidly fell to
27 per cent in 1792, and collapsed to 9 per cent in 1794. Without a doubt,
the systems of state finance devised by the National Assembly and perpe-
tuated by its successors produced the worst of all possible fiscal worlds. It
proved much easier, and fatally tempting, for the state to fund its needs
and initiatives by printing more of the assignat paper currency.

Late 1790 had also marked the beginning of the sale of church lands,
nationalised a year earlier. By fortunate coincidence for those concerned,
this took place just as the many thousands of privileged judges, provincial
officials and other office-holders of the Old Regime were receiving large
payouts in assignats as compensation for their abolished posts. Although
some disgruntlement was caused by these sums being paid out at the
tax-assessed values of the offices, unchanged for twenty years, rather than
their inflated pre-revolutionary market prices, some 800 million livres were
issued in this way – itself an inflationary measure against the paper currency.[6]
Unsurprisingly, since it was one of the explicit aims of the system, many
of the recipients immediately poured these funds into land, and often very
good land, as the church had had centuries to refine its holdings. The hold
of the middle classes (and some of the former aspiring nobility) on the
countryside was thus considerably extended, while the peasantry frequently
had to stand by and watch the best plots in their communities go to outside
landlords. Rural inhabitants who were too poor to contemplate redeeming
their feudal dues were certainly also too poor to consider bidding for the
substantial plots in which lands were sold at this point – another grievance
amongst many.[7]

At the end of 1790, to add insult to injury, the National Assembly also
voted through a measure of blinkered social prejudice. In early December,
it decreed that landowners with pre-existing contracts would receive, from
their tenants' harvests, the value of the abolished tithe on top of the rents
they charged.[8] The value of the old direct tax, the *taille*, was to be treated
in the same way in those southern regions where it had been levied on the
land. The underlying logic was the claim that the new land tax was paid
by the owners of property, whereas earlier arrangements often placed the

burden on the leaseholder; the state was now accessing the same resources, merely in a different fashion. This was not seen in this light by tenants, however, and it added more fuel to existing social and political antagonisms. Although the measure noted that new tenancy agreements need not include this surcharge, it gave official sanction to a process of cranking up rents which some landlords had already begun, claiming that tenants were now able to pay more, thanks to the abolition of indirect taxes. In some regions, where the abolished feudal dues had been particularly high, peasant tenants and sharecroppers might still come out a little ahead, but elsewhere there is no doubt that they were being battened on in a way that would have seemed entirely familiar – the abuses of the feudal regime replaced (or, worse, added to) by the same masters, and the same sums (if not more) merely paid under new headings. Both small landholders oppressed by tax demands, and tenants and sharecroppers harassed by rising rents, could now claim solid economic grounds for grievance against the new order. This may have lurked in many minds as they confronted the changes imposed on the church.

In early January 1791, after the usual Sunday mass, in church and before their congregations, tens of thousands of priests had to make up their minds about the drastic changes being imposed on the church and on their lives.[9] The result was a huge rift, a chasm of dissent that slashed across the revolutionary landscape. Overall, around half of all priests refused the oath. Provinces where the number taking it was above half covered two large contiguous areas: the far south east, from Lyon down the eastern side of the Rhône valley to the coast, including areas such as the mountainous Dauphiné, where oath-taking was near unanimous in many districts; and a larger north-central zone, a rough wedge starting at Bordeaux and expanding north eastwards, reaching the coast near Dieppe, the northern border in the Ardennes, and as far east as Dijon. Smaller patches dotted the south west. Zones of below-average acceptance were principally the north-eastern zone of the old provinces of Alsace, Lorraine and the Franche-Comté, the far west, including western Normandy, Brittany and adjacent departments, and the south-central region roughly bounded by Toulouse, Marseille, Clermont-Ferrand and Limoges. The far south-west coastal zone and the far north, around Lille, added two other substantial, if smaller, regions of majority refusal. In the most resistant areas, such as the Moselle in the east and the Vendée in the west, as few as a quarter of all priests took the oath in some districts.

The social, political and ideological stakes of this moment were huge – far greater, indeed, than the revolutionary authorities understood at this point. The vast bulk of the upper church hierarchy refused the oath – only eight bishops took it, and there was little doubt at this point that the papacy would not accept the new situation (as indeed time proved, with explicit papal condemnation coming in the spring). For many priests, the roots of their faith lay as much in the notion of obedience to proper ecclesiastical authority and acknowledgement of hierarchy as in any other theological issue; every oath-taker was turning away from this. The objections of some went further: for them what the oath required was little less than a deal with the devil. On the fringes of the oath-refusing or 'non-juror' cohort, some priests and bishops argued that the Revolution was the fruit of the Enlightenment, which was a plot by Jews, Protestants and freemasons to destroy the true religion and to damn the souls of their innocent flocks. It is notable, however, that many more priests found the demands of the Revolution to be entirely compatible with their clerical duties. Passive obedience to the ecclesiastical hierarchy was not the only model of the priestly role in circulation within the church. Many felt that their role as pastors to their flocks required them to be attentive to the wishes of the community, and many others felt that the Revolution's proposals were a welcome reform of a church that was bloated with wealth and privilege, and that had grown too far apart from its primary mission of salvation. Some priests took the oath proudly, and indeed many communities made a show of the ceremony, with municipal officers and National Guard in full regalia in attendance, and feasting and music on offer.

Other communities experienced the oath-taking episode in ways which reveal a little more about how rural society, in particular, was responding to the wider revolutionary agenda. In a number of places there were riots and risings when the first news arrived at the end of November about the oath requirement: isolated outbreaks from the Pas-de-Calais to the region of Nîmes, a wider brief flare-up in the Vendée, and significant disturbances in southern Brittany. Here municipal authorities in some cases returned the text of the decree to their local districts, refusing to accept it. The local capital, Vannes, was the target of protest marches, and there was a veritable rural mobilisation after a rumoured assassination attempt on the local non-juring bishop in early February. This region was particularly inflamed over the effects of the new tax regime, which overturned ancient Breton privileges. Meetings to protest this issue had already been taking place when the oath added to the locals' grievances.[10]

Across large parts of the western zone of refusal, rural communities actively endorsed their priests' rejection of the oath – an activity that went as far as intimidating some priests into refusal, and abusing and victimising some who went ahead with it. One Breton cleric, who had served his parish for forty years, complained that he had been pelted with stones as he tried to swear, and one priest in the Vendée was actually shot for taking the oath. The vision of the relationship between church and community that was deeply rooted into the regional culture could not tolerate the proposed changes. They threatened the traditional role of the church as the central organising feature of moral and social life for what were often scattered hamlets and farmhouses, in what seemed to be the alien product of illegitimate urban intruders. Many parts of this region, especially in its southern reaches, bordering onto the Loire valley, already suffered from considerable structural tensions between urban and rural populations. This attitude was immediately reinforced in the context of the oath by the response of some local, town-dominated, authorities, who labelled the non-jurors as counter-revolutionary fanatics from the outset, and who persecuted them and their followers over the coming months and years in ways which exceeded, or at least ran well ahead of, official anticlerical policies.

Vicious conflict was not confined to the west. Alsace saw scenes of abuse and humiliation of newly 'constitutional' clergy, and in the Lozère, just north of the sectarian hotbed of the Gard, knife-wielding female gangs were reported to be hounding constitutionals from their parishes. Around the country, some priests tried to justify their refusal of the oath in terms of just such sentiments – it was simply impossible to live as a constitutional priest in a community that saw the new arrangements as a plot to change their religion, and where oath-takers were condemned as 'Judases, traitors and tyrants', as one priest complained from the Haute-Loire.[11] What would make the fault-lines created by the oath so permanent and dangerous for France as a whole was that such anti-oath sentiments and violence in some areas were mirrored in other regions by an almost equal intensity of rage against non-jurors.

In Paris itself, the church of Saint-Sulpice, a suspected hotbed of counter-revolutionary clergy, was overwhelmed by a huge crowd on the occasion of its priest's oath-taking choice. He defied them, and publicly refused to swear, after which only rapid intervention by the National Guard prevented him from being carried away by the stampede that swamped the altar, yelling threats to hang him. Other Parisian parishes saw confrontations that were similarly stark, if less immediately violent. Around half the Parisian clergy refused the oath, and through the following months crowds pursued non-jurors and their supporters, as they attempted to hold legally sanctioned alternative services. In April, men vented their fury on groups of nuns with public floggings, and in June men and women stormed a church to prevent its use for 'refractory' services.[12] The city of Lyon saw a similar pattern of violence and intimidation to Paris, and there, as in the capital, the authorities trod a delicate path between closing down religious buildings that were thought to shelter illegal gatherings, and allowing the freedom of worship that the law provided for. Much of the Paris Basin also shared the capital's popular scorn for non-jurors, and priests further north and east in the Aisne and the Moselle reported violence, intimidation and mockery. Near Laon, three non-jurors suffered a beating, and one a bullet in the arm, from a crowd of over two hundred men and women who tried to make them swear. Although the non-jurors were legally supposed to continue in their duties until the could be replaced, some communities in the Parisian region barred them from the church, and many wrote to higher authorities demanding immediate replacements.

In some cases purely local grievances can be detected in the antagonisms over this issue. Many newly elected village municipalities were now run by men who might have been at odds with their priests for years, or even decades, but had previously been powerless to act. All manner of personal and professional hostilities might be at work – priests accused the new authorities of 'despotism' in some parishes, a charge levelled by other municipalities against their priests. In the village of Bléville in Calvados, the priest was locked in conflict with the municipality over the latter's desire to install a special pew for itself before the altar – symbolically seizing the place of the seigneur. In one village in the Sarthe the priest complained that the new mayor had tried to enforce his right to precedence in seating with National Guard troops, and demanded that the priest burn incense for him as he had done for the seigneur. A petition for the removal of a priest might list any number of a series of failings: immoral lifestyle, vex-atious litigation against parishioners, politically suspect remarks, abuse of the confessional relationship, excessive charges for services. In one region, such as the Aisne or Seine-et-Marne, this might lead up to the demand for the removal of a non-juror. In another, such as the Haute-Loire, it might be the precursor to the rejection of a constitutional priest. Villages in at least three departments attempted either to prevent their priest taking the oath, or to deny that he had taken it properly, specifically to get rid of him.

While it is possible to paint some of the fine detail of this episode as coming down to personalities, clearly there were much larger issues at stake. The oath created several tens of thousands of priests who had publicly declared themselves unable to accept state policy, and a substantial minority of these viewed that policy as heretical, if not satanically inspired. A sizeable proportion of the French population shared those views at least to a degree. Educated patriot commentators reached immediately for simplistic answers: the fanaticism of ignorant peasants was being manipulated by unscrupulous priests in the service of organised counter-revolution. The future would show how easy it was to turn that assumption into a self-fulfilling prophecy, as communal resistance to religious change dug itself in as the bedrock for more generalised opposition. A foretaste of this could be found in the south east throughout the rest of 1791, around the enclave of papal territory known as the Comtat Venaissin. Here, agitation led by the city of Avignon for incorporation into France set into effective localised civil war with pro-papal communities led by Carpentras. Skirmishing and the occasional massacre continued up to, and beyond, the area's annexation in September, with members of every urban class to be found on both sides. Political tensions between Catholics added to the south east's existing sectarian divide over revolutionary allegiances.

The increasingly tense national (and frequently local) context was one reason for the accelerating tendency of the 'political class' to group itself into clubs and societies, of which the Parisian Jacobins and their many regional affiliates were the clearest manifestation. Jacobinism, however, was not the furthest extent of radical politics, especially in Paris. Groups with even more forthright demands for popular and direct democracy had agitated a number of the Parisian electoral districts in 1789–90. When these were amalgamated into new 'sections' in May 1790, a group centred on the Cordeliers district on the Left Bank decided to keep the ultra-radical banner alive by forming their own club. They too used rooms in a monastery, the one that the old district had been named after, and soon became known as the Cordeliers Club. Their official title was the Society of Friends of the Rights of Man, which marked out an allegiance to principles of social equality that they felt had already been undermined by the planned new constitution.[13]

There was not much to distinguish the leadership of the Cordeliers from many Jacobins – indeed, a number of individuals were members of both groups. Lawyers, other professionals, the occasional clergyman, and the new breed of political journalists and activists were a mixed bag, but were still from the 'educated' classes. The movement they founded, however, sought, and rapidly found, a rank and file of more plebeian origin. Moreover, the all-male membership of the clubs was soon joined by an audience that included women, who, at the Cordeliers at least, might contribute to debate. At the end of 1790, a cadre from this movement went a stage further and began forming genuinely 'popular' societies. The first of these was the 'Fraternal Society of Both Sexes, meeting at the Jacobins', which took a room on the floor below the 'great' club. Initially led by an ex-schoolmaster, Claude Dansard, with a didactic approach to enlightening the population about political affairs, this society moved in the early months of 1791 towards adopting a vociferously radical stance. As it did so, it was joined by other societies, often founded by Cordeliers members, who adopted the principle of dual-sex and relatively unrestricted membership – among the most notable were the Carmes and Minimes, which both met in convents, the Société des Halles, which met in the market district, and that of the Indigents, which paraded its collective poverty as a political virtue.[14]

In one sense, the Parisians were latecomers to the club movement. Alone amongst the great cities of France, Lyon had produced a movement of neighbourhood-based popular societies from late 1790, that claimed some four to five thousand members by the spring of 1791. This was far more of a formal federation than the Parisian movement, with a central club staffed by regularly rotated delegates, and had a tight linkage to the administrative geography of the city. It also echoed this by being a male-only network, and was in some senses a voice for neighbourhood leaders, not necessarily the most radical in the population. From the end of 1790, however, the clubs had succeeded in rallying electoral opinion behind a group of 'patriot' notables, who had thereby taken charge of the municipality from the old oligarchs by early 1791. The links between the artisanal rank and file of the clubs and the municipality were reinforced when silk workers, who had been approached to join a counter-revolutionary insurrection in December 1790, denounced the plotters to the authorities. The breaking of this 'Lyon Plot' was a brief national *cause célèbre*, though in the longer run it proved counter-productive for the Lyon patriots, helping to associate their city, especially in Parisian minds, with aristocratic conspirators.[15]

News such as this, and the agitation of popular societies generally, reinforced an anxious groundswell of opinion that saw the Revolution in danger of drifting into the hands of its enemies. In Paris the elite municipal leadership of Bailly and Lafayette had never been popular on the streets, and Lafayette had besmirched his revolutionary credentials further in August 1790 by supporting the suppression of a military mutiny at Nancy against 'counter-revolutionary' officers. Official support for the continued toleration of non-juror priests after January 1791 added to the radicals' list of grievances. So too did their suspicion that the authorities were too close to the royalist response to the Jacobins, the Society of Friends of the Monarchical Constitution, that had come into existence – or emerged from underground, in some eyes – in recent months. The population was fed a continual diet of alarm on these fronts, and others, by the burgeoning press. In the form both of regular journals and occasional pamphlets, the publishing industry had boomed since 1789, and although the production of new titles slackened in 1790, early 1791 saw a new rise, as ever-more divergent political opinions spilled out into print.

Such productions, especially the more ephemeral pamphlets, were well

within the budgets of the artisan classes. Even those who could not or
would not afford them could often hear them read out in the squares and
gardens of the city, where crowds continued to congregate, as they had in
1789, for the latest political news. In 1790 a trend had begun amongst writers
and publishers, initially of right-wing pamphlets but joined by their com-
petitors to the left, to produce material aimed at a plebeian audience. The
device they chose was that of the burlesque dialogue or monologue – words
put into the mouths of stock characters from the pre-revolutionary popular
stage, sprinkled with oaths, innuendo and the occasional slang phrase.
Characters like the Père Duchesne, a sturdy furnace-maker, or his wife,
the shrewd Mère Duchesne, turned their hands to homespun advice for the
supposedly bewildered populace, or even got into extended dialogue with
different series of pamphlets with divergent opinions. There is no doubt
that this material sold, with the number of individual authors resorting to
such mouthpieces reaching a peak of over a dozen in 1791, but it sold
alongside a great deal more material that did not have to resort to patronising
parodies of popular speech to get its message across.[16]

One of the greatest popular journalists of the age was Jean-Paul Marat.
A largely self-taught doctor and aspiring scientist, Marat had long nurtured
a hatred of oppression, aggravated by his failure to enter the closed circles
of the scientific elite in the 1780s. The Revolution provided him with the
opportunity and audience for a four-year career of relentless and dedicated
harrying of the people's enemies – in the course of which he had to flee
arrest more than once at the hands of the authorities. In his longest-lived
journalistic incarnation, he was L'Ami du Peuple, 'The People's Friend', and
he espoused their cause by returning time and again to the theme of
counter-revolutionary conspiracy – its pervasive presence, and nefarious
effects, and the urgent need to extirpate it with blood. His language made
no concession to alleged popular semi-literacy, and he put on no pantomime
mask, but it was Marat more often than anyone else that the most radical
groups wanted to hear read out in the Palais-Royal or the Tuileries gardens,
and it was he with whom many corresponded – he was one of the first
political journalists to make effective use of readers' letters to create a sense
of community between himself and his audience.[17]

Marat's paper had its own imitators – amongst them the L'Orateur du
Peuple, 'The People's Orator', which spent far less time developing a view
of the political situation and far more simply regurgitating appalling
prophecies of counter-revolutionary slaughter – but even the least of these
papers was able to attract popular readers. Moreover, a whole swathe of
more sober, but little less anti-aristocratic, journals also had a popular and
public readership, and the ephemeral pamphlets that claimed to offer all

the 'Great Details' of a new political shock every few weeks had an equally discerning approach to their vocabulary. The mock-comic oaths and simplified language of the *Père Duchesne* titles went down well enough, if the particular version in question suited its readers' views, but the popular classes of the capital were not dependent on such fabrications for their political information.

By the spring of 1791, the flood of political information that was reaching the Parisian (and other) streets continued to be highly alarmist. Rumours of menacing foreign troop movements on the borders were reported as fact, as was every last fragment of anticlerical and anti-aristocratic scaremongering about plots and rebellion. Readers of the press in early 1791 had every right to believe themselves to be facing imminent invasion and uprising, and the overthrow of all the Revolution's gains. As this kind of news provided the background of life, so the everyday activities of the general population provided cause for further concern.

The assignats that the state had begun to issue over a year earlier, attempting to regulate its debts through the credit of the church's lands, were becoming a monetary disaster. Within months of their origin, they had slipped from being government bonds to become paper money, first by general practice and later by official decree. By late 1790 two parallel monetary systems were developing, in which good old-fashioned coins circulated at a premium against an increasing weight of paper, and in which a spreading group of *marchands d'argent*, 'money merchants', controlled the interchange between the two. Money became a commodity, and paper money began a devaluation slide – merchants were charging a 5 per cent premium for coin in January 1791 but approaching 15 per cent by May. Workers paid in assignats could not always get change for them – inns and shops refused transactions, and were unwilling to yield up their own coins. The press and popular opinion turned on anyone seeking to change paper for coins in large quantities – they were, at best, financial speculators, if not counter-revolutionaries bent on destabilisation.[18]

The National Assembly ordered the printing of more assignats in smaller denominations, and even created a shortage of copper by attempting to mint a new issue of small change – the raw material became so valuable in the short term that it was profitable for some to hoard the coins, melt them down and sell the scrap to the mint. Local authorities and even some popular societies attempted to ease the situation by producing *billets de confiance* – 'notes of trust' – that could circulate as small-denomination currency. Trust, however, was in short supply. Printing techniques even for the official assignats were primitive, and even more so for the *billets*, which meant that forgery was rife and the fear of it especially so. The demand for coins encouraged forgers, and some minting took place even within the prisons themselves, as a series of police raids in the summer proved. Aristocratic plotting was continually raised as a cause of the money shortage and of the circulation of forgeries, and scarcely a week went by when the press did not retail some new alleged conspiracy or suspect activity.

A further crisis at the centre burst out on Palm Sunday, 17 April 1791, when a patriotic witness reported that the king had taken communion from a non-juror priest inside the Tuileries. This shocking act came the day before the royal family were due to leave for the château of Saint-Cloud, outside the city. This visit, although a regular feature of the royal summer itinerary, was suspiciously early this year, and allowed the king to evade the public performance of his usual Easter communion in the church of Saint-Germain-l'Auxerrois. Public concern at this evasion mushroomed once news of the non-juror's role got out, and on the morning of the 18th, the royal family found themselves blockaded inside the Tuileries by a crowd of thousands. Even relatively hostile accounts agree that there was no violence directed towards the king and his family, but there was a stubborn refusal to yield a path for their coaches. The Paris municipality and the commanders of the National Guard tried in vain to exercise their authority over the citizens – reinforcing, in radical eyes, their dubious association with the forces of the right – but in the end the king yielded and agreed to stay. The radical press, convinced that the royal family would only have paused at Saint-Cloud before fleeing towards one or other of the frontiers, hailed the popular victory, but it sowed the seeds of a far greater crisis a mere two months later.

As the king and queen, and their supporters, brooded on what looked increasingly like their imprisonment at the hands of the mob, the working population was being convulsed by new disputes with authority. The National Assembly had initially excluded the trade guilds from the abolition of privilege in 1789, seeing their economic policing role as important. By the second half of 1790 this role was being openly disputed across the country. A Dieppe candlemaker proclaimed in September that he could work without a mastership 'by virtue of the liberty of men decreed by the National Assembly', and a month later a group of several traders in the same town observed that, in the context of the Rights of Man, 'there must not exist an enormous abuse like that of masterships'. Journeymen tailors from Rennes made a detailed case in December 1790 that a 'criminal resistance' was being waged by the privileged masters against all those who wished to set up for themselves, or just to work as free individuals without vexatious regulations. In January 1791 no fewer than 2316 Lyonnais craftsmen demanded the abolition of such 'gothic and ruinous institutions'.[19]

Throughout this period, guild patrols continued to exercise their own policing, seizing tools and goods from 'illicit' workers and inhibiting free trade from Paris to Rouen, Grenoble to Nantes, Lyon to Limoges. By the end of 1790 workers' groups in Paris had begun to organise resistance to this continued oppression. Journeymen stonemasons, carpenters, locksmiths and print workers followed the lead of the more overtly political popular groups and formed 'fraternal societies'. These echoed all the political language of the Revolution, while offering much the same services to members as the old compagnonnage. The print-workers' group, for example, published its rules under the heading 'general regulations for the typographical *corps*, composed by the committee of the general assembly of representatives of the print-workers of Paris'.[20]

Such activity was looked on fearfully by the authorities as just another pretext for popular disorder, and those fears were stoked ably by the existing guild masters, who revived memories of the 'insubordination' of the Turgot experiment of 1774–75. Economic individualism won, however, and the guilds were officially abolished by the D'Allarde Law of 2 March 1791. In the aftermath of this, Paris in particular was struck by a further wave of conflict, as both employers and workers began to test their strength under the new arrangements. Groups of artisans, most prominently in the construction carpentry trade, but embracing a range of others, began to seek a bottom-up regulation of their working conditions and wages. Construing themselves as rights-holding citizens, they met in assemblies and formulated minimum pay-rates, while also offering a structure to guarantee contractors that they would finish any job started under these conditions – reference to the labour-poaching that was so endemic in the guild system.

Such manoeuvres were immediately condemned by groups of employers as factional cabals, seeking to hold them hostage to their workers' demands. Much was also made of the tensions and occasional violence that had marked the first skirmishes between workers and employers – intimidation of those who wished to carry on working was the most common charge. The view of the workers' actions as disorder was that taken up by the municipal authorities, who pursued a strategy of denouncing the protests in printed orders, and of policing them vigorously with the National Guard. Workers' groups themselves entered the print arena, protesting there, and in petitions to the National Assembly, that there was nothing intrinsically unfair about their proposed conditions: while the workers were accused of 'caballing', it was the employers who were self-evidently doing this, both to hold wages down initially and to condemn the workers' actions.

Such an argument held no water with the politicians of the National Assembly, nor even with relatively radical commentators. The newspaper

The Revolutions of Paris, normally a supporter of popular societies, argued in May that workers' groups were different: 'An assembly which can only admit men who exercise the same profession injures the new order of things; it casts a shadow on liberty; in isolating the citizens, it makes them strangers to the fatherland.'[21] With even 'advanced' patriots taking a sharply individualist interpretation of the Rights of Man, the social insubordination implied by the workers' stance finished off their cause, and on 17 June 1791 the Le Chapelier Law was passed, specifically removing the right of assembly and association from groups of urban workers, and criminalising any effort to exercise collective influence over individual wages or conditions of work. A month later the measure was extended to farm workers and domestic servants. This reflected the continually hostile tone amongst the political class towards popular activity of all kinds. Five weeks before the Le Chapelier enactment, on 10 May, the new popular societies had had their activities curtailed by a law which banned the petitioning of public authorities on behalf of groups rather than by named signatories. The societies were becoming an increasing irritant to the leadership of the Assembly, as they questioned and challenged the conservative tone of its deliberations, and its eagerness to draw the constitution to a close without taking further decisive action against counter-revolution.

Just as the societies saw counter-revolution within the Assembly, so its leadership was inclined, as it had always been, to see brigandage at work in any and all popular demonstration, protest or alleged disorder. Brigandage, to elite eyes, was itself counter-revolutionary, even if only indirectly, as the gullible mob spurned what was good for it through its own stupidity, listening to the voices of irresponsible firebrands with no practical conception of political realities. In a further circularity, many continued to suspect radical agitators of being no more than aristocrats or their agents themselves – some viewed Marat's outpourings, for example, as the product of a committee, not able to credit one man with so much bile or to believe it could be sincerely meant. In late April the Paris municipality observed to the National Assembly that 'the enemies of the constitution have placed their hopes in anarchy', and that these figures were using 'the exaggeration of patriotism ... impatient ardour' and 'habit of mistrust of a people always abused' to stir up agitation against 'the legitimate powers conferred by a free people'.[22]

These suspicions and antagonisms had turned Parisian politics into a boiling cauldron of mutual malevolence even before the city, and the nation, was struck by yet another critical and decisive moment. The royal family's Flight to Varennes on 21 June 1791 threw national politics into turmoil, and also provoked yet another deadly confrontation between popular agitation and the forces of order. Even as the National Assembly propagated the myth of the king's 'kidnapping' to the nation, it also put the National Guard on high alert to suppress dissent – which was not long in coming. Although Parisians were frequently themselves stunned into quiescence by the news that the long-feared flight had actually happened, a few were eloquent on its causes – more than one was arrested for demanding the heads of Mayor Bailly and General Lafayette, even while local authorities spent more time worrying about disorder from the 'brigands' inside the prisons and lodging-houses of the capital. Individuals who read the word 'kidnapping' in official notices and either sought to erase or denounce it as a falsehood were seized as inflammatory agitators. Nevertheless, on 22 June, the Cordeliers Club struck a republican stance in a printed deliberation, concluding that 'royalty, hereditary royalty above all, is incompatible with liberty'.[23]

News of the king's capture reached Paris within a day, and the National Assembly hastily dispatched a party of deputies to escort the royal family back to the capital: the ingratiating tone the deputies adopted towards the king further enraged radical opinion when it emerged. The royal family arrived back in Paris on the 25th, greeted by huge crowds who looked on in silence – acts of approval and displeasure alike having been banned by municipal order. Such orders could not conceal the fact that, on the previous day, a 30,000-signature petition endorsing the Cordeliers' position had been handed to the Assembly. Across the country, there was less overt republicanism on display, but an equal determination to head off the counter-revolution that the king's flight seemed to presage. Regions on the eastern and northern frontiers, convulsed by rumours of Austrian and émigré armies, entered a state of effective martial law, while similar rumours about Spanish invasion ran through the Pyrenees. In Brittany, rumours of an English invasion fleet landing thousands of brigands sparked a panicked mobilisation and alarm that spread as far south as Bordeaux. A rash of 'permanent committees' that united all government functions echoed the crisis of July 1789, and Lyon, the Nord and the Ariège acted against non-juror priests, closing churches and making arrests. There were isolated incidents of further attacks on châteaux, with at least two killings of particularly hated and 'counter-revolutionary' seigneurs.

Meanwhile, back in Paris, the political elite of France was locked away from the population, concocting a deal to save all their skins. What emerged, and was ratified by the Assembly on 15 July, was as preposterous as it was unavoidable. The kidnapping myth was sanctified, but nonetheless the king was to remain officially suspended from his executive functions until he had accepted the finished constitution. Other than that temporary arrangement, and a vain promise to prosecute the already-emigrated villains of the piece,

all was to be forgotten. Radical opinion, amongst every class of the population, but especially the popular societies, had spent several weeks building
up a head of steam on this issue, and was not prepared to tolerate such a
fait accompli.

On 16 July there were various attempts to get together a mass protest
petition, hindered by lack of coordination and by the refusal of the Jacobin
Club officially to support a text that defied the expressed will of the National
Assembly. Indeed, at this moment the Jacobins decisively split, with the
vast majority of its members who sat in the Assembly moving to form a
'centrist' club at the Feuillants monastery. Individual radicals from the
Jacobins, along with the Cordeliers Club, settled on a text for a renewed
effort on the 17th, and word went out to all corners of the city that everyone
was welcome. The key demand was for a national consultation on the king's
position. It was couched in language, however, which took his abdication
as fact, and spoke of 'the organisation of a new executive power', so there
was little doubt of the underlying republican sentiment.[24] The text was to
be available for signature on the 'Altar of the Fatherland' erected the year
before on the Champ de Mars for the Festival of Federation. A crowd
estimated at up to 20,000 gathered through the day on Sunday 17 July, and
reaped, in their collective innocence, the whirlwind that months and years
of escalating suspicion had sown.

Two men who had hidden under the altar were discovered by the crowd
around noon. They were immediately assumed to be plotters, perhaps
preparing to blow up the platform. When local authorities dithered over
their fate, they were seized again by the crowd and lynched. Word of this
incident reached the municipality and the National Assembly, and a decision
was taken to declare martial law against the whole gathering. National Guard
battalions marched on the Champ de Mars from several directions, con-
verging around 7 p.m. A confused stand-off, in which a number of stray
shots were fired and elements in the crowd began stoning some of the
Guards, turned into an undisciplined charge by the National Guard – as
their own officers admitted to the official enquiry, which was intended to
inculpate the radical leadership, the Guards had been out of control. Fatal-
ities were almost certainly over a dozen, possibly closer to fifty, and estimates
ranged from there upwards into the hundreds, depending on how lurid the
imagination of the writer was.

Witnesses and participants in the crowd retailed their stories through
the public spaces of Paris in the coming days, denouncing the wickedness
of the Guard and its leadership, and associating such a deed with counter-
revolution. Two of the first to be arrested, in separate incidents on the evening
of the 17th, were Philippe Chapelle, a cockade-maker, and Jean Le Gueulx,

an innkeeper. Both were in their thirties, established in the artisan milieu, and both were or had been National Guard sergeants, but both were arrested as suspected agitators as they bewailed the massacre in distraught tones on the streets. Ardent protestations of their patriotism did not save them from spending the rest of the summer in prison. These two were in many ways typical of those detained over the following days – members of the artisan classes, with a record of patriotic commitment, who could not equate the enraged forces of 'order' on the 17th with the Revolution they believed in.[25]

Reinforced Guard patrols and a steady suppression of public discussion under martial law regulations saw relative calm restored to Paris within a few days. What is most striking about the reaction to this 'Champ de Mars Massacre' overall is the unanimity of reference to counter-revolution and brigandage in the commentary of the press and the political class. For the conservative centrist revolutionaries the events had been the defeat of a pack of brigands, funded by the aristocracy to stir up unwarranted discord. For those on the left centre, the crowd had largely been innocent, but brigands within it had lured the National Guard, itself also blameless, into its attack. On the extreme left, Marat decided that the counter-revolutionary Assembly and municipality had plotted the entire course of events, and had paid brigands to shoot blanks at the Guard to give them a pretext for attacking the crowd. The massacre demonstrated that the political class of the French Revolution was unable to conceive of dissent and opposition outside the framework of counter-revolution – and such counter-revolution was clearly assumed to be irreconcilable and implacable, as well as rooted deep in the social structure.

The fear of brigandage from below that coloured these perceptions is shown by events which had paralleled the post-Varennes political evolution in Paris, as the municipal authorities wrestled to disperse over 20,000 unemployed men who had been kept working at public expense over the previous months. Official and unofficial commentaries harped on the danger that these public workshops posed. Mass protest meetings by the workers in the last week of June had heightened fears, and armed force had already been used to disperse gatherings and occupations of the workshops in the first week of July, while the press spread rumours of nocturnal plots and agitation. Only the continued growth of more overtly political agitation pushed these alarms down the public agenda, but any former workers from these institutions were automatically doubly suspect in the round-ups that followed 17 July.

In Lyon, the aftermath of the Flight to Varennes triggered a similar outburst of social suspicion in the neighbourhood club movement. As early as February wealthier members had attempted to close the movement to non-active citizens, drawing a retort from the plebeian Croix-Rousse neighbourhood that such people continued to serve in the National Guard, and that 'at a time when our manufactures are languishing the views of non-active citizens are certainly worthy of being taken into consideration'.[26] The foundation of the city's social divisions, in the contest between merchants and weavers over control of their industry, was thus pointedly highlighted. Such arguments defeated the proposal, but allegations abounded in the following months that poorer members were being driven out of clubs in the wealthier quarters of the city. News of Varennes prompted a strong wave of republican popular sentiment, provoking protest from several wealthier clubs and driving one into a violent split. By the end of the summer somewhere between six and eleven clubs were no longer actively cooperating with the central club. All of these were in well-to-do areas, and viewed the growing domination of the centre by radical activists as a dangerous abuse of their supposedly subordinate coordinating role, and as the building of a personal power-base for social disruption.

Across the country at large, unrest with a specifically social agenda also continued. On 20 July 1791 a veritable army of peasants, some three to four thousand strong, confronted a military detachment in the Pays de Caux, near Rouen.[27] Parading under the National Guard banners of twenty-two communes, and with mayors and councillors at their head, they demanded the withdrawal of military forces from their region, the reduction of taxation, and the control of the grain trade. This temporary rally soon dispersed, but there were reports of more overtly violent incidents elsewhere. Across the summer in the *grande culture* grain baskets of the Paris Basin, a different issue, that of wages for harvest labourers, occasioned strikes and protests that sometimes gathered up to a thousand men, demanding that local authorities decree and enforce higher pay. Troops were sent to guard many farms in the region of Soissons and elsewhere, after several had been pillaged and local forces driven off. This was the context for the extension of the Le Chapelier Law to rural labour in mid July, which was followed by a wave of arrests, especially around Soissons.[28]

Ironically, the national political agenda of the late summer of 1791 took reconciliation as one of its key themes, for so long as most of the population was quiescent, scathing judgments about it could be subsumed under a veneer of optimism. Nevertheless, restrictive and exclusive currents ran through the final works of the National Assembly. Legislation tightened the socially exclusive rules for membership of the National Guard, and even attempted – at the last moment before the dissolution of the Assembly – to ban political clubs from public activity, though this measure was never enforced. The array of measures against sedition was expanded still further, and the property franchise for voting in future elections was raised at the end of August – though this did not affect the delayed elections then under way for the new Legislative Assembly.

The middle of 1791 also saw the final stages of the Constituent Assembly's response to the problem of poverty. The mendicity committee offered no grand solution, although it claimed that the doctrine of *bienfaisance* would be infinitely more healthy for society than church charity. Many of the responses to this issue remained at an emergency level. Municipal *bienfaisance* commissions were officially summoned into existence in May 1791, as it became apparent that the parish organisation of charity was collapsing under the weight of religious dissidence and aristocratic withdrawal. The Paris commission only started operating properly in October, such were the tangled issues of funding and the management of former church assets.[29]

The Mendicity Committee's work was continually threatened by the wider context, especially of religious reorganisation. Besides the purely administrative entanglements, the Assembly's treatment of the personnel of charity was fundamentally disruptive. It had been decreed as early as February 1790 that monastic vows were an absurd anachronism, to be abolished, but this had also embraced nuns, the majority of whom were in fact charity and health workers – of 55,000 nuns, at least two-thirds were active in this sense. Over 8000 were members of one such order alone, the Sisters of Charity, which worked in some 2000 separate establishments for the sick and aged. There were many other such orders, and an entire further network, of perhaps 150,000 women *béates*, who had taken less stringent 'simple vows' and lived in local communities, visiting the sick, collecting clothing for the poor, running soup-kitchens, organising needlework workshops for impoverished girls, and teaching.[30]

The Assembly ordered all such charitable orders to keep working on a provisional basis, but both their ability and their willingness to do so were placed under increasing strain by events. Unable to take on new novices, since their vows had been prohibited, the nuns of the Hôtel-Dieu in Paris reported in 1791 that their numbers had already fallen from 172, including sixty-seven novices, to only seventy-five, including eleven novices. All such women were now expected to work for a token annual salary of only 9 livres – the vow of poverty, although formally abolished, was taken for granted by the revolutionaries, unable to contemplate funding public welfare at commercial rates. Some nuns would later convert themselves to *citoyennes de secours*, 'citizen helpers', but many more would either shun revolutionary organisation altogether, or go further and join an underground current of resistance, even if they continued to try to help those who were their immediate charges. Efforts to recruit lay replacements over the coming years produced only a trickle of women, mostly those who could find no work elsewhere, and who lacked either the experience or the moral commitment to tend the sick properly.

An underlying economic complacency, which would remain in place throughout all the Revolution's future vicissitudes, led the Assembly to agree that there was no structural economic issue about the wider problem of poverty. Two working parents could support themselves, and one or two children, come what may – and the assumption was that such work would always be available, barring brief seasonal crises. Larger families might need some marginal support payments, in this view, as would the old and sick, but it was vital that levels of support should never be sufficiently generous to discourage work. Indeed, there was widespread agreement that work was exactly what should be provided for the able-bodied poor, and workshops continued to operate on this basis throughout the Revolution.

The conjunction of such supposedly temporary unemployment with plans for valuable public works attracted most support from the state: 600,000 livres were granted in 1791 to the department of the Yonne, for example, for major canal works, and sums of 150,000 livres for deepening the harbour at La Rochelle, and navigation works on the upper Rhine. Heavy unskilled labour was the lowest common denominator of relief work, and many such schemes using it were also put forward for Paris, only to be aborted by political fears. Despite all such measures, throughout the years to come, communities large and small alike consistently reported 10 per cent or more of their populations in need of immediate aid, and bemoaned the inadequacy of their economic resources to meet this demand. Paris continued to pay out over 400,000 livres per year to its non-working poor – no less than it had under the Old Regime. If the Constituent Assembly succeeded in codifying the treatment of the poor, it singularly failed to arrive at a means of stopping them being poor.

This period also saw an effort to codify the relationship of peasants to the land, a problem that went far beyond the issue of 'feudal' relations. In June 1791 the Assembly had struck a blow for individualism by abolishing the practice of enforced crop rotation – the classic pattern of the three-field system where individual holdings consisted of strips or patches within large community fields, and the type of crops grown in each field was shifted from year to year. Individualism was the message that emerged even more strongly in late September, when what became known as the 'rural code' was passed, attempting to regulate this and many other aspects of land use. It was an individualism that looked after individual possessions, however, not individual needs.

Landlords and local authorities had begun to complain from early in the Revolution that peasants were despoiling important communal resources in search of crop-growing plots. Especially in the south, where much land was steep and of marginal utility, such areas had been kept out of cultivation by seigneurial and communal rules. Where such land was also forested, the authority of lord and king was conjoined to defend it from pillage in the name of public utility. Naturally, such authority had lapsed in 1789–91, when a great deal of 'wild' tree-felling, clearance, grazing and planting had gone on. Administrators bewailed this at the time, and later, as a form of pillage, and an environmental tragedy – deforested slopes losing their soil to rain and wind, flash-floods becoming more common, crops failing in inappropriate soils, and so on. The Assembly had issued repeated warnings about the illegality of forest clearances in particular, but these fell on deaf ears, and in the circumstances of the Revolution punishment was certainly unenforceable in any community where such deeds had occurred.[31]

The general rural and specific forest codes, passed on consecutive days, struck an uneasy balance between the value of communal stewardship and the reinforcement of individual property rights. Thus no one was any longer to be forced to pasture their animals in a common flock, if they wished to make other arrangements, nor could individuals be prevented from enclosing their own lands by pre-existing claims of passage and forage for such flocks. At the same time, communal lands, and especially forests, were to be defended against damaging individual incursions. Such a uniform code could not hope to please everyone – for every peasant community that had sought to seize and enclose seigneurial commons since 1789 there was another that had broken down the lord's enclosures to restore free passage. Issues such as these were to be revisited again and again in coming years, and it was only the passage of time itself that finally erased some of the most damaging conflicts that emerged over the land.[32] Many of the other issues that continued to divide the leadership of the Revolution from its people could not be thus eased away, and the coming months and years produced only a sharpening of antagonisms that led through war and uprising towards civil war and terror.

8

The Politics of Conflict

The story of high politics in the first six months of the Legislative Assembly is swiftly told: stalemate at home and looming war abroad. Measures passed by the Assembly in October and November 1791 to sequestrate the lands of émigrés, to enforce oaths on non-juror priests, and to exclude the king's émigré brothers from the succession were all vetoed by Louis XVI, using his new constitutional powers. Meanwhile, from the end of October, political radicals such as the journalist and newly-elected deputy Jacques-Pierre Brissot and his emergent 'Brissotin' or 'Girondin' faction began calling for a war to cleanse the frontiers of the émigré threat. By mid December, such political pressure had obliged Louis publicly to demand the dispersal of émigré groups in the Rhineland. Ultimatums to the Holy Roman Emperor to renounce previous threats were issued in January 1792, and again in late March, by which time Marie-Antoinette's brother Leopold II had been succeeded as emperor by his more fervently counter-revolutionary son Francis II. Patriot rhetoric within France escalated steadily as these ultimatums and other measures were ignored, and also in the light of continued suspicion about the royal family's relationship to the émigré community and to Austrian power.[1]

Louis, Marie-Antoinette, and the whole court and émigré network were themselves increasingly of the view that only military defeat would curb the pretensions of the revolutionaries and restore royal freedom, while the patriots saw only the prospect of victory in the confrontation between free men and the slaves of tyranny. The former provincial barrister Maximilien Robespierre, who had established a reputation for extreme radicalism in the National Assembly, was one of the few voices on the national scene to cry out against this fatal conjunction. From his base in Parisian municipal politics, in print, and at the tribune of the Jacobin Club, he warned that France could be fatally imperilled by war, especially a war so eagerly sought by her enemies. He was ignored, sidelined by a patriotic bellicosity that brooked no hesitation. Thus it was that, on 20 April 1792, the Legislative Assembly voted on a motion – ostensibly at the king's request, but extracted from him by a Brissotin set of ministers installed in late March – to declare war on the 'king of Bohemia and Hungary', in an attempt to restrict the war to a conflict with Austria, rather than the whole empire. This measure of limitation failed, and within months France was at war with all the forces of central Europe, including the formidable might of Prussia.

The tone for these months was set in the second week of the campaign, on 29 April 1792, when the French general Dillon was killed by his own troops, suspecting treachery after an unsuccessful skirmish near the northern frontier town of Valenciennes. There were successful advances in the east, on the Swiss border, but after four weeks of war the three senior army commanders were all calling for peace negotiations, horrified by the potentially catastrophic outcome of committing their troops to battle. They were also discussing amongst themselves possible intervention in the internal politics of the capital (one of the three was Lafayette, who had deserted those politics after losing a mayoral election in November), and generally disregarding many of the orders coming from the Brissotin War Ministry. Nevertheless, a month later, in mid June, the French attempted to resume the offensive, only to find themselves steadily driven backwards within their frontiers over the following weeks, to a critical point by mid August.

What followed was a second revolution, in some ways more radical and decisive than the first of 1789. Continuing activity by radical groups, increasingly dissatisfied with the royal executive, and suspecting, quite rightly, that the court was plotting the patriots' defeat, built up a head of steam for violent political change. National Guard forces from Paris and the provinces came together, under the leadership of Jacobins, Cordeliers and municipal politicians, to topple the monarchy on 10 August 1792. Within three weeks, continued alarm at the progress of enemy forces towards the capital had led to the September Massacres – an unprecedentedly bloody settling of accounts with a supposed aristocratic fifth column lurking in the prisons of Paris. Such actions were the background to elections for a new National Convention, to govern the country and to give it, yet again, a new constitution. Under the circumstances, it is hardly surprising that the men chosen were virtually all ardent revolutionaries and republicans. They included Brissot and a strong contingent of Girondins alongside the more radical Robespierre, the journalist Marat and Georges Danton – a Cordeliers Club member and Parisian politician who as justice minister had been the organising hero of resistance during the weeks after 10 August. Time would show that, despite their shared republicanism, much also divided these new *conventionnels.*[2]

The military situation took a dramatic turn for the better almost at once. On 20 September 1792, at Valmy, in the wooded hills of the Argonne between Verdun and Chalons, a mixed French force of regulars and newly raised volunteers finally faced the advancing Austro-Prussian army, and pushed them into retreat after an artillery exchange. The enemy assumed that they could retreat unmolested into winter quarters, in the civilised manner of eighteenth-century warfare, but the French followed them, within a month advancing into the Austrian Netherlands (modern Belgium) and the Rhineland. Basle in Switzerland and Savoy to the south east also fell (the latter being annexed later in November), and on 6 November a major victory at Jemappes secured the French position in the north, paving the way for an advance into Holland.

With these events as a background, the National Convention, which had proclaimed France a republic on 22 September, succeeded in adding remarkably little to the fortunes of the country. Within days of this proclamation, the conflict between the formerly dominant Girondins and their more radical opponents had burst out into accusations of conspiracy and corruption that slowly dragged the Convention into mortal internecine confrontation. Radical Jacobins held that the Girondins had attempted to save the monarchy, while the Girondins believed fervently that radical leaders such as Robespierre and Marat had tried to sweep them into the September Massacres. It would be only a matter of months before leaders on both sides openly concluded that their opponents were counter-revolutionaries. Such attitudes were mirrored across France. A wave of purges had brought avowed republicans to power at all levels, and additional elections were used to consolidate this changeover through the autumn. The new republican rulers, however, were already divided. In major cities such as Lyon, Bordeaux and Marseille, the solid bourgeoisie, who had gone along with, and in many cases led, patriotic mobilisation and club membership, now found themselves on the more conservative side of a growing divide. As in Paris, the forces of popular radicalism would come to be seen by such groups as the harbingers of anarchy – and that anarchy as but a step on the road to bloody aristocratic revenge.

For much of the autumn, the national political agenda was also taken up with hesitation and argument over what to do with 'Citizen Capet', the former Louis XVI. The Convention finally agreed on 3 December to his trial and judgement by its own members, over the protests of some radicals who thought Louis should be executed out of hand.[3] Meanwhile, of the relatively little legislation passed in this period, much concerned the perennial threat of the émigrés. They were decreed to be outlaws on 23 October, permanently banished from French soil and subject to execution if they returned. On the 24th the movable property of all émigrés was declared subject to confiscation, their lands having already been seized the previous February, and arrangements to sell them put forward in July and September. A month later, any émigrés who had already returned to France, following the repeated earlier appeals to do so, were told to leave the country within a week.

Agreement on such issues, and on the need to keep the war effort going, was almost all that held the Convention together by the winter of 1792–93. Violent disputes amongst its membership reflected a growing tension within the country at large. From initially seeing France in 1789 as a nation united in resistance to Old Regime tyranny, perceptions in the following years had increasingly focused on the currents that divided the country. Believing implicitly in the conjoined threats of aristocrats, fanatics and brigands, the revolutionary leadership moved from a paternalist, authoritarian, but still inclusive model of the polity, towards one in which many, if not most, inhabitants of France were losing the right to be members of the revolutionary people. In the year 1793 this shift in attitudes accelerated dramatically, unleashing what must be recognised as a full-scale civil war, a conflict from which would emerge a ruthless new approach to the shaping of political and social conformity.

On 21 January 1793 the French Republic executed the man who had been king. Citizen Capet accepted his fate stoically, comforting his grieving family in the Temple before being driven in a coach to the guillotine (and becoming amongst the first, and perhaps most eminent, of its political victims, the 'humane' machine having been introduced in April 1792). On the scaffold Louis announced his forgiveness of his people, before a roll of drums drowned him out and the executioner did his work. The remains were hurried away for disposal, the site of which was kept secret to hinder any move to make relics of them. The king's fate had continued to divide the Convention until almost the last moment, with Girondin-led efforts to put his sentence to a referendum provoking further infighting amid accusations that it was a plot to save him. The perils of the republican position had been thrown further into sharp relief on the day before the execution, when one of the leading lights of the Jacobins in the Convention, the ex-noble Michel Lepeletier, was assassinated by a royalist in a Parisian restaurant. His remains, unlike those of the king, were made the subject of a public tableau of grief and a painting by Jacques-Louis David that hung in the Convention itself. It was a stark reminder, if any were needed, that the enemies of the Revolution were everywhere. The coming year was to be full of such reminders, as the list of the Revolution's martyrs, and its enemies, grew ever longer.

The leadership of the Republic could be said to have done their best to lengthen that list themselves. A fundamental belief that the crowned heads of Europe were all in concert against France led them to declare war on Holland and Great Britain on 1 February, and on Spain on 7 March, interspersing this with declarations against various of the smaller Italian states, and the annexation of Belgium, Nice, Monaco, Mainz and Basle, all completed by 23 March. The revolutionaries' belief that Britain in particular had been supporting counter-revolution had some truth in it, but by these acts they gave France the appearance of a voracious beast, spreading a regicide doctrine by force on all fronts. This image was matched with a vigorous and early start to the new military campaigning season. French forces moved out of Belgium into Holland in February, and initially seemed to be repeating the successes that had crowned the previous year. A well-planned Austrian counter-attack from the east forced the French to withdraw to defend their rear, however, and led them into a serious defeat at Neerwinden on 18 March. At the same time, forces under the duke of Brunswick drove the French out of the Rhineland.[4]

The next six months saw France plunged into civil war. Attempts to recruit new levies of troops by conscription led to uprisings in the areas of the west that had been at odds with authority since the imposition of the oath on the clergy. In the south east, similar tensions simmered in a series of smaller uprisings. Meanwhile, intensified hostilities between radical Jacobins and the Girondins, not merely in Paris, but embracing France's three other largest cities – Lyon, Marseille and Bordeaux – led to a second, overlapping outbreak of hostilities soon named the 'Federalist revolt'. At the beginning of June, the Girondin leadership was thrown out of the Convention and the government by an orchestrated Parisian rising, at virtually the same moment that radical leaderships in Marseille and Lyon were confronting militant discontent with their divisive policies.[5]

Under these circumstances, the completion by the Convention in June of a highly democratic new constitution, with manhood suffrage and annual elections, was effectively irrelevant. By September, with further campaigns looming in the general war, and hard fighting in the west, pressure from within the Convention and from the wider radical circles of Parisian politics moved the Jacobin leadership towards the creation of a system of government that they openly defined as Terror. Moves towards a more centralised and ruthless deployment of state power had already been made during the crisis of the spring, often with the acquiescence of many amongst the Girondins. A Revolutionary Tribunal for political crimes, whose only sentence was death, had been established, draconian powers against rebels captured under arms were introduced, and roving commissioners or 'representatives-on-mission' from the Convention had been invested with sweeping powers. At the start of April, the Convention gave final form to a Committee of Public Safety, having toyed for several months with different versions of a central governing council. Although formally only one committee of the Convention amongst many, this group, which from the summer numbered twelve, had power to oversee all administrative and military functions, and to issue any necessary decrees on its own authority. Robespierre was voted onto the committee on 27 July, bringing his aura of irreproachable radical virtue, and reinforcing the drive to a ruthless treatment of dissent – all such acts being increasingly branded as *incivique*, unworthy of a citizen.[6]

The need for the kind of power the committee represented seemed to be borne out by the immediate aftermath of the Girondins' expulsion. Several of their leaders fled to Caen in Normandy, rallying a small army and briefly threatening lines of communication with the war zone of the Vendée. While pressure or persuasion from the Convention's commissioners was bringing into line other centres that had dabbled with revolt, such as Toulouse and Montauban, and several department administrations that had protested against the events of 2 June, the threat was still dire. The Caen Federalists' declared intention to march on Paris made them seem a greater threat than they actually were; and, although easily dispersed by government forces on 13 July, (the same day that Marat was killed by a Girondin sympathiser in Paris) this movement and events in Lyon pushed the Federalist episode into a new dimension.[7] Convention representatives had tried hard to keep channels of communication between Paris and Lyon open, but political pressures from within the rebel city led on 17 July to the execution of the Jacobin ex-mayor, Chalier. From a Parisian perspective, he was now a 'martyr of liberty' alongside Lepeletier and Marat, and the military option for settling accounts with Federalism now seemed the only way forward.[8]

Such action seemed all the more necessary as the situation in the west became more of a significant threat to the state every day. The rebellion centred on the department of the Vendée, and the 'Vendean Revolt' had rapidly consolidated into a peasant army, led by a mixture of genuinely plebeian activists and sympathetic local nobles. This force had a series of successes against both local National Guards and regular troops in May and June, taking a number of regional urban centres. Meanwhile, the Republic's external war continued to go very badly indeed. The Austrians had defeated French armies near the significant northern fortress towns of Condé and Valenciennes in May, and placed them under siege. Both fell in July, as did Mainz, besieged in the east by Brunswick's Prussian forces. The Spanish and Piedmontese also advanced over the south-western and south-eastern frontiers, the latter particularly weakened by troops drawn into the anti-Federalist campaign.

In the face of all this, on 5 September 1793 another orchestrated *journée*, or day of Parisian action, pushed through the Convention the outline of a Terrorist agenda. A wide-ranging series of acts to control, contain and oversee the population, and especially those deemed for any reason 'suspect', counterpointed the dramatic measure that had been agreed two weeks earlier to raise a 'mass levy' of the citizenry – deploying military discipline across the population to form a huge army, and to feed, clothe and equip it. The measures of September 1793 were followed in October by further decisive acts. On the 10th, acting on the recommendation of the Committee of Public Safety, the Convention declared that the government of the Republic would be 'revolutionary until peace'. They thus confirmed the suspension of the 1793 constitution, and the continued rule of the committee, where Robespierre increasingly exercised an effective political dominance. He, like many leading Jacobins, was by now convinced of the need to remake France completely if the Republic was to endure. Paradoxically existing alongside continued reference to the virtue of the people, the language of corruption, of a people morally weakened by life under tyranny, led necessarily to ideas of renewal, and of a 'regeneration' that would be almost physical, as well as cultural, political and spiritual. The radical leadership of France came to believe that a total change in the environment could create, or restore, a virtuous republican citizenry.[9]

On 24 October the Convention took another step in this direction, shattering the 'Christian' Gregorian calendar, with its week based on the days of creation, and its litany of saints, in favour of a new order which began the year with the day of the Republic's declaration, 22 September. There were to be twelve thirty-day months, named after features of the seasons and the agricultural year, and five extra feast days at the end. This was now, therefore, early Brumaire Year II, although the nomenclature was not finally established by decree until late November (or early Frimaire). Eventually, an entire panoply of special designations and festivals marked this calendar, aiming to replace the morality of the church with lessons in civic pride, patriotism and homely virtues.

These measures were part of the ongoing war against the counter-revolutionary church, which within a month of the new calendar's promulgation had become a war against religious belief itself.[10] Some representatives-on-mission, such as Fouché in the Nièvre, had already begun in the summer to close down churches, ban worship, force 'constitutional' priests to renounce their vocations, and campaign against the 'superstition' of Catholicism. This became in the autumn a favourite cause of the ultra-radicals still to be found in the Cordeliers Club and the Paris Commune and sections. On their prompting, the Convention decreed on 6 November that municipalities could renounce Catholicism formally, and the following day a wave of such activity began in Paris as the city's archbishop, Gobel, was persuaded to resign his priesthood. Three days later, the cathedral of Notre-Dame was renamed the Temple of Reason during a festival of liberty. There was little opposition to all this in the capital. Parisian popular culture had been anticlerical for decades, and had reacted sharply against the non-jurors; in any case, so dominated was the city now by radical revolutionary institutions and groups that resistance to such a policy in the name of religion was unthinkable – or at least suicidal.

The Parisian ultra-radical movement was most visibly associated with the name of Jacques-Réné Hébert, the successful journalist and Cordeliers Club activist who had become one of the Paris Commune's chief prosecutors in late 1792, and who took a vicious part in the show trial of Marie-Antoinette in October 1793. Followers of his line had also taken over the War Ministry in early 1793, and were especially prominent in provoking and praising the bloodiest actions again the western rebels. Hébert's brand of verbal violence was all too easily translated into real violence on the streets and in the villages of France. The adoption of a 'dechristianising' agenda by radical groups, and particularly by the groups of militants formed into *armées révolutionnaires* by the measures of September, led to a spiralling wave of aggression, particularly against rural communities. The alienation of rural producers that inevitably followed made the job of provisioning so difficult (even with the ever-present threat of force) that the leaders of the Revolution could not long let it continue. This dechristianising fervour was symptomatic of a bottom-up spontaneity of action, so typical of revolutionary development throughout this decade, and as problematic for central authority under the Terror as it had been in earlier years.

The practical problems caused by such action meshed with personal and ideological confrontations evolving within the highest echelons of the Jacobin leadership. The overt political enemies of the Jacobins had already been disposed of under what Hébert liked to call the 'hot hand' of the guillotine – Marie-Antoinette on 16 October 1793, the leading Girondins *en masse* on the 31st, and the duc d'Orléans, probably harmless but with royal blood and alleged Girondin connections, on 6 November. With these figures gone, and the Federalist menace under control, the radical leadership began to turn in on itself, seeking new enemies to blame as final victory seemed as distant as ever. Through the winter of 1793–94, the ultra-revolutionary dechristianisers succeeded in alienating Robespierre and his closest followers with their intemperate atheism, while creating tensions with the military and technocratic planners on the Committee of Public Safety through the disruptive impact of their continual calls for purges and greater 'revolutionising' of administration. Meanwhile, others linked to Danton were calling for the abrupt reining-in of all internal Terror, seeing it as increasingly counter-productive, and as breeding more enemies than it crushed. At the same time, Robespierre and his allies heard reports of the personal corruption of both Hébert and Danton, and some of their followers, a corruption that was linked, through specific individuals and by its very nature, to foreign counter-revolution.

On 4 December 1793 the Law of 14 Frimaire had already bureaucratised Terror, ordering the dissolution of all *armées révolutionnaires* except that of Paris, reinforcing central control of representatives-on-mission, and placing appointed 'National Agents' at district and municipal level in a key administrative role, bypassing elected local and department authorities. The independent local initiative that had formed so many militia units and irregular ultra-revolutionary committees was formally crushed, and the 'anarchic Terror' was progressively taken in hand in the first months of 1794. With general control achieved, and with Robespierre and his followers believing implicitly in the counter-revolutionary nature of all dissent, the Hébertist leadership were seized on 13 and 14 March 1794. They were executed ten days later as conspirators against the Republic.[11]

Any suggestion of a more general political swing to the right was countered, however, by the arrest of the 'Dantonists' or 'indulgents', and their execution on 5 April after a four-day show trial.[12] With the 'factions' suppressed, the Robespierrist leadership went further still through April and May, pressurising the popular societies of the Paris sections into dissolving themselves, and recalling to Paris many of the leading representatives-on-mission. On 10 June the Law of 22 Prairial introduced measures to ensure almost-certain conviction of anyone sent before the Revolutionary Tribunal, and for the next seven weeks a 'Great Terror' reigned. Most convictions now came from the investigation of the huge numbers already held in the prisons as suspects, upon whom a population of spies worked to weed out – or to provoke – counter-revolutionary sentiments, remarks and ambitions. Unsurprisingly, they were eminently successful, and batches of men and women of every social condition passed swiftly to the guillotine under increasingly improbable pretexts.

The impression all this might give, that Robespierre was secure at the centre of power, is misleading. The less fanatical members of the Committee of Public Safety had no commitment to the more extreme measures introduced, while many members of the subordinate Committee of General Security were coming to oppose the centralisation of powers in Robespierrist hands. Many powerful and influential representatives had been recalled from their missions, knowing they were under a cloud of suspicion for their less than clean hands – not a few had interpreted the role of the provincial proconsul as entitling them to the personal benefits of power, as well as its responsibilities. Many also felt more personal loyalty to the

dead Hébert or Danton than to Robespierre or his equally fanatical young
protégé Saint-Just. The additional fact that a great victory on 26 June at
Fleurus saw the French armies overrunning Belgium by late July, accompanied by victories on many other fronts, left many *conventionnels* feeling
that the emergency which had justified the Terror was waning.

The Great Terror fell apart at the end of July 1794. Robespierre, unaware
of the totality of his isolation, returned from a bout of ill health to the
Convention on 26 July, and made a speech in which he more than hinted
at a purge of that body itself. The next day, 9 Thermidor, his enemies
rounded on him, led by men such as Fouché and Tallien, once arch-terrorists
themselves. The majority of *conventionnels*, who had always remained relatively uncommitted in the ideological disputes of the previous year, needed
little persuading. Robespierre, Saint-Just and the wheelchair-bound Couthon
were ejected from the Committee of Public Safety and declared outlaws,
liable to immediate execution upon arrest. They were taken that night as
they vainly tried to rally support from a Paris Commune they had stuffed
with their nominees in previous months – the National Guard almost, but
not quite, summoned the political will to rise up, though failure to act did
not save its leaders from proscription and death in the coming days.[13]

The 'Thermidorian Reaction' is commonly presented as the decisive turn-
ing-point of revolutionary history, particularly by left-leaning scholars.[14] It
represents the moment when the Revolution's basic commitment to social
justice went into reverse, and when the enemies of the people began a slow
creep back to power. There is much in the revolutionary story, however,
to suggest that no such decisive turnaround was possible, because no such
laudable ambitions existed, except in the most ephemeral, not to say phan-
tasmal, form. Many of the conflicts that five years of revolution had brought
showed no profound alteration after July 1794 – the guerrilla war in the
west dragged on unabated, and Thermidor marked no change in the external
war either. There was a 'reaction' against the activists and foot-soldiers of
the Terror, one which focused heavily on those who had risen from below
as the Jacobins had sought out a popular constituency. This attack, however,
was directed as much against the image of the popular activist projected
by the Jacobins, as it was a genuine act of social revenge. Through the
period of both terror and reaction, the political leadership of France continued a pattern of behaviour that had developed since 1791–92 – prioritising
'the people' in their pronouncements, for good or ill, but imposing on the
real people of France the consequences of an almost dream-like conception
of who such 'people' should and could be.

In August 1795 the Convention finished the job it had been first summoned for, and published a new constitution for the Republic. A bicameral

legislature safeguarded against the excesses of any one faction, and a five-man panel took on the role of chief executive to block any monarchic ambitions. Returning to some of the principles of 1791, the constitution created a simple taxpayer franchise for the basic voter, and an elevated version – the value of over one hundred days' labour – for 'electors', who did the real job of selecting administrators and representatives. Thus the unpropertied were cut out of anything but a token role in politics, and membership of the real political nation became confined to a wealthy elite – an exclusion that was to endure in various forms for a further half-century. If that matter seemed settled, almost nothing else was. Terror and reaction had created a political class which, even when restricted to substantial property-owners, was so riven between unrepentant Jacobins and vengeful royalists that the Republic's survival tottered on a knife-edge through the remainder of the decade.

9

War and Republic

The movement from peace to war was another decisive stage in the evolution of this turbulent decade. It turned resistance of any kind into outright treason in the face of the enemy, and enabled the call of pure patriotism (and an increasingly chauvinistic nationalism) to be added to the other motors of revolutionary commitment. What it did not do, however, was to pacify any of the conflicts that already raged within France, and the demands of war on the population, however enthusiastically some embraced the call to arms, generated only further conflicts in the coming years. Many of the population also found that, even as political leaders made increasingly explicit calls for popular mobilisation and bids for popular support, those leaders' vision of what 'the people' should want remained radically at odds with what they actually did want.

While the Legislative Assembly wrestled with its relationship to the constitutional monarch, other embittered conflicts continued to sweep the nation. There had been no significant let-up in the agitation over the clergy since the imposition of the oath in January 1791. By the autumn of 1791, the situation in north-western France was so disturbed as to occasion a formal investigation by the Assembly. A cultural gulf had opened up in this region – most of the deputies it sent to the Assembly, for example, were of the left, because no one but the minority of fervent revolutionaries bothered to vote. The town-based and culturally 'bourgeois' local administrators increasingly felt themselves to be under siege from a 'fanatical' peasant population. Many elements conspired to produce this alienation: not only were priests still seen by many western peasants as their natural community leaders, but their previous experience of the bourgeoisie was often solely in the role of rapacious landlords, who were now taking advantage of the taxes and tithes that the National Assembly had allowed them to add to their rents. That Assembly had also imposed an ever-growing burden of taxation on a region which had complained in its *cahiers* that it was already overtaxed. By contrast, seigneurialism here had a relatively light touch, and habits of deference had not been strained by overt pre-revolutionary conflict.[1]

In early November, the departmental administrators of the Maine-et-Loire wrote that 'assemblies of three to four thousand armed men form at several points [with] all the delirious excesses of superstition and fanaticism'. Such gatherings, they claimed, began with 'nocturnal processions led by seditious priests', who denounced all instruments of revolutionary authority as enemies of religion. The administrators reported that three district capitals within the department were effectively besieged, 'in danger of night attacks, of being pillaged and burnt by these brigands'. While swearing to 'die here rather than abandon' their posts, the administrators also noted their belief that 'the interest of religion' was only a veil used by counter-revolution to animate resistance – it was inconceivable to them that they could really be perceived as the enemies of faith.[2]

If the Maine-et-Loire was in an extreme state of agitation, things were little better elsewhere. In the summer of 1791 alone, a quarter of all departments either petitioned the centre for a law exiling non-jurors, or took arbitrary action to eject or intern such men. Administrators in the Rhône-et-Loire (which embraced Lyon) argued that there was a state of 'latent insurrection' that needed to be curbed, while in the Haute-Garonne (around Toulouse) liberty of religion was declared to be something only 'the honest citizen' was fit to exercise, in association with a necessary 'respect for public order'.[3] In the following months, local sweeps by urban-based and patriotic National Guards arrested non-jurors' supporters, closed churches and pillaged 'enemy' property in Brittany, the Ardèche and the Nord – where the 'non-juror' village of Berlaimont was attacked by forces from fifteen other communities and its convent pillaged. After the king's veto of official measures against non-jurors, such unofficial initiatives spread even further, so that by the end of April 1792 half of all departments had acted to exile or detain such priests. Official violence and sanctions were accompanied in many areas by 'missionary' activities led by local Jacobins. From towns such as Angers, Besançon, Montauban and others, so-called 'ambulatory clubs' went out in early 1792 to bring liberty trees, patriotic songs, speeches and revolutionary almanacs to the rural population. In general, such efforts were a resounding failure – the language of the publications was obscure, when it was not patronising to a peasant audience, and the speakers and activists of these groups often matched the perceived 'fanaticism' of rural attachment to the priesthood with an equally unyielding anticlerical dogmatism. Many of the areas where such clubs were most active later gave themselves over almost entirely to counter-revolutionary sympathies.[4]

As religion continued to foment trouble and attract suspicion of counter-revolution, overt counter-revolutionaries were also working to extend their networks, with the avowed aim of creating a nationwide uprising against the patriots when the émigrés came to their aid. The ever-active François Froment of Nîmes, who had secured new funds from the émigré princes, established committees to this end in Arles, Carpentras and Avignon, and planned to unite organised counter-revolutionary forces from at least five departments when the time was ripe. Aristocratic conspiratorial networks formed in Brittany and Normandy, and intelligence of movements, collections of arms and correspondence left vigilant local and national authorities with no doubt of their goals, even if their membership remained shadowy.[5]

Such threats from 'above' clearly intersected with the threat from 'below' occasioned by clerical resistance and southern sectarianism, but there were also other veins of dissatisfaction. In Brittany and Normandy, for example, not only had many communities enjoyed an extremely privileged position in regard to taxation in the Old Regime, a good number had made a solid living from exploiting the system. The classic case is that of salt smuggling, a supplement to the incomes of many peasants who took salt from Brittany and the western third of Normandy, where it was almost or entirely untaxed, and sold it in the other regions immediately to the east, where most of the normal price of salt was made up of the hated *gabelle* tax. Such activities had of course pitted these people against the royal *maréchaussée* and the paramilitary agents of the tax farmers, but they represented a livelihood that had now vanished. Both early rumour and later established fact placed these groups, with their well-known grievance, at the heart of counter-revolutionary brigandage in these regions. One group in the Mayenne department, in the old province of Maine bordering both Brittany and Normandy, was following just such a path by late 1792. They were led by a certain Jean Cottereau, an ex-smuggler known as 'Chouan' – the local word for the *chat-houant* or owl, whose call was imitated by the smugglers as a nocturnal rendezvous signal. Cottereau lent his nickname to what became in later years a popular guerrilla movement against the Revolution spanning much of the north west.[6]

Other economic grievances should not be overlooked. Many of the abolished bishoprics, for example, had supported extensive retinues of servants, craftsmen and labourers, and the loss of these was felt especially in the south, where there were clusters of small dioceses. More generally, many religious houses, even those with only a few members, had been generously endowed and supported the labouring population through their consumption and largesse. The inhabitants of Lagrasse in the Corbières, for example, had benefited from its abbey's charity to the tune of a hundred sackfuls of wheat and 300 livres annually (even if, at the same time, the absentee abbot of this major foundation had taken 18,000 livres a year from its wide landholdings).[7] All these established channels of support had now dried up, the revenue vanishing into the national coffers as the lands passed into the hands of the grasping bourgeoisie.

Communities also had to look on as the wider resources of charity and support were pressurised. Although local hospitals had been exempted from the immediate conversion of their lands to *biens nationaux*, they suffered from the general economic and political climate. State funds that were voted for their maintenance from 1791 – several million livres per year – were hopelessly inadequate, especially as they were now taxed on their buildings and property; from 1792, their rights to income from lands were withdrawn. State payments in the following years often did not arrive, or at best arrived late and partially, and a spiral of inflation saw hospitals always remain worse off than they had been before 1789, and providing a poorer service to their communities. Many fell into partial or complete dilapidation, even as dedicated staff struggled to work on.[8] For all the complaints made about the abusive wealth of the church in the *cahiers* and elsewhere, and all the attacks on such institutions in 1789, some of the consequences of their reordering had not been foreseen.

Economic decline was a real political concern for some in the elite. When the king made a speech to the newly constituted Legislative Assembly in early October 1791, he called for measures of economic regeneration to be a priority. Radical critics, however, denounced this as a ploy to divert the Assembly's energies into debating long-term schemes for the economy, at a time when the émigrés and the non-juring priests continued to pose an immediate threat.[9] For the political class at large, this perspective remained dominant, even as further economic difficulties struck the general population. Late 1791 and early 1792 saw a further source of anxiety and disorder on this score, as the harvest proved less than bountiful, and as revolt in France's Caribbean colonies provoked shortages of imported goods, notably of sugar and coffee. These were by now staples of the urban diet, valued by workers for their stimulant quality as much as their taste – the appetite-suppressing ability of a well-sugared morning cup of coffee was useful when a larger breakfast was beyond the reach of one's pocket. Thus it was that Paris in particular saw episodes of *taxation populaire* directed at grocers' shops in January and February 1792, while educated commentators expressed disbelief at the rage occasioned by this apparent 'luxury'.[10]

The shortage of grain, a more acceptably basic commodity, was occasioned (as in 1789) by the vagaries of climate. Rain poured down in the autumn of 1791, interfering with winter wheat-sowing, and causing devastating floods on the slopes below the Massif Central and along the Rhône valley. Grain prices rose by between 25 and 50 per cent across the country, a rise made worse by the continued decline in the value of assignats against 'real' money. Still worth around 85 per cent of their face value in late 1791, they slid steadily towards 60 per cent in the spring of 1792, and dipped below that in the summer. A 50 per cent rise in the notional price of grain might therefore amount almost to a doubling of what actually had to be paid. In rural areas it was becoming increasingly common for assignats simply to be refused, while the purely local circulation of all the various *billets de confiance* hindered commerce still further. Such economic disruption became a vicious circle: in 1791 unemployment was already a serious problem in Paris, and by early 1792, across the cities and towns of France, there was less and less of a manufacturing economy to offer work, while the service economy also sagged deeper into depression as the social elite continued to emigrate.[11]

Taxation populaire burst out again through the winter and early spring of 1791–92, notably in the north, to the east of the capital in the Haute-Marne, and across many of the same territories around Paris that had seen the Flour War of 1775. Along the rivers Aisne and Oise, barges were held up and pillaged by groups of artisans and workers, while throughout the spring groups numbering in their thousands marched on market towns, often led by village mayors in full regalia. Just as half a generation before, they seized control of markets and even raided private premises to secure goods. Now, however, they dealt in 'just prices' not only for grain and bread but also eggs and butter, and for basic raw materials of everyday life such as wood, iron and cloth. Urban workers, both male and female, joined in such action with the rural population (which itself included many such as pin-makers, weavers and charcoal-burners afflicted by the decline of rural industries), as sometimes did community notables such as forge-masters, forest stewards or lawyers.

A scattering of patriot constitutional priests also joined their ranks, some of whom drew on biblical language to denounce private property itself as being in conflict with the prior needs of the community. Although such rhetoric probably owed more to apocalyptic sermons than to proto-socialism, this movement also saw widespread demands for fair rents and wages, and vigorous denunciations of individual greed and excess. It was a powerful sign of the persistent currents of economic discontent that underlay the simple opposition of patriots and aristocrats. The language of famine plots continued, however, to associate such grievances with fear of counter-revolution, and the independent movement of protest subsided noticeably as France entered war – the northern regions being a prime site of invasion scares and military mobilisation.

Across southern France there were more explicitly political uprisings. These included peasant attacks in the Lot on châteaux of émigrés suspected of joining the counter-revolutionary armies in January 1792, and a wider assault on both non-jurors and former seigneurs in the Tarn in February, including the disarmament of counter-revolutionary suspects by local National Guard detachments. Around Toulouse in late February, peasants gathered up to a thousand strong, and pursued a wide-ranging agenda that included not only *taxation populaire*, attacks on châteaux and the harassment of non-jurors, but also the burning of feudal titles and the extortion of a revolutionary 'contribution' from their victims. In the following month, the Cantal in south-central France saw a wide-ranging anti-aristocratic rising after a crowd of patriotic volunteers for military service attacked a known counter-revolutionary's home in the local capital, Aurillac. This violence gave rise to rumours of aristocratic attacks on the peasantry, and was translated into a rural revolt that turned against the patriots' initial victim – the man in question was lynched and decapitated by a peasant mob (which included the local National Guards). The unrest spread across the department, attacks on supposed aristocrats and fanatics merging with anti-feudal pillage, and with a *taxation populaire* that on occasion turned into the carnivalesque consumption of châteaux's stocks of food and drink.[12]

Similar, if less Rabelaisian, events occurred in at least three other central departments around this time, sometimes taking on the more structured approach of placing 'suspects' under observation and warning – with armed force always on hand to push the message home. In the Manche department of Normandy, and the Ille-et-Vilaine in Brittany, a series of similar actions by urban patriot crowds against non-jurors and their supporters reflected the steadily growing divisions in the west, where rural support for the non-jurors remained strong and widespread. In the south east, violent confrontation developed an ever-more overt and structured place within local life. In the department of the Gard, around Nîmes, sectarianism and social prejudice continued to form an explosive mixture, as the Protestant mercantile elite tightened its grip on most administrative functions. This contrasted sharply with the situation at Lyon, where the mercantile elite, having lost the battle to control the clubs, seems to have backed away from municipal politics in this period, leaving a dedicated band of radicals in charge, who at least had the virtue of not provoking popular unrest. Such passivity, however, interpreted by patriot activists (largely correctly) as scorn for popular political engagement, only encouraged the increasing suspicion that Lyon was the haunt of counter-revolutionaries, and in particular the refuge of seigneurs fleeing the more hostile and less anonymous environment of departments such as the Gard and its neighbours.

Catholic royalists in and around Nîmes denounced all supporters of the Revolution as 'Calvinists', while the ruling elite itself showed equal scorn for both Catholic and Protestant textile-workers and peasants throughout this period, warning back in July 1791 that 'anarchy is the greatest of all

evils, worse than despotism itself', and that such a state would loom large
if various groups were allowed to continue social and political agitation.[13]
Political clubs, both on the Jacobin model and of a more popular tone,
spread through the whole region of the south east, with its many medium-
sized towns and strong manufacturing links between town and country
fostering social intercourse and an engaged political culture. Political polarisation became ever-more intense and armed confrontation ever-more
likely. An attempt to convene a second gathering of counter-revolutionary
National Guards at Jalès was partially thwarted by the interception of posted
invitations, but sufficient numbers gathered on 20 February 1792 for some
of their leaders to suggest a march on Nîmes and Uzès – though cooler heads
prevailed and the forces dispersed. Two days later, Protestant detachments
that had mobilised in response reached the area and clashed with locals,
leaving seven dead. A few days after this, one of the counter-revolutionary
local leaders was found dead near the Rhône – drowned accidentally, or
murdered, according to one's political taste.

As winter turned to spring, the twin threats of counter-revolution and
popular uprising gripped the south-eastern authorities. The provisioning
situation was serious, as were rumours of plots and mobilisations. As early
as 31 January there was a major outbreak of *taxation populaire* in Nîmes,
followed by further disturbances as a protesting crowd forced the authorities
to release two of the three ringleaders they were holding. Relatively reliable
National Guard detachments were shuffled around the region to control
both urban and rural unrest: on 25 March sixty-nine of these Guards were
drowned as they tried to cross the swollen Rhône in a boat. Malicious
royalist rejoicing was met with patriot charges of sabotage and conspiracy,
and divisions grew still more profound. Small-scale popular protest had
broken out across both the Gard and the Ardèche through March, but it
was a week after the drowning incident, on Sunday 2 April, that a full-scale
wave of unrest swept the Gard. It was mainly Protestant communities that
rose up and pillaged, burnt and demolished several dozen châteaux over
the course of the next week, while Catholic communities joined in as that
wave subsided.[14]

Destruction of counter-revolutionaries' property seems to have been a
main goal of the Protestant wave, along with *taxation populaire* where food
reserves were located, while the later Catholic risings concentrated on land
seizures and the destruction of feudal records. Overall, such actions were
complex: lawyers' houses were frequently targeted, though whether for their
role in collecting feudal dues or their current revolutionary leadership is
unclear. In another sense, of course, the motives were quite simple: crowds
attacked the many and varied symbols of a social and political system that

brought them nothing but strife and hunger. The communal nature of the actions is highlighted by the routine participation of enrolled National Guards in a number of areas, and the drawing in of community leaders of various types, as in previous months further north. Such events in the last weeks of peace reflected the extent to which revolutionary politics had succeeded in creating an active sense of engagement amongst the common people, yet had also failed comprehensively to channel that engagement anywhere other than into hostility. Continuing economic instability left individuals and communities anxious and alarmed, while recurrent waves of both rumoured and real counter-revolutionary action incited those on both sides of the political divide to rising levels of aggression.

Such disturbing conflicts were pushed aside, at least temporarily, by the resort to war, but this itself brought to the forefront of attention a problem which had simmered since 1789 – the condition of the army. The story of military-civilian relations over the previous three years had been a turbulent one. Troops had frequently been used, if not always actively to confront disorder then certainly to pacify otherwise agitated regions, while at the same time soldiers had been gradually integrated into the political nation. Those who qualified as active citizens were allowed from 1790 to vote in their home community. From May 1791 there was official encouragement to involve soldiers in patriotic political societies in their garrisons, and from July soldiers were able to be active citizens of those garrison towns. Such innovations helped to solidify a growing disaffection amongst the rank and file with the military hierarchy itself. Troops who had sided with Revolution in 1789 looked askance at an almost exclusively noble officer corps who made no secret of their royalist sympathies. Every one of the latter who emigrated (and a trickle became a flood after the Flight to Varennes), intensified the suspicion directed at those who remained.[15]

Through 1790 a series of mutinies in garrison towns across France, from Brest to Perpignan to Metz, and at many points in between, seemed to threaten a total military breakdown. The answer by the revolutionary authorities was the suppression by force of one such mutiny, at Nancy in August 1790. An abortive National Assembly measure to ban political groups within the army had been only one element of a complex agenda of grievances, including material charges of misappropriation and mismanagement of soldiers' funds placed in regimental care, that had brought three regiments to mutiny. A disciplined attempt to put grievances before the officers of the Swiss Châteauvieux regiment was met with a order for the whipping of the delegates, sparking full-scale revolt. The National Assembly ordered the marquis de Bouillé to retake the town with four thousand loyal troops, which he did, inflicting a hundred casualties in the process. Twenty-three executions and dozens of other heavy sentences followed. These measures, which horrified many more radical patriots, secured the temporary subordination of the troops, but rumblings of discontent, and officer emigration, continued.

The parlous state of the army by the time of the Flight to Varennes led to a first major emergency measure: volunteers were called upon to enrol for a year, and serve in special all-volunteer units, at preferential rates of pay. Unsurprisingly, in an atmosphere of both political and economic crisis, the response was overwhelming, and the total number of volunteers raised, 100,000, was four times the original target. Men of almost every social class joined up, as did some who were either too young or too old to be of real use. Some came because of fervid patriotism, others in search of steady pay, but almost all viewed their service as a purely temporary expedient in which fighting, if there were to be any, would involve routing the demoralised slaves of despotism.

This enrolment nearly doubled the effective strength of the army, but it also created divisive differentials of pay, organisation and even uniform – the *bleus* of the volunteers against the *culs-blancs*, 'white-arses', of the regulars. The regular army, meanwhile, haemorrhaged over two thousand officers in late 1791, and remained short of its nominal strength by some fifty thousand men. Some of these, of course, had deserted to take up the better offer of volunteer service, just as many had deserted in 1789 to join the salaried companies embodied within each urban National Guard battalion. Thus France went to war in 1792 with an army split down the middle, led by aristocrats whose loyalty was suspect, with gaps in the regular officer corps filled by hastily promoted NCOs, and in the volunteer units by the dubious merits of election. It is scarcely surprising that the first campaigning season was a disaster.

In Paris, as elsewhere, the outbreak of war and the crises which immediately accompanied it stimulated a patriotic radicalisation. The Jacobin Club achieved a moral ascendancy in politics, aided by the various popular societies that had recovered from the repression of the previous summer, rising to new heights of activity. The societies' influence was increasingly felt in the sections, the forty-eight administrative divisions of the city that had been created in 1790 to take the heat out of grassroots democracy, but which were now home to a revival of popular radicalism. Section general assemblies became more frequent, and alarmed and urgent petitions were dispatched to the municipality and the Legislative Assembly, protesting at aristocratic subversion in the court and military command.[16]

Wartime patriotism also accelerated the trend for politics to be discussed in terms of the 'people' and their supposed interests. Jacques-Pierre Brissot, in his guise as editor of the newspaper the *French Patriot*, commented in May 1792 on the three 'parties' he saw as operating within revolutionary politics:

*Patriote*Friend of the people, friend of the constitution.
*Modéré*False friend of the constitution, enemy of the people.
*Enragé*False friend of the people, enemy of the constitution.[17]

Although such language made the centrality of the people more apparent than the debates in 1789 that took the nation as their reference point, it also assumed that the 'patriotic' friends of the people had a duty to keep them on the right path. For Brissot, as for many of the political class, rectitude in politics meant holding together the people and 'their' constitution, even while others – implicitly sinister – tried to pull the two apart. The people still needed to be led, and led firmly.

It was at this time that a new social and political label was beginning to be adopted amongst urban radicals in Paris. Patriotic members of the common people were increasingly referred to, and began to refer to themselves as, *sans-culottes*.[18] Literally, the phrase means 'without breeches', identifying those who wore workers' long trousers rather than the respectable costume of breeches and stockings. It originated in satirical, and frequently right-wing, commentary, belabouring the *sans-culottes* as the gullible foils of radical scaremongering (with a hint of stage farce about their breechless condition). It was a variant on the even more scathing *va-nu-pieds*, the 'barefooted', who were by definition indigent, and hence dangerous. But as so often, a derogatory label was picked up and began to be used with proud assertion by some of its targets.

Although the *sans-culotte* ideal was far more self-consciously radical than the assumptions of Brissot and his followers, it was still not a straightforward reflection of a popular identity. It is certainly true that, amongst the Parisian sections, *sans-culotte* soon came to stand for the involvement of an artisanal rank and file in politics, and it undoubtedly represented an aggressive repudiation of the cultural values of a more 'refined' elite. None of this, however, ensured that leadership of the sectional movement passed out of the hands of those relatively prosperous artisans who had dominated neighbourhood politics in many areas since before 1789. The *sans-culotte* ideal could be used to give artisans and other town-dwellers a more assertive sense of their entitlement to political participation, but it did not necessarily ensure that they could exercise that involvement free from the tutelage of more established radical leaders.

Within a few weeks and months of the troubles of this period, the term *sans-culotte* began almost to rival reference to the 'people' in radical assertions about the sovereignty of the population, although it remained a word mostly connected to the urban artisan classes, signifying independence, patriotism, and a collection of largely masculine and pseudo-martial virtues. In some senses, it actually hindered the engagement of ordinary people with politics – the definition of what it meant to be a 'true' *sans-culotte* came to rest in the hands of radical leaders, journalists and political activists, who tended to reserve it for groups with ideas similar to their own, while continuing to denounce other initiatives as the product of those 'led astray' (*égaré*) by counter-revolutionary subversion. Men such as the doctor Marat and the barristers Danton and Robespierre would have no difficulty lauding the *sans-culottes*, or being accepted as their leaders and inspirations, regardless of their own non-plebeian lifestyles.

A key moment for the emergence of the *sans-culotte* on to the political stage came when war emergency measures that the Assembly had proposed, notably the deportation of suspect priests and the gathering of 20,000 'federated' provincial National Guard troops near Paris, were vetoed by the king on 19 June 1792. On the following day, a demonstration arranged by leaders from the Cordeliers Club showed the mobilising power of the radical movement. The crowd penetrated the Tuileries palace itself and harangued the king face to face, forcing him to put on a red cap, the newly-adopted symbol of liberty (borrowed from ancient Rome), and demanding the retraction of his veto. He did not yield, but such an event showed the critical point that politics had reached. A week earlier the king had sacked his Girondin ministers and appointed more conservative ones, who were at loggerheads with the Assembly. A week after the 20 June demonstration, General Lafayette left his army and returned to Paris, demanding that the Assembly punish the demonstrators.

Early July in fact saw something of a conservative reaction against what was widely perceived as anarchic popular protest: there were 20,000 signatures on a petition denouncing the 20 June events handed to the Assembly on 1 July. Two days earlier, an address from the active citizens of Rouen, one of many similar documents, had demanded punishment for 'these agitators who, even within the sanctuary of legislation, dare to deify revolt and murder'. On 1 July, however, an address from the Bonne-Nouvelle section of Paris called the National Guard headquarters of the city an 'aristocratic corporation' full of 'traitors' who were responsible for poisoning opinion against measures such as those the king had vetoed.[19] Neither side backed down, and politics throughout July were a morass of charge and counter-charge, in which the conservative ministry fell, and the mayor of Paris was first removed and then reinstated by different authorities.

The perils of the military situation nevertheless brought forth decisive action. A measure to declare 'the Fatherland in Danger' was devised on 5 July and enacted six days later, calling administrative bodies (including the Paris sections) into daily 'permanent' session, overriding the royal veto and fully militarising the National Guard for front-line service – and also authorising the gathering of the 20,000 'federated' troops demanded in June. This came as news arrived in Paris that Prussian forces were preparing to join the conflict in strength on the eastern frontiers. Political deadlock continued through the rest of the month and into August, but by the last week of July, the first explicit calls for the overthrow of the monarchy had already come from provincial National Guard delegates, now arriving in the city and meeting with the Jacobins. On 27 July, leading radicals and municipal politicians began to meet in the Hôtel de Ville to plan just such an event.[20]

It was clear to all who cared to see that the king was plotting the defeat of France with his European 'cousins'. In the last days of July, word reached Paris of what that would mean, in the form of the 'Brunswick Manifesto' issued by the commander of the allied armies (and written by a vengeful émigré). National Guardsmen and any other irregulars who took part in fighting were liable to be shot as rebels under arms, and if the king and royal family were not restored to unfettered power and safeguarded in their persons, 'an exemplary and long-memorable vengeance shall be taken, in giving Paris over to military execution and total destruction'.[21] Needless to say, this did not cow the Parisians but helped spur them on to resistance.

The sections were by this time becoming the focus of a clear structural democratisation, admitting non-active citizens to their debates, and enrolling them in their National Guard battalions. Although this expansion of their ranks was probably less the cause than the effect of growing republican ferment, it certainly consolidated it, and on 3 August, all but one of the sections banded together and formally petitioned the Assembly for the king's overthrow. The assembly postponed debate until the 9th, and on that day refused to reach a decision. Radical leaders that night formed an 'Insurrectionary Commune' to take charge of the city, and on the next day, 10 August, National Guard forces from the sections, joined by provincial detachments, attacked and defeated the Swiss Guards at the Tuileries, forcing the king to take refuge with his family in the Assembly. It then voted to suspend him, to enact all vetoed legislation, and to call a National Convention to decide on a future constitution. With a nod towards egalitarianism, all independent adult males were allowed to vote and to be chosen as second-stage electors, expanding the electorate by a half, but domestic servants and the transient or indigent were still excluded. Meanwhile, to run the beleaguered country, a Provisional Executive Council of left-leaning figures was appointed as a temporary government.

The 10 August rising had cost the lives of some six hundred troops loyal to the king, including a number, perhaps as many as a hundred, who had been executed summarily. In return, some three hundred Parisians, from forty-four of the forty-eight sections of the city, had been killed or wounded, along with nearly ninety of their comrades from other regions. The rank and file of the attackers came from the core of the Parisian working population. Counter-revolutionaries condemned them as brigands, bandits and the dregs of society, but the lists of the dead and wounded were a roll-call of respectable working men, master craftsmen, shopkeepers and other small traders. Between a third and a half of the casualties appear to have come from the two great artisan districts of the city, the Faubourgs Saint-Antoine and Saint-Marcel, spanning all ages of the adult population, and including many who left behind dependent spouses, children and aged parents. These were archetypal *sans-culottes*, and they and their surviving comrades were lionised as such by the new authorities.[22]

On the other hand, in those regions of France that were increasingly turning against the policies of the Parisian government, popular unrest against the new order had begun even before it came fully into being. Non-juror priests continued to be a focus of discontent, and more than half a dozen departments were engaged in July and early August 1792 with detaining or deporting them. Wherever this happened, from Lyon to Brittany, divisions between revolutionaries and the priests' supporters became further entrenched. Meanwhile, the patriotic mobilisation of the National Guard ordered as part of the 'Fatherland in Danger' measures was not accepted everywhere. When there was a further call for 50,000 new volunteer troops later in July, areas of the west saw major disorders. The estate of a departmental administrator in the Deux-Sèvres was sacked on 19 August by rural protestors, and the local capital invaded three days later by a crowd of ten thousand, who destroyed administrative files, voicing claims that the foreign enemy was in fact acting to protect religion. National Guards from cities across the region were needed to defend other centres from such bands. In Brittany, there were battles in two departments, while in the Mayenne, protestors declared that they would 'never consent to send soldiers against the king and the priests'.[23]

Such movements had not yet coalesced into a longer-term organisation, and the revolutionary authorities of the west in particular were learning how to mobilise military force to contain and quell short-term unrest. Active counter-revolutionary organisations, in contrast, continued to prove inept at seizing such opportunities, and all too prone to penetration and dispersal – a conspiratorial cell discovered at this point in Rennes unravelled a network extending across several departments. Furthermore, measures of largely rural popular resistance to the actions of authority were counterpointed by simultaneous acts of popular 'justice' against suspected counter-revolutionaries, especially in urban centres. In Vans in the Ardèche on 12 July 1792, five captured counter-revolutionary agents, escorted into the town by numerous National Guardsmen, were set upon, lynched and decapitated by a large crowd. The following day, a priest and a noble met the same fate in the nearby town of Joyeuse, while on the 14th, in Alès in the Gard, the prison was forced open by a crowd who killed four counter-revolutionaries detained there, while others turned again on the houses of 'aristocrats' in the neighbourhood. On the eve of the Parisian uprising itself, a National Guard detachment in the Lozère killed an associate of the chief agent lynched in Vans the previous month.[24]

Most dramatically, a third attempt to organise a counter-revolutionary rising centred on Jalès was attacked by battalions of volunteers raised by local authorities. The royalists were routed on 12 and 13 July, with up to two hundred killed and 'suspect' villages in the area put to the torch. Such clashes, although most intense in the rural south east, had their parallels elsewhere. In July, two non-jurors were lynched in Bordeaux, while at Port-en-Bessin in Normandy no fewer than a hundred priests were saved from massacre after 10 August by the intervention of the authorities, their gathering for emigration having been inflated by local alarm into an invasion attempt. Militant action from both ends of the political spectrum had thus become ingrained into French political life by the summer of 1792. The 10 August battle could only widen such rifts, especially when seen in conjunction with its aftermath.

The fall of the monarchy was accompanied in Paris by a round-up of large numbers of suspected counter-revolutionaries. This included several hundred non-jurors, along with discredited figures from the city's administrative hierarchy, officials of the royal court, and associates of the royal family. The most eminent of these was the princesse de Lamballe, a former favourite of the queen, and often portrayed as her lesbian lover in scurrilous pamphlets, who was confined in La Force prison with a small group of other court ladies. The royal family themselves were locked up in the keep of the Temple, a fortified building in the north of the city that had once housed the Paris chapter of the Knights Templars. Less distinguished prisoners were either crammed into existing prisons, or housed in temporary quarters, mainly in former monastic buildings. All of these individuals were viewed with the most intense suspicion by the radicals who had led and carried out the overthrow of the monarchy. All the history and rhetoric of the past four years had insisted that such figures were agents of internal subversion, and that it was down amongst the dregs of society, in the prisons, that they were most likely to find the rank and file of their brigand armies.

Such fears were fanned by the general situation, which did not get better as August wore on. Austro-Prussian military forces pushed on into eastern France, subduing fortresses methodically, and nearing the point at which the road to Paris would be open to them. The tone of the messages put out by the Provisional Executive Council was grim, as this example from 25 August shows: 'Our enemies prepare the last blows of their insane rage ... they wish to open a route to Paris, they may succeed.' The Interior Ministry was even more alarmist, noting that the French 'should expect the cruellest vengeance if they weaken before the atrocious men who have meditated this revenge for so long', and that 'Every measure of preservation is good in the extreme crisis of our danger'. The press went a stage further, the *People's Orator* observing that 'The first battle we shall offer will take place within the walls of Paris, and not outside. All the royal brigands that this unhappy city shelters shall perish in one day.'[25] In so doing it echoed rumours that had been in circulation since 10 August that unspecified popular radical forces planned to do away with the enemies in the prisons.

On 2 September, as news of the hopeless position of besieged Verdun, the last fortress before Paris, ran through the city, action was taken. Within five days, around half the entire prison population, some 1500 people in all, had been executed in the September Massacres, an episode which set the seal on the shattering transformation of the summer. Almost as they were happening, accounts of these events were set down – to be added to by a growing chorus in the following months and years – all of which enshrined the massacres as a moment of uncontrolled popular bloodlust, in which furious gangs of sword- and axe-wielding ruffians were unleashed on innocents by shadowy radical leaders, and where any and all imaginable sadistic tortures were used in the dispatch of their helpless victims. The episode was held up again and again as a crowning revelatory example of the bestial forces unleashed by popular revolutionary fury.

It is easy to show the unreality of these perceptions. Although the precise identities of the *septembriseurs* who carried out the killings were obscured by later claims and counter-claims, it is probable that they were activists of the sectional *sans-culotte* movement, and equally probable that large sectors of the local and national political leadership knew something of what was to happen – and certainly did little to stop it by force once it had begun.[26] It is also clear that the *septembriseurs* were neither indiscriminate butchers nor sadistic torturers. In the incident with the highest proportion of deaths, when chain-gang prisoners were the victims, only three of the seventy-five prisoners were spared – but nonetheless, three were spared. At the other end of the scale, when killers visited the Salpêtrière women's prison, only thirty-seven of some 270 inmates were executed, and even these victims were fewer than half of the branded felons singled out for judgement. At the temporary prison of the Abbaye Saint-Germain-des-Près, some 250 of the 450 priests, nobles, officials and others held there were spared, and anywhere between a quarter and two-thirds of those held in half a dozen other centres were likewise released, or sometimes even held elsewhere in protective custody until the events ended. Impartial justice was clearly not on the agenda – career criminals and forgers were singled out as 'brigands' for summary judgement, as the killers identified those presumed to represent the rank and file of counter-revolution. Nevertheless, records were scrutinised everywhere, and tribunals were improvised in many of the prisons to hear prisoners' attempts at self-justification. In well over 40 per cent of cases, such pleas were successful.

For the less fortunate, punishment was immediate and bloody. With firearms needed at the front and ammunition in short supply, swords, pikes and axes were turned on the victims, usually by a gauntlet of killers directly outside the room where the cases were heard. What followed was butchery, but it was almost certainly quicker than any of the Old Regime's favoured modes of execution. Nevertheless, it is this element which contributed most to the 'black legend' of the massacres. The princesse de Lamballe, most notoriously, was reported as being subject to revolting sexual mutilations after her death, with her naked and eviscerated corpse paraded through the streets and her severed head taken to 'greet' Marie-Antoinette in the Temple. Every genre from private letters to academic painting recorded stages of this legendary demise, but legendary it was, because her clothed body was actually held discreetly by the local authorities until collected by members of her household. Its severed head very probably was paraded to the Temple, but such acts were part of the established repertoire of execution.[27]

The violence of Paris, if unequalled in magnitude, was mirrored everywhere from the great cities to the villages. Radicals in Marseille had already lynched a number of counter-revolutionaries as early as July, and four more died in September. The city established an unofficial popular tribunal to judge the region's suspects, and its militants seized control of the department administration, based in Aix, and transferred the arrested personnel under armed guard to the port. In Lyon on 9 September, crowds stormed the prisons, killing three non-jurors and eight military officers held for links to the émigrés. The largest number of deaths outside Paris came on that same day in Versailles, when a National Guard escort brought into the town a group of counter-revolutionary suspects formerly held for trial in Orléans. The escort had instructions from the national authorities to move this group to Saumur, for their own safety, but passed through Versailles on their own initiative. An alert having gone out to neighbouring communities, peasants and townsmen set on it as the convoy left town, killing fifty of the fifty-three prisoners.

In many areas, action against counter-revolutionaries was mixed with the enthusiasm of volunteers gathering to march to war. In the Orne department, a noble and eight priests were killed in the course of such gatherings in six separate centres between 15 August and 10 September. In Reims, news of the fall of Verdun caused a two-day uprising on 3–4 September that claimed the lives of two 'suspect' local officials, six priests and a noble. Rural and urban volunteers for the front were again at the heart of this, as they were in the Aisne, at Coucy, where around a thousand gathered from surrounding villages to enrol and put to the sack two houses of a notable local 'suspect', who fled with his life. There were in total over sixty separate fatal incidents across France in this wave of popular unrest, retribution, justice, or preventative measures – and it was in this latter sense that many participants clearly viewed the killings. Added to them was continued unrest against the properties of the elite and against feudal exactions. This took place, to a greater or lesser extent, in some seventeen departments during this critical period. In one of the more pointed juxtapositions, in the Jura, rural National Guards broke into the state office charged with administering the feudal rights of nationalised lands and burnt its records.[28]

Even the fervour of revolutionary war mobilisation could not prevent clashes with authority over what rural inhabitants regarded as their rightful liberation from oppression. That fervour, moreover, was not necessarily expressed everywhere, even when counter-revolution was entirely absent – many local authorities filled their quotas of volunteers slowly and with difficulty, often resorting to cash bounties (a standard sum was 80 livres for the infantry and 120 for cavalry). Some 'volunteers' emerged from community ballots, others were unhappy youths effectively blackmailed into leaving their villages after quarrels and misdemeanours.[29] Three-quarters of the 1792 recruits were under twenty-five, and a good number under eighteen. Their defining attribute was rural poverty, and their willingness to serve sharply delimited. The one-year term they had agreed to was interpreted by many to mean one summer's campaigning.

The violent episodes which formed the backdrop to this recruitment, and which helped to make the 'second revolution' of August–September 1792 so thoroughgoing, did little in the end to consolidate the new republican order. Amongst those who now came to power, there were many whose concern for their own lives and property caused them to look in horror at the September Massacres. This sentiment was allied to the conviction, held by the beleaguered Girondins in Paris and more widely amongst the political class of a number of other centres, that radical Jacobins were indeed 'anarchists'. Their intention to destroy the national Girondin leadership was widely assumed, and their followers might be expected to try the same locally. In Lyon, where radicals had long seized control of the central club, and where the municipality was closely linked to the Girondin minister Roland, an extensive outbreak of *taxation populaire* following on from the anti-aristocratic attacks of early September led to a breakdown in local authority. Orders from Paris to hold new elections a month early, in October, produced a council dominated by extreme radicals, many of whom originated in the artisan classes. For the richer and more moderate citizens, this seizure of power seemed part and parcel of an ongoing anarchist conspiracy and further entrenched social conflict in the city.

Revolutionary commitment amongst the bulk of the population was a difficult asset to manage effectively, and hesitant and self-contradictory moves by the legislature over issues affecting peasants' lives produced further protest in the autumn and winter of 1792–93, even as the Revolution's armies turned the tide of defeat into victory. Following petitions presented to them after 10 August, the Legislative Assembly, in one of its last definitive acts, had struck down all feudal dues for which the seigneur could not provide the 'original title'. This was a real victory for the thousands of peasant communities who had never ceased to petition the authorities over this issue, as well as a mark of the force of their more physically expressed demands. Nevertheless, it was an incomplete victory, for two reasons. Firstly, the Assembly yet again allowed landowners to increase their rents by the value of such abolished dues.[30] Meanwhile, and secondly, many well-attested 'original titles' to feudal rights had survived peasant bonfires, and the authorities themselves continued to collect payment for rights owned by the church (and hence now by the state) and other defunct bodies. At Bordeaux, for example, revenues were collected on a considerable feudal holding accrued by the Old Regime city corporation in its hinterland. Many individual seigneurs may now have been afraid to take action, but state administrators were less hesitant about pursuing rural communities and individuals for payments due until a further measure of complete abolition in July 1793. Moreover, individual bourgeois proprietors who had invested in the 'infeudated tithe' of the church, which was abolished outright in August 1792, would feel aggrieved enough to petition (albeit unsuccessfully) for redress. The sacred rights of private property were still a force in the political culture, even if the national authorities had partially yielded in practice.

In the final two months of the year there were again, as in 1791, serious outbreaks of *taxation populaire* in the socially polarised grain-growing lands to the south of Paris. In the middle of this, on 8 December, the Interior Ministry attempted again to deregulate the market for grain. The scorn this implied for popular views was clear again in the deaf ear that the authorities turned to a wave of petitions for division of commons, or *partage*, in late 1792. The Convention had suspended on 11 October a sketchy decree allowing for the division of common lands the Legislative Assembly had passed on 14 August, but a measure of 28 August, which allowed for the revocation of any and all seigneurial land seizures that had occurred since 1667 (the date of the original enabling legislation), was still theoretically operative. Disputes over demands for the enforcement of both these measures was to culminate in a law of 18 March 1793, imposing the death penalty for advocating the *loi agraire* or 'agrarian law' – a classical Roman tag for the enforced egalitarian redistribution of land.[31]

This draconian measure had become necessary, in the eyes of the Convention, because peasant demand for such a redistribution was threatening the fabric of society. In the previous months, individual activists had begun touring the villages of Picardy and the Paris Basin urging communities to rise up and seize all land, so often in this region held in large farms growing grain for the cities. Reversion to peasant subsistence farming would be a demographic and a military calamity, notwithstanding the challenge it posed to the still inviolable principle of private property. Nevertheless, the view from below was different, and petitions to the Convention from various parts of France in the wake of the legislative about-turns of the autumn made some brutally clear points about the social order. One commune in the Gard expressed what was a common view:

> Royalty, clergy and nobility have been abolished for ever, but the great landed proprietors remain to be destroyed, for it is in this very moment that they bear down with their full weight upon the poor inhabitants of the countryside.[32]

A notary from a village in the Somme indicted the 'rich class who have seen with pleasure the former nobles become their equals, [but] who have not admitted those unfortunates below them as equals'. From the Haute-Garonne came the accusation that 'the Constituent and Legislative Assemblies have done nothing' to help the poor; 'they have been preoccupied only with property-owners'. Petitions and correspondence of this kind also made use of an abusive vocabulary, once confined to the agents of counter-revolution, but now increasingly commonplace in a wider range of conflicts. Like the nobles and priests before them, rich proprietors were condemned as 'tyrants' and 'despots', 'agents of the aristocrats', 'vultures' and 'vampires thirsting for human blood'. *Sangsue*, 'leech', was another common denunciation. Their economic actions in husbanding their own resources and selling at a profit became 'speculation' and 'hoarding', which in their alliterative originals, *agiotage et accaparement*, became staple charges in the social conflict and disorder of the following year – in the cities and the countryside.

It is important to note that the *partage* agitation actually produced no large-scale risings. There were hundreds of small-scale episodes of illegal invasion and subdivision of commons, along with the illegal opening-up of previously enclosed lands and the reversal of alleged seigneurial seizures on dubious grounds of recollection. Such conflicts could be long drawn out and occasionally violent: in the commune of Tuchan in the eastern Pyrenees two municipal officers were stoned, one fatally, as they tried to intervene in a scuffle caused by one such extended grievance over the commons back in November 1791. In this region, the main dispute was over the ongoing peasant 'pillage' of formerly seigneurial and now communal forested lands, stripped of their produce for firewood, charcoal and other industrial products. By 1792, small detachments of troops were being shuffled from village to village in this region by the departmental authorities in a vain attempt to maintain order and respect for property.[33]

Episodes such as this show the deep-seated bitterness of many rural antagonisms. At the same time, for all the grief they caused, the vast majority provoked no specific alarm outside their own communal boundaries and brought about no institutional change. Pressure for the more formal division of common lands was in fact a regional phenomenon, confined to the north-eastern quarter of France, with only two exceptional patches elsewhere: the Lot and Haute-Garonne in the south west, and the Drôme and Gard in the south east. Likewise, agitation over the concentrated ownership of land, although extending in various forms to some twenty-five departments, was almost entirely confined to a quadrilateral with Paris at its centre and Lille, Cherbourg, Dijon and the Indre department at its corners. Although the Parisian region was at the heart of both agitations, it never succeeded in raising the same momentum of revolt as did the forces of urban politics, religion and counter-revolution elsewhere.

A central reason for this was that in most localities the property-owners held the levers of power. Only in a few dozen or hundred communes did the poorer peasantry and their sympathisers establish sufficient political dominance to threaten real change. Occasionally, as in the commune of Givry-sur-Aisne in the Ardennes in December 1792, such groups succeeded in ejecting old municipal officials to insert others with a more *partageux* attitude.[34] In far more localities, however, those owning or leasing enough property to have at least some concern for stability were in the majority. They were quite able if necessary to stall demands for radical change, or to point the way to action against the now-powerless seigneur for the reclamation of seized lands. This was by far the most popular option, with thousands of individual cases launched. A second, and equally important, reason was that large-scale disruption, especially of the commons system, was seldom in the interests even of poorer villagers. Customary conceptions of property, based on communal deliberation and the distribution of usage rights to commons, still had more meaning for many than the chance to own what might be a small plot of land outright. Many peasants had a pragmatic recognition that village commons were often little use for much beyond rough grazing and forage – this was especially true in the drier uplands of the south, helping to explain the lack of agitation there, though thickly wooded or boggy ground in the damp north could be equally worthless.

In some senses, the death penalty decreed against advocates of the *loi agraire* can be seen as disproportionate, but it came in the context of a series of crises and agitations in which deadly force was rapidly becoming the authorities' only resource, and at times close to being their first resort. The authorities, both at the centre and in particular localities, had profoundly ambivalent attitudes to the revolutionary engagement of ordinary peasants and townspeople. The persistence of such attitudes through the winter of 1792–93 led France closer to a state of civil war – a state which would then reinforce those same prejudices.

10

The Year of Civil War

Having executed the king, and launched an aggressive wave of new hostilities, the French Republic was faced by the early spring of 1793 with a catastrophic collapse in both its external and internal fortunes. Military disaster at Neerwinden struck as the administration of France was being plunged into further chaos, much of which continued to revolve around ordinary citizens' relations to authority. Within the capital, agitation over food prices led some sections to demand strict new controls in mid February, and lack of action on such issues helped to prompt a wave of *taxation populaire* at the end of the month. Prices of sugar and soap in particular had inflated to more than double their 1790 levels, with other items up by 20 per cent or more. The response was on an even larger scale than that of a year earlier, embracing almost every quarter of the city, with basic goods of all kinds being seized. Shopkeepers reported that sometimes as much as 30 to 40 per cent of the full price was paid, but more often a mere tenth or nothing at all. Arrested participants, against whom the authorities took action despite the occasional resistance of their own National Guards, constituted a cross-section of the working population, with dozens of detainees ranging from artisans and shopkeepers to labourers, servants, water-carriers and market-women. Just as a year earlier, the revolutionary leadership condemned this, the radical idol Robespierre speaking later of such crowds being not 'the people of Paris', but 'a mob of women, led by valets of the aristocracy'. Bertrand Barère, a moderate who would progress leftwards over the next year, spoke in the Convention of 'the perfidious incitement of aristocrats in disguise', and noted that 'where I see no respect for property, there I can no longer recognise any social order'.[1] Yet again aristocrats and brigands were invoked to explain popular actions that disturbed authority – even as that authority claimed to act in the most radical fashion on behalf of the people.

Meanwhile, as the Republic struggled to feed its people, it was also struggling to man its armies for a war with all the powers of Europe. The volunteers of 1791 and 1792 had been called up under the proviso of one season's service. If many had stayed on this long, many had also been released, haemorrhaging the country's military strength at a critical moment. The army now counted some 350,000 effectives, double the pre-revolutionary total, but far fewer than it needed to wage war on every frontier. On 21 February, the Convention decreed that all military forces would begin to be amalgamated, breaking down the distinction between line and volunteer units by brigading them together. On 24 February it took a more radical step, and ordered departments and districts to raise their share of a new call-up of 300,000 men to fill the ranks. The concept of volunteering was retained in this new levy, but it was made clear that other methods would be resorted to in order to meet the quota, including compulsion by drawing of lots or by ballot.[2]

The Convention was entirely unprepared for the hostility that the measure engendered. Although much of the north, north east and south east succeeded in raising most of the required numbers without great difficulty, it was rare enough to be noteworthy when this was done entirely with volunteers; or when, as in the Haute-Saône and the Doubs departments, volunteers of 1791 agreed to return to the colours. In many places, a sullen acceptance of the urgent situation, and of the coercive power of authority, was more apparent than patriotic enthusiasm, even in a successful levy. By 9 March the situation in a number of regions was so evidently problematic that the Convention dispatched special commissioners from its own ranks to rally support for the military effort. The levy eventually raised perhaps half the men it had set out to find, but it set off a chain of events far more destabilising than a mere manpower shortage.

There were understandable grievances behind much of the discontent. All unmarried men aged forty or below were eligible as potential recruits, but unmarried National Guards and public officials were exempted: it seemed to many as if the class of propertied activists who had done best from the Revolution were avoiding the need to defend it. In the town of Beaune, near Dijon, the eligible men gathered and demanded that public officials, purchasers of *biens nationaux* and members of the local Jacobin club should be the first to be selected. Other nearby towns made similar demands, and at Semur-en-Auxois the ballot was used to nominate the sons of the town's wealthy elite for service. At one centre near Lyon, the young men gathered under arms and voted for the constitutional priest and fourteen other local radicals to fill their quota – a problem which elsewhere led to newly arrived commissioners insisting on the less easily manipulated recruitment by lottery.[3]

Further to the south, many selected for service from individual villages disappeared into the hills, often with the backing of their families, the start of a tradition of *insoumission* that became a major drain on the Revolution's resources in later years. In the Aveyron there was more direct opposition. A riot of potential conscripts in Rodez on 17 March left the mayor wounded and one rioter dead, and on the eastern fringes of the department more serious troubles saw several thousand insurgents threaten the local centre, only to be driven off by troops and artillery, with eighteen dead and a further twenty executions. This movement had been in part fomented by an emissary for a royalist conspiracy centred in the neighbouring Lozère, which burst briefly into life in May but was crushed by coordinated military action and arrests. Such events were made to seem mere skirmishes, however, by the crisis looming in the west.

The whole of France west and north of Poitiers, covering parts of at least twelve departments, saw violent protest wherever that recruitment was attempted. The Breton peasantry rose up, especially in the Morbihan and Ille-et-Vilaine, threatening over half a dozen district capitals, and even the major city of Rennes. National Guard mobilisation by the region's pro-revolutionary towns and cities took several weeks to bring the situation under control, after several major skirmishes and cannonades. Military patrols continued through the spring, and over fifty captured rebels were tried and executed, but the local authorities were sufficiently confident to attempt the recruitment process again in April and to complete it without undue disturbance.

Such confidence proved to be misplaced. Rural Breton popular attitudes were now firmly anti-revolutionary. One speaker in the town of Champeaux in the Ille-et-Vilaine summed up the views of many: 'We shouldn't pay taxes any more; since there is no more king, there are no more laws ... The nation is fucked, and all the laws it made are only good to be fucked.'[4] Those who had marched on the district capitals had openly sought the restoration of religion, the abolition of the hated bourgeois-dominated local authorities, and a royal restoration as well – which implied the return of their provincial privileges. Many had begun their protests by stripping out revolutionary and republican symbols from their localities – uprooting 'liberty trees' and ripping tricolour cockades from patriots' hats. All that was 'national' was to be banished from the community, and some patriots had been forced to take an oath 'No longer to be national'. From this point onwards, the guerrilla *Chouannerie* that had begun in a few isolated places at the end of the previous year swelled to a regional movement that would make normal political activity impossible.

It was to the south of Brittany, however, below the line of the Loire, that resistance to recruitment immediately became a more overt war against the Revolution.[5] A region covering the southern half of the Loire-Inférieure, the south-western corner of the Maine-et-Loire, the north-western sector of the Deux-Sèvres, and three-quarters of the Vendée burst into open insurrection almost as soon as word of the levy reached them. As early as

3 March, the town of Cholet had heard cries for the National Guard 'bluecoats', a description which in this region designated all partisans of the Republic, to be the ones to leave for the war, and for the administrators of district and department to take the lead. It took little more than a week for such feelings, coupled with underlying long-term hostility to the revolutionary intruders, to gather into forceful action. Armed bands of peasants seized the strategic Loire crossing at St-Florent-le-Vieil on 12 March, and pillaged patriots' houses and the offices of the district administration, publicly burning all its papers.

Leaders of this nascent force were appointed the next day, and on the 14th the rebels overran Cholet, the most significant centre in the disturbed region. A gamekeeper and former soldier named Stofflet led around ten thousand rebels, who crushed opposition, leaving three hundred dead and injured. The explosive momentum of the rebellion was checked shortly after by a failure to seize Saumur, but an initial attempt to move government troops into the heart of the rebel area was repulsed at Pont-Charrault in the Vendée on 19 March, and a civil war was born. Other local towns fell to the rebels in the course of the month, although they failed to gain control of the port of Sables-d'Olonne, cutting themselves off from seaborne aid.

The bald narrative of military events, however, disguises the real nature of this rising. Massacre and revenge killings were on the agenda from the start. One of the fiercest episodes came at Machecoul, a district capital in the Loire-Inférieure with some four thousand inhabitants.[6] The town was overrun by peasant bands numbering more than a thousand on 11 March, and the local constitutional priest and a National Guard lieutenant were amongst those killed at once – the priest's body being mutilated. Around twenty republicans died that day, and more the next, while a broad sweep of over a hundred soldiers, National Guards and officials from the town and its neighbouring communities were taken captive. This initial massacre was part of a wider pattern – in at least half a dozen other centres, twenty or thirty of the leading local republicans were executed out of hand when the rebels gained control.

Events in Machecoul then went a stage further. In the following days, the insurgent forces in the town swelled to some six thousand, and those republicans and their families who were still free began to escape to Nantes and other 'blue' strongholds. In such places, when news arrived, especially of the defeat of 19 March, many counter-revolutionary suspects were rounded up, and there were further massacres by republicans: in La Rochelle, six priests were hacked to death and their heads and other body-parts paraded through the city. Meanwhile, the forces gathered at Machecoul seized the neighbouring town of Pornic on 23 March, but were surprised by republican forces after celebrating their victory with looted wine. Some two to three hundred were killed, not all during the fighting. When the survivors got back to Machecoul, they began to take the detained republicans out in batches and shoot them, a long drawn out process over the next week, with a few further killings as late as mid April. Some 150 were executed in the town overall, with republican reports putting the figure at five hundred, with tales of brutality which, in a few cases, may have been true. The rebels were demonised for such acts, but the underlying complexity of events is hinted at by the survival of twenty-two 'blues' from the parish of Bouin, saved from execution at the request of their own insurgent neighbours. A handful of others were even cleared by the tribunal set up by the rebels to preside over the executions.

There is no doubt that the Revolution's interference in the religious life of this region had been deeply significant in preparing the ground for such violent dissent, which was rapidly christened the 'Vendean Revolt'. Many of the local population would have been hard put to itemise any concrete personal gains for themselves since the initial risings of 1789, and there was entrenched hostility to department and district authorities, chosen by the bourgeois-dominated electoral assemblies and overtly hostile to peasant desires. As recently as the late summer of 1792, many such authorities had turned the direct force of the National Guard on recalcitrant rural communities. Although the rebels are easiest to characterise as 'peasants', we should note that perhaps over a third of their rank and file was made up of rural artisans and proto-industrial textile workers – it was not so much their mode of economic existence as the whole culture of their communities that put them at odds with revolutionary authority.[7]

Clergy and local seigneurs were willing and able to blame the Revolution for damaging interference in local ways of life, and to call for the return of church and king to their earlier eminence, adding fuel to the fire. By May the rebellion had consolidated as a 'Royal and Catholic Army', but each step in that direction only hardened the resolve of the Convention to crush the rebellion. As early as 19 March (a day after its measure against the *loi agraire*, and with news of the Neerwinden defeat just arrived, but before news of events such as Pont-Charrault and Machecoul), the Convention voted for the death penalty without appeal for all rebels captured under arms.

Even in peaceful areas of the country, the active presence of the Convention's commissioners had a profound impact on local political life. Two of these, Chabot and Bo, led a sweep through the rural departments of the Aveyron and Tarn that was amongst the more vigorous, but it was not entirely exceptional. In the month of April alone, they appointed special

delegates and local commissioners to oversee recruitment and disarm suspects, ordered the forced collection of a war tax from aristocrats and wealthy
moderates, annulled many local elections, and purged all local bodies of
unreliable members. Such 'incivic' citizens were deprived of their political
rights, and the National Guard was reorganised, with an additional military
force raised to pursue non-juror priests and émigrés. New surveillance
committees were filled with suitably reliable patriots. By the end of the
month, suspects were being held as hostages in district capitals, lists of
charges were being compiled for Parisian scrutiny, and house to house
searches had been authorised wherever necessary. The local framework of
political life was overturned by the snap decisions and sweeping initiatives
of the Convention's agents, often with no more than a cursory appreciation
of the real situation on the ground. They believed they were bringing 'the
people' to the fore, but the future was to show that to be a problematic
assumption. Moreover, although special powers had been granted to the
commissioners, there were grave doubts amongst many Girondins as to the
legality of such deeds, and also about their political implications, carried
out as they were by a largely radical cohort.[8] Concerns such as these were
fuel for a rising spiral of political infighting in the Convention.

As the Vendean rebels became an ever-larger threat, the Convention also
found itself beset from within and outside by political rivalries and over
social and economic demands. The journalist and *conventionnel* Marat had
rehearsed some of the key points in his new *Journal of the French Republic*
on 25 February:

> It is incontestable that the capitalists, the speculators, the monopolists, the luxury
> merchants, the instruments of chicanery, the old judges, the ex-nobles, etc., are
> all, more or less, instruments of the Old Regime, who miss the abuses that they
> profited from to enrich themselves from the public spoils ... I see that only the
> total destruction of this cursed breed can bring tranquillity to the state ... Today
> they redouble their zeal to desolate the people through the exorbitant rise in
> prices of goods of the first necessity, and the fear of famine.[9]

Language like this undoubtedly had a role in provoking the 'dangerous'
taxation populaire which followed it immediately, but Marat's role in this
was played down by his radical colleagues, as he was a valuable figurehead
in a more overtly political struggle. Marat spoke for the Jacobin Montagnards
or 'Mountain', a nickname derived from the radicals' habit of sitting high
on the Convention's tiered benches, and also an emblem of their independence and austerity. He also spoke at this point for many in the sectional
movement of the capital, and against the Girondins, whom his rhetoric
associated explicitly with the 'capitalists' and other profiteers of revolution.

Open conflict burst on to the streets of Paris on 9 and 10 March, when crowds smashed the printing presses of pro-Girondin journals, and unsuccessfully attempted to coordinate a more thoroughgoing attack on the political leadership. Within the sectional movement itself, the near unanimity of the overthrow of the monarchy had progressively broken down, and *sans-culotte* and 'moderate' sections were at odds. The spring of 1793 saw overt intimidation brought to bear in many section assemblies, with 'fraternal' delegations from more radical sections arriving to install committees with the appropriate political views. The political fashion of the year was for votes by acclamation, with a careful eye kept on those who might try to dissent.[10] The assertion that the organised 'popular movement' of the *sans-culotte* sections represented (or just was) 'the people' was imposed on Parisian politics by brute force.

Within the Convention the Girondins were at bay. In their view, recent events confirmed what they had proclaimed since September, that Parisian anarchists were trying to destroy the Revolution from within for personal gain, perhaps bribed by the counter-revolution. On 13 March one leading Girondin, Vergniaud, spoke out in the Convention to denounce the plotters behind the recent riots, expressing the view shared with his fellows that the real people of France were

> divided into two classes, of which one, delirious in the excess of exaltation to which it has been carried, works each day towards its own ruin; and the other, struck by stupor, drags out a troubled existence, in the anguish of terrors that no longer have an end.[11]

But circumstances continued to conspire against the Girondin perspective. At the end of March, General Dumouriez, who had been war minister in a Girondin government the previous year, crowned his failure on the northern front by denouncing the authority of the Convention and trying to lead his troops against it. A few days later, on 1 April, he captured and handed to the enemy the current war minister and four members of the Convention who had gone to arrest him. On 5 April, he fled to the Austrian lines.

In the face of such treachery, the Montagnards stepped up their anti-Girondin campaign, Marat calling on Jacobin clubs to denounce and recall all Convention deputies who had voted for the Girondins' attempted referendum on the king's fate in January. For this act, the Girondins succeeded in impeaching Marat before the newly established Revolutionary Tribunal, but it acquitted him on 24 April. The initial impeachment had prompted three-quarters of the Parisian sections to protest, and to demand that twenty-two Girondin leaders be themselves expelled from the Convention.

The acquitted Marat was carried in triumph from the Tribunal to resume his seat in the Convention, and the radical agenda was carried further on 4 May by the passage of a 'Maximum on Grains' – formal price restrictions on grain, flour and bread. On 18 May, however, political initiative in the Convention seesawed again, reflecting the fact that committed Montagnards and Girondins together formed a minority amongst its members, and the majority could be swayed either way by rhetoric or external alarms. On this occasion the Girondins drove through the formation of a 'Commission of Twelve' within the Convention to investigate subversive acts by the Paris Commune and the sections.

The Commune, Paris's municipal government, had indeed been a hotbed of radicalism since the fall of the monarchy. The journalist Hébert, author of the most staunchly radical and popular of the *Père Duchesne* papers, held ideological sway from his post as deputy prosecutor, and his allies filled many other senior posts. Hébert and two others were arrested by the Twelve on 24 May. Petitioners for their release were rebuffed by the Girondin Isnard from the chair of the Convention the next day with a dire warning: if order was not restored to the streets, 'Paris will be destroyed ... Soon one will search the banks of the Seine for a sign that Paris existed.'[12] With this echo of the Brunswick Manifesto, open political warfare was declared. By 29 May radical leaders had formed a Central Revolutionary Committee at the Commune to plan the Girondins' overthrow, and two days later a massive Parisian demonstration succeeded in winning the abolition of the Twelve, though not the expulsion of the Girondins. On 2 June this aim was realised through a more coordinated offensive, with military forces from the sections surrounding the Tuileries. After a tense stand-off, in which even some of the more radical leaders quailed at what was under way, the Convention yielded, and twenty-nine Girondin members were expelled and placed under house arrest, along with two ministers.[13]

On the surface this was a victory of the Parisian people (though clearly a misled, or indeed vicious, people, according to their critics). Indeed, it bore out what many provincial critics had been saying since the events of 20 June 1792, that the national representation was not safe in Paris. The Paris Commune had called on the sections to raise special battalions of *sans-culottes* to supplement the National Guard for the insurrection, and the call had been answered vigorously – records survive of over 22,000 claims for special payments for workers who had lost earnings as a result of participation, with some sections in the Faubourg Saint-Antoine recording over two thousand names each.[14] The hornets' nest of internal social and political division had once again been stirred.

To make matters worse, as the Montagnards had been consolidating their links with the Parisian local authorities, they had also been engaging with radicals across the country, stirring discontent in populations fearful of the anarchic implications of such an association. In Marseille, for example, the local Jacobins had been extremely active, in liaison with commissioners sent from the Convention, in purging the administrations in neighbouring towns and generally pursuing suspected counter-revolutionaries. But this behaviour was too close to home for many of the Marseillais. Many of those purged were less visibly guilty of royalism than of being rich, or of having antagonised some newly self-appointed popular tribune. There was an increasing fear that local Jacobins were combining with unknown outsiders, and possibly with anarchist brigands, to make war on property. A petition to the Convention with no fewer than 25,000 signatories made just this point on 25 May. Even local activists who had been ardent revolutionaries, and supporters of the Jacobins in disputes with the Girondins as late as February 1793, were becoming disillusioned, and the propertied were taking refuge in sectional assemblies to voice their grievances. Something very similar was happening in Lyon, except here the Jacobins were in charge of the municipality, and in control of the regular army garrison. Furious rhetoric and a growing climate of suspicion of property itself – dwelling on the political lassitude of the Lyonnais propertied classes in the past two years – drew the latter group back into an active concern for the city's future, as at Marseille, finding a voice in sectional organisation.[15]

It has been tempting for many years to depict these events in Lyon and Marseille, and to a lesser degree elsewhere, as a take-over of those cities' sections by a social elite, while seeing in Paris the example of a sectional movement genuinely dedicated to popular ends. There were undoubted social antagonisms at play on all sides of the provincial and national political divides, but it is not clear that a popular rank and file wholly committed to the radical side was to be found anywhere. The sectional movement in Lyon rose up on 29 May, at least partially in response to word that the Jacobin municipality had called for major military reinforcements, and in anticipation of the purge that would follow their arrival. It did so in significant strength, mobilising the city's National Guard, which itself had been 'democratised' since the fall of the monarchy. There was open battle for two hours around the Hôtel de Ville that afternoon, with sniping, cannon fire from the Jacobin side, and several dozen casualties. Two Convention members who had been sent to support the municipality were besieged by crowds in the fortified arsenal overnight until they agreed to endorse the actions of the insurgents.

The role of Convention representatives in Marseille had been even more inflammatory, having early in May attempted to suppress the growing sectional agitation, explicitly branding it as counter-revolutionary. In response, the sections declared that they were rising up in the name of resistance to oppression as proclaimed in the Rights of Man, and had effectively taken over the running of the city through a central general committee by 9 May. A purge of leading Jacobin club members on the night of 18–19 May, when some twenty were arrested and others fled to the capital, consolidated opposition. Repeating the pattern of previous waves of activity, the city sent emissaries to the towns of the department, their reports often speaking of the 'liberation' of these places from the grip of small cliques of dangerous men put in place by the club and the representatives.

Events in Marseille were welcomed by the authorities in the department of the Gard, which continued to suffer the effects of its deep-seated social antagonisms. Here the elite mercantile membership of the Nîmes Society of Friends of the Constitution had been at odds with the more radical members of a second club, the Popular Society of Friends of the Constitution. The former had seen its partisans placed in positions of authority at departmental level through 1792–93, while the latter had campaigned vigorously for action over the economic plight of the weavers and peasants of the region – such independent master-workers making up the core of its membership. The latter society had made the running in sending troops to the federated gathering of 1792 in Paris that took part in the fall of the monarchy, and in coordinating popular societies into a network across the region. Their rhetorical war against the alleged Girondins of the department administration had grown in intensity, while these leaders maintained control of the sections of Nîmes, and brought them into daily session on 20 May 1793. The Nîmes popular society was closed down on 11 June, when news of the Parisian rising reached the area.[16]

Trying to understand the social dynamics of this period can lead into an abyss of complexity. It is clear, for example, that men of property in Lyon, Marseille and Nîmes, and other centres such as Bordeaux, viewed the direction of events of that spring in Paris as a threat to property and social order, and that such men came to the fore in leading anti-Jacobin activity that would shortly receive the label of 'Federalism' (thus tainting with counter-revolution a word with hitherto positive attributes of unity). Their rhetoric combined condemnation of anarchism, Maratism and the *loi agraire* effortlessly into a picture of politically motivated seditious disruption from below, in which the propertyless of all kinds were inherently suspect. It is equally clear, however, that in the centres where most effective resistance to Montagnard control was mounted, major sectors of the population were mobilised against local Jacobins and then against national forces. Lyon fell to the armies of the Republic on 9 October, after a nine-week siege – but such resistance was unthinkable without the support of several thousand of the city's inhabitants in arms, and the acquiescence of many more.

This popular element in anti-Jacobin resistance is counterpointed by clear signs of a divide between the radical leadership and elements of their Parisian rank and file after the fall of the Girondins. The origins of this went back to the struggles of February, when spontaneous popular action for economic goals had attracted damning criticism from Montagnard elites. A small group of journalists and activists continued to agitate over such issues, including a 'red priest', Jacques Roux, and a group of advanced feminists called the Society of Revolutionary Republican Women – the last word in French, *Citoyennes*, being the untranslatable feminine version of 'citizen'. This latter group, which was formed officially in early May 1793, seems to have split off from the long-established 'Fraternal Society of the Two Sexes' at the Jacobins, being in some senses a paramilitary organisation. It took on a repertoire of symbols, including tricolour ensigns and the red cap of liberty, that almost added up to a uniform, and some of its members wore trousers and went armed with pistols and daggers. They numbered at least a hundred, and claimed the support of between 200 and 4000 sympathisers – the latter a definite exaggeration. The leading lights of the *Citoyennes* included Pauline Léon, a twenty-five-year-old *chocolatière* who had taken part in revolutionary demonstrations since at least 1791, and claimed to have fought in July 1789. She had certainly petitioned in early 1791, and again a year later, for the formation of a 'legion of women' to defend the nation, and had been involved in the turbulent demonstrations of Parisian radical politics throughout the period. Alongside her stood Claire 'Rose' Lacombe, an actress of some talent and renown, who had forsaken the stage since her arrival in Paris in 1792, putting her glamour to work as a symbolic heroine for the federated forces in Paris that summer, and her rhetorical talents into fiery speechmaking.[17]

Labelled by their more moderate opponents as *enragés*, or 'madmen', Roux, the *Citoyennes* and a few others picked up the rhetoric of Marat and tried to develop it into a programme. They were marginal to the actual course of events in the spring, although the role of individual orators in touching off collective action is unclear. Roux was a well-known figure on the council of the Commune, trusted with monitoring the detention of the king in late 1792, but he never managed to build a solid political following outside his own section, Gravilliers. The *Citoyennes* acquired a key place in Girondin rhetoric, being branded by Isnard as a 'regiment' formed for the 'iniquitous work' of stirring disorder as a prelude to massacre.[18] Parisian rumour, as reported by the Interior Ministry police, accorded them the same role, and their flamboyant appearance, bloodthirsty rhetoric and assiduous attendance in the public galleries of the Convention undoubtedly played on the anxieties of their political opponents. When it came to actual insurrection, however, they were sidelined by the more organised forces of mainstream radicalism.

The *enragés* were to become an increasing thorn in the side of authority, not least because by June one of the key concerns of the newly enthroned Montagnard supremacy was to restore the kind of social order that would reassure the nervous provincial elites. Assignats were plunging, trading at scarcely more than a third of their face value by this time, falling to less than a quarter over the rest of the summer. Mutterings on the streets of Paris had warned of more action against shopkeepers: sugar was now four times as costly as it had been in 1790, and butter almost double, with meat prices, for those who could afford them even in normal times, now almost 50 per cent up on the years of peace. In the face of the possible consequences of this, figures in the Paris Commune such as Hébert, who had been vociferous in opposition to the Girondins, now reined in their rhetoric as the Convention worked swiftly to draft a new constitution – work that had been deadlocked by the political clashes of the spring.

Putting the country on a constitutional footing was seen as the first step to quelling the Federalist charge of 'Parisian anarchy'. The offensive against intemperate radical and *enragé* demands that followed can be seen either as breathtaking hypocrisy or as a demonstration that the Montagnard leadership and its Parisian allies were in fact skilled politicians, manipulating the 'movement' below them towards strategic ends. Hébert's *Père Duchesne* railed against those who 'preach murder and carnage to us', and used the voice of an aged bourgeois in conversation with the *Père* to remark that 'I had thought you a man of faction, a disorganiser, I see to the contrary that you organise the Republic well, you *sans-culottes*, since you safeguard my property'. His character went on to claim that the rich should 'sansculottise themselves', or else foreign invasion would follow on the heels of internal dissent, 'and then what will become of my houses, my precious possessions?' [19] In this context, a continued campaign, led by Roux, to denounce hoarders and speculators, and to call for exemplary punishments and draconian measures of economic regulation, seemed dangerously counter-productive to the new masters of the Convention.

Roux and his associates, notably in the Cordeliers Club and the Gravilliers section, agitated continually over this issue, dominating a club session on 22 June with calls for a petition to the Convention, and a rising if their demands were not met: 'we need a tenth of August, the heads of the scoundrels must roll!' [20] Three days later, on the day set aside to celebrate the promulgation of the new constitution, Roux appeared before the

Convention at the head of a delegation from the club and the section. A lengthy speech began with a resounding summary of their complaint:

> Liberty is but a vain phantom when one class of men can starve another with impunity. Equality is but a vain phantom when the rich exercise the power of life and death over their fellows through monopolies. The Republic is but a vain phantom when the counter-revolution is accomplished daily through the price of provisions which three-quarters of the citizens cannot pay without shedding tears.[21]

In a condemnation of the political and economic laxity of the Convention, Roux effectively warned of another insurrection: 'it is only by putting foodstuffs within the reach of the *sans-culottes* that you will attach them to the Revolution ...'

Such a threat could no longer go unnoticed, especially when a sporadic wave of *taxation populaire* over the price of soap hit the Paris streets between 25 and 28 June. On 30 June Robespierre and Hébert joined forces to have Roux expelled from the Cordeliers. On the following day, the Commune passed a motion of censure, and on 4 July Marat himself inveighed in print against Roux and other 'false patriots'. A public argument between the two followed, and when Marat was assassinated by the Girondin sympathiser Charlotte Corday, on 13 July, Roux was rounded up for questioning. He remained at liberty for a further month, and produced a newspaper in the guise of 'the Shade of Marat' to attempt to redeem his reputation, but he was increasingly marginalised. Imprisoned in early September, Roux committed suicide the following February rather than face the public humiliation of a trial before the Revolutionary Tribunal as a counter-revolutionary.

A dedicated priest and ardent revolutionary, serving an inner-city parish with a population of over fifty thousand, many of whom lived in near destitution, Jacques Roux was perhaps too idealistic for the politics of the Jacobin Republic. Robespierre would go down in history as the high priest of revolutionary virtue, but he served his own purified version of 'the people', and in practical politics was a very sharp operator until his final weeks. Although, in the wider scheme of things, Roux's rhetoric was as bloodthirsty and intransigent as anything Robespierre was to utter, it clearly emerged from his efforts to serve the real people of the slums of Paris, and was sufficiently inconvenient to those who claimed to share his ideals to have him struck down. The ideological machine that was Jacobinism gathered strength as it fought a growing civil war, crushing, with less and less compunction all who stood in its way.

That machine, in addition to its major national features, such as the Revolutionary Tribunal and the representatives-on-mission, had begun to spread into every corner of the country (or at least, those that remained in contact with Paris). 'Surveillance committees' were formed in every individual commune and urban section, charged with issuing (and denying) the good-conduct certificates (*certificats de civisme*) that were increasingly essential for engagement in public life and for movement around the country. This measure itself helped to reinforce the sense of mass mobilisation amongst the population. To staff such committees involved finding as many men as the military levy of the spring, drawing yet more ordinary peasants and artisans into the orbit of revolutionary administration.

The summer of 1793 saw a fundamental crisis in the survival of the Republic and the Revolution, with counter-revolutionary armies rampant in the west and south east, and enemy forces seeming to pour across every frontier. As it was now essential for the Montagnard leadership to reach out to the mass of the population for its support, their policy steadily swung towards further egalitarian measures. The struggle with the Girondins and their regional supporters had already shown that the rhetoric of a 'war on property', even if less clearly defined than some claimed, could rally supporters as well as opponents. It is clear that there was a line of agreement on a basically egalitarian, if property-owning, social structure between radical Jacobins, urban *sans-culottes* and a considerable portion of the rural population. That agreement proved rather hazy and fragmentary in practice, but it is noteworthy that amongst the first legislative acts of the 'purged' Convention in early June were decrees that ordered the sale of confiscated émigré lands in small plots and confirmed a procedure for the division of common lands – though this measure was ironically much more moderate in tone than that passed hastily in August 1792. To crown its alliance with the 'revolutionary' peasantry, the Convention declared the formal and final abolition of all feudal obligations without compensation on 17 July 1793, ordaining the public burning of title deeds – if many châteaux's registers had succumbed to peasant militancy, there were still sheaves of legal documents in notarial offices across the country that bound the peasantry to such dues. Even this measure, however, was not the unequivocal end of the feudal burden for all. In the Charente-Inférieure, for example, communities which had somehow missed out on the antiseigneurial message could still be found paying redemption-fees in September 1793, and elsewhere there were isolated cases of payment as late as January 1794.[22]

Such continuity may have something to do with the alarm that the 17 July law itself caused in the rural bourgeoisie, since it seemed to threaten the existence of any lease which included an element of feudal rights. In many regions, it had become customary in the late Old Regime to insert token or near-token amounts of such obligations into otherwise purely commercial

long-term leases, which were now potentially imperilled. Many local administrators quailed at these implications, to the extent that peasant
communities in some regions wrote to protest later in the summer about
their inaction. The Jacobin Convention grew increasingly unsympathetic to
such opposition. As the Federalist crisis progressed towards armed confrontation, there seemed little more to be gained from efforts to mollify wealthy
opinion. It is worth noting, however, that far less sympathy was shown to
short-term leaseholders, and the many varieties of sharecropper, who continued to protest at the addition of tithe and *taille* payments to their rents.
From the Gers in the south to the Yonne near Paris complaints and
sometimes violent protests emerged around the harvest from late July
onwards. This challenge from the entirely unpropertied, lacking any anti-
feudal resonance, was not so easily answered – except by silence.
Anti-feudalism gained another symbolic victory in early August, when the
Convention ordered its representatives-on-mission to demolish fortified
châteaux, both as an act of security against internal rebellion and as a blow
against the feudal order – but this was a 'victory' against the aristocrats,
not for the peasants.[23]

Meanwhile, continued agitation over prices and shortages in Paris produced their own political responses, with bitterly ironic timing in light
of the demonisation of the *enragés*. The closure of the stock exchange on
27 June was a largely symbolic measure against speculation, but a more
material law imposing the death penalty for hoarding was passed a month
later on 26 July. This empowered communes and sections to create further
commissioners with special powers of search and seizure – alongside the
surveillance committees, a further step to complete regulation of social and
economic life, and a new wave of public employment for those drawn to
the *sans-culotte* ideal. An abortive measure to establish public granaries in
every district on 9 August came amidst fresh waves of agitation, both about
spiralling prices and the increasingly desperate military situation.

As the summer wore on, with further critical news arriving from the
internal and external war fronts, the Jacobin and *sans-culotte* leadership
began unashamedly to lean towards the very actions they had denounced
the *enragés* for proposing a few weeks before. On 16 August, the Convention
agreed in principle to the Paris Commune's call for a universal conscript
army, while the Montagnard leadership began to look more favourably on
other aspects of ultra-radical demands. Dictatorial powers, although not in
the hands of one man, were put clearly on the agenda. On 10 August, during
the celebrations commemorating the fall of the monarchy, it had been
announced that a plebiscite had overwhelmingly ratified the new constitution published in June, but only days later suggestions in the Convention

that new elections should now be held were blocked by the Committee of Public Safety, citing the emergency situation.

At this point, Lyon had just been placed under siege. Although some minor Federalist centres had already fallen, Marseille remained in rebel hands until the end of the month, Bordeaux for a further five weeks, and the military port of Toulon, home to the Mediterranean fleet, for another four months – at the end of August came the crushing news that the rebels there had surrendered the fleet to the British. At Lyon and Toulon in particular, the Federalists proved the Montagnards' point by allying (partly at least out of desperation) with open counter-revolutionaries and foreign powers. It was all the proof anyone in Paris could need that the Republic's enemies were indeed all in concert against it, and that any deviation from the line of revolutionary rectitude led to aristocratic royalism, and all its immoral horrors.

Horror is an appropriate word for the summer of 1793, because it was at this point that the Republic began to unleash a truly merciless response on its enemies. Ironically, one trigger for this came from its adherence to the laws of war elsewhere. The large garrison of Mainz, which had yielded to siege in July, had surrendered on terms which forbade their use in combat against the Prussians and their allies. On 1 August the Convention decided to employ these same troops in the Vendée. It simultaneously, with these additional forces at its disposal, ordered a policy of devastation in the rebel areas, denying the enemy shelter and resources by destroying all dwellings and crops. All non-combatant women, children and old men were to be seized and deported from the rebel area; the rebels themselves, of course, were all under sentence of death. Proposals to depopulate the region had already been made by some speakers as early as June, and similar things would be said a few months later about Lyon.[24] Jacobin rhetoric, unable to cope with the concept of real principled resistance from ordinary workers and peasants, resorted increasingly to a language of 'contamination' and 'vice', and of a population either diseased or corrupted by 'aristocracy' and the 'fanaticism' of the priests.[25]

In response to the desperation of the national situation, truly unprecedented measures were now called for by the leadership of the Convention. On 23 August it decreed a mass levy (*levée en masse*), which in its first article managed both to prefigure the mass warfare of the twentieth century and hark back to picturesque legends of ancient Rome:

Henceforth, until the enemies have been driven from the territory of the Republic, the French people are in permanent requisition for military service. The young men shall go to battle; the married men shall forge arms and transport provisions;

the women shall make tents and clothing, and shall serve in the hospitals; the children shall turn old linen into bandages; the old men shall go to the public places, to stimulate the courage of the warriors and preach the unity of the Republic and the hatred of kings.[26]

The decree went on to requisition 'national buildings', former church property, as barracks, and other public buildings for conversion to arms workshops. All weapons other than light shotguns were to be requisitioned, as were all saddle-horses and as many draught-animals as possible. A national network of arms manufactories was to be set up, and all single men between eighteen and twenty-five were instructed to report immediately to district capitals to form the first battalions of the levy – there to drill daily until further orders. No substitutes were permitted, although 'the public functionaries will remain at their posts'. To feed these armies, farmers were ordered to pay their taxes for the year, and any arrears, in kind at once. To coordinate this effort, further waves of representatives-on-mission were appointed, being specifically granted the unlimited powers which those that accompanied the armies into combat zones had been exercising since earlier in the year.

The *levée en masse* was a great statement of the potential for national unity against external enemies, but of course the Republic was not united. Action against internal enemies continued, with the suppression of joint-stock companies on 24 August striking a further blow against 'capitalist' speculators. Two days later came a decree for the immediate and unconditional deportation of all non-juring priests, regardless of their activities or lack thereof. This was still not enough to satisfy the radicals of the Paris Commune and sections, who in collusion with some of the Jacobin leadership began to pressurise the Convention for more decisive action against the counter-revolutionaries within France, and for a wider control of social and economic life. Sectional demonstrations at the Hôtel de Ville to this effect on 4 September were transformed by the Commune's leaders into a peaceful, but massive, mobilisation on the 5th, when the Convention was again surrounded by the evidence of Parisian strength and wide-ranging new measures were agreed. It was at this point that 'Terror' was decreed to be 'the order of the day', although what that meant exactly would emerge only gradually over the following weeks and months.[27]

If the rank and file of these mobilisations again consisted of the artisans and workers of the city, they continued to be recognised as 'good *sans-culottes*' by the political establishment only when they conformed to its own models of political activity. The session of the Commune on 4 September, which agreed to march on the Convention the next day, also voted to use the National Guard to disperse building workers who were demonstrating for higher wages. Ambiguities of this kind ran through the measures voted for in principle by the Convention on 5 September and passed into law throughout the month. A General Maximum on prices was formalised on 29 September, restricting them to 1790 levels, plus one-third, plus transport allowances and a 15 per cent sellers' premium – something over a 50 per cent increase. The measure covered thirty-nine categories, but excluded staples such as firewood, salt, fish, poultry and milk. A Maximum on wages accompanied this, at a rate of only 50 per cent over 1790 levels, at a time when even official statistics showed that the going rate for labour was up to 150 per cent more than in 1790. Any gains achieved by free bargaining in a time of labour shortage were immediately undercut – though private employers were widely forced to ignore this restriction to keep their workers. The pay of the many who passed into the employ of the state under the *levée en masse* was tightly regulated. It was paid in assignats which, despite rallying from 22 per cent in August, were worth only 48 per cent of their face value in December 1793.[28]

Sectional assemblies and the *sans-culotte* movement in politics were also curtailed after 5 September. Such bodies were to meet only twice weekly, although workers were to be paid 40 sous for the time they took to attend them, leading to ironic (but predictably paranoid) accusations that sturdy independent *sans-culottes* might be outnumbered by paid hirelings. As if in recompense, the most ardent were given the chance to prove themselves by joining new *armées révolutionnaires* – not true armies, but paramilitary bands designed to monitor the provisioning of the cities by patrolling the country-side and searching out counter-revolution and hoarding. Like all other revolutionary institutions, these groups were to watch for 'suspects' defined by a law voted on 17 September. Ex-nobles and non-juring priests had for some time been subject to official and unofficial surveillance, but this measure was sweeping, it ordered the indefinite internment of all such individuals and a wide range of others. It embraced anyone who 'by their conduct, associations, speech or writings have shown themselves partisans of tyranny or federalism and enemies of liberty', but also anyone unable to justify their means of support or their patriotism to a surveillance committee, anyone to whom such a committee had refused a *certificat de civisme*, any public officials who had been dismissed from their posts, especially after 10 August, and all former nobles, including women and children, and other 'agents of the émigrés', along with anyone declared to have emigrated at any point since 1 July 1789, regardless of their date of return.[29] Surveillance committees were ordered to list such individuals immediately, issue arrest warrants and have them detained, either in existing prisons or under house arrest, until sufficient 'national buildings' could be requisitioned to the task.

The Law of Suspects was harsh enough in itself, but to see the effect it had, we must look a little closer at its interpretation. On 11 September, in anticipation of the new law, the Paris Commune had voted a new regulation on persons to be refused *certificats de civisme* – who after 17 September would therefore automatically be suspects:

1. Those who, in assemblies of the people, arrest its energy by crafty discourses, turbulent cries and threats.

2. Those, more prudent, who speak mysteriously of the misfortunes of the Republic, are full of pity for the lot of the people, and are always ready to spread bad news with an affected grief.

3. Those who have changed their conduct and language in line with events ...

4. Those who pity the farmers and greedy merchants against whom the law is obliged to take measures.

5. Those who have the words Liberty, Republic and Fatherland constantly on their lips, but who consort with former nobles, counter-revolutionary priests, aristocrats [and] moderates, and show concern for their fate.

6. Those who have taken no active part in revolutionary affairs ...

7. Those who received the republican constitution with indifference and have given credence to false fears concerning its establishment and duration.

8. Those who, having done nothing against liberty, have also done nothing for it.

9. Those who do not attend the meetings of their sections and who give as excuses that they do not know how to speak or that their occupation prevents them.[30]

To this list were added those who had actually defamed the authorities, or associated with 'counter-revolutionary' petitions or groups, but these seem almost an afterthought in what is a barrage of denunciation against anyone who had simply tried to get on with their life through the Revolution, or who had ever offered an opinion not precisely in accord with the *sans-culotte* orthodoxy prevailing in September 1793. Applied without prejudice, such a measure would have seen every Parisian arrested, including the revolutionary leadership itself. Of course, it was to be applied with selective amnesia – and extreme prejudice.

That amnesia and prejudice can be seen, from another direction, in the remarks of the Jacobin leader Danton during the Convention debate on the *armées révolutionnaires* on 5 September. He announced that 'the people are great', as attested by their supposed lack of response to the ongoing 'false famine, arranged to lead them into counter-revolution'. He went on, to rapturous applause from his fellow representatives: 'You fast for liberty, you must get it. We march with you, your enemies shall be confounded; you will be free.'³¹ In part purely circumstantial rhetoric, the reception of this sweeping and patently false generalisation points to the blinkered and patronising view of the French people to be found throughout the revolutionary political establishment. The *sans-culotte* concept itself, with its parodic and theatrical origins, was in some senses merely a more refined manifestation of this approach.

The autumn of 1793 was to be the apogee of the *sans-culotte* movement, although cracks in the relationship of *sans-culottes* with the state had already appeared, witnessed by the limitations on their sectional meetings. Parisian activists, and those of their provincial counterparts who could effectively ape the *sans-culotte* social and ideological ideal, nonetheless were the first point of reference for the agents of the state in search of supporters as they fanned out on their renewed missions. That ideal leant heavily, as already noted, on a strongly plebeian sense of identity with the people, frequently articulated through a hatred of the rich. These, however, are imprecise terms. Over a quarter of those who staffed the regular civil committees of the Paris sections in 1793, a body largely renewed in the radical atmosphere of autumn 1792, lived on an independent income, without working – though most of these, it must be admitted, were employers and business investors rather than pure *rentiers*. Even amongst the surveillance committees, created in the ferment of March 1793, and often known in Paris under the more fiery title of *comités révolutionnaires*, almost 5 per cent of members had such an income, and some two-thirds of them were independent artisans or shopkeepers. There were more clerks, artists, teachers and lawyers than there were workers, apprentices or journeymen – 10 per cent of the latter, about 12 per cent of the former.³²

Some of those who described themselves as artisans were undoubtedly not particularly well off, and many hairdressers, wigmakers, shoemakers and other luxury tradesmen later pleaded that they had taken on roles within the sections for the daily expenses that were paid, having lost their clientele to emigration and economic collapse. Unemployed servants sometimes followed a similar route, being noteworthy amongst the activists in the Faubourg Saint-Germain, the former haunt of the purest nobility. On the other hand, some who defined themselves as fanmakers, plasterers or joiners employed dozens of workers, or owned property worth tens of thousands of livres. Even looking outside the ranks of committee members, to some five hundred activists who can be identified as participating in a more general way in militancy, only a fifth can be described even loosely as being wage-earners – from journeymen to office boys, servants and waiters. Some 15 per cent were professionals or clerks and a similar number shopkeepers. The largest proportion were artisans, at almost 42 per cent – but again, such a label hid a similar range of fortunes to those on the committees.

It is instructive to compare the profile of these *sans-culottes* with that of the activists of the rebellion of Lyon. As a proportion of the two cities' populations, active political participants were in both cases tiny minorities – under 1.4 per cent for Lyon, scarcely more for Paris, even on the most generous estimation. Although only a few dozen individual identities can be confirmed for Lyonnais anti-Jacobin militants, they too were spread across the ranks of society. When the Lyon sections formed bodies of 'surveillance commissioners' in May 1793, preparatory to acting against the municipality, 28 per cent of these were from the upper bourgeoisie, and 25 per cent merchants, but almost 19 per cent were silk weavers, and 22 per cent other artisans and shopkeepers. Some 20 per cent of those who continued to hold sectional office during the siege were clerks, artisans or weavers. In the Federalist army formed to defend the city, artisans, shopkeepers, weavers, labourers and servants all enrolled in substantial numbers, making up over half the rank and file, but also over a third of officers holding the rank of captain or higher. Some in the ranks may have been seeking employment rather than expressing a political commitment, but then some Parisian *sans-culottes* later claimed likewise, and who is to judge either way?[33]

The evidence of other major urban centres points to the same ambiguities. In Bordeaux the majority of sections adhered firmly to the relatively short-lived regional Federalist movement – domination of local office by a propertied and literate elite was one factor here, but even some of the poorest areas continued to follow that lead into rebellion. Although countervailing support for the Jacobin cause was generated most strongly in a minority of the poorer sections, this may be equally attributed to a well-organised campaign focused on these 'natural' *sans-culottes* by local club members, including wealthy merchants and brokers, state employees, bookkeepers and others of the educated elite. In Marseille where, as in Lyon and Bordeaux, a wealthy mercantile elite would be superficially blamed for Federalism, the sections that rose up and governed the city seem also to have had a wide social composition. The Revolutionary Tribunal that restored order there executed eighteen wholesale merchants, ten lawyers, and forty-two *propriétaires*, but also three bakers, three butchers, one carpenter, eleven clerks, eighteen farmers and market gardeners, two hatters, one news-hawker, five shoemakers, one journeyman sweetmaker, three tailors, and an array of others of every social class.[34]

Outside the main urban centres, the stresses of the summer of 1793 pulled different groups and localities in a variety of directions. The three districts of Roanne, Montbrison and Saint-Etienne formed until August 1793 the western half of the Rhône-et-Loire department, which included Lyon on its eastern edge. On 12 August, they were cut off from the rebel city by decree of the local representatives-on-mission and formed into the department of the Loire. The tensions which created the Federalist movement were reproduced in this area, but in a wide variety of ways. The departmental administration had attempted in June to bring the whole area to revolt, but fell apart as many delegates backed away in the face of approaching military force and punitive decrees. As authority crumbled, forces from Lyon occupied Saint-Etienne and its neighbouring towns on 11–12 July, purging Jacobins from the local administration. A pro-Federalist council in Montbrison responded to local clashes by calling on aid from newly 'Federalised' Saint-Etienne, which arrived in force on 22 July, allowing them to seize their own Jacobins.

The district of Saint-Etienne was subsequently 'liberated' from Federalist occupation by a rising of its own National Guards, starting in the industrial town of Rive-de-Gier on 26 August. Federalist forces withdrew to consolidate in Montbrison, where they held out until the second week of September, many finally slipping through the hills to Lyon as regular troops and battalions of the levée en masse raised in the nearby Auvergne closed in. The district of Roanne, furthest from Lyon, had played a waiting game, refusing to commit itself to revolt, or to Jacobin countermeasures, until the arrival of representatives-on-mission forced their hand. National Guards from Roanne had helped to subdue Montbrison, and the area's response to the levée en masse had been eager enough to draw a written testimonial from one of the representatives.[35]

Different profiles of social and political allegiance could be drawn for each of these areas. Around Saint-Etienne there was a great deal of industry, with strong mercantile links to Lyon; Montbrison was a former judicial centre, and its elite was somewhat 'Old Regime' in composition. Roanne, by contrast, was a mercantile centre for trade down the Loire and had no strong connection to Lyon. Around Saint-Etienne, the population lived mainly from working coal, iron and silk, with very little purely local agricultural provision – villages on the neighbouring highlands were themselves scarcely self-sufficient and were unable to feed the towns. Montbrison was in a more agricultural zone, and its urban elite were far more likely to live from rents. Its lowland agricultural surroundings were actually more thinly populated than the isolated mountains that ringed them, and more landlords tied than the merchants lead – spinning and weaving for the latter was what kept the overpopulated uplands alive. Around Roanne, furthest north, the uplands were also impoverished, while the lower surrounding land held many vineyards, often in absentee ownership. The town elite had little connection with the area around them, being focused on the river trade, as was the small working population.

It was in Montbrison, with its quota of ex-seigneurs, that tensions had run highest before June, but it was in Saint-Etienne, with its concentrated working population perhaps most amenable to being 'led astray', that the Federalists struck first. Both Federalists and Jacobins launched a hail of propaganda, the one against the 'anarchy' that loomed, the other equating wealth with speculation and thence counter-revolution. As elsewhere, ordinary people were drawn into conflicts started by others: with armed forces being raised on both sides, they found themselves serving – sometimes as volunteers, sometimes not. There can be little doubt that the message of the Jacobins was more attractive to the interests of the urban and proto-industrial workers, helping to explain the genuine uprising that finally pushed the Federalist forces out of Saint-Etienne, but there is also little doubt that individuals of every social class were involved on all sides. Some of the bitterest antagonisms at Montbrison involved almost no ordinary peasants or workers at all, while a rural anti-Federalist force raised nearby in September was led by a former noble who held the Old Regime Order of Saint-Louis. Many areas held back from all commitment for as long as they could, community leaders seeing no virtue in plunging themselves into civil war. This was particularly the case in upland villages. In many senses the turbulent events of the Loire were a battle between the towns, with the peasantry looking on until the final stages.

The Loire encapsulated in miniature many of the key features of the Federalist civil war. It was a fundamentally urban phenomenon, with only the passage of troops, and the growing demands for requisitions to support them, penetrating the countryside. It was on the surface a war between 'the rich' and the 'enemies of property'; but when looked at more closely it was riven with social ambiguities and many participants were drawn in against their wills. It was an episode in which subtleties of social or political distinction rapidly became erased by the crushing force of a national and international armed struggle, driving political allegiances in one of only two possible directions. Out of the conjunction of Federalism with the Vendée and the wider war came the institutions of the Terror, which for the next year sought to impose a cultural revolution on the inhabitants of France.

11

Terror and Reaction

With the measures of a practical political and economic Terror in place from September 1793, the Montagnard Convention had also in the following month established the groundwork for its programme of cultural Terror. With government declared 'revolutionary until peace', the moral and psychological transformation of the French people was to be accomplished by breaking the mental hold of the Old Regime, as expressed everywhere from the days of the week to the names of individual communities. The new calendar, with its rationalised framework, was an immediate step in this direction. From the outset, however, the structures of the calendar demonstrated the distance between Montagnard sensibilities and working life. The calendar of the church made Sunday a holiday for every worker. It has also been estimated that, in the cities at least, perhaps as many days again were given over to feasts each year – the occasions for fairs and markets as well as general celebration. The republican calendar restricted its holidays to the *décadi*, the tenth day of its new 'week'. Cutting the workers' days off from perhaps a hundred (and at least fifty-two, even for the peasants) to under forty was unlikely to endear this model to them.[1]

The wider effort to break the hold of the church, later dubbed 'dechristianisation', had many aspects.[2] There was an element of coordinated economic Terror to the forced stripping out of valuables from churches to support the war effort – and even more directly to the removal of bronze church bells to be cast into cannon, a measure specifically ordered on 3 August 1793. The execution of this order provided the opportunity for literally thousands of small confrontations, often involving the population of the parish, men and women alike, rallying around a vital timekeeping mechanism of community life, as well as a religious symbol of great potency. Many local authorities indeed shied away from enforcing this order until the more starkly confrontational atmosphere of the autumn made it unavoidable. Beyond such directed motives, many dechristianisers, especially in the *armées révolutionnaires*, relished the opportunities for pillage and destruction unleashed by a general hostility to religion. Statues of saints and the Holy Family were a favourite choice for target practice or decapitation, as were the images of kings that often lined cathedrals. At Saint-Denis, north of Paris, the resting-place for centuries of French kings, havoc was wreaked on their memorials and their very bones were dragged up from the crypt. Such was the extent of iconoclasm that a report to the Convention, bemoaning the loss of France's cultural heritage, invoked a classical reference to the fall of Rome and called it *vandalisme*.

Priests themselves were persecuted. Non-jurors were of course often under arrest, or had fled into hiding by now, but loyal constitutional priests were pressurised, like Archbishop Gobel, into renunciation of the cloth, or even into forced marriages – most satisfactorily, from the ultra-revolutionaries' perspective, to former nuns driven out of the cloister. It has been estimated that there were something like thirty thousand such renunciations, and six thousand marriages. Dechristianisers also actively preached atheism. From some, this might mean long discourses on Enlightenment philosophy, from others grotesque and blasphemous parodies of religious rites – dressing a donkey in episcopal robes was only one of many classic anticlerical images revived and acted out. Either mode of action was likely to elicit a disgusted and appalled reaction from the peasantry; but such responses were further evidence, if a good *sans-culotte* needed it, that the peasantry were fanatics under the thumb of the counter-revolutionary servants of throne and altar. Every refusal to stop following the priests prompted a new move to prevent such behaviour, and reinforced the sense amongst revolutionaries that the beliefs and loyalties of such peasants were in themselves iniquitous and threatening. There was a self-aggravating tendency to this opposition, and an element of fear – every church that the revolutionaries stripped and closed saw a larger crowd gather for worship at the ones that remained open, and months of war in the Vendée had taught every good republican what a peasant mob could do.

The overt assault on religion in the country at large was therefore one more nail in the coffin of urban–rural relations. The autumn of 1793 saw a proliferation of groups and organisations that might almost have been designed to promote disharmony between peasants and townsfolk. The phenomenon of the 'popular society' was spread through the towns of France, large and small alike, by the passage of representatives-on-mission, who encouraged activists to band together, just as Parisians were doing, to form permanent groupings of patriots – in the Parisian case transparently to evade the limitations on the frequency of section meetings. These groups, led by those most keen to create an active relationship with the emissaries of the Republic, and coloured by the press and propaganda that poured out of the capital, tended towards extremism; far more so than the societies that had existed in many towns since 1790 or 1791, and especially in the smaller towns where they represented an isolated minority amongst close-knit and often feud-riven communities.[3]

There was also a real movement towards opening the ranks of local administration, especially to the artisan classes. Even in the recaptured Federalist cities and other large towns, however, such men never amounted to more than a substantial minority amongst Jacobin lawyers, merchants and men of property.[4] Even this limited social opening later provoked a violent backlash. In 1793 restructuring of political and administrative life swept up those who were susceptible to the appeal of the *sans-culotte* image, and encouraged a belligerent and denunciatory style of politics. Society, even in relatively peaceful rural areas, became divided in revolutionaries' minds ever more clearly along political lines. As the National Agent of the district of Cany (Seine-Inférieure) noted at the end of 1793, 'rich egoists' were everywhere, outnumbered, admittedly, by the 'true *sans-culottes*', but these latter were themselves heavily outweighed by 'the indifferent, of whom the countryside counts a great number, incapable of having an opinion of their own'.[5] Getting through to this indifferent mass meant a constant hectoring effort of propaganda, taken up as the patriotic duty of many popular societies and local committees. Denouncing counter-revolution, either to the locals or to higher authorities, became a compulsion – partly perhaps because the alternative, fighting it, would have implied enrolling in the armies.

In the autumn of 1793 counter-revolution, where there was not overt civil war, most often meant failure efficiently to feed and supply the militarised, town-led machinery created by the *levée en masse* and the General Maximum. In more than a dozen departments neighbouring Paris, as far afield as Normandy, such a failure might bring the intervention of one of the most feared and hated instruments of Terror, the Parisian *armée révolutionnaire*. Formed immediately after 5 September, this body of some six thousand infantry and cavalry was made up for the most part of classic *sans-culottes*, aged in their thirties or older, with a wide range of occupational backgrounds. The infantry were vetted for service by the sections and their societies, and incarnated the Parisian prejudices against hoarders, speculators and aristocrats. Ironically, and notoriously, the cavalry component, which was recruited with particular haste, disorganisation and patronage, hid a number of men of prime age for military service, and a number of others who by any reckoning were aristocrats. The prince of Rohan-Rochefort was caught the day after enrolling (and later sent to the guillotine) when a faithful former servant called him 'monseigneur' in conversation, but the marquis de Baudelaire successfully hid in the *armée* throughout its existence. By contrast, the 1200 artillerymen also enrolled were the cream of the *sans-culottes*, drafted straight from the companies of the Parisian National Guard that had fought on 10 August 1792 and purged the Convention on

2 June 1793 – they, however, tended to be deployed in real trouble spots, and hence encountered the ordinary peasant somewhat less frequently than the infantry.[6]

The infantry of the *armée révolutionnaire* was sent out to police the gathering of provisions for Paris. In their own eyes, this meant confronting the egoism and ill will of the peasant – a figure whom they saw almost entirely through the lens of caricatural propaganda. For aid, they actively sought out the popular societies in the areas to which they were posted. In the environs of Paris, such societies tended to be composed of those on the bottom end of the sharp antagonisms between large farmers and labourers that had characterised this region since the time of the Flour War. These *sociétaires* were all too willing to point the finger at the fat proprietors who were a cliché of radical rhetoric, and likely to make up the local administration. Such officials faced growing structural as well as political pressures. The urban provisioning systems put in place by the Convention were chaotic – it was not unknown, for example, for villages to be expected to supply two or even three urban centres with grain, when they had little enough of it to send to one. The repeated peremptory demands of urban authorities ate into any residual active loyalty that peasant communities and leaders might have felt to the Republic. At the sharp end of this antagonism were the men of the *armée*, whom individual towns often ordered into action against their suppliers on their own 'revolutionary' authority, adding to the chaos surrounding their overall deployment.

Due to the vast area it had to cover, and the intricate networks of transport and marketing within that area, the Paris *armée* was most often deployed in small detachments – as few as a handful of men. Such handfuls, armed, uniformed and sent off with ringing urban denunciations of hoarders and speculators in their ears, entered a hostile world, where it was the grasping hand of the hungry town that posed the greatest threat to the inhabitants. Only too aware of this hostility, the men of the *armée* responded in kind. Regarding themselves as true revolutionaries, patriots and self-sacrificing warriors, they took every opportunity to vex those who seemed opposed to them, by actions such as routine gorging and swilling at village taverns, to loud and brutal denunciations, to the varied excesses of soldierly free quarter, and on in some cases to violent assaults and worse crimes. The latter, however, were rare in the ranks of the *armée* itself, which for all its brutality prided itself on being a *corps d'élite* amongst revolutionaries. Unfortunately, the activities of the *armée* provided cover for the actions of real brigands. The Parisian basin had been home to robber bands throughout the century, and it is no surprise to find them active at this point – in October at Corbeil, for example, one such band, twenty-five strong, was reported to have adopted revolutionary uniform to help them get away with armed robbery of isolated farms. Between the two extremes of criminality and the Paris force, other local groups of militants, whose activities might waver between virtue and crime, clouded relations still further.[7]

Ironically, given its existence as an instrument of Terror, the Paris *armée révolutionnaire* never stopped being denounced to the Convention by peasants, for both its real and mythical excesses. At the same time, the Parisians responded by denouncing both individuals and local authorities as 'hoarders, men of the law [a very *sans-culotte* accusation], priests and agents of former nobles', as one wrote about the district of Pontoise.[8] Of course, as outsiders, the men of the *armée* were prone to manipulation, and capable of interpreting the struggles of village factions through the distorting lens of *sans-culotte* virtue – frequently dependent on which side got to them first. Fat proprietors or feckless brigands might be made the target of their wrath, when in fact the dynamics of local relations were far more subtle, or more factional.

Many villages had a political life little less turbulent than the case of Tonnerre, a small town in the Yonne where two factions, both led by former seigneurial agents and bailiffs, had fought for political power all through the Revolution in a vendetta that went back to the 1760s, and enrolled over a hundred active partisans on each side. No nuance of intimidation or electoral fraud was beyond either of these. In 1793, when open violence between them had broken out, the two factions were labelling themselves as 'montagnards' and 'sans-culottes', formed opposing popular societies, and sought to outbid each other in radical rhetoric. September 1793 saw a further outbreak of significant violence over the recruitment of the *levée en masse*, following which a commissioner from Paris arrived and gave full powers to the faction leader who presented the most revolutionary face, Cherest, who then seized many of his opponents as suspects. Those who escaped fled to Paris, appealed to the Jacobins and the Convention, and had these arrangements overturned by another commissioner in November. Only the detention of many faction leaders throughout the Terror kept a fragile peace in this community of some 3500 souls, in a region of France untroubled by any of the larger causes of revolutionary conflict.[9]

The Revolution had nurtured an evolution of conflict in Tonnerre that became increasingly violent, even without the input of external agents. Elsewhere, in the extraordinary atmosphere of the time, it often took little to bring the corrosive tensions of the Revolution down to the level of the individual village and farmstead, in what were otherwise peaceful backwaters of the Republic. It required little prompting for revolutionary bodies, and men to lead them, to spring up. In the Nièvre, for example, a local magistrate,

Chaix, who called himself 'Marat' Chaix, established an ill-defined position for himself as a *commissaire civil* during and after the mission of the *conventionnel* Fouché in the department. Chaix led his own personal reign of terror for several months in late 1793 in his home district of Lormes. He ably exploited pre-existing tensions between village and town, and between local centres, and might be seen as no more than the equivalent of Cherest in Tonnerre. But Chaix also embodied something found in many such men who rose to spontaneous or manipulated positions of leadership at this moment – he was an ultra-revolutionary. Chaix preached war on moderates of every stripe in local administration: he spoke out for rapid, categorical, revolutionary justice against suspects, and called for the forbidden *loi agraire* in the name of the poor *sans-culottes*. He supposedly once said that 'he would prefer to be a dog ... than to be a bourgeois', due to their selfish and counter-revolutionary ways.[10]

Chaix gathered a small armed force around himself, drawing on the local popular societies, and went some way to redistributing wealth by terror, although largely only in terms of forcing requisitions that were state policy anyway. Where he acquired his political and social position is not clear, and it may have been a rationalisation of more personal vendettas. That he was himself a comfortable landowner, and some of his terrorist followers were his employees, clouds the picture further. He was far from alone, however, and similar speculation could be made about many other such figures in this and other departments. They and their fragments of *armée révolutionnaire* and other irregular forces conjured up an image of total social war and the spoliation of the rich, even while actually doing little more than carrying out the state's intentions – requisitioning food, clothing, blankets, cutlery and valuables for the war effort. They made their share of arrests of 'suspects', but their efforts at repression were brutal and unco-ordinated. Such lack of coordination, which had allowed many of them to seize power, in the end became a threat to the Republic itself, and was stamped out in the spring of 1794. The gleeful participation of provincial ultra-revolutionaries in the campaign of dechristianisation encouraged this crackdown, even as it solidified rural opposition to the Revolution itself.

It was the initiative of locals such as Chaix that most radically redrew the map of France under the Terror, seconded by the initiative of the representatives-on-mission, and given their example by the Convention, which was to rename both Lyon and Marseille as marks of their treachery. The verbal relics of feudal slavery and religious superstition were swept away in an orgy of onomastic innovation. The sections of Paris had led the way here over the previous year. Some changes were obvious – the Palais-Royal and Louvre sections became Butte-des-Moulins 'Mill Hill' and Muséum as royal associations became iniquitous, and the section Henri-IV, around the Pont Neuf, became Révolutionnaire. The Place-Vendôme section renamed itself after the *sans-culottes'* favourite weapon, and became section Piques. Section Théâtre-Français, home to the Cordeliers Club, had first renamed itself Marseille, after that city's heroic fighters of 10 August, but in 1793 found the martyred Marat a more fitting appellation. Other changes were more obscure, though explicable – the tongue-twisting Mutius Scaevola adopted by the former Luxembourg section was a republican Roman leader who burned his own hand in the brazier of his royal torturers to defy them. The Hôtel de Ville section renamed itself Maison Commune, to strike a more radical note, but then had to become section Fidelité (Loyalty) when the ultra-radicals of the Commune lost favour in 1794. One noteworthy point is that the three sections of the Faubourg Saint-Antoine, strongholds of radical fervour since 1789, felt no need to rename themselves. They had earned their own fame, but it is also the case that such renaming often accompanied the victory of radical factions, and the extremism of the new name sometimes marked also the relative social isolation of those victors.[11]

Out in the countryside, it was the marks of religion that most often had to be scoured away. Countless villages had been named after the local saints, and countless more, in one fashion or another, after the Virgin Mary. Sainte-Marie translated easily to Sainte-Montagne, almost anything could be changed to 'Marat', and any mention of château or king could go in favour of 'Bonnet Rouge' (Red Cap) or 'Liberté'. Some imagination could also be shown. In the Loire, the representatives-on-mission and their cohorts who restored order after the Federalist episode undertook a whole-sale revolutionisation of the local geography. Saint-Etienne became Commune d'Armes, marking its concentration of gunsmiths. Montbrison, which had stubbornly resisted 'liberation', was renamed Montbrisé (Mount Broken). Dozens of villages had the 'Saint' shorn from their names, and other sites were renamed more politically, and sometimes more cryptically. Saint-Just-en-Chevalet became Montmarat, and Saint-Germain-Laval, Montchalier-Laval, after the Lyonnais martyr. Charlieu was easily re-named simply Chalier. Saint-Chamond became Vallée-Rousseau after the philosopher, Sainte-Polgues simply Roche-Libre (Free Rock), and Saint-Haon-le-Châtel even more laconically Bel-Air.[12]

It was not only places that were renamed – Chaix in the Nièvre was far from the only activist to rename himself 'Marat'. French naming practices in the eighteenth century were remarkably narrow – many male children were called either Louis or Jean-Baptiste, and a substantial proportion of girls were Marie, Anne or Catherine. The names of the few favoured and familiar saints were by far the commonest choices, and this was problematic for the ardent dechristianiser. Roman names offered one route out – the favourite was probably Brutus, as both the assassin of the tyrant Caesar and an austere hero of the earlier republic celebrated in one of Jacques-Louis David's paintings. Those who renamed themselves in this period would usually choose such a heroic association, but for those who had children to name the choice was wider. Many unfortunates went out into the world bearing the name of a military victory, one of the homely virtues of the revolutionary calendar, or worse, a favoured animal or plant – for, to revolutionary eyes, all that was natural was good.[13]

Not every revolutionary approved of the thoroughgoing nature of this process. From Cany, near Rouen, the National Agent of a district wrote to his superiors that a 'disorderly mania' for municipal renaming had taken hold locally by the spring of 1794. He lamented that 'most of [the communes] make these changes without reflection, and abandon insignificant names only to take on others even more insignificant'.[14] Even what now seem to be almost comical episodes of individual and collective rebranding could possess a deadly seriousness during the Terror. Aristocracy and fanaticism lurked behind every suspicious act, every failure to follow revolutionary policy à outrance. All revolutionary action of this period was coloured by perceptions of the desperate situation in the west, and scarcely less desperate one of the south east. Such zones of conflict were, of course, seen as part and parcel of the larger struggle, where unremitting warfare was waged on all fronts. In the north there were no major advances, but important victories in September and October 1793 halted the retreat, and some territory was liberated after the Austrians were beaten at Wattignies. In the south, steady pressure throughout the autumn pushed Spanish forces back over the Pyrenees, while light resistance from Federalist forces around Bordeaux had been mopped up in September. An offensive in the east ground to a halt in November, but regrouped French forces fought stubbornly on into the depths of winter, liberating Alsace from the Prussians. The other major front, around the Alps, was paralysed by the diversion of forces to the sieges of Lyon and Toulon – the latter in particular merged war and civil war as the British occupied the port until finally driven out on 19 December 1793.[15]

The Vendeans had suffered mixed fortunes in September, winning one battle and losing another. In mid October, the heart and origin of the rebellion, Cholet, was the site of a major defeat for them, and the Republic's noose began to tighten.[16] Thanks in part to the policy of devastation and deportation, the rebel army became increasingly like a migrant mass, with women, children and other non-combatants following the fighters. The last two months of 1793 saw a tragedy of misguided hopes, as the Royal and Catholic Army set off to force a passage northwards to the Channel coast, believing that they could unite with British forces and raise the whole west in their support. They succeeded in drawing in some hundreds of Chouans to open insurrection, and for a brief period revolutionary civil authority was overturned across a wide area. The military forces of the Republic were able to clamp down on the surrounding territory, however, and, after several weeks of futile manoeuvring, the Vendeans turned back southwards. They were driven off by the republican defenders of Angers, and forced out of Le Mans by savage street-fighting on 13 and 14 December. The plight of this peasant army, embattled in the depths of winter, need only be imagined. Far worse was to come, after the failing forces of the Vendeans were crushed at Savenay, midway between Nantes and the mouth of the Loire, on 23 December. The rebels surrendered in droves, along with their families, while others attempted to flee to their homes. Trapped as they were on the north bank of the Loire, this in itself was no easy task, and many were hounded to their deaths by patrols. All the rebels were under predetermined sentence of death, of course, and by this time the willingness of the Republic to carry out such sentences *en masse* had already been demonstrated.

Three weeks before the victory at Savenay, the Republic had accelerated its persecution of the defeated Lyonnais. Several thousand had been taken into custody when the city fell, and if at first there were lachrymose reports of the reunion between republicans and a rank and file of Federalists constrained into rebellion, the Convention steadily hardened its line, intending to make Lyon an unforgettable example of the price of treachery. This aim was marked by a decree on 12 October, the day news of the city's fall arrived: Lyon was to be physically destroyed, with the exception of the dwellings of the poor and of public buildings useful to industry or public welfare. On its remains a monument was to be erected, inscribed: 'Lyon made war on liberty, Lyon is no more'.[17] The city was formally renamed Ville-Affranchie, 'Freed Town'. The first Montagnard leaders in Lyon seem to have regarded this as hyperbole, but the Convention sent others in November who took it very seriously. To intensify their intimidatory message, they had some 270 men executed by cannon fire on 4 and 5 December. The revulsion of the troops who had been forced to finish off the mutilated victims of the first salvoes led to a return to more conventional firing-squads, but these two days were enough to brand the legend of the *mitraillades* on the public consciousness. Some 1900 Lyonnais rebels were executed in total – although here, as in many other Federalist centres, at least as many were acquitted, able to plead ignorance or oppressed patriotism.

It was in the Vendée that revolutionary justice came closest to indiscriminate slaughter. Acts were committed there that even the most zealous partisans of the Terror would in later decades prefer to pass over in silence.

Such a reaction was not immediate, however, and the groundwork for what followed had been clearly laid throughout the preceding year. In October 1793, speaking for the Committee of Public Safety, Barère had asserted that 'the brigands are in service from the age of ten to sixty-six ... The women are their scouts, the whole population of this revolted land is in armed rebellion.'[18] Thus after Savenay, the victorious general Westermann could write to the Committee in self-congratulation that 'I have crushed children beneath my horses' hooves, and massacred the women, who thus will give birth to no more brigands ... We take no prisoners, they would need to be given the bread of liberty, and pity is not revolutionary.'[19] Hundreds of rebels who threw down their arms were shot or bayoneted out of hand, hundreds more were rounded up and shot in batches.

In Nantes thousands of prisoners, men, women and children, accumulated, all of them marked for death. Surrounded by vanquished foes, but terrified of a reignition of the rebellion, and determined to mete out truly 'revolutionary' punishment, the representative-on-mission Carrier and a small band of associates – who called themselves the 'Marat Company' of the *armée révolutionnaire* – began to take bargeloads of bound prisoners into the wide estuary of the Loire and sink them. They began with priests, but soon became more indiscriminate. These mass drownings, *noyades*, were another marker in the legend of the Terror, as were the occasional 'revolutionary marriages' that punctuated them – men and women (most symbolically priests and nuns) were bound face-to-face, naked, before being tossed into the river. Their ultra-terrorist executioners, amidst the carnage, practised a gallows-humour that could be taken as the last refinement of cruelty, or as the desperate psychological accommodation of men close to the edge. Several thousand, at least, died in the city.[20]

Worse still was to come. To implement the logical outcome of an already-existing policy, the republican general Turreau sent a wave of parallel *colonnes infernales*, 'hell columns', across the heartland of the revolt in January 1794, each detachment of troops destroying farms and killing all those in their path – the mere fact of such people being there, in a region swept clean of patriots, making them proscribed rebels. The representative-on-mission Lequinio wrote a year later, in his own account of the Vendean war, that

> We saw republican soldiers rape rebel women on the stones piled by the sides of the main roads, and then shoot or stab them as they left their arms. We saw others carry nursling infants on their bayonets, or on the pikes which had pierced mother and child with the same blow.[21]

Sexual brutality, he noted, was also meted out to the unfortunate wives and daughters of local patriots: these 'were often placed under requisition, that was the term used'. Lequinio's account offers what is probably an accurate description – he wrote not to condemn such massacres, but believing the whole Vendean campaign had been a necessary measure of public safety. Two other representatives, Hentz and Francastel, were explicit on this at the time: 'We are convinced that the Vendean war will be finished only when there will no longer be a single inhabitant in this miserable land.' [22] Although the methods used owed much to earlier precedents – notably the savage repression of the Camisard revolt of 1702–5 – the republican forces elevated them to a new order of magnitude.

After the passage of the infernal columns, the torment was not over for the Vendée and its neighbouring departments. Guerrilla war continued, with the same exterminatory mentality, for another three years. The conflict probably accounted for the astonishing total of more than 220,000 deaths. A proportion of these were due to a dysentery epidemic, albeit one aggravated (even if not ultimately caused) by the dislocations of the conflict.[23] Nevertheless, the war in the west involved the deliberate killing of a civilian population on a scale not seen again in western Europe for over a century. The killings in the Vendée did not require the direct outside intervention that the acceleration of executions at Lyon had. Those involved in the fighting themselves, once victory was assured, went on to commit unashamed butchery on an unprecedented scale. Although it is worth remembering that this brutality was not 'popular' or 'spontaneous', but emerged in the context of both hard fighting and exterminatory military and political orders, it is also clear that a profound and dehumanising alienation stood between the republican killers and their victims. Unlike at Lyon, where the revolutionaries and the *sans-culottes* confronted a well-understood urban landscape in which wickedness could be rooted out in the form of the individual egoist, speculator and Federalist, the forces in the west were at war with a whole culture, almost with the landscape itself.

The stereotypical countryside of the western revolt was the *bocage*, marked by sharecropper farmsteads isolated amongst a dense network of small fields, each with their own hedgerows. These could be several metres high and impenetrably thick, turning the roads and trackways between them into sunken tunnels of vegetation. Significant towns were few and far between, and, with its patches of dense woodland for shelter, this was ideal country for ambush by those who knew its byways. Even outside the *bocage*, in the coastal marshes fringing the Loire estuary, or up onto the heathlands of the Breton peninsula, all of these landscapes were alien to the town-dwelling troops and agents of the Republic, closed in on themselves, if not always literally by vegetation, then as often by the rain and mists of the Atlantic climate. The Vendean peasant and his Breton and Norman cousins seemed,

to republican eyes, to be the product of this landscape and its darknesses
– cultural as well as physical. Attacks came as if from the woods and hedges
themselves, especially as the rebels who continued the struggle were forced
away from habitation and into guerrilla activity. In the minds and mouths
of those who fought them, the rebels were defined by their religious fanaticism, seen as the product of a profound and almost bestial ignorance, and
by a more overt demonisation that likened them to images of 'savages' from
the four corners of the earth.

At the centre, and in the minds of representatives-on-mission, there was
little to distinguish the rebels from aristocratic counter-revolution, expressed
in the language of corruption and infection. Of the Vendeans, it was said
in one proclamation to the inhabitants of the Mayenne that they would
'bring back the Old Regime and with it the tithes, the *taille*, the salt-tax,
the customs-duties, the hunting and milling privileges, all the feudal exactions and all-consuming trickery that we have had so much trouble to get
rid of'. They were led, allegedly, by 'insolent and haughty nobles, crafty
and avid priests who miss their insulting prerogatives and their scandalous
wealth'.[24] Another representative, commenting on the Chouan activity that
had flared again in Brittany and Normandy in late 1793, wrote to the
Committee of Public Safety that this 'army' was composed of

> refractory priests, customs-agents, bankrupts, cellar-rats, procurators' clerks, émi-
> grés' valets, monks, nuns, marquises, countesses, [and] former nobles, [leaving]
> behind itself such a moral and physical infection that it is known throughout
> the country it crosses as the army of the *puants* [stinkers].[25]

Such an image was almost wholly false. The Chouans would trouble the
order of the Republic for several years after the defeat of the Vendean army.
Although those who actively took part probably numbered only a few tens
of thousands, of whom only a small minority had firearms, they drew on
the resources of the whole population, and their tactics made much of this
region ungovernable in any normal sense. Chouannerie expanded in parallel
with the emergence of the Terror, and most specifically in response to the
levée en masse. Fundamentally alienated from the Republic, and unable to
take a chance on not being called up, as had been possible even in March
1793, many young men, like those further south, took to the woods. There
they came into the orbit of a hard core of Chouans already carrying out
intermittent local attacks, and provided the rank and file of a viable guerrilla
force. That viability largely depended, ironically, on the small and fluctuating
size of Chouan bands. Many never numbered more than a few dozen, and
even these only reached peak numbers occasionally, as their members
depended on regular trips home for food and rest. A few of the 'captains'

and 'generals' who led such bands were nobles, but most, like the original 'Jean Chouan', were ordinary rural inhabitants.

In their heartlands, most Chouans were integrated members of their communities until the time came to stage a raid or a retaliation. It was impossible for them to be pinned down by conventional military action, and it took the Republic years to amass sufficient available forces for the kind of brutal punitive action that had brought the Vendée to a devastated state of semi-peace. In the meantime, the Chouans traded in fear and the humiliation of isolated patriots. In late 1793, one outraged individual reported that he had been made to climb the local church tower and cry *Vive Louis XVII!* – the royalists' title for Louis XVI's surviving son, languishing in a republican prison. On another occasion, a female victim had been made to kneel before an image of the Sacred Heart of Jesus, the adopted emblem of the more devout amongst the rebels. Public renunciations of revolutionary faith under threat of death were common, often accompanied by ritualised public abuse and beatings.

Much about this pattern of Chouan activity indicates clearly that they were attempting to defend a pre-existent set of local community norms against the alien republican values of those they fervently denounced as *intrus* or intruders. When 'converted' local patriots betrayed them again by reporting such acts to the authorities and appealing for aid, a more embittered confrontation set in, and between early 1794 and mid 1796 the Chouans assassinated hundreds of local republican officials, and persecuted those they saw as profiting from the spoliation of the church through *biens nationaux*. In the later stages of their existence, they went so far as to collect the rents due on such property from the peasant tenants, diverting funds from patriots' pockets to the Royal and Catholic Army in whose name they issued receipts. The towns of the region became effectively armed camps, with the thin lines of the main highways kept open between them by military force alone. If active Chouan militants constituted a tiny minority of the population, like active political militants of all colours, it is clear that in the villages of the west they enjoyed a solid, if largely passive, popular support.

The same could not be said of the Republic. Yet it did have a great deal of support, outside rebel areas at least, for its war on the Revolution's original enemies. One reason for the continual harping on the aristocratic nature of counter-revolution was that it corresponded to genuine fears and hatreds in the minds of many. Counterpointing this, the language of patriotism generated enormous popular effort, and identification with the *patrie*. Whatever the real views of the elite about their popular supporters, they could still tell them that they were now citizens and not subjects, and that the revenge of the aristocrats would subjugate them in even worse fashion than before. The continuing struggle for economic survival that life had become could thus be blamed very firmly on the counter-revolution, and the incessant rain of republican propaganda undoubtedly consolidated this view. Meanwhile, for those prepared to become *sans-culotte* activists, especially in Paris, revolutionary mobilisation may have been a veritable boon. Many formerly insignificant figures accumulated impressive-sounding job titles, military rank and arrays of intimidatory powers. They also gained secure work, and many an entrepreneur in the locksmithing or joinery trades reinvented himself as an *armurier*, or gunsmith, and successfully managed part of the huge weapons factory that the capital had become. In this way, the path of the Old Regime master artisans to neighbourhood power and influence through the guilds and the parishes was reproduced in a new form.[26]

Despite appeals to patriotism and the continual reminders of the aristocratic threat, the real and perceived burdens of mass mobilisation on the population at large were severe, and increasingly problematic. For the mass of the rural population the Republic became the force that stole their crops, under the guise of requisition, having stolen their sons, under the guise of conscription. For the ordinary city-dweller, besides those subjected to the military and political repression of Federalism, life was increasingly regimented and arduous. The *levée en masse* put many of them to work under what amounted to military discipline. The General Maximum and its many enforcing *commissaires* kept a trickle of food coming into the towns; but, ever since the outbreak of war, provisioning a family had become a matter of endless queues. There is evidence to suggest that the enforcement of the Maximum itself, through the encouragement of denunciation and the actual prosecutions undertaken, targeted small retailers in a successful effort to divert popular discontent from the larger questions of economic relationships, or the responsibility of local officials who might themselves be involved in wholesale trade.[27]

Women with families to feed had to queue at the doors of local bakers for many hours – eating into the time that most had to work for their living – and the disputes and mutterings of dissent that emerged from such gatherings helped to further tarnish all women in the eyes of the republicans. Women of every social and political stripe were increasingly distrusted by the Montagnard revolutionaries, who had read in Rousseau a message that only 'natural' women, in the guise of the breast-feeding brood-mother and helpmate, should have a place in the ideal society. Peasant women, with their fanatical attachment to their priests, had already placed themselves beneath contempt from this viewpoint. Prostitutes, associated in Montagnard eyes with a vice that was implicitly aristocratic, were banned from the

streets of Paris by an order of 2 October 1793, subjected to instant arrest,
and the surveillance of all 'republicans who are austere and friends of
morality'.[28] Aristocratic women were perceived to be the worst of all, and
on 16 October 1793 Marie-Antoinette was sent to the guillotine, after a trial
in which Hébert and his fellow prosecutors heaped sexual slanders upon
her, the worst of which being that she had sexually abused her own young
and sickly son in an effort to hasten his demise. Madame Roland, wife of
a Girondin minister and the hostess of his salon gatherings, and the symbol
of a clever and meddling woman, was executed on 9 November (following
most of the leading Girondins, executed together on 31 October. Her husband, on the run, committed suicide when he learned of her death).

By the time Madame Roland died, all women had been banished formally
from public life. On 30 October 1793 the Convention heard a report occasioned by the activities of the revolutionary republican *Citoyennes*, who for
reasons best known to themselves had launched a divisive and self-destruc-
tive campaign to force all women in the capital to adopt first the tricolour
cockade and then the red bonnet of liberty. The Convention had in fact
supported the first of these measures with a decree of 21 September, but
the latter had resulted in brawls between the *Citoyennes* and the redoubtable
market-women of the city, who heartily despised these 'Amazons'. This
justified, for the Convention, wholesale repression. They voted to confirm,
on principle, the total exclusion of women from formal political activity,
and to follow this up in practice by a complete ban on female membership
of political organisations and clubs.[29]

Even as the Convention progressively alienated more and more of its
citizens, it embarked on ever-more lavish attempts to demonstrate the
citizens' fundamental unity. Urban inhabitants were regularly supposed to
turn out *en masse* for festivals affirming civic values, where they would
often parade in mock-classical garb, arranged in divisions by age and sex,
and listen to pontificating speeches of patriotic platitudes and Rousseauistic
rhetoric.[30] Participation was organised through local municipalities and
sections, and refusal to join in was a suspect act. During the Terror, upwards
of a third of a million people were confined as 'suspects', so the choice of
the ordinary citizen was clear. Representatives-on-mission were especially
fond of festivals as devices for demonstrating the unity and patriotism of
areas they administered. The pattern of the festivals, in which participation
and spectating were mingled, echoed and adopted some of the most successful elements of the Catholic parades of saints and relics (though for the
anticlerical revolutionaries the model they had in mind was ancient
Greece).[31] Paris saw some enormous public occasions, stage-managed in
large part by the painter and Montagnard *conventionnel* Jacques-Louis David.

The last major festival under the Terror was on 8 June 1794, when Robespierre personally inaugurated the public worship of the 'Supreme Being', in a bizarre effort to distance the Republic from what he saw as the immorality and atheistic excess of dechristianisation. Even some of his fellow *conventionnels* sniggered as he seemed to be making himself the pope of the Republic, marching at the head of the parade, and setting light to a vast effigy of counter-revolutionary superstition to reveal the figure of wisdom within.

The Cult of the Supreme Being was part of the Montagnard plan for the complete regeneration of France. This also included massive plans for public buildings, recasting the urban landscape away from the monuments of kings towards the celebration of the people. Laws and moral injunctions were to be carved into the façades, and the whole city was to become a didactic instrument for the social and cultural regeneration of the population.[32] Plans for education, all of which again fell by the wayside, varied from the idealistic and enlightened to the positively Spartan – one extreme proposal from the Montagnard ideologue Saint-Just was to remove all children from their parents to republican boarding-schools, to ensure that fanaticism and corruption could not be passed down the generations. All such measures seem to have combined a basic hostility to what ordinary people actually were with a stridently didactic vision of what they could (and should) become. The idealisation of the independent citizen as the bedrock of society resulted in the Ventôse Decrees of 26 February and 3 March 1794, in which Saint-Just set out a plan to distribute the lands of suspects to poor patriots. This measure was stillborn due to provincial indifference and administrative complications – and, more basically, to a lack of clarity about how one qualified as a 'poor patriot'. A further plan was presented on 11 May 1794 for a 'Great Register of National Welfare' to support the rural poor – this was more successful in the short term, making modest but reasonable payments to the elderly and widows in its first year, but funds and political enthusiasm petered out, and it was abolished in the Year V, having already ceased to function effectively.[33]

The immediate reason for the failure of the overall plans for the regeneration of France, besides their being in many cases fantasies of an authoritarian utopia, was that the Jacobin Republic was steadily tearing itself apart. The descent of the republican leadership into mutually destructive factions had much to do with the personal enmities and shady dealings of many amongst that leadership. The fall of the Hébertists nevertheless also illustrated the increasingly brutal pragmatism that coexisted with even the most radical plans for regeneration within the Committee of Public Safety. One of the underlying reasons for the elimination of the Hébertists, and the abolition of the Paris *armée révolutionnaire* immediately afterwards, was the increasing tension over the operation of the Maximum in Paris. Black-marketeers on both small and large scales widely evaded its controls, selling butter, for example, at twice the controlled price, and eggs at twice what they had cost even in the critical summer of 1793. Pragmatic committee members recognised that the Maximum should probably be amended to increase profit margins within legal trading, but crowds continued to resort to protest – in late February and mid March 1794 there were small-scale *taxation populaire* episodes over butter and eggs, and widespread mutterings of discontent recorded by police agents.[34]

The Hébertist solution to all this had been to propose increased Terror, more action by the *armées révolutionnaires* and more executions of speculators – and, indeed, to hint, as some had hinted since late 1793, of a further purge of the Convention and its committees. That solution had support at street level too, as an anonymous placard observed on 6 March 1794:

> *Sans-culottes*, it is time to beat the drum, sound the tocsin and arm yourself and be quick, for you see that they are pushing you to your last breath, if you want to believe me it's better to die defending your Glory for the *patrie* that dying in a famine, where all the Representatives want to plunge you, don't trust them it is time, civil war is being prepared, turn the tables on all the scoundrels who say they govern the republic, they are all conspirators and all merchants of Paris I denounce them, some of those who will read my few words written, which are the pure truth will say that I am a conspirator because I speak the truth.[35]

The arrest and execution of the Hébertists put paid to the open expression of such sentiments, with reports of section meetings and public gatherings suggesting a loyal (or prudent) acceptance of the authorities' line.[36] The approach to all popular dissent rapidly toughened. The fate of a petition from hundreds of women working in the municipal spinning-workshops shows this clearly. In late February 1794 they had sought the help of two nearby radical popular societies for the improvement of their wages, payment in cash instead of assignats (which they dismissed as 'false bills'), restoration of a recently withdrawn bread ration, and the extirpation of a number of 'abuses' they claimed permeated the workshop's management. By the time the affair was made public in May, Hébert's fall had sharply altered the balance of power in the city. The management of the workshop were able to put down dissent with accusations of *Hébertisme* against the ringleaders of the women, and one of these was subsequently arraigned before the Revolutionary Tribunal in June (she was, unusually, acquitted). Ironically, only a matter of weeks earlier this woman had been amongst those instrumental in having two female workshop supervisors arrested, tried and executed on charges of counter-revolutionary sympathies. The fact that the spinners were of course now engaged on war work made the dismissal of their allegations all the more urgent, and the fact that Hébert did seem to have sympathised in person with their plight made that move much easier.[37]

The changed atmosphere of Parisian politics had enabled the Convention to approve a new higher set of Maximum prices at the end of March. The removal of Hébertist influence in the Paris Commune also allowed the Convention to begin to squeeze wages in the capital – the Commune had been dragging its feet over its municipal responsibility to publish approved rates of pay. Workers in the state-controlled arms workshops had been limited to 5 livres (100 sous) per day since the previous autumn, while outside direct government control wages were exorbitant – even unskilled labour reportedly demanded 100 sous a day, and some bakers even refused to work for a package worth 300 sous, including board. By April, the new 'Robespierrist' Commune was invoking the 1791 Loi Le Chapelier to ban workers' protests, and arresting ringleaders of such protest amongst tobacco-workers, bakers, plasterers and others.[38]

Such actions, however, ultimately contributed to the downfall of the Terror. Although it was the dissent within the Convention, and Robespierre's own political isolation, that prompted his outlawry, it was the alienation of the Parisian rank and file that removed all hope of a rally against the Convention. The publication of a table of ruthlessly reduced wage rates on 23 July, threatening workers with a loss of half their earnings, had already led to protests and disturbances, and events only three days later found the Parisians confused and embittered about which leaders to trust. On 27 July, 10 Thermidor, Robespierre and his colleagues were guillotined before celebratory crowds, happy to join in condemning him as an aspirant Caesar. When his partisans in the Commune followed him a day later, they were cheered to the scaffold, according to some reports, by crowds acclaiming the end of the 'fucking Maximum'.[39] The change of leadership brought the workers relief in the short term, as two weeks later they saw the wage scales of July replaced by others some 50 per cent higher. A renewed spiral of price inflation soon ate up this gain, however, and the economic future looked increasingly grim.

The new Thermidorian regime, despite its reputation for 'reaction', could not divert many of the main streams of revolutionary conflict. The leaders were still republicans. Although this meant that the surviving Girondins could look forward to reintegration into politics, it equally meant that the new rulers were no better than the old, in the eyes of Catholic and royalist rebels and counter-revolutionaries. If dechristianisation had already been abandoned, there was still no reconciliation with the church, which meant on the one hand a continued conflict over worship in every corner of

France and, on the other, a continued sale of *biens nationaux*.[40] The lands of both the church and the émigrés continued to be parcelled out to speculators, to the upwardly mobile and even to some genuine peasants throughout the following years. Yet the more radical attempt to offer *partage* of commons to the peasantry continued to attract at best a lukewarm response.

Despite legislation which said that a local vote had to be held on the request of only a third of householders, and a wide spread of such voting, it is rare to find a district or department where more than a third of eligible communities voted for division – the figures were as few as one in seven in the Nord, and one in six in the Oise. Even lower were the numbers that actually went forward to a share-out – perhaps half those initially approving the idea, some of whom later revoked the arrangements. When we note that the community of Rousies in the Nord shared out just 0.22 of a hectare to each of its 215 households, we can see one reason for avoiding *partage*. During the Terror, Montagnard-oriented National Agents and others had lamented the egoism of the rich peasants who feared 'to lose the pastures which serve only to fatten their flocks of sheep, while the poor man's cow dies of hunger', as the Calvados department claimed in February 1794.[41] Nevertheless, such concerns did nothing to accelerate the acceptance of *partage*, and on this (as on so many other issues) the Jacobin Republic had remained alienated from the majority of the population. The measure's final suspension in June 1796 provoked little response.

There was one area, however, where the Thermidorian regime introduced change that both grievously alienated the urban working population and provoked nostalgia for 1793. It backed steadily away from enforcement of the General Maximum, raising prices in October 1794, and effectively abolishing the system entirely on 24 December. A bread and meat ration at controlled prices was retained for urban inhabitants, but these rapidly shrank to pitifully inadequate amounts, and all other goods had to be bought on the open market. One reason for the shrinkage of the ration was an abominably harsh winter, already setting in when these measures were announced. The callous indifference of the Thermidorians to the fate of the populace through the next year was counterpointed by their own behaviour. Montagnard worship of virtue had gone out of the window – wealth was respectable again, and political leaders had begun to flaunt their relationships with the social elite, itself becoming rejuvenated in a more relaxed political atmosphere, with tens of thousands of 'suspects' released from prison and ready to heap scorn on the upstart 'terrorists' who had put them there.

Thus it was that this winter, and the whole terrible year that followed it, passed into legend as *nonante-cinq*, 'ninety-five' in the dialect of the northern regions where its effects were felt most harshly. Farmers, reluctant to grow crops that would be stolen from them, had cut back on their planting, and what was grown was assailed by heavy autumnal rains. As winter drew in, what food had been saved in rural areas from the ruthless requisitions of the previous year rapidly ran out. Temperatures plummeted, adding to the near impossibility of transporting supplies on ice-bound rivers and snow-clogged roads. In the cities, artisans found themselves bereft of candles or firewood to light their workshops or fire their furnaces – they were thus unable to work and scarcely able to live. The economy was still catastrophically disrupted by the decline of the assignat, and hundreds of thousands found themselves effectively indigent, with no communal resources to fall back on. Old people stumbled out into the cold to die. Infants found no milk at their starving mothers' breasts. Suicides amongst the working people of Paris became so common that the authorities ordered the suppression of published figures, to avoid panic. Recorded death rates in Rouen, normally under two hundred per month, soared to over four hundred in midwinter 1794–95, remained elevated all year, and peaked again at nine hundred in the late autumn.[42] The birth rate, especially in the north, plummeted in the next year, as many women's menstrual cycles broke down due to chronic malnutrition, a condition which continued through another very poor harvest in late 1795.

In this context of popular suffering, the Thermidorians' political scorn for the formerly lauded *sans-culottes* developed beyond public pronouncements. At every level, from the individual village to the small town, the cities and Paris itself, scores began to be settled. In Paris this meant attacks on radicals by the *jeunesse dorée*, young dandies coordinated by the ex-terrorist Fréron. They aped the manners of the now acceptable upper classes, while in fact many came from an artisanal milieu. They also brawled with more conspicuously plebeian activists, and simple passers-by, as well as launching organised attacks on the Jacobin Club and 'Terrorist' sections. In almost any part of the country, the wives and widows of 'Terrorists' might be singled out for ostracism, and in some places for ridicule and assault – in Montbrison in the Loire, for example, such women were flogged on their bared buttocks by royalist gangs and made to recant their 'sins' on their knees. In the cities of the south east, a more bloody and programmatic 'White Terror' began to emerge, and over the following year several hundred local Jacobins who had been rounded up after Thermidor were massacred in their prisons by gangs that flaunted a fierce Catholic royalism. From the towns, this spread to the villages, in a region where the vendetta had long been accepted as part of life, and savage tit-for-tat killings stretched on far beyond the end of the decade.

The White Terror was assisted in the summer of 1795 by a systematic disarmament of former Terrorists – a process which meant not merely a literal confiscation of weapons, but the barring from citizenship activities which followed exclusion from the National Guard. This decisive measure was prompted by the last major radical uprising of the Parisians, which itself was a product of their economic desperation as much as their political demands. The plight of ordinary workers in the capital can be shown by a few simple numbers. In April and May 1795 no more than half a pound of bread per person, and often much less, was being offered each day at the ration price. The assignat was hovering somewhere between 10 and 15 per cent of its face value, and heading downwards. Meanwhile the price of open-market bread was going through the roof: from 25 sous a pound in late March, to 65 in early April, 120 sous two weeks later, and an astonishing 320 sous (16 livres) in mid May. Ever since the annulment of the Maximum, there had been waves of uncoordinated discontent, and arrests for individual outspoken attacks on the authorities. By March police reports revealed a litany of complaint and desperation from men and women alike. Between 16 and 31 March there were at least five marches to the Convention to protest at shortages, one of which, on the 28th, was violent, being dispersed by the National Guard. The previous day had seen *taxation populaire* break out in two sections, and illegal assemblies formed in several others. Further rioting occurred on the 30th, and a strike for bread broke out on the 31st.[43]

On 1 and 2 April this movement escalated into a general, albeit uncoordinated, rising. The Convention itself was invaded by a crowd of both sexes demanding 'Bread and the Constitution of 1793' – the latter having acquired totemic power as a democratic document.[44] There was little difficulty in dispersing these protestors without further violence, once some loyal National Guards and *jeunesse dorée* had been collected. Parisians who had almost worshipped the 'national representation', and cheered the fall of the various alleged factions that threatened it, could not yet muster sufficient contempt for the Convention as an institution to challenge its existence. This abortive 'Rising of 12 and 13 Germinal' succeeded in the short term only in provoking the Thermidorian leadership to arrest more Montagnards suspected of Terrorist sympathies, and to make a token commitment to supplement bread rations with rice. This had little effect.[45]

Outside Paris, the rising prompted an upsurge in a pattern of rural *taxation populaire* in the Paris Basin that had become almost routine during this bitter season, and also led to major rioting in Rouen and Amiens. In the former, civil authority effectively broke down for two days after news from Paris arrived, although here, as in Amiens, the crowds were anti-republican in their slogans and attacks on officials. Smaller urban protests occurred as far afield as Caen and Honfleur. Despite the obvious material motives for protest, the authorities were as keen as ever to see evidence of counter-revolutionary conspiracy in such allegedly simultaneous risings.

Continued desperation, as prices escalated to the levels noted already, produced a more intense Parisian insurrection on 20 May, or 1 Prairial. For weeks, the streets had rung to rumours of suicides by the starving, and even official documents noted that rations were running short daily, leaving thousands across the city with no food for days on end. Women, as ever at the forefront of subsistence anxieties, seem to have taken the lead, gathering in popular areas from the early hours, and acting to summon men from their work, rounding up others from bread queues, and even breaking into section meetings. By early afternoon, normal life in many sections had been suspended, and from the Faubourg Saint-Antoine, a column headed by women, and including many armed men, was making for the Convention. Insurgents forced open section armouries, even while the National Guards of other sections struggled to arm themselves and also headed for the Convention. When the crowds burst again into the assembly hall, they bore with them on a pike the head of a *conventionnel*, Féraud, who had tried to bar their path.

Despite this brutal display of their determination, the naive faith of the protestors in the Convention meant that they lost all momentum once it agreed to release some prisoners and look into the food supply situation. The aimless lull that ensued was enough for loyal troops to be gathered and the crowds driven out. Forced back into the eastern faubourgs, and perhaps regretting their earlier mistakes, the insurgents rearmed, appearing the next day in central Paris with as many as twenty thousand under arms, to face twice that number of government troops. Even when some of these forces deserted to them the insurgents did not press the issue, and there was no fighting. They were once again fobbed off with promises. Over the following few days, the Thermidorian leadership took no more chances, mustering their military forces and surrounding the Faubourg Saint-Antoine, the heart of the insurrection, and forcing an ignominious surrender.[46]

What followed was a thoroughgoing political and social purge. Once again, the opportunity was used to dispose of a few more recalcitrant Montagnard *conventionnels*, and over a hundred people were tried by a special military commission. Many were acquitted or given only brief sentences, especially women who chose to plead that they had been 'impregnated with opinions and maxims' by 'impostors who seduced [them] with apparent patriotism'.[47] Such disingenuousness was gratefully taken at face value by the judges, confirming as it did their own prejudices and avoiding the total rejection of their regime by both sexes. New laws nevertheless banned all women from attending political assemblies, even as spectators, and they were prohibited from gathering outdoors in groups of more than five, under pain of arrest.

Thousands of male activists, however, suffered individually when the sections were ordered on 24 May to denounce all suspected Terrorists. Old scores were settled, and many found the safest route to political acceptance was through the denunciation of others. As many as five thousand individuals may have been detained in the capital, and perhaps as many more sentenced to the civil death of 'disarmament'. It was this process which then rippled out to the country at large, and saw as many as a hundred thousand disarmed, most of whom were also arrested, and a significant proportion of them imprisoned for several months.[48] Even in a quiet medium-sized town like Le Havre in Normandy, at least fifteen men were arrested, and in the nearby small town of Ingouville, with only two thousand inhabitants, reason enough was found to lock up eight artisans for having supported the Terrorist former mayor.

The purges of the 'Year III' (which had begun in September 1794) ironically helped to establish a somewhat misleading image of the sans-culotte as a profoundly plebeian type. Thermidorian rhetoric, picking up themes prevalent at all stages of the Revolution, looked to the bottom of the social ladder for those to blame for upheaval, and the Terrorist emerged from this as a caricatured marginal creature, led on into excess by the evil leaders who, again, had taken this role in explanations at every stage of events. When individuals had to explain themselves, they frequently chose (like the Parisian women after Prairial) to emphasise their own ignorance – and to assert that much of that ignorance came from their own low status. This is one reason why historians have had to dig behind the self-definitions of so many as locksmiths or joiners to find their employees and their property portfolios. At the same time, the real animus of the Thermidorians against social upstarts ensured that those of the poorer classes who had entered the ranks of the Terror were clearly labelled as dangerous men – who might suffer persecution as a result for decades to come.

A minority of activists who were genuinely marginal stood out. Nicolas Guénot, originally from the Yonne, had drifted to Paris in the 1780s, joined and left the Gardes Françaises, gone home and lived as a poacher, returned to Paris before the Revolution, become a police informer, and briefly a prison warder, before embarking on a career as a Terrorist enforcer, working for the Committee of General Security. In early 1794, aged forty, he was an eager and vigorous Terrorist, producing a steady stream of individual denunciations. An embezzlement charge nearly sent him to the guillotine, but he was saved, ironically, by Thermidor. A career that hovered somewhere halfway between policing and crime continued for several more years, until another brush with the law saw him exiled back to the Yonne in 1801. There he went back to living in the woods, a bogeyman for local children, having survived a lynching-party on December 1802 which cornered him on the roof of a cottage owned by one of his few friends. They shot at him for an hour and a half until he fell to the ground, wounded in a dozen places, and he was only saved from being finished off by a police officer, an outsider, who put him on a cart to the local hospital. The savage treatment of this bizarre figure, who seems to have almost lost the power of speech during his sojourn in the woods, was orchestrated by the local mayor, a timber merchant whose clique ruled the village, having ousted the Terrorists headed by the local notary. The blatant illegality of Guénot's persecution would continue to be ignored by higher authority through every subsequent change of regime. His internal exile continued until his death, hardened perhaps by the outdoor life, at the ripe old age of seventy-eight in 1832.[49]

If Guénot fitted almost too well the profile of the Terrorist that later regimes wanted to stigmatise, another individual, Claude Barthélemy Jurie, shows the limits of a reading of the Terror as a movement solely from below.[50] Jurie too died ruined and broken by his connections to the *sans-culotte* movement of the Year II, but he began as a scion of the provincial squirearchy, became a barrister in Paris, and married into the bourgeoisie, with a dowry of eight urban and two rural properties from his father-in-law in the Faubourg Saint-Antoine. Aged thirty in 1789, he had a meteoric rise in the politics of the faubourg, being elected as a police *commissaire* and a member of the Commune, serving as National Guard battalion commander and section secretary, and holding several other posts, along with membership of the Jacobins. Only the Thermidorian reaction reversed this trajectory, and led to an obscure death. If the Terror had ended differently, or gone on, it is very likely that Jurie's prospects would have been as bright as a true *sans-culotte* as they were as a prosperous noble bridegroom.

Other 'respectable' ex-Terrorists often managed to slip back into a property-owning life, at least outside the regions where 'White Terror' was more entrenched. 'Marat' Chaix, scourge of the rich in the district of Lormes, was arrested early in 1794 as an Hébertist, but was free again in the Year III to resume his properties, even while defending his former actions in correspondence. In Roanne in the Loire, a more thoroughgoing pattern of continuity prevailed – the radical *sans-culottes* of the town's revolutionary committee in 1794 were the same cautious businessmen who had weathered the Federalist storm so adroitly a year earlier, who had run the town through every previous phase of revolutionary change, and who would slip through the net of Thermidorian revenge equally successfully.[51]

As the Republic's massive armies of peasants and workers embarked from 1794 on what became increasingly a war of conquest, they did so in the name of a regime, and a social structure, that was doing its best to repudiate all popular engagement with public life. The efforts of all phases of the Terror had been directed towards creating and maintaining the armies above all else, and some 800,000 men were under arms at the peak of mass mobilisation. They came from all sectors of society in the wake of the levy of 300,000 and the later *levée en masse*; and since April 1793, when Hébertists took over the war ministry, they had been subjected to a barrage of politicising propaganda and directives. Military political clubs were initially encouraged (although later suppressed like all other popular societies), and the printed rantings of the *Père Duchesne* and other similar papers were distributed at state expense (making a fortune of over 100,000 livres for Hébert along the way).

It is not surprising that, under the direct eye of Montagnard representatives-on-mission, and in the face of the 'real' counter-revolutionary enemy, the army became a stronghold of Jacobinism. Both the Great Terror and the Thermidorian reaction mostly passed the troops by, though there were predictable purges in the higher ranks and civilian administration. So long as they actively fought the internal and external enemies of the Republic itself, a radical patriotism was both self-reinforcing, and detached them from much of the bitterness of civilian politics.[52] As time went on, however, that patriotism became translated into both a chauvinistic nationalism and a willingness to intervene in the name of the Republic in the squabbles of civilian politics. Under the banners of the nation, troops resumed the unquestioning suppression of dissent that had been so lacking in 1789. The support of the army allowed the regime that emerged as the Convention finalised the 'Constitution of the Year III' in the summer of 1795 to endure a further four years, when everything else about the politics of those years pointed to imminent collapse.

12

Revolution against the People?

Political life under the new Directorial regime, named after the five-man presidency of the Executive Directory, was never peaceful. It was born in the shadow of yet another Parisian uprising, this time by the National Guards of the more 'moderate' sections, who had by now become decidedly royalist in character. They launched an attack on the Convention on 5 October 1795, 13 Vendémiaire IV, when it became clear that new elections had no hope of bringing in a royalist majority. This highly probable outcome had been blocked by the simple device of the Convention selecting two-thirds of the new legislators itself, from its own membership. The ex-Terrorist Thermidorian leader Barras, assisted by troops led by General Bonaparte, drove off the insurgents.

Only a month later, the ultra-radical François-Noël Babeuf began publishing a new left-wing journal, only to be forced into hiding himself by December. Babeuf, a feudal lawyer by profession, had been a minor activist in the early years of the Revolution, and later an agent for the enforcement of the General Maximum. He changed his first name to Gracchus, the name of two brothers who had been murdered in ancient Rome for proposing the agrarian law. Imprisoned by the Thermidorians in 1794–95, Babeuf rose to prominence now as one of the few prepared to take a public stand for radical Jacobinism. Through early 1796, Babeuf and a small group of co-conspirators tried to establish the groundwork for a new *sans-culotte* rising. This 'Conspiracy of the Equals' was broken by arrests in May 1796, which also licensed a new persecution of unrepentant Terrorists within Paris and elsewhere.[1]

Although the 'Babouvists' had established long lists of the good *sans-culottes* they expected to rise up and then occupy leadership positions, their network of support was largely imaginary – an attempted rising amongst troops encamped near the capital was snuffed out easily in September. It nevertheless offered the Directory the chance to show off its law and order credentials to propertied opinion. There were hundreds of arrests, and a mass show trial of the leading Babouvists, conducted safely outside Paris in Vendôme. This was mismanaged, however, leading to the acquittal of most of the sixty-four defendants, and press exposés of intimidatory prosecution tactics. The trial dragged on until Babeuf and his leading co-conspirator were sentenced to death and executed on 27 May 1797, by which time the political foundations of the government were crumbling for other reasons.

As the Vendémiaire and Babouvist episodes show, the relatively centrist politics followed by the Directory still required it to deploy armed force and the resources of an increasingly well-developed police state against enemies on both flanks. The tightrope that was being walked became increasingly precarious, until a balance became impossible to maintain, and policy began to swing violently from left to right. September 1797 saw a *coup d'état* of the executive against the electorate, annulling an alarming wave of royalist electoral gains and initiating a further wave of punitive legislation against priests, royalists and émigrés. Less than a year later a resurgence of the left amongst the electorate, prompted in part by these measures, was itself snuffed out by a further coup. Electoral politics were shamelessly, if increasingly ineffectively, manipulated until the coup of 9 November 1799, 18 Brumaire VIII, which brought Napoleon Bonaparte to political power.[2]

The Directory had little in its political arsenal beyond savage measures against both émigrés and Terrorists and their families, combined with a slow-motion game of cat-and-mouse with political clubs and publications, repeatedly banning and unbanning groups and journals to left and right as the political see-saw rose and fell. All attempts at political stabilisation failed, as did the search for a stable relationship with other states. The knowledge that, as republicans, they remained anathema to the European powers, and to the émigrés who egged the latter on, forced the Directory to pursue a military solution. The most spectacular success, driving Austria herself out of the war in October 1797, came as the climax of Bonaparte's Italian campaign. This opened a brief period of French supremacy before general war was renewed in late 1798 and early 1799. The avid desire of the regime for revenue from the conquered territories – which sometimes was all that stood between them and total collapse – was one reason for the fatal instability of the chain of 'sister republics' erected from Naples to Holland throughout this period. Forcible incorporation into the territory of the nascent French Empire provided a longer-term solution, and one entirely typical of the expansionist military-political machine that the revolutionary state had become.

Overall the Directorial era witnessed political chaos, even though the social elite steadily re-established its uncontested dominance. That dominance was accomplished, however, only by clamping down persistently, if with fluctuating success, on a population which continued to challenge the elite in various ways.³ The impact of this period on the lives of the common people can be seen in several key areas: economic policy and taxation; the peasantry and the land; military service and public order; and popular religious expression. The Directorial economy is hard to portray other than as a disaster. As early as 1795 there had been emergency measures to protect capital as the assignat collapsed: landlords were authorised to demand half their rents in kind, and a decree prohibited the early repayment of loans in devalued paper. The state also demanded at the same time that half of all taxes should be paid in grain, but still the assignat fell. In Brumaire IV, a few months later, some 800 billion livres, at face value, were printed – demand was so overwhelming that a political crisis nearly ensued when the printers threatened a strike. For some in the elite this had its advantages: artisans who tried to revive their fortunes by servicing the new extravagances of fashion might find themselves paid off with worthless paper. Everyday trading, in contrast, especially in the countryside, was reduced to barter and the small supply of carefully hoarded coins. Only the power of the state could force people to transact significant business in paper, except where, as with rent and debts, it was to their advantage.

In a desperate attempt to remedy the situation, a new currency, the *mandat territorial*, intended to have a value firmly fixed against national lands, was introduced in March 1796, when the assignat printing-plates were ceremoniously broken. It lasted four months before the fixed rate for its value had to be abandoned. Thereafter it collapsed to total worthlessness, being formally withdrawn in February 1797. It was after this that indirect taxes, so hated in 1789, were reintroduced – a stamp tax on documents and transactions, and a door and window tax, followed in late 1798 by a tobacco tax. The greater certainty of collection represented by such measures began to ease the state's finances. They were accompanied by a partial state bankruptcy, as two-thirds of all state debts were forcibly transferred into bonds, the value of which soon evaporated.⁴ Nevertheless, this led slowly to stabilisation, since there was now no paper money to devalue, and by November 1798 the payment of tax in kind was replaced by cash.

The task of stimulating a wider economic recovery was almost insurmountable. The dominant industries of the eighteenth century had all been hit hard. Trade with the Caribbean, and merchant shipping generally, was effectively non-existent while war with England lasted. Its replacement, privateering, made fortunes for some but was hardly a productive enterprise. The networks that supported the dispersed textile industries of Normandy, Anjou and other regions across the north and south were shattered by war and civil war. Half the looms of Cholet, devastated by the Vendean war, were still idle in 1798. Lyon's silk-weavers had already been in crisis in 1789, but still operated some 10,000 looms. This number fell to only 3500 after the 1793 siege, and only reached 6500 by 1801. Towns across the country told the same tale: in Carcassonne in the far south, textile production in 1800 was below one-third of its 1789 level. Stimulation of the cotton industry, as elsewhere the most advanced industrial sector, led to the revival of tentative experiments with machines first begun in the 1780s, but continual problems of supply and labour made such investments hard to justify.[5]

The newer forms of industrialisation, as Britain was discovering, required new kinds of discipline (or brutal regimentation, from a worker's perspective). As early as 1789, machine-breaking had been the response in several regions to attempted mechanisation. There seemed little prospect of workers accepting this forceful intrusion into their working lives, so long as a spark of the sans-culotte spirit of independence was alive. The total disarray of the country's finances also discouraged capital investment, and the state had neither the financial resources to support industrialists in long drawn out struggles against recalcitrant workers, nor the political will to induce new bitter conflicts when so many old ones continued to rage. Its reliance instead on the relatively inexpensive promotion of intellectual innovation amongst the higher ranks of society, and the recreation of the Old Regime's structures of elite schools and academic institutes, provided France with a new generation of notable scholars, scientists and innovators, but many of the products of this endeavour had to wait for the new century before being disseminated.[6]

Even though the economic situation held back its immediate expansion, the educated, 'enlightened' revolutionaries had nonetheless carried forward a project which was in many ways an integral part of the history of modern European society. All the restructuring since 1789 had brought modernity to France, creating a single, rational, hierarchical system of administration, and bringing uniformity to taxation, weights and measures. The metric system, passed into law on 7 April 1795, was one of the most profound innovations in human history, replacing a myriad local and disputable measures with one national, and ultimately global, standard.[7] The revolutionaries had also begun to export this system by military force into the Netherlands, the Rhineland and Italy. Over the coming Napoleonic era these benefits were disseminated even more widely by similarly coercive means.

It is worth recalling, however, that this magnificent act of creation was also an act of great violence in itself. It wrenched the population, without consultation, from the comfortable convolutions of its time-honoured ways into a society reconstructed as if from a blank canvas. The ways of the Old Regime, oppressive though they were, were at least well understood by the population, who had had time to develop an appreciation of the gaps and absences, contradictions and lapses in the patchwork of duties imposed on them. The new order, with its model of a single stable framework of state operations, could only be resisted by open defiance. A system made simple, for the convenience of state administrators, the admiration of intellectuals and the profit of capitalists, was alien to most people's lives, and it would take generations for the majority to unwillingly accept the new vocabulary of measurement, analysis and quantification that parcelled out their existence and activities.[8]

The peasantry, although bullied by the state in this and many other respects, continued nonetheless to reap the benefits of the end of feudalism and the sale of *biens nationaux*. Desperate for money, the Thermidorians had in May 1795 authorised buyers to bypass the usual auction sales if they could put up seventy-five times the 1790 income of the property within three months. Since this was the face-value figure, it added up in hard-cash terms to only some four times the income, if paid in assignats. Superficially, this was a victory for speculators, who could now turn piles of almost-worthless paper into land worth a fortune on the open market. To realise such fortunes, however, the lands were frequently disposed of again, when the buyers were often peasant landholders. Auction sales were reinstated in November 1796, but by this stage the vast majority of lands had already been disposed of. Around three-quarters of all purchases were completed between 1790 and 1795; many of those that followed were not of land at all, but buildings, such as vicarages, that had previously been part of the state church.[9]

Around a tenth of all land changed hands, two-thirds of which came from the church, the remainder coming from the confiscated royal domains and émigré lands. Somewhere over half a million individual purchasers were involved: perhaps a tenth of all households. Overall figures show wide disparities in the proportion of lands that peasants were able to acquire for themselves – in the Nord department, they secured 52 per cent of all sales, and peasant holdings here rose from some 32 to 42 per cent of the land, in a region where the church had owned over a fifth of all land. Nevertheless, in this densely populated region, some three-quarters of peasants were still left holding a hectare or less, and remained unable to be self-sufficient without common lands and other employment. Around Toulouse, only some 15 per cent of land went to peasants, despite their making up over two-thirds of all individual purchasers. In the Seine-et-Oise, close to Paris, the figures were even lower, around 13.5 per cent for several districts.[10] Nevertheless, it seems probable that the peasantry overall secured something over a third of the lands on offer, plus those later resold by speculators, and that these gains pushed the overall peasant share of land in France from under 45 per cent to around a half.

Peasants continued to work the other half as well, of course, and if they remained subject to the prejudicial assignment of the old tithe and *taille* to their rents, they also came to be in an increasingly advantageous position towards their landlords. Even the landless benefited from rising wages in a period of labour shortages, when dislocation and the demands of war pulled so many young men from the fields.[11] Overall there was, perhaps ironically, more justice than progress in the agricultural system that emerged by the late 1790s. Progress towards modernisation, as understood then and since, meant the consolidation of enclosed large farms able to be worked intensively, the expansion of agricultural wage labour to work them, and a consequent movement of such labour, when surplus, into the towns – there to provide the fodder for industry's new machines. None of this happened. It was noticeable that the rich continued to invest their profits in substantial landholdings, but even these were rarely turned into the arable factories of the economists' dreams. When landholding was an ambition in itself, what motivation was there to stir unrest amongst the community by challenging existing practices, perhaps only to see one's property torched by the vengeful peasantry?

Every force acting on agriculture, except the stubborn will of a few innovators, pulled in the direction of inhibiting growth and maximising returns for peasants, who still preferred the traditional methods, and whose aim was to survive and pass on their lands to their offspring, not to boost the national economy. This aim had a further structural effect, as one of the few surviving pieces of radically egalitarian revolutionary legislation required land to be divided between all children upon inheritance.[12] The French peasantry would exacerbate a long-term labour shortage by resolutely refusing to have large families in future – within half a generation average family size had shrunk from around six children to four or fewer.

One other dramatic gain for the average French family is revealed only by the close analysis of later statistics. Although family size shrank, life expectancy at birth rose over the following generation from under thirty to almost forty, and the number of children surviving to age fifteen from under half to almost two-thirds. This happened in no other country on such a dramatic scale, so general trends such as improvements in medicine can be discounted. There can be no doubt that the French peasantry's persistent refusal to accept anything other than a complete removal of the feudal yoke was ultimately a great victory for them, and made a real difference to the lives of their children and grandchildren.[13]

Ironically, of course, this gain was accompanied by the burden of providing Napoleon with his famed 'income' of 100,000 men a year. This helps account for another demographic anomaly of the next generation, a soaring marriage rate that coincided with the introduction from 1798 of a nationwide system of regular military conscription for young single men. In bidding to avoid service, one of the easiest manoeuvres was to take a wife – even in some cases an old one, and one that could be divorced later, thanks to another piece of revolutionary legislation (this right would later be curtailed by Napoleon). Early marriage was not available to all, however, and in any case, by the end of the 1790s, the relationship between military service and the rural majority had already become complex and tormented.

The simplest recourse of those summoned to serve, especially if they came from more remote parts of the countryside, was not to go, disappearing either before or after the initial muster. This *insoumission* had already begun with the levy of 300,000 in early 1793, rising to epidemic levels later. The town of Aurillac in the Cantal sent seventy-one men away to the nearby centre of Saint-Flour for this first levy, but by the end of the summer the authorities could only locate nineteen of them. In the Creuse, 1314 men were called up under the new laws in 1800, but only 300 reached their assigned units. Further to the west, the marshy coastal plains of the Landes had been supposed to provide 1200 men in 1799, but only sixty could be found the day after the muster. Regions like this, thinly-populated and with impenetrable countryside, were ideal territory for young men called to the colours to simply remain with their families, melting into the hills or marshes if the forces of order ever happened to appear.[14]

The problem of recruitment was made far worse by the parallel issue of desertion. Young men called up in the two great levies of 1793 had no set term of service and, until the new conscription, there was no general system for replacements and reinforcements. The consequences of endless campaigning and the financial plight of the state were spelled out in brutally pragmatic terms by General Bonaparte when he took charge of French forces in Italy, in a proclamation of 27 March 1796:

> Soldiers, you are naked, ill fed! The government owes you much; it can give you nothing. Your patience, the courage you display in the midst of these rocks, are admirable; but they procure you no glory, no fame is reflected upon you. I seek to lead you into the most fertile plains in the world. Rich provinces, great cities will be in your power. There you will find honour, glory, and riches.[15]

Those triple temptations, set before troops who often had only the scraps of worn-out uniforms, and who were fortunate if they had wooden clogs on their feet, some of their comrades making do with plaited straw, would inspire a campaign of lightning victories. The troops who stayed with the colours through this period developed a hardened professionalism, alloyed with a continued republican devotion and *élan* that helped claw them to victory even against the steepest odds.

Those who stayed in the front line of victorious campaigns, rather than manning the other long frontiers or garrisoning conquered territories, were nonetheless a minority. There was little recompense in glory, or gold, for most. Many soldiers, worn out or disillusioned by continual service, began to drift away from the army at any opportunity. Individuals could easily disappear home from garrison or reserve camps, and even more easily from military hospitals, from where convalescents were expected to return to their units individually and on foot. Some reintegrated into home communities, much like the *insoumis*, but this was often not possible, especially as the most disaffected soldiers were likely to be those who had been shunted out by their home villages in the first place, who would hardly be welcomed back. Even those whose families might shelter them ran the risk of denunciation by jealous or vindictive neighbours.[16]

Many deserters and *insoumis* had little choice but to turn to crime. From the later 1790s, through far into the Napoleonic period, individuals and groups created an internal security problem that was both criminal and political. Revenge attacks on the property, crops and persons of revolutionary local authorities were commonplace. Administrative buildings that housed the registers of births were frequent targets for arson from 1798, since it was one's recorded date of birth which held the key to conscription. In the west, revived Chouan bands found a major source of both personnel and weapons in desertion. In the south east, in particular, long-lived and determined forces of brigands with a distinctly counter-revolutionary flavour found many of their recruits in this way.[17]

Some of this activity shaded into counter-revolutionary insurrection. Royalist gangs in the south east attempted to seize towns ranging from Saint-Etienne to Montpellier in the winter of 1795–96. This activity terrified local republicans, and created a siege mentality, especially as atrocities against isolated activists were well documented. Nevertheless, on a national scale these raids were little more than a nuisance to the authorities.[18] In the west, the guerrilla war that had settled over the Vendée and its neighbouring departments remained a far more serious concern – so much so that in 1796 the Army of the Ocean Coasts deployed over 100,000 men in garrisons and columns to hunt the rebels down, three times more than Bonaparte led into Italy. Driven beyond the bounds of habitation, the rebels were isolated and increasingly desperate. Stofflet, the ex-gamekeeper who had been one of the Vendeans' first leaders, was reduced to a few hundred followers in January 1796. He attempted to launch a new campaign, but was swiftly captured and shot. Another former 'general', Charrette, who had negotiated as an equal with republican commanders over an earlier truce, was paraded in chains through Nantes before his execution in March.[19] Overwhelming force crushed resistance in the Vendée, and across the west, thereafter.

If royalists' activity was mostly a problem for the authorities, and quite often seen in something of a heroic light by disaffected locals, there were plenty of more grimly self-interested deserters at work. Violent crime of all kinds rose dramatically in the late 1790s. The disruption of the previous years, and the near total collapse of endeavours to operate public welfare schemes, swelled the existing ranks of robbers and bandits, who were then joined by military renegades in many areas. Some of these bands preyed on state services, robbing the mailcoaches of public funds but leaving passengers alone. In the Aisne in 1795 bands of deserters were raiding public granaries. Others turned on known 'patriots' and well-off purchasers of biens nationaux, adding nocturnal raids and extortions to the more public ostracism meted out by some communities. In the Drôme, a known counter-revolutionary led a band which seized arms from at least sixty 'patriots' around Taulignan in 1796–97. How far any of this was idealistically political, and how far a question of hitting soft targets without generating too much local opposition, is a moot point, but it clearly reflects the alienation from the Republic, and its most overt and often wealthy supporters, felt in many areas throughout this period.

Nevertheless, much crime in this period had no shred of political justification. All but the poorest farmers in some areas came to live in fear of nocturnal raids. In the northern regions, long-standing bandit patterns of terror and extortion revived sharply. The sommation minatoire, written blackmail demands for cash on pain of arson and pillage, became widespread in Picardy, reviving a practice that had been fought against by the authorities as far back as the 1720s. In this and many other areas, chauffage became epidemic – bandit gangs who tortured farmers into revealing their hidden valuables by 'warming' their feet in their own fires. Some such gangs became veritable private armies. The Bande de Salembrier numbered over sixty, and roved at will between the Pas-de-Calais, the Nord and the Belgian territories in 1795–97.[20] The Bande d'Orgères, more formidable still, was not broken by the authorities until 1799, after a reign of terror in the Beauce, in and around the Eure-et-Loir department south of Paris. This had begun with isolated incidents in 1791–93, been interrupted by the state's Terror in 1794, and exploded to a peak of seventy-one crimes in 1796–97.[21] Almost 120 people, thirty-eight of them women, were indicted over a total of ninety-five incidents. There was evidence of a fully-functional 'anti-community' at the core of the gang, which according to members' testimony recruited its thieves as young as ten or twelve years old, using these *mioches* to spy out likely targets. Certainly, few members could give any identifiable former profession, beyond some who claimed military service, and many may have been driven to a life of crime even before 1789. Most were the rejects of rural society, and often carried scars, mutilations and deformities – from hernias to missing toes and fingers – that might have made them useless for work. Some even had to walk with sticks or crutches, and one was an epileptic.

Their behaviour, however, robbed such ill-shaped figures of any pity. Although they sometimes camped in the woods, and did most of their work under cover of darkness, they used their contacts and stolen resources to ensure that they more often slept in rural inns and wanted for little. Their methods were unhesitatingly brutal. Seventy-five murders were attributed to the gang, including four incidents where victims were first raped. On several occasions they were charged with having slaughtered whole households in isolated farms before sitting down to a meal, and more debauched entertainments, amongst the corpses. They also murdered each other – on several occasions killing individuals who had disobeyed or failed on some mission, and at least twice killing women who had refused sex to male leaders. In general, however, the women seem to have taken part in carnage on equal terms with men, and in some cases gave the lead in cruelty, before routinely bedecking themselves with whatever finery they had seized on their raids. Two women and twenty men were executed and a total of twenty-four imprisoned. These were the core of the captured gang. Another thirty were on the run, and twenty-three had died awaiting trial in the awful conditions of a Directorial prison. This may not even have been the largest criminal network operating in the region – the Rouen courts condemned sixty-four *chauffeurs* to death in a series of trials between January 1798 and March 1799.

Even much smaller gangs could exercise intimidation that left whole communities powerless. In mid December 1796, one such group of fifteen men broke into a farmhouse near Remiremont in the Vosges, not at midnight but at five in the afternoon.[22] After smashing down the door, they systematically destroyed all the crockery and glassware, cooked a huge meal with all the provisions of the house, ate it at their leisure, and left with all the cash they could find, smashing the windows as they went. No one tried to stop them, or to summon help, as a wave of such attacks had terrified the community into silence. Even the lone deserter could very easily be transformed into a violent and desperate criminal simply by his situation. Prison or firing-squad awaited him on recapture, and many became brutalised by their fugitive status, if they had not already been so by army life. Violence, of course, was in any case never far from the surface of eighteenth-century life. Beyond the theft which was their only resource for survival, such men were sometimes guilty of rapes, murders and other assaults that appalled whole districts, so that communities became even more wary of strangers than they had been before the Revolution. The terrible price of the Republic's ongoing wars was paid in blood and fear, very far from the battlefields where such activities were dignified with the pall of glory and patriotism.

Fear and uncertainty could drive people to cooperate with authority as well as to shun it, and it would be wrong to suggest that French civil society collapsed under the Directory, though it undoubtedly teetered on the brink. Many villages continued to function as they always had done, as organic communities, even if this now included the tacitly acknowledged presence of a non-juring priest or an *insoumis* somewhere in the vicinity. Such places tended to respond to the more unwelcome demands of authority by simply ignoring them, and many a local official who sought to investigate irregularities in taxation or requisitioning was met with closed doors, behind which stood a united front of monosyllabic proclaimed ignorance, until they went away in despair. The towns were more amenable to a generally authoritarian form of policing, in which the National Guard of property-owners reverted to the main aim of safeguarding that property, as its original founders had envisaged. Although the centralised police powers of the Terror were formally abolished in April 1795, by December of that year the central government had again empowered itself to appoint agents in all communes of fewer than 5000 inhabitants, and created a formal Ministry of General Police in January 1796.[23] Local government was closely scrutinised thereafter, and its personnel were subject to change and control from above. Robust military action, placing many departments under forms of martial law, brought some of the more lawless areas under a semblance of control. Even in its closing months, however, the Directory was challenged by royalist rebellions in the Haute-Garonne and the west, and endeavours to finally solidify social control needed to go on scarcely abated for a decade or more.[24]

Not all opposition, or support, focused around such brutally physical conflicts, however, and in the sphere of religion this period reveals some significant subtleties, even amidst a tale of ongoing fundamental dispute. Religious policy stood on foundations laid down on 21 February 1795. Then the state had formally renounced its financial support for, and organisational ties with, the constitutional church, and thus its support for any one form of public worship. Formal freedom of religion, *la liberté des cultes*, was proclaimed. It had not been intended with this decree to reopen the confiscated and closed churches, but such was the wave of popular demand that this had to be permitted three months later. Many citizens had not waited for permission. In Auxerre a massive demonstration on 29 March 1795, Palm Sunday, opened up the cathedral of Saint-Etienne. Men and women of all ages set to work stripping out the vestiges of the *décadi* cult, and burnt painted classical images that had been used in it. A delegation to the local authorities demanded that formal access to the building be allowed, while also proclaiming their revolutionary and republican loyalties. The Altar of the Fatherland and the national flag were preserved from the destruction, and the delegation concluded their address with 'Glory to God! Respect to the Convention and the constituted authorities! *Vive la République!*'[25]

This bold assertion that Catholicism was compatible with republicanism was widely held: in the towns of the west, for example, where the two had seemed in sharp conflict, urban populations now regularly demanded that their religious rights should be respected. In June 1796 the village of Gahard in the Ille-et-Vilaine explicitly claimed that their collective patriotism in the face of 'the furor of the Chouans' now entitled them to worship freely.[26] This assertion came in the face of another wave of official anticlericalism: non-juring priests had been subjected to renewed penalties in October 1795 after the Vendémiaire rising, which were not withdrawn until December 1796. Until that point, many remained imprisoned, and many others remained in emigration even after this. The pendulum swung even more violently in 1797, with all legislation against non-jurors being repealed on 24 August, only to be reinvoked after the 4 September coup. Over 1500 priests were deported in the following year, and a concerted effort was made by the authorities to reinvigorate the scheme of national festivals, and to make the *décadi* once again the day of worship.

In February 1798 French troops took Rome, proclaiming a republic there. The pope died eighteen months later in French custody at Valence. This period for many French Catholics seemed to be a final test of their faith, with their religion subject to implacable and increasingly unjustifiable persecution. Of course, to the committed men of the Enlightenment who ruled France, nothing had changed since the church was first condemned as bloated and aristocratic in 1789–90, and as evidently counter-revolutionary in 1791–93. Only the more pragmatic, and militarily secure, regime of Napoleon would feel able to deal with the church as a problem of practical politics, agreeing in 1802 to restore Catholic worship under state supervision in return for effective papal recognition. Until that change, priests remained the bogeymen of opposition, and their hold over their deluded flocks, especially the female half, was taken for granted.

Thousands of ordinary Frenchwomen did indeed support both the non-jurors and the wider campaign for religious freedom in the 1790s. Many objected profoundly to the Revolution's intrusion, and were not afraid to show this, even in the absence of any of their alleged clerical ringleaders. In the small town of Montpigié in the Haute-Loire, a representative-on-mission summoned what he called 'a large assembly of stupid little women' in February 1795 to witness their local *béates*, the quasi-nuns who lived under simple vows, take a revolutionary oath.[27] The *béates* instead pro-claimed their immediate willingness to be guillotined for their faith, to loud cheers from all present. The representative's attempt to enforce his control with arrests led to a full-scale uprising, led by women, that emptied the prison and incarcerated the local officials. Even at the height of Terror, such collective defiance had sometimes rendered officialdom powerless. In the community of Saint-Vincent in the same department, June 1794 had seen the whole population gathered in church to hear an oration on the Supreme Being, when the female population stood *en masse* in their pews, turned and showed the orator their bared backsides – an act of scorn so successful that it was repeated in neighbouring parishes as word spread.

Religious women lived through a dramatic period that tested their faith in a variety of ways. Even when not confronted by overt conflict, they lived with the scorn and opposition of the authorities. They reclaimed church buildings, scouring them clean of any of the varied functions they had been used for, in effectively penitential acts of labour. They invited and sheltered priests, protecting them from arrest, and heard clandestine masses in thousands of individual places. The revolutionary leadership's basic belief in their irrationality may, ironically, have sheltered such women from individual persecution, but there is no doubt that many found a new strength in their faith and a new role in combatting the challenges to it.[28]

Women were not alone in this, of course, despite the efforts of republican propaganda to separate their actions from those of 'real', male, citizens. In a remarkable expression of the enduring force of popular religiosity, hundreds of communities which had lost their priests replaced them with laymen, sometimes humble artisans or peasants, often former parochial schoolmasters and other church assistants, who could perform the cere-monies that tradition required.[29] Even in the centre and north, far from violent counter-revolution, such practices had begun as soon as the Terror ended, and expanded as the reclaiming of the churches was given official sanction from 1795. Rural and small-town inhabitants continued to dwell in a universe where the rituals of the liturgy had real sacred power: for many, the awful conditions of *nonante-cinq* were clear evidence of divine wrath against those who had forgotten their faith. Being forced, especially in 1798–99, to parade for a Festival of Old Age, Industry, Fruitfulness, or any of the other insipid idols of the late Directory was no substitute for their traditional rites. Still less was the meaningless mishmash cult of Theophilanthropy that a few republican leaders attempted at that point to foist on them. Even the constitutional church itself, stripped of state funding since 1795 but contaminated with a republican image (and desperately short of willing clergy), struggled to find worshippers outside the cities. Many shifted for themselves in matters of ritual, and many others were either awaiting the return of their true priests, or sheltered such men amongst them.[30]

Assessing the final impact of the Revolution on the ordinary people of France is a difficult task. The period that began with universal hopes ended with the dominance of a new elite, and a military dictatorship that would transform itself by 1804 into a sterile reproduction of monarchy, complete with a newly minted imperial nobility. For the common people, even the allegedly radical institutions of the Terror had brought great suffering. A grand total of 16,594 death sentences were meted out across France during that period. Of some 14,000 for whom a social identity is recorded, fewer than 9 per cent came from the ranks of the nobility. This was of course a statistical over-representation of this relatively small social elite, but it reminds us that even the official, judicial Terror was far from the later clichéd image of aristocrat-laden processions of tumbrils. Around a quarter of executions were of the middle classes, and 6.5 per cent clergy, but almost a third were of the urban working classes, and 28 per cent were of peasants. The vast majority of these, and of the other hundreds of thousands of casualties of civil war and more generalised repression, came from the country-dwelling agricultural and labouring classes of the west.[31]

The Revolution, as it turned its ardour on its own political class, may have guillotined 433 lawyers, but it also executed ninety-two tailors, eighty-two shoemakers, and 106 day-labourers. Forty-six blacksmiths joined fifty-six carpenters on the scaffold, alongside sixty-seven wigmakers, who lost more than their livelihoods to changing fashions in dress and politics. Twenty-four butchers met a bloody fate, while 122 bar-owners learnt the cost of being host to public gatherings. One hundred and sixty-two clerks, suspiciously literate individuals in a time of plots and secret correspondence, also went under the knife. As if to emphasise that no occupational group was immune, the Terror also took the lives, amongst others, of a pinmaker, a ratcatcher, a chestnut-seller, a ship's caulker, a violin-string-maker and a stable-boy.

Even in Paris, home to the most spectacular trials and 2639 executions, the guillotine was more likely to fall on a worker's or an artisan's neck (493 executions) than on one of the military nobles (490). The capital also saw ninety-four peasants, sent from all over the country, done to death in what were often examples of the near-mindless bureaucratic persecution of dissent. Two of these came from the village of Romain-sur-Colle in the Dordogne. On 29 April 1794 the inhabitants of the village had been gathered outside the 'temple of Reason' – the parish church – to hear the reading of new laws that made up an integral part of the *décadi* routine. The peasant-farmer Leonard Meynard and his sister, Paule, exasperated at the intrusions of revolutionary authority, tore a decree from the hands of an official as he tried to read it and called on their fellow-villagers to resist. They succeeded in stirring a brief clamour, especially, according to the official report, amongst the women. All this petty act of defiance earned them, however, was a slow journey to Paris, a stay in a revolutionary prison, and execution during the most merciless phase of the Terror, only ten days before the fall of Robespierre.[32]

Even for those who survived the Revolution unscathed, these years had brought at least as much suffering as achievement. The semi-literate memoirs of one such ordinary man, the Parisian glazier Ménétra, who had strolled with Rousseau in 1770, tell a sorry tale. Only the last twenty of some 240 pages are taken up with the Revolution, which 'came suddenly and revived all our spirits. And the word liberty so often repeated had an almost supernatural effect and invigorated us all.' He wrote, however, at the end of the decade, when revolutionary politics had brought him nothing but grief:

> Everything moved forward. They flattered the ambitious and all the ills came gradually to a head. Murder drowning everything was allowed. Intriguers monopolised all the offices. Good men could only mutter for if they spoke they were lost. Hatred vengeance everything was permitted and nobody dared open his mouth.[33]

Ménétra lamented the fates of friends and colleagues fallen to the guillotine – victims, according to him, of personal intrigue, grudge-bearing and corruption. Monsters and barbarians had roamed the streets, 'The French breathed blood. They were like cannibals', and things scarcely improved after Thermidor:

> This National Convention in which everyone had the greatest confidence was and one can say so nothing but a den of slanderers of vindictive men seeking to slaughter one party so as to replace it with another. They made the people march according to their passion.[34]

Ménétra's tone of regret and recollected fear conceals, however, his own active role in *sans-culotte* politics. He seems to have successfully minded his own business until the fall of the monarchy, although serving as an ordinary National Guard. By late 1792, however, he was a lieutenant in his section's battalion, and went on to hold a number of other posts on the section's various committees. He was named president of the section assembly at least once – though here, as with many other posts, he claimed 'I tried to get out of it. I was so to speak carried to the bureau'.[35] He also claimed to have lost an election to a man who was later guillotined as one of the 'Robespierrist' Commune, and had various other narrow scrapes with the political infighting of the period. Clashes from the fall of the Gironde to the Vendémiaire rising of 1795 appear in his text as events which Ménétra survived, rather than participated in – although clearly, from what he says, he did participate in all the radical mobilisations of 1793–95.

Seeking peace he sold up his business for 10,000 livres at the height of the Directorial inflation, getting 2000 in paper at once, 'the rest payable after six months when it was no longer worth the trouble to collect'. He went to work as a foreman for his son-in-law, an iron founder with armaments contracts, but ill-feeling between his wife and daughter saw him move back to Paris by the end of the decade. His final thoughts were elegiac: 'The fires of my youth are quenched. When I am with old friends I think about all that has happened … the good and the evil that the Revolution has done, all the assaults, the days, the nights, the punishments and the fate of our unfortunate friends.' Thinking of his children, he asked only that 'I may see them in my old age free of the suffering that the Revolution has made all of us feel'.[36]

Reading such words, one cannot help wondering if, indeed, there was anything about the Revolution that made it worth enduring its undoubted horrors. Yet Ménétra, 'ordinary' as he was, had been doing very much better than most before 1789, as an established master craftsman in a trade unchallenged by new techniques or semi-skilled usurpers. With that, and with all his regrets, he could still recall that the Revolution had been a beacon of hope for release from the rule of 'inept outrageous liars who thought only of their pleasures', and nobles who 'could not imagine that a man who was not of this class was made for anything but to serve their whims'.[37]

Even for Ménétra, therefore, some appreciation of the worth of the Revolution and its goals endured. The same must be said for the country at large, where many had had a great deal more to complain of than him. Throughout all the vicissitudes of the decade, few even in the heartlands of counter-revolutionary revolt had looked for a return to the unalloyed Old Regime. So manifest were the injustices of that system that harping on the threatened return of aristocracy, even if prompted more by paranoia than by psychological insight, remained one of the Republic's most effective weapons. Some amongst the Vendeans and the Chouans may have genuinely felt that they had been better off when the state left them alone to enjoy their provincial privileges, but most recognised that they now enjoyed a new status, even if it was one that sometimes seemed honoured only in the breach. It was the Republic and its interfering agents that they scorned, not their own freedom from feudal dues, monopolies and obligations.

On 4 July 1799 in Villethierry in the Yonne, on the stump of a republican tree of liberty newly severed by Catholic protestors, a certain 'Suzanne *Sans Peur*' posted a blunt message:

> Wake up people of France. No government is as despotic as ours. They tell us, 'You are free and sovereign', while we are enchained to the point where we are not allowed to sing or play on Sundays, not even allowed to kneel down to offer homage to the Supreme Being ... After this, are we sovereign? Isn't this playing with the people? [38]

Even coming as it did expressed in scorn for the posturings of republican politicians, this unabashed claim to popular sovereignty, not from the mouth of a caricatured *sans-culotte* icon but from a Catholic woman seeking to worship as she chose, marks the clear change brought on by the events of the decade.

In January 1789 the French had been summoned as subjects to address their monarch through the Estates-General. Their response had ultimately made them into citizens. The irony is that the regime which turned that word into a form of address, the Jacobin Republic of 1793–94, was the one which turned the resources of the state most savagely against the people. The political and cultural apparatus and heritage of the Terror – from the republican calendar and the anticatholic scorn it embodied, to the increasingly robust militarisation of the state – soon stood between many of the common people and their alleged political inclusion. But of course, no leaders had done more than the Terrorists to make the claim of such inclusion a structural reality, at least for adult males. Those who repudiated Terror, and turned the Terrorist into a clichéd plebeian ogre, used that as an excuse to exclude the majority once more from politics, long before their own divisions ended the attempt to build a liberal polity on a new non-noble elite.

In the end, a fundamental point remains. The common people of France had made the French Revolution, even if its meaning and course had been taken from them by successive waves of leaders confident in their own misguided rectitude. Everything that the people gained they had to fight for, not just against the Old Regime but against almost every phase of the

Revolution itself, as defined by its leaders. What they did gain was less than what they sought, and perhaps than what they deserved. The sovereignty of Suzanne *Sans Peur*, so eloquently proclaimed, was not enacted securely for all Frenchmen, even at the most basic structural levels of voting, for three-quarters of a century.[39] Suzanne's daughters had to wait 145 years for their inclusion in the body politic. That great gulf of time is the measure of how far ahead the impetus of popular revolution had flung France, only to be dragged back again by those who claimed to know better.

Notes

Notes to Introduction

1. These remarks cited in George Rudé, *The Crowd in the French Revolution* (Oxford, 1959), pp. 2–3.
2. Cited in Morris Slavin, *The Hébertistes to the Guillotine: Anatomy of a 'Conspiracy' in Revolutionary France* (Baton Rouge, 1994), p. 3.
3. On this topic in general, see Geoffrey Best (ed.), *The Permanent Revolution: The French Revolution and its Legacy, 1789–1989* (London, 1988), and Noel Parker, *Portrayals of Revolution: Images, Debates and Patterns of Thought on the French Revolution* (Carbondale, 1990), esp. chapters 5 and 6.
4. These are the basic conclusions of Rudé, *The Crowd in the French Revolution*, and also of Albert Soboul, *Les sans-culottes parisiens en l'an II: mouvement populaire et gouvernement révolutionnaire* (original publication 1958; Paris, 1968).
5. Simon Schama, *Citizens: A Chronicle of the French Revolution* (New York, 1989), pp. xv, 467.
6. Schama, *Citizens*, pp. 859–60.
7. The official exchange rate between the French *livre tournois* and the pound sterling ran at somewhere over 20:1. Real purchasing-power is harder to compare: a French craftsman on perhaps 500 livres per year can be contrasted with English wage-rates of £30 per year for many crafts, rising to over £50 per year for the more skilled. English agricultural labourers generally made less than £20 per year. None of these people starved, but none was affluent either. See John Rule, *Albion's People: English Society, 1714–1815* (London, 1992), pp. 166–86, for the English figures.
8. See Rudé, *The Crowd in the French Revolution*, appendix 7, pp. 251–52. Labour in Paris commanded a premium, largely because local taxes and rent-rates made it impossible to live in the city on less. Across the country, urban labour earned perhaps 30 per cent less, on average, than the Parisians. Rural labour, as discussed in more detail in Chapter 1, was often not paid anything that approaching a 'living wage'.
9. For a study of the public image of the queen, see Chantal Thomas, *The Wicked Queen: The Origins of the Myth of Marie-Antoinette* (London, 1999).
10. For a history of one such family, see Christine Adams, *A Taste for Comfort and Status: A Bourgeois Family in Eighteenth-century France* (University Park, Pennsylvania, 2000). For a more general overview, see William Doyle (ed.), *Old Regime France, 1648–1788* (Oxford, 2001).

11. See, for a brief introduction, Dorinda Outram, *The Enlightenment* (Cambridge, 1995).

12. For a more detailed overview of such developments, see my *French Society in Revolution, 1789–1799* (Manchester, 1999), chapter 2, and William Doyle, *Origins of the French Revolution* (3rd edn, Oxford, 1999). See also Roger Chartier, *The Cultural Origins of the French Revolution* (Durham, North Carolina, 1991).

13. Amongst others cited in the course of this study, see for example Daniel Roche, *The People of Paris: An Essay in Popular Culture in the Eighteenth Century* (Leamington Spa, 1987); D. M. G. Sutherland, *The Chouans: The Social Origins of Popular Counter-Revolution in Upper Brittany, 1770–1796* (Oxford, 1982); and Michael Sonenscher, *Work and Wages: Natural Law, Politics and the Eighteenth-Century French Trades* (Cambridge, 1989). On women, see for example Olwen Hufton, *Women and the Limits of Citizenship in the French Revolution* (Toronto, 1992); and Dominique Godineau, *The Women of Paris and their French Revolution* (Berkeley, 1998).

14. See for example Gwynne Lewis, *Life in Revolutionary France* (London, 1972); and Jean Robiquet, *Daily Life in the French Revolution* (London, 1964).

15. Cited in Peter McPhee, *The French Revolution 1789–1799* (Oxford, 2002), p. 57.

16. See Anthony F. Upton, *Europe, 1600–1789* (London, 2001), chapter 10; and Euan Cameron (ed.), *Early Modern Europe: An Oxford History* (Oxford, 2001), Part III.

17. A brief note on general sources: there are many excellent overview accounts of the events of the revolutionary period, which have necessarily been drawn upon in what follows. In addition to those noted above, these include William Doyle, *The Oxford History of the French Revolution* (Oxford, 1989); François Furet, *The French Revolution, 1770–1814* (Oxford, 1996); Albert Soboul, *The French Revolution* 2 vols (London, 1974); D. M. G. Sutherland, *France, 1789–1815: Revolution and Counterrevolution* (London, 1985), recently updated as *The French Revolution and Empire: The Quest for a Civic Order* (Oxford, 2002). A non-narrative source with much essential information is Colin Jones, *The Longman Companion to the French Revolution* (London, 1988). For those interested in historiographical debates in more detail, two useful recent collections are Gary Kates (ed.), *The French Revolution: Recent Debates and New Controversies* (London, 1998), and Ronald Schechter (ed.), *The French Revolution: The Essential Readings* (Oxford, 2001).

Notes to Chapter 1: Peasants

1. Work on the French rural population in the run-up to the Revolution is ably condensed in Peter M. Jones, *The Peasantry in the French Revolution* (Cambridge, 1988), chapters 1 and 2.

2. For the latter, see Abel Poitrineau, *La vie rurale en Basse-Auvergne au XVIIIe siècle (1726–1789)* (Marseille, 1979).

3. Peter McPhee, *Revolution and Environment in Southern France, 1780–1830: Peasants, Lords and Murder in the Corbières* (Oxford, 1999), chapter 1.
4. See the extensive discussion of historiography on this issue in Jill Maciak, 'Of News and Networks: The Communication of Political Information in the Rural South West during the French Revolution', *French History*, 15 (2001), pp. 273–306.
5. Debates over language and 'nation' are discussed in David A. Bell, *The Cult of the Nation in France: Inventing Nationalism, 1680–1800* (Cambridge, Massachusetts, 2001).
6. On the science of midwifery and the rigours of birth, see Nina Gelbart, *The King's Midwife: A History and Mystery of Madame du Coudray* (Berkeley, 1998).
7. Serge Bonin and Claude Langlois (eds), *Atlas de la Révolution française*, viii, *Population* (Paris, 1995), pp. 14–19.
8. See Jean-François Poulet, *La vie quotidienne dans les Pyrénées sous l'ancien régime* (Paris, 1974).
9. The contract is translated and analysed in detail in Robert and Elborg Forster (ed.), *European Society in the Eighteenth Century* (London, 1969), pp. 130–33.
10. Serge Bianchi, Michel Biard, Alan Forrest, Edouard Gruter and Jean Jacquart, *La terre et les paysans en France et en Grande-Bretagne du début du XVIIe à la fin du XVIIIe siècle* (Paris, 1999), pp. 174–75.
11. Poitrineau, *La vie rurale,*, ii, p. 134, map.
12. Georges Lefebvre, *Les paysans du Nord pendant la Révolution française* (1924; reprinted Paris, 1972); and Liana Vardi, *The Land and the Loom: Peasants and Profit in Northern France, 1680–1800* (Durham, North Carolina, 1993).
13. Cynthia Bouton, *The Flour War: Gender, Class and Community in Late Ancien Régime French Society* (University Park, Pennsylvania, 1993), chapter 2.
14. Gwynne Lewis, *The Advent of Modern Capitalism in France, 1770–1840: The Contribution of Pierre-François Tubeuf* (Oxford, 1993), chapter 1.
15. The phrase is Olwen Hufton's, used as a chapter heading in her *The Poor of Eighteenth-Century France, 1750–1789* (Oxford, 1974), pp. 69ff. See pp. 245ff for the observations of Roland.
16. Guy Cabourdin, *La vie quotidienne en Lorraine aux XVIIe et XVIIIe siècles* (Paris, 1984).
17. Charles Tilly, *The Vendée* (London, 1964).
18. Cited in Charles Leroy, *Paysans normands au XVIIIe siècle: la vie rurale* (1904; reprinted Brionne, 1978), pp. 140–41.
19. Jean-Pierre Gutton, *La sociabilité villageoise dans l'ancienne France* (Paris, 1979).
20. Leroy, *Paysans normands*, pp. 149–50.
21. André Bendjebbar, *La vie quotidienne en Anjou au XVIIIe siècle* (Paris, 1983).
22. Vardi, *The Land and the Loom*, p. 64.
23. Gutton, *Sociabilité villageoise*, pp. 141–51.
24. Olwen H. Hufton, 'Attitudes towards Authority in Eighteenth-Century Languedoc', *Social History*, 3 (1978), pp. 281–302.
25. Bianchi et al., *La terre*, pp. 202–4.

26. Ibid., *La terre*, pp. 199–201.
27. Cynthia Bouton, 'Les syndics des villages du Bassin parisien des années 1750 à la Revolution', in Roger Dupuy (ed.), *Pouvoir local et révolution, 1780–1850: la frontière intérieure* (Rennes, 1995), pp. 55–69.
28. John McManners, *Church and Society in Eighteenth-Century France* 2 vols (Oxford, 1998).
29. Alain Corbin, *Village Bells: Sound and Meaning in the Nineteenth-Century French Countryside* (London, 1998), pp. 80–92.
30. Nigel Aston, *Religion and Revolution in France, 1780–1804* (Basingstoke, 2000), chapter 2.
31. Timothy Tackett, 'The West in France in 1789: The Religious Factor in the Origins of the Counter-Revolution', *Journal of Modern History*, 54 (1982), pp. 715–45.
32. Cited in Laura Mason and Tracey Rizzo (eds), *The French Revolution: A Document Collection* (Boston, Massachusetts, 1999), p. 136.
33. Robert Darnton, *Mesmerism and the End of the Enlightenment in France* (Cambridge, Massachusetts, 1968).
34. Bianchi et al., *La terre*, pp. 194–96.
35. See, for example, Steven G. Reinhardt, *Justice in the Sarladais, 1770–1790* (Baton Rouge, 1991), and more generally, John Markoff, *The Abolition of Feudalism: Peasants, Lords and Legislators in the French Revolution* (University Park, Pennsylvania, 1996).
36. Lewis, *The Advent of Modern Capitalism*, pp. 81–83.
37. McPhee, *Revolution and Environment*, pp. 28–29.
38. Cited in Forster, *European Society*, pp. 73–75.
39. Hilton Root, *Peasants and King in Burgundy: Agrarian Foundations of French Absolutism* (Berkeley, 1987), chapter 5.
40. Stephen S. Miller, 'Lords, Peasant Communities and the State in Eighteenth-Century Languedoc', *French Historical Studies*, 26 (2003), pp. 55–86.
41. McPhee, *Revolution and Environment*, pp. 33–34.
42. Guy Astoul, 'Solidarités paysannes au pays des croquants au XVIIIe siècle', *Annales historiques de la Révolution française*, 311 (1998), pp. 25–48. See also McPhee, *Revolution and Environment*, pp. 37–39.
43. Bianchi et al., *La terre*, pp. 196–98.
44. Ibid., *La terre*, pp. 168–74.

Notes to Chapter 2: Artisans

1. Excellent overviews of urban life, albeit from a Parisian perspective, can be found in Jeffry Kaplow, *The Names of Kings: The Parisian Laboring Poor in the Eighteenth Century* (New York, 1972); Daniel Roche, *The People of Paris: An Essay in Popular Culture in the Eighteenth Century* (Leamington Spa, 1987); and Arlette Farge, *Fragile Lives: Violence, Power and Solidarity in Eighteenth-Century Paris* (Cambridge, 1993).

2. Thomas McStay Adams, *Bureaucrats and Beggars: French Social Policy in the Age of the Enlightenment* (Oxford, 1990), pp. 103–4.

3. David Garrioch, *Neighbourhood and Community in Paris, 1740–1790* (Cambridge, Massachusetts, 1986).

4. Daniel Roche, *A History of Everyday Things: The Birth of Consumption in France, 1600–1800* (Cambridge, 2000).

5. Michael Sonenscher, *Work and Wages: Natural Law, Politics and the Eighteenth-Century French Trades* (Cambridge, 1989). Much of this chapter is indebted to this pioneering work.

6. Alain Thillay, *Le Faubourg Saint-Antoine et ses 'faux-ouvriers': la liberté du travail à Paris aux XVIIe et XVIIIe siècles* (Seyssel, 2002).

7. Paul Butel and Jean-Pierre Poussou, *La vie quotidienne à Bordeaux au XVIIIe siècle* (Paris, 1980).

8. Sonenscher, *Work and Wages*, pp. 266–70.

9. Steven L. Kaplan, 'La Lutte pour la contrôle du marché du travail à Paris au XVIIIe siècle', *Revue d'histoire moderne et contemporaine*, 36 (1989), pp. 361–412.

10. Cited in Sonenscher, *Work and Wages*, p. 248.

11. Steven L. Kaplan, 'The Character and Implications of Strife amongst Masters in the Guilds of Eighteenth-Century Paris', *Journal of Social History*, 19 (1985–86), pp. 631–47.

12. David Garrioch and Michael Sonenscher, '*Compagnonnages*, Confraternities and Associations of Journeymen in Eighteenth-Century Paris', *European History Quarterly*, 16 (1986), pp. 25–45.

13. Cited in Robert Forster and Elborg Forster (eds), *European Society in the Eighteenth Century* (London, 1969), p. 234.

14. Sonenscher, *Work and Wages*, pp. 306–8.

15. Daryl Hafter, 'Female Masters in the Ribbonmaking Guild of Eighteenth-Century Rouen', *French Historical Studies*, 20 (1997), pp. 1–14.

16. See also Judith G. Coffin, 'Gender and the Guild Order: The Garment Trades in Eighteenth-Century Paris', *Journal of Economic History*, 54 (1994), pp. 768–93; and Clare Crowston, 'Engendering the Guilds: Seamstresses, Tailors and the Clash of Corporate Identities in Old Regime France', *French Historical Studies*, 23 (2000), pp. 339–71.

17. Elizabeth C. Musgrave, 'Women in the Male World of Work: The Building Industries of Eighteenth-Century Brittany', *French History*, 7 (1989), pp. 30–52.

18. David Garrioch, *The Formation of the Parisian Bourgeoisie, 1690–1830* (Cambridge, Massachusetts, 1996).

19. Arlette Farge, *Subversive Words: Public Opinion in Eighteenth-Century France* (Cambridge, 1994).

20. Thomas Brennan, *Public Drinking and Popular Culture in Eighteenth-Century Paris* (Princeton, 1988).

21. Jacques-Louis Ménétra, *Journal of My Life* introduction and commentary by Daniel Roche, translated by Arthur Goldhammer (New York, 1986), pp. 181–84.

22. Farge, *Subversive Words*, pp. 175–92.

23. Steven L. Kaplan, 'Social Classification and Representation in the Corporate World of Eighteenth-Century France: Turgot's "Carnival"', in Steven L. Kaplan and Cynthia J. Koepp (ed.), *Work in France: Representations, Meaning, Organization and Practice* (Ithaca, New York, 1986), pp. 176–228.

24. Steven L. Kaplan, *La fin des corporations* (Paris, 2001).

25. Michael Sonenscher, 'Journeymen, the Courts and the French Trades, 1781–1791', *Past and Present*, 114 (1987), pp. 77–109.

26. Cited in Kaplan, *La fin des corporations*, pp. 299–300.

27. Cited in Kaplan, *La fin des corporations*, p. 300.

Notes to Chapter 3: The Margins

1. Alan Williams, *The Police of Paris, 1718–1789* (Baton Rouge, 1979).

2. Robert M. Schwartz, *Policing the Poor in Eighteenth-Century France* (Chapel Hill, North Carolina, 1988).

3. Clive Emsley, 'La Maréchaussée à la fin de l'ancien régime: note sur la composition du corps', *Revue d'histoire moderne et contemporaine*, 33 (1986), pp. 622–44.

4. Olwen H. Hufton, *The Poor of Eighteenth-Century France, 1750–1789* (Oxford, 1974), pp. 62ff.

5. Alan Forrest, *The French Revolution and the Poor* (Oxford, 1981), chapter 1.

6. Jean-André Tournerie, *Criminels et vagabonds au siècle des lumières* (Paris, 1997).

7. Schwartz, *Policing the Poor*, chapters 2–4.

8. Peter M. Jones, *The Peasantry in the French Revolution* (Cambridge, 1988), chapter 1; Abel Poitrineau, *La vie rurale en Basse-Auvergne au XVIIIe siècle (1726–1789)* (Marseille, 1979); Georges Lefebvre, *The Great Fear of 1789* (1932), translated by Joan White, London, 1973), pp. 7–10; David Garrioch, *The Making of Revolutionary Paris* (Berkeley, 2002), p. 48.

9. Both officials are cited in Thomas McStay Adams, *Bureaucrats and Beggars: French Social Policy in the Age of the Enlightenment* (Oxford, 1990), pp. 36 and 41.

10. Cited in Adams, *Bureaucrats and Beggars*, p. 49.

11. Cissie Fairchilds, *Domestic Enemies: Servants and their Masters in Old Regime France* (Baltimore, 1984), and Sarah C. Maza, *Servants and Masters in Eighteenth-Century France: The Uses of Loyalty* (Princeton, 1983).

12. Cited in Maza, *Servants and Masters*, p. 30.

13. Ibid., p. 108.

14. Serge Bonin and Claude Langlois (ed.), *Atlas de la Révolution française*, viii, *Population* (Paris, 1995), pp. 20–21.

15. André Burguière, 'La Révolution française et la famille', *Annales ESC*, 1991, pp. 151–68, especially pp. 154–55.

16. Arlette Farge, *Fragile Lives: Violence, Power and Solidarity in Eighteenth-Century Paris* (Cambridge, 1993), chapter 3, 'Seduced and Abandoned', and Hufton, *The Poor of Eighteenth-Century France*, chapter 12.

17. Hufton, *The Poor of Eighteenth-Century France*, chapter 11.
18. Erica-Marie Benabou, *La prostitution et la police des moeurs au XVIIIe siècle* (Paris, 1987).
19. Arlette Farge and Jacques Revel, *The Rules of Rebellion: Child Abductions in Paris in 1750* (Cambridge, 1991), chapter 2.
20. Robert Darnton, *The Forbidden Bestsellers of Prerevolutionary France* (New York, 1995).
21. Cited in Hufton, *The Poor of Eighteenth-Century France*, p. 313.
22. Archives nationales, Series Y, carton 15684, 8 April 1790, *déclaration de grossesse* before *commissaire* Sirebeau; carton 11287, 19 August 1790, complaint by sieur d'Escherny before *commissaire* Carré.
23. Cited in Farge, *Fragile Lives*, p. 74.
24. Jeffrey Merrick, 'Commissioner Foucault, Inspector Noël, and the "Pederasts" of Paris, 1780–83', *Journal of Social History*, 32 (1998), pp. 287–307.
25. Farge, *Fragile Lives*, pp. 159–65.
26. Cited in Jeffry Kaplow, *The Names of Kings: The Parisian Laboring Poor in the Eighteenth Century* (New York, 1972), p. 147.
27. Julius R. Ruff, *Crime, Justice and Public Order in Old Regime France: The Sénéchaussées of Libourne and Bazas, 1696–1789* (London, 1984).
28. David Garrioch, *Neighbourhood and Community in Paris, 1740–1790* (Cambridge, 1986), chapters 1 and 2.
29. Roderick Phillips, 'Women, Neighborhood, and Family in the Late Eighteenth Century', *French Historical Studies*, 18 (1993), pp. 1–12.
30. Michel Foucault, *Discipline and Punish: The Birth of the Prison* (Harmondsworth, 1977), pp. 3–6.
31. David Garrioch, *The Making of Revolutionary Paris* (Berkeley, 2002), pp. 84–85.
32. Olwen Hufton, 'Attitudes towards Authority in Eighteenth-Century Languedoc', *Social History*, 3 (1978), pp. 281–302.
33. Cited in Robert Forster and Elborg Forster (eds), *European Society in the Eighteenth Century* (London, 1969), p. 346.
34. Steven L. Kaplan, *The Famine Plot Persuasion in Eighteenth-Century France* (Philadelphia, 1982).
35. Cited in Cynthia Bouton, *The Flour War: Gender, Class and Community in Late Ancien Régime French Society* (University Park, Pennsylvania, 1993), p. 83.
36. Louis-Sébastien Mercier, *Le tableau de Paris*, selected by J. Kaplow (Paris, 1979), pp. 316–18.

Notes to Chapter 4: From Crisis to Constitution

1. Bailey Stone, *Reinterpreting the French Revolution: A Global-Historical Perspective* (Cambridge, 2002), chapter 1.
2. William Doyle, *Origins of the French Revolution* (3rd edn, Oxford, 1999).
3. Jean Egret, *The French Prerevolution, 1787–1788* (Chicago, 1977).
4. On the deputies, their attitudes and behaviour, see Timothy Tackett, *Becoming*

A Revolutionary: The Deputies of the French National Assembly and the Emergence of a Revolutionary Political Culture (1789–1790) (Princeton, 1996), and Norman Hampson, *Prelude to Terror: The Constituent Assembly and the Failure of Consensus, 1789–1791* (Oxford, 1988).

5. Cited in John Hardman, *The French Revolution Sourcebook* (London, 1999), p. 117.

6. Isser Woloch, *The New Regime: Transformations of the French Civic Order, 1789–1820s* (New York, 1994), chapters 1 and 2; and Malcolm Crook, *Elections in the French Revolution: An Apprenticeship in Democracy, 1789–99* (Cambridge, 1996).

7. Woloch, *New Regime*, pp. 26–31, and Ted W. Margadant, *Urban Rivalries in the French Revolution* (Princeton, 1992), pp. 84–140.

8. Jacques Godechot, *The Counter-Revolution: Doctrine and Action 1789–1804* (Princeton, 1971).

9. Florin Aftalion, *The French Revolution: An Economic Interpretation* (Cambridge, 1990), and François Crouzet, *La grande inflation: la monnaie en France de Louis XVI à Napoléon* (Paris, 1993).

10. M. Albertone, 'Une histoire oubliée: les assignats dans l'historiographie', *Annales historiques de la Révolution française*, 287 (1992), pp. 87–104.

11. Patrice Higonnet, *Goodness Beyond Virtue: Jacobins during the French Revolution* (Cambridge, Massachusetts, 1998).

12. Michael L. Kennedy, *The Jacobin Clubs in the French Revolution: The First Years* (Princeton, 1981).

13. Marcel Reinhard, *La chute de la royauté* (Paris, 1969), Part 1.

14. Cited in Hardman, *French Revolution Sourcebook*, pp. 128–36.

15. David Andress, *Massacre at the Champ de Mars: Popular Dissent and Political Culture in the French Revolution* (Woodbridge, 2000)

16. Michael P. Fitzsimmons, *The Remaking of France: The National Assembly and the Constitution of 1791* (Cambridge, 1994).

17. C. J. Mitchell, *The French Legislative Assembly of 1791* (Leiden, 1988).

Notes to Chapter 5: Collapse and Revolt

1. Georges Lefebvre, *The Great Fear of 1789* (1932, translated by Joan White, London, 1973), pp. 12–13.

2. George Rudé, *The Crowd in the French Revolution* (Oxford, 1959), pp. 29ff.

3. David Andress, *Massacre at the Champ de Mars: Popular Dissent and Political Culture in the French Revolution* (Woodbridge, 2000), pp. 47–48.

4. Cited in Lefebvre, *Great Fear*, p. 29.

5. John Markoff, *The Abolition of Feudalism: Peasants, Lords and Legislators in the French Revolution* (University Park, Pennsylvania, 1996), chapters 1 and 2.

6. Cited in Colin Jones, *The Great Nation: France from Louis XV to Napoleon, 1715–99* (London, 2002), p. 404.

7. This and the following *cahier* are translated in David Andress, *French Society in Revolution, 1789–1799* (Manchester, 1999), pp. 168–69.

8. Translated in John Hardman, *The French Revolution Sourcebook* (London, 1999), pp. 82–83.

9. Lefebvre, *Great Fear*, pp. 14–21.

10. Cited in Alfred Cobban, *The Social Interpretation of the French Revolution* (2nd edn, Cambridge, 1999), p. 136.

11. Cited in Cobban, *Social Interpretation*, p. 137.

12. Alexis de Tocqueville, *The Ancien Régime* (London, 1988), p. 114.

13. Cited in Lefebvre, *Great Fear*, p. 41.

14. Cited in Jacques Godechot, *The Taking of the Bastille, July 14th 1789* (London, 1970), p. 134.

15. Cited in Cobban, *Social Interpretation*, p. 142.

16. This and remarks in following paragraph cited in Godechot, *The Taking of the Bastille*, p. 135.

17. Remarks in this paragraph cited in Godechot, *The Taking of the Bastille*, pp. 139–40.

18. Cited in Rudé, *The Crowd in the French Revolution*, p. 37.

19. Remarks in this paragraph cited in Lefebvre, *Great Fear*, p. 44–45.

20. Cited in Lefebvre, *Great Fear*, p. 40.

21. This and following remarks cited in Lefebvre, *Great Fear*, p. 39.

22. Jean-Paul Bertaud, *La Révolution armée: les soldats-citoyens et la Révolution française* (Paris, 1979), introduction and chapter 1; Alan Forrest, *The Soldiers of the French Revolution* (Durham, North Carolina, 1990), chapter 2.

23. Cited in Godechot, *The Taking of the Bastille*, p. 176

24. Ibid., p. 188.

25. Cited in Paul G. Spagnoli, 'The Revolution Begins: Lambesc's charge, 12 July 1789', *French Historical Studies*, 17 (1991), pp. 466–97, see p. 471.

26. Cited in Godechot, *The Taking of the Bastille*, p. 193.

27. Ibid., p. 199.

28. Colin Lucas, 'Talking About Urban Popular Violence in 1789', in Alan Forrest and Peter Jones (ed.), *Reshaping France: Town, Country and Region during the French Revolution* (Manchester, 1991), pp. 122–36.

29. Bibliothèque Nationale de France, MS n.a.f. 2665, fol. 259. It is highly probable that this was the same Collenot d'Angremont who was executed on 21 August 1792, the first 'political' victim of the new guillotine, for his role as an alleged royalist agent in the intrigues around the fall of the monarchy.

Notes to Chapter 6: Revolution and Reordering

1. Georges Lefebvre, *The Great Fear of 1789* (1932, translated by Joan White, London, 1973), Part 3; and also Clay Ramsay, *The Ideology of the Great Fear: The Soissonnais in 1789* (Baltimore, 1992).

2. Cited in William D. Edmonds, *Jacobinism and the Revolt of Lyon, 1789–1793* (Oxford, 1990), pp. 45, 46–47.

3. Anatoli Ado, *Paysans en révolution: terre, pouvoir et jacquerie 1789–1794* (Paris, 1996), pp. 124–39, esp. p. 138 n. 28.
4. This translation is cited in John Hardman, *The French Revolution Sourcebook* (London, 1999), p. 111.
5. Dale L. Clifford, 'The National Guard and the Parisian Community', *French Historical Studies*, 16 (1990), pp. 849–78.
6. Barry M. Shapiro, *Revolutionary Justice in Paris, 1789–1790* (Cambridge, 1993), pp. 89–90.
7. William H. Sewell Jr, 'Historical Events as Transformations of Structures: Inventing Revolution at the Bastille', *Theory and Society*, 25 (1996), pp. 841–81, see p. 859.
8. George Rudé, *The Crowd in the French Revolution* (Oxford, 1959), pp. 64–68.
9. Cited in Rudé, *The Crowd in the French Revolution*, p. 67.
10. Cited in Sigismond Lacroix, *Actes de la Commune de Paris pendant la Révolution* first series, i (Paris, 1894), pp. 423–25.
11. David Garrioch, 'The Everyday Lives of Parisian Women and the October Days of 1789', *Social History*, 24 (1999), pp. 231–49.
12. Jeff Horn, 'The Legacy of 14 July 1789 in the Cultural History of French Industrialisation', unpublished paper presented to the Society for French Historical Studies, 47th Annual Meeting, 8–10 March 2001, Chapel Hill, North Carolina.
13. Edmonds, *Jacobinism and the Revolt of Lyon*, pp. 40–62.
14. Peter M. Jones, *The Peasantry in the French Revolution* (Cambridge, 1988), pp. 83–85.
15. Cited in Ado, *Paysans en révolution*, p. 160.
16. Guy Astoul, 'Solidarités paysannes au pays des croquants au XVIIIe siècle', *Annales historiques de la Révolution française*, 311 (1998), pp. 25–48; pp. 38–40.
17. Cited in D. M. G. Sutherland, *France, 1789–1815: Revolution and Counterrevolution* (London, 1985), p. 109.
18. Malcolm Crook, *Elections in the French Revolution: An Apprenticeship in Democracy, 1789–99* (Cambridge, 1996), and Patrice Gueniffey, *Le nombre et la raison: la Révolution française et les élections* (Paris, 1993).
19. Melvin Edelstein, 'Les administrateurs du Haut-Rhin en 1790: aspects sociaux', *Annales historiques de la Révolution française*, 327 (2002), pp. 75–81. See also Lynn Hunt, *Politics, Culture and Class in the French Revolution* (London, 1984), chapter 5.
20. Alan Forrest, *The French Revolution and the Poor* (Oxford, 1981), chapter 2.
21. Ibid., pp. 108–11.
22. Jones, *Peasantry*, pp. 103ff.
23. Cited in Jones, *Peasantry*, p. 108.
24. Peter McPhee, *Revolution and Environment in Southern France 1780–1830: Peasants, Lords and Murder in the Corbières* (Oxford, 1999), pp. 61ff.
25. Paul d'Hollander, 'Les Gardes nationales en Limousin (juillet 1789 – juillet 1790)', *Annales historiques de la Révolution française*, 290 (1992), pp. 465–89.

26. Antoine de Baecque, *The Body Politic: Corporeal Metaphor in Revolutionary France, 1770–1800*, translated by Charlotte Mandel (Stanford, 1997), pp. 249–54.
27. Archives de la Prefecture de Police, Paris, series AA, carton 81, fos 180–84.

Notes to Chapter 7: The Widening Gulf

1. William D. Edmonds, *Jacobinism and the Revolt of Lyon, 1789–1793* (Oxford, 1990), pp. 55–62.
2. Cited in Jacques Godechot, *The Counter-Revolution: Doctrine and Action 1789–1804* (Princeton, 1971), p. 233.
3. D. M. G. Sutherland, *France, 1789–1815: Revolution and Counterrevolution* (London, 1985), pp. 103–4.
4. D. M. G. Sutherland, 'Peasants, Lords and Leviathan: Winners and Losers from the Abolition of French Feudalism, 1780–1820', *Journal of Economic History*, 62 (2002), pp. 1–24; see pp. 7–11.
5. Cited in Peter McPhee, *Revolution and Environment in Southern France, 1780–1830: Peasants, Lords and Murder in the Corbières* (Oxford, 1999), p. 80.
6. William Doyle, *The Oxford History of the French Revolution* (Oxford, 1989), p. 408.
7. Peter M. Jones, *The Peasantry in the French Revolution* (Cambridge, 1988), pp. 154ff.
8. Anatoli Ado, *Paysans en révolution: terre, pouvoir et jacquerie, 1789–1794* (Paris, 1996), pp. 190ff.
9. Timothy Tackett, *Religion, Revolution and Regional Culture in Eighteenth-Century France: The Ecclesiastical Oath of 1791* (Princeton, 1986).
10. T. J. A. Le Goff and D. M. G. Sutherland, 'The Revolution and the Rural Community in Eighteenth-century Brittany', *Past and Present*, 62 (1974), pp. 96–107.
11. Cited in Tackett, *Religion, Revolution and Regional Culture*, p. 168.
12. David Andress, *Massacre at the Champ de Mars: Popular Dissent and Political Culture in the French Revolution* (Woodbridge, 2000), pp. 100–108.
13. Albert Mathiez, *Le Club des Cordeliers pendant la crise de Varennes et la massacre du Champ de Mars* (Paris, 1910, repr. Geneva, 1975).
14. Isabelle Bourdin, *Les sociétés populaires à Paris pendant la Révolution* (Paris, 1937), and R. B. Rose, *The Making of the Sans-Culottes: Democratic Ideas and Institutions in Paris, 1789–1792* (Manchester, 1983).
15. Edmonds, *Jacobinism and the Revolt of Lyon*, pp. 108–11.
16. Andress, *Massacre at the Champ de Mars*, chapter 4.
17. Olivier Coquard, *Jean-Paul Marat* (Paris, 1993).
18. Andress, *Massacre*, pp. 122–30, and E. S. Brezis and F. Crouzet, 'The Role of Assignats during the French Revolution: An Evil or a Rescuer?', *Journal of European Economic History*, 24 (1995), pp. 7–40.
19. Cited in Steven L. Kaplan, *La fin des corporations* (Paris, 2001), pp. 429, 431.

20. Cited in Andress, *Massacre at the Champ de Mars*, p. 131.

21. Ibid., p. 134.

22. Ibid., p. 114.

23. Ibid., p. 153.

24. Cited in Keith M. Baker, *The Old Regime and the French Revolution* (Chicago, 1987), pp. 275–76.

25. Andress, *Massacre at the Champ de Mars*, pp. 8–10.

26. Cited in Edmonds, *Jacobinism and the Revolt of Lyon*, p. 98.

27. Ado, *Paysans en révolution*, pp. 236–37.

28. Ibid., pp. 241ff.

29. Isser Woloch, 'From Charity to Welfare in Revolutionary Paris', *Journal of Modern History*, 58 (1986), pp. 779–812.

30. Forrest, *French Revolution and the Poor*, chapter 3.

31. Peter McPhee, '"The Misguided Greed of Peasants"? Popular Attitudes to the Environment in the Revolution of 1789', *French Historical Studies*, 24 (2001), pp. 247–69.

32. Jones, *Peasantry*, pp. 128–36.

Notes to Chapter 8: The Politics of Conflict

1. T. C. W. Blanning, *The Origins of the French Revolutionary Wars* (London, 1986); and Bailey Stone, *Reinterpreting the French Revolution: A Global-Historical Perspective* (Cambridge, 2002), pp. 162–68.

2. Alison Patrick, *The Men of the First French Republic: Political Alignments in the National Convention of 1792* (Baltimore, 1972).

3. David P. Jordan, *The King's Trial: The French Revolution versus Louis XVI* (Berkeley, 1979); and Andrew Freeman, *The Compromising of Louis XVI: The Armoire de Fer and the French Revolution* (Exeter, 1989).

4. T. C. W. Blanning, *The French Revolutionary Wars, 1787–1802* (London, 1996).

5. Morris Slavin, *The Making of An Insurrection: Parisian Sections and the Gironde* (Cambridge, Massachusetts, 1986).

6. R. R. Palmer, *Twelve Who Ruled: The Year of the Terror in the French Revolution* (original publication 1941; Princeton, 1970).

7. W. D. Edmonds, '"Federalism" and Urban Revolt in France in 1793', *Journal of Modern History*, 55 (1983), pp. 22–53; Alan Forrest, 'Federalism', in Colin Lucas (ed.), *The French Revolution and the Creation of Modern Political Culture*, ii, *The Political Culture of the French Revolution* (Oxford, 1988), pp. 309–25; Paul R. Hanson, *The Jacobin Republic Under Fire: The Federalist Revolt in the French Revolution* (University Park, Pennsylvania, 2003).

8. William D. Edmonds, *Jacobinism and the Revolt of Lyon, 1789–1793* (Oxford, 1990), pp. 226–32.

9. Lucien Jaume, *Le discours jacobin et la démocratie* (Paris, 1989), and Patrice Gueniffey, *La politique de la terreur: essai sur la violence révolutionnaire, 1789–1794* (Paris, 2000).

10. Michel Vovelle, *The Revolution against the Church: From Reason to the Supreme Being* (Cambridge, 1991).
11. Morris Slavin, *The Hébertistes to the Guillotine: Anatomy of a 'Conspiracy' in Revolutionary France* (Baton Rouge, 1994).
12. Norman Hampson, *Danton* (London, 1978).
13. Richard Bienvenu (ed.), *The Ninth of Thermidor: The Fall of Robespierre* (London, 1968).
14. Bronislaw Baczko, *Ending the Terror: The French Revolution after Robespierre* (Cambridge, 1994).

Notes to Chapter 9: War and Republic

1. Claude Petitfrère, 'The Origins of the Civil War in the Vendée', *French History*, 2 (1988), pp. 187–207; see pp. 196–201.
2. Cited in David Andress, *French Society in Revolution, 1789–1799* (Manchester, 1999), pp. 177–78.
3. Cited in D. M. G. Sutherland, *France, 1789–1815: Revolution and Counterrevolution* (London, 1985), p. 133.
4. Marcel Reinhard, *La chute de la royauté* (Paris, 1969), pp. 234–35.
5. Jacques Godechot, *The Counter-Revolution: Doctrine and Action, 1789–1804* (Princeton, 1971), pp. 208–13.
6. D. M. G. Sutherland, *The Chouans: The Social Origins of Popular Counter-Revolution in Upper Brittany, 1770–1796* (Oxford, 1982), p. 7.
7. Peter McPhee, *Revolution and Environment in Southern France, 1780–1830: Peasants, Lords and Murder in the Corbières* (Oxford, 1999), pp. 30, 76.
8. Alan Forrest, *The French Revolution and the Poor* (Oxford, 1981), pp. 44ff.
9. Reinhard, *La chute de la royauté*, pp. 217–20.
10. Colin Jones and Rebecca Spang, 'Sans-culottes, *Sans Café, Sans Tabac:* Shifting Realms of Necessity and Luxury in Eighteenth-Century France', in Maxine Berg and Helen Clifford (ed), *Consumers and Luxury; Consumer Culture in Europe, 1650–1850* (Manchester, 1999), pp. 37–62.
11. Sutherland, *France, 1789–1815*, pp. 139ff.
12. Anatoli Ado, *Paysans en révolution: terre, pouvoir et jacquerie 1789–1794* (Paris, 1996), pp. 261–73.
13. Cited in Gwynne Lewis, *The Second Vendée: The Continuity of Counter-Revolution in the Department of the Gard, 1789–1815* (Oxford, 1978), p. 43.
14. Lewis, *The Second Vendée*, pp. 45–50.
15. Alan Forrest, *The Soldiers of the French Revolution* (Durham, North Carolina, 1990), pp. 19–22, 45–46.
16. R. B. Rose, *The Making of the Sans-Culottes: Democratic Ideas and Institutions in Paris, 1789–1792* (Manchester, 1983).
17. Cited in Jacques Guilhaumou, *L'avènement des porte-parole de la République (1789–1792): essai de synthèse sur les langages de la Révolution française* (Lille, 1998), p. 214.

18. Michael Sonenscher, 'Artisans, Sans-culottes and the French Revolution', in Alan Forrest and Peter Jones (eds), *Reshaping France: Town, Country and Region in the French Revolution* (Manchester, 1991), pp. 105–21.
19. Both these texts cited in Andress, *French Society*, pp. 181–82.
20. Leigh Whaley, 'Political Factions and the Second Revolution: The Insurrection of 10 August 1792', *French History*, 7 (1993), pp. 205–24.
21. Cited in John Hall Stewart, *A Documentary Survey of the French Revolution* (New York, 1951), pp. 309–10.
22. George Rudé, *The Crowd in the French Revolution* (Oxford, 1959), pp. 104–08.
23. Cited in Sutherland, *France, 1789–1815*, p. 153.
24. Ado, *Paysans en révolution*, p. 311.
25. Cited in Pierre Caron, *Les Massacres de septembre* (Paris, 1935), pp. 418–19, 422.
26. Frédéric Bluche, *Septembre 1792: logiques d'un massacre* (Paris, 1986).
27. Antoine de Baecque, *Glory and Terror: Seven Deaths under the French Revolution* (London, 2001), chapter 3.
28. Ado, *Paysans en révolution*, pp. 312–19.
29. Forrest, *Soldiers of the French Revolution*, pp. 66–67.
30. Petitfrère, 'Origins of the Civil War', p. 200.
31. Peter Jones, 'The "Agrarian Law": Schemes for Land Redistribution during the French Revolution', *Past and Present*, 133 (1991), pp. 96–133.
32. This and the following quotation cited in Ado, *Paysans en révolution*, pp. 325–26.
33. McPhee, *Revolution and Environment*, pp. 87–89.
34. Peter M. Jones, *The Peasantry in the French Revolution* (Cambridge, 1988), p. 146.

Notes to Chapter 10: The Year of Civil War

1. Robespierre's remark is cited in Carol Blum, *Rousseau and the Republic of Virtue: The Language of Politics in the French Revolution* (Ithaca, New York, 1986), p. 198; Barère's in George Rudé, *The Crowd in the French Revolution* (Oxford, 1959), p. 118.
2. Alan Forrest, *The Soldiers of the French Revolution* (Durham, North Carolina, 1990), pp. 68–71.
3. Peter M. Jones, *The Peasantry in the French Revolution* (Cambridge, 1988), pp. 223–25.
4. This and the following quotation cited in D. M. G. Sutherland, *The Chouans: The Social Origins of Popular Counter-Revolution in Upper Brittany, 1770–1796* (Oxford, 1982), pp. 260–61.
5. Claude Petitfrère, 'The Origins of the Civil War in the Vendée', *French History*, 2 (1988), pp. 187–207. See also Alain Gérard, *'Par principe d'humanité': la Terreur et la Vendée* (Paris, 1999), and Jean-Clément Martin, *La Vendée et la France* (Paris, 1987).

6. Jean-Clément Martin, 'Histoire et polémique: les massacres de Machecoul', *Annales historiques de la Révolution française*, 291 (1993), pp. 33–60.

7. Jones, *Peasantry*, p. 230.

8. Ibid., pp. 232–33.

9. Cited in David Andress, *French Society in Revolution, 1789–1799* (Manchester, 1999), p. 186.

10. Albert Soboul, *Les sans-culottes parisiens en l'an II: mouvement populaire et gouvernement révolutionnaire* (original publication 1958; Paris, 1968).

11. Cited in H. Morse Stephens (ed.), *The Principal Speeches of the Statesmen and Orators of the French Revolution, 1789–1795* (Oxford, 1892), i, p. 347.

12. Cited in John Hardman (ed.), *French Revolution Documents* (Oxford, 1973), ii, p. 67.

13. Morris Slavin, *The Making of An Insurrection: Parisian Sections and the Gironde* (Cambridge, Massachusetts, 1986).

14. Rudé, *The Crowd in the French Revolution*, pp. 123–24.

15. William Scott, *Terror and Repression in Revolutionary Marseille* (London, 1973), pp. 71–87; William D. Edmonds, *Jacobinism and the Revolt of Lyon, 1789–1793* (Oxford, 1990), chapter 5.

16. Gwynne Lewis, *The Second Vendée: The Continuity of Counter-Revolution in the Department of the Gard, 1789–1815* (Oxford, 1978), pp. 56–59, 63–64.

17. R. B. Rose, *The Enragés: Socialists of the French Revolution?* (Sydney, 1965).

18. Cited in Rose, *The Enragés*, p. 58.

19. Jacques-René Hébert, *Le Père Duchesne*, reprinted in 10 vols. (Paris, 1969), no. 243, p. 7.

20. Cited in Andress, *French Society*, pp. 187–88.

21. This and the following quotation cited in John Hardman, *The French Revolution Sourcebook* (London, 1999), p. 179.

22. Anatoli Ado, *Paysans en révolution: terre, pouvoir et jacquerie 1789–1794* (Paris, 1996), p. 359.

23. Ibid., pp. 380–85.

24. Edmonds, *Jacobinism and the Revolt of Lyon*, pp. 279–80; Jean-Clément Martin, *Guerre et répression: la Vendée et le monde* (Nantes, 1993).

25. Christian A. Muller, 'Du "peuple égaré" au "peuple enfant": le discours politique révolutionnaire à l'épreuve de la révolte populaire en 1793', *Revue d'histoire moderne et contemporaine*, 47 (2000), pp. 93–112.

26. Cited in Keith M. Baker, *The Old Regime and the French Revolution* (Chicago, 1987), pp. 340–41.

27. Diane Ladjouzi, 'Les journées de 4 et 5 septembre 1793 à Paris: un mouvement d'union entre le peuple, la Commune de Paris et la Convention pour un exécutif révolutionnaire', *Annales historiques de la Révolution française*, 321 (2000), pp. 27–44.

28. Rudé, *The Crowd in the French Revolution*, pp. 125–30.

29. Cited in Baker, *Old Regime*, pp. 353–54.

30. Ibid., pp. 338–39.

31. Cited in Muller, 'Du "peuple égaré"', p. 98.
32. Soboul, *Sans-culottes*, pp. 442–51.
33. Edmonds, *Jacobinism and the Revolt of Lyon*, pp. 321–23.
34. Alan Forrest, *Society and Politics in Revolutionary Bordeaux* (London, 1975); Scott, *Terror and Repression*, pp. 346–50.
35. Colin Lucas, *The Structure of the Terror: The Example of Javogues and the Loire* (Oxford, 1973), chapter 2.

Notes to Chapter 11: Terror and Reaction

1. Serge Bianchi, 'La "Bataille du calendrier" ou le décadi contre le dimanche: nouvelles approches pour la réception du calendrier républicain', *Annales historiques de la Révolution française*, 312 (1998), pp. 245–64.
2. Michel Vovelle, *The Revolution against the Church: From Reason to the Supreme Being* (Cambridge, 1991).
3. Serge Bonin and Claude Langlois (eds), *Atlas de la Révolution française*, vi, *Les sociétés politiques* (Paris, 1992).
4. Lynn Hunt, *Politics, Culture and Class in the French Revolution* (London, 1984), chapter 5.
5. Cited in Philippe Goujard, 'L'homme de masse sans les masses ou le déchristianisateur malheureux', *Annales historiques de la Révolution française*, 58 (1986), pp. 160–80; see p. 163.
6. Richard Cobb, *The People's Armies: The Armées Révolutionnaires, Instruments of the Terror in the Departments April 1793 to Floréal Year III* (New Haven, 1987), book 1, chapter 3.
7. Ibid., book 2, chapters 3 and 7.
8. Ibid., p. 271.
9. Patrice Gueniffey, *Le nombre et la raison: la Révolution française et les élections* (Paris, 1993), pp. 386–92.
10. Cited in Cobb, *The People's Armies*, p. 432.
11. Rudé, *The Crowd in the French Revolution* (Oxford, 1959), p. 241, for a full listing of changes.
12. Colin Lucas, *The Structure of the Terror: The Example of Javogues and the Loire* (Oxford, 1973), pp. xiv–xv.
13. Pierre-Henri Billy, 'Les prénoms révolutionnaires en France', *Annales historiques de la Révolution française*, 322 (2000), pp. 39–60.
14. Cited in Goujard, 'L'homme de masse', p. 171.
15. Malcolm Crook, *Toulon in War and Revolution: From the Ancien Régime to the Restoration, 1750–1820* (Manchester, 1991), chapter 6.
16. Claude Petitfrère, 'La Vendée en l'An II: defaite et répression', *Annales historiques de la Révolution française*, 300 (1995), pp. 173–85.
17. Cited in William D. Edmonds, *Jacobinism and the Revolt of Lyon, 1789–1793* (Oxford, 1990), p. 280.
18. Cited in Christian A. Muller, 'Du "peuple égaré" au "peuple enfant": le discours

politique révolutionnaire à l'épreuve de la révolte populaire en 1793', *Revue d'histoire moderne et contemporaine*, 47 (2000), pp. 93–112; see p. 100.

19. Cited in Alain Gérard, *'Par principe d'humanité': La Terreur et La Vendée* (Paris, 1999), p. 23.

20. Ibid., chapters 12–14.

21. This and the following quotation cited in Gérard, *'Par principe'*, p. 26.

22. Cited in D. M. G. Sutherland, *The French Revolution and Empire: The Quest for a Civic Order* (Oxford, 2002), p. 217.

23. Serge Bonin and Claude Langlois (eds), *Atlas de la Révolution française*, viii, *Population* (Paris, 1995), pp. 32–33.

24. Cited in Muller, 'Du "peuple égaré"', p. 101.

25. Cited in D. M. G. Sutherland, *The Chouans: The Social Origins of Popular Counter-Revolution in Upper Brittany, 1770–1796* (Oxford, 1982), p. 291.

26. Richard M. Andrews, 'Social Structures, Political Elites and Ideology in Revolutionary Paris, 1792–4: A Critical Evaluation of Albert Soboul's *Les Sans-Culottes Parisiens …*', *Journal of Social History*, 19 (1985–6), pp. 71–112.

27. Margaret H. Darrow, 'Economic Terror in the City: The General Maximum in Montauban', *French Historical Studies*, 17 (1991), pp. 498–525; see also Andrews, 'Social Structures', for similar suggestions about Paris.

28. Cited in David Andress, *French Society in Revolution, 1789–1799* (Manchester, 1999), p. 191. See also Susan P. Conner, 'Politics, Prostitution and the Pox in Revolutionary Paris, 1789–1799', *Journal of Social History*, 22 (1988), pp. 713–34.

29. Hunt, *Politics, Culture and Class*, esp. chapters 3 and 4; and Dominique Godineau, *The Women of Paris and Their French Revolution* (Berkeley, 1998), chapter 7.

30. Mona Ozouf, *Festivals and the French Revolution* (Cambridge, Massachusetts, 1988).

31. Jean-Pierre Gross, *Fair Shares for All: Jacobin Egalitarianism in Practice* (Cambridge, 1997), pp. 193–99.

32. James A. Leith, *Space and Revolution: Projects for Monuments, Squares and Public Buildings in France, 1789–1799* (Montreal, 1991).

33. Alan Forrest, *The French Revolution and the Poor* (Oxford, 1981), pp. 82–85.

34. Rudé, *The Crowd in the French Revolution*, pp. 131–32; Godineau, *Women of Paris*, chapter 8.

35. Cited in Andress, *French Society*, p. 193.

36. Morris Slavin, *The Hébertistes to the Guillotine: Anatomy of a 'Conspiracy' in Revolutionary France* (Baton Rouge, 1994), pp. 144–50.

37. Lisa DiCaprio, 'Women Workers, State-Sponsored Work, and the Right to Subsistence during the French Revolution', *Journal of Modern History*, 71 (1999), pp. 519–51; see pp. 534–40.

38. Rudé, *The Crowd in the French Revolution*, pp. 132–36.

39. Cited in Rudé, *The Crowd in the French Revolution*, p. 140.

40. Jacques Bernet, 'Les limites de la déchristianisation de l'an II éclairées par le

retour au culte de l'an III: l'exemple du district de Compiègne', *Annales historiques de la Révolution française*, 312 (1998), pp. 285–99.

41. Cited in Anatoli Ado, *Paysans en révolution: terre, pouvoir et jacquerie 1789–1794* (Paris, 1996), pp. 377–78.

42. Richard Cobb, *Terreur et subsistances, 1793–1795* (Paris, 1965), pp. 321–26.

43. Rudé, *The Crowd in the French Revolution*, chapter 10.

44. Cited in Rudé, *The Crowd in the French Revolution*, p. 149.

45. Godineau, *Women of Paris*, chapter 14.

46. Ibid., chapter 15.

47. Cited in Olwen Hufton, *Women and the Limits of Citizenship in the French Revolution* (Toronto, 1992), p. 48.

48. Richard Cobb, *The Police and the People: French Popular Protest, 1789–1820* (Oxford, 1970), part 2, chapter 10.

49. Richard Cobb, *Reactions to the French Revolution* (London, 1972), pp. 75–93.

50. Sophie Faguay, 'Bourgeois du Faubourg Saint-Antoine, 1791–1792', in M. Vovelle (ed.), *Paris et la Révolution; actes du colloque de Paris I, 14–16 avril 1989* (Paris, 1989), pp. 89–95, see p. 92.

51. Cobb, *The Police and the People*, pp. 63–64.

52. Alan Forrest, *The Soldiers of the French Revolution* (Durham, North Carolina, 1990), chapter 4.

Notes to Chapter 12: Revolution against the People?

1. R. B. Rose, *Gracchus Babeuf: The First Revolutionary Communist* (London, 1978).

2. Malcolm Crook, *Napoleon Comes to Power: Democracy and Dictatorship in Revolutionary France, 1795–1804* (Cardiff, 1998).

3. Gwynne Lewis and Colin Lucas (eds), *Beyond the Terror: Essays in French Regional and Social History, 1794–1815* (Cambridge, 1983).

4. Denis Woronoff, *The Thermidorean Regime and the Directory, 1794–1799* (Cambridge, 1984), pp. 91–97.

5. Martin Lyons, *France Under the Directory* (Cambridge, 1975), pp. 175–88.

6. Woronoff, *The Thermidorean Regime*, pp. 125–37.

7. Ken Alder, *The Measure of All Things: The Seven-Year Odyssey and Hidden Error that Transformed the World* (London, 2002). See also Daniel R. Headrick, *When Information Came of Age: Technologies of Knowledge in the Age of the Information Revolution, 1700–1850* (Oxford, 2000), pp. 40–49.

8. James C. Scott, *Seeing Like a State: How Certain Schemes to Improve the Human Condition Have Failed* (New Haven, 1998), chapter 1, 'Nature and Space', esp. pp. 27–33, 36–37.

9. Bernard Bodinier and Éric Teyssier, *L'événement le plus important de la Révolution: la vente des biens nationaux* (Paris, 2000).

10. Colin Jones, *The Longman Companion to the French Revolution* (London, 1988), p. 283.

11. D. M. G. Sutherland, 'Peasants, Lords and Leviathan: Winners and Losers from the Abolition of French Feudalism, 1780–1820', *Journal of Economic History*, 62 (2002), pp. 1–24.

12. Suzanne Desan, '"War Between Brothers and Sisters": Inheritance Law and Gender Politics in Revolutionary France', *French Historical Studies*, 20 (1997), pp. 597–634.

13. Paul G. Spagnoli, 'The Unique Decline of Mortality in Revolutionary France', *Journal of Family History*, 22 (1997), pp. 425–61.

14. Alan Forrest, *The French Revolution and the Poor* (Oxford, 1981), chapter 8, and idem. *The Soldiers of the French Revolution* (Durham, North Carolina, 1990), pp. 82–88.

15. Cited in Corelli Barnett, *Bonaparte* (London, 1978), p. 41.

16. Alan Forrest, *Conscripts and Deserters: The Army and French Society during the Revolution and Empire* (Oxford, 1989), esp. chapters 5 and 6.

17. Gwynne Lewis, 'Political Brigandage and Popular Disaffection in the South-East of France, 1795–1804', in Lewis and Lucas, *Beyond the Terror*, pp. 195–231.

18. Colin Lucas, 'Themes in Southern Violence after 9 Thermidor', in Lewis and Lucas, *Beyond the Terror*, pp. 152–94.

19. D. M. G. Sutherland, *The French Revolution and Empire: The Quest for a Civic Order* (Oxford, 2002), pp. 274–77.

20. Forrest, *Conscripts and Deserters*, p. 124.

21. Richard Cobb, *Reactions to the French Revolution* (London, 1972), chapter 5.

22. Forrest, *Conscripts and Deserters*, pp. 133–34.

23. Lyons, *France Under the Directory*, pp. 161–67.

24. Jonathan D. Devlin, 'The Army, Politics and Public Order in Directorial Provence, 1795–1800', *Historical Journal*, 32 (1989), pp. 87–106; see also Howard G. Brown, 'From Organic Society to Security State: The War on Brigandage in France, 1797–1802', *Journal of Modern History*, 69 (1997), pp. 661–95.

25. Cited in Suzanne Desan, *Reclaiming the Sacred: Lay Religion and Popular Politics in Revolutionary France* (Ithaca, New York, 1990), p. 154.

26. Cited in Desan, *Reclaiming the Sacred*, p. 159.

27. Cited in Olwen Hufton, *Women and the Limits of Citizenship in the French Revolution* (Toronto, 1992), pp. 116–17.

28. Olwen Hufton, 'The Reconstruction of a Church, 1796–1801', in Lewis and Lucas, *Beyond the Terror*, pp. 21–52.

29. Desan, *Reclaiming the Sacred*, chapter 3.

30. Lyons, *France Under the Directory*, chapter 7, and Woronoff, *The Thermidorean Regime*, pp. 119–24.

31. Donald Greer, *The Incidence of the Terror during the French Revolution: A Statistical Interpretation* (Gloucester, Massachusetts, 1966), esp. totals on p. 163.

32. Jill Maciak, 'Of News and Networks: The Communication of Political Information in the Rural Southwest during the French Revolution', *French History*, 15 (2001), pp. 273–306; see pp. 297–98.

33. Jacques-Louis Ménétra, *Journal of My Life* introduction and commentary by

Daniel Roche, translated by Arthur Goldhammer (New York, 1986), pp. 217–18. The original text is unpunctuated throughout. Minimum punctuation has been added here for clarity.

34. Ménétra, *Journal*, pp. 219, 222–23.
35. Ibid., p. 223.
36. Ibid., pp. 236–37.
37. Ibid., pp. 217–18.
38. Cited in Desan, *Reclaiming the Sacred*, pp. 142–43.
39. Developments after 1800 are outside the remit of this book, but for some thoughtful overviews, see Peter McPhee, *A Social History of France, 1780–1880* (London, 1992); Robert Tombs, *France, 1814–1914* (London, 1996); and Malcolm Crook (ed.), *Revolutionary France, 1788–1880* (Oxford, 2002).

Bibliography

Adams, Christine, *A Taste for Comfort and Status: A Bourgeois Family in Eighteenth-Century France* (University Park, Pennsylvania, 2000).

Adams, Thomas McStay, *Bureaucrats and Beggars: French Social Policy in the Age of the Enlightenment* (Oxford, 1990).

Ado, Anatoli, *Paysans en révolution: terre, pouvoir et jacquerie, 1789–1794* (Paris, 1996).

Aftalion, Florin, *The French Revolution: An Economic Interpretation* (Cambridge, 1990).

Albertone, M., 'Une histoire oubliée: les assignats dans l'historiographie', *Annales historiques de la Révolution française*, 287 (1992), pp. 87–104.

Alder, Ken, *The Measure of All Things: The Seven-Year Odyssey and Hidden Error that Transformed the World* (London, 2002).

Andress, David, *French Society in Revolution, 1789–1799* (Manchester, 1999).

—, *Massacre at the Champ de Mars: Popular Dissent and Political Culture in the French Revolution* (Woodbridge, 2000).

Andrews, Richard M., 'Social Structures, Political Elites and Ideology in Revolutionary Paris, 1792–4: a Critical Evaluation of Albert Soboul's *Les Sans-Culottes Parisiens* …', *Journal of Social History*, 19 (1985–86), pp. 71–112.

Aston, Nigel, *Religion and Revolution in France, 1780–1804* (Basingstoke, 2000).

Astoul, Guy, 'Solidarités paysannes au pays des croquants au XVIIIe siècle', *Annales historiques de la Révolution française* 311 (1998), pp. 25–48.

Baczko, Bronislaw, *Ending the Terror: The French Revolution after Robespierre* (Cambridge, 1994).

Baecque, Antoine de, *The Body Politic: Corporeal Metaphor in Revolutionary France, 1770–1800* (Stanford, 1997).

—, *Glory and Terror: Seven Deaths under the French Revolution* (London, 2001).

Baker, Keith M., *The Old Regime and the French Revolution* (Chicago, 1987).

Barnett, Corelli, *Bonaparte* (London, 1978).

Bell, David A., *The Cult of the Nation in France: Inventing Nationalism, 1680–1800* (Cambridge, Massachusetts, 2001).

Benabou, Erica-Marie, *La prostitution et la police des moeurs au XVIIIe siècle* (Paris, 1987).

Bendjebbar, André, *La vie quotidienne en Anjou au XVIII$_e$ siècle* (Paris, 1983).

Bernet, Jacques, 'Les limites de la déchristianisation de l'an II éclairées par le retour au culte de l'an III: l'exemple du district de Compiègne', *Annales historiques de la Révolution française*, 312 (1998), pp. 285–99.

Bertaud, Jean-Paul, *La Révolution armée: les soldats-citoyens et la Révolution française* (Paris, 1979).

Best, Geoffrey (ed.), *The Permanent Revolution: The French Revolution and its Legacy, 1789–1989* (London, 1988).

Bianchi, Serge, 'La "bataille du calendrier" ou le décadi contre le dimanche: nouvelles approches pour la réception du calendrier républicain', *Annales historiques de la Révolution française*, 312 (1998), pp. 245–64.

—, Michel Biard, Alan Forrest, Edouard Gruter and Jean Jacquart, *La terre et les paysans en France et en Grande-Bretagne du début du XVIIe à la fin du XVIIIe siècle* (Paris, 1999).

Bienvenu, Richard (ed.), *The Ninth of Thermidor: The Fall of Robespierre* (London, 1968).

Billy, Pierre-Henri, 'Les prénoms révolutionnaires en France', *Annales historiques de la Révolution française*, 322 (2000), pp. 39–60.

Blanning, T. C. W., *The French Revolutionary Wars, 1787–1802* (London, 1996).

—, *The Origins of the French Revolutionary Wars* (London, 1986).

Bluche, Frédéric, *Septembre 1792: logiques d'un massacre* (Paris, 1986).

Blum, Carol, *Rousseau and the Republic of Virtue: The Language of Politics in the French Revolution* (Ithaca, New York, 1986).

Bodinier, Bernard, and Eric Teyssier, *L'événement le plus important de la Révolution: la vente des biens nationaux* (Paris, 2000).

Bonin, Serge, and Claude Langlois (eds), *Atlas de la Révolution française*, vi, *Les sociétés politiques* (Paris, 1992).

—, *Atlas de la Révolution française*, viii, *Population* (Paris, 1995).

Bourdin, Isabelle, *Les sociétés populaires à Paris pendant la Révolution* (Paris, 1937).

Bouton, Cynthia, *The Flour War: Gender, Class and Community in Late Ancien Régime French Society* (University Park, Pennsylvania, 1993).

—, 'Les syndics des villages du Bassin parisien des années 1750 à la Révolution', in Roger Dupuy (ed.), *Pouvoir local et révolution 1780–1850: la frontière intérieure* (Rennes, 1995).

Brennan, Thomas, *Public Drinking and Popular Culture in Eighteenth-Century Paris* (Princeton, 1988).

Brezis, E. S., and F. Crouzet, 'The Role of Assignats during the French Revolution: An Evil or a Rescuer?', *Journal of European Economic History*, 24 (1995), pp. 7–40.

Brown, Howard G., 'From Organic Society to Security State: The War on Brigandage in France, 1797–1802', *Journal of Modern History*, 69 (1997), pp. 661–95.

Burguière, André, 'La Révolution française et la famille', *Annales ESC*, 1991, pp. 151–68.

Butel, Paul, and Jean-Pierre Poussou, *La vie quotidienne à Bordeaux au XVIIIe siècle* (Paris, 1980).

Cabourdin, Guy, *La vie quotidienne en Lorraine aux XVIIe et XVIIIe siècles* (Paris, 1984).

Cameron, Euan (ed.), *Early Modern Europe: An Oxford History* (Oxford, 2001).

Caron, Pierre, *Les Massacres de septembre* (Paris, 1935).

Censer, Jack, *Prelude to Power: The Parisian Radical Press, 1789–1791* (London, 1976).

Chartier, Roger, *The Cultural Origins of the French Revolution* (Durham, North Carolina, 1991).

Clifford, Dale L., 'The National Guard and the Parisian Community', *French Historical Studies*, 16 (1990), pp. 849–78.

Cobb, Richard, *Reactions to the French Revolution* (London, 1972).

—, *Terreur et subsistances, 1793–1795* (Paris, 1965).

—, *The People's Armies: the armées révolutionnaires, instruments of the Terror in the departments April 1793 to Floréal Year III* (New Haven, 1987).

—, *The Police and the People: French Popular Protest 1789–1820* (Oxford, 1970).

Cobban, Alfred, *The Social Interpretation of the French Revolution* (2nd edn, Cambridge, 1999).

Coffin, Judith G., 'Gender and the Guild Order: The Garment Trades in Eighteenth-Century Paris', *Journal of Economic History*, 54 (1994), pp. 768–93.

Conner, Susan P., 'Politics, Prostitution and the Pox in Revolutionary Paris, 1789–1799', *Journal of Social History*, 22 (1988), pp. 713–34.

Coquard, Olivier, *Jean-Paul Marat* (Paris, 1993).

Corbin, Alain, *Village Bells: Sound and Meaning in the Nineteenth Century French Countryside* (London, 1998).

Crook, Malcolm, *Elections in the French Revolution: An Apprenticeship in Democracy, 1789–99* (Cambridge, 1996).

—, *Napoleon Comes to Power: Democracy and Dictatorship in Revolutionary France, 1795–1804* (Cardiff, 1998).

—, *Toulon in War and Revolution: From the ancien régime to the Restoration, 1750–1820* (Manchester, 1991).

— (ed.), *Revolutionary France, 1788–1880* (Oxford, 2002).

Crouzet, François, *La grande inflation: la monnaie en France de Louis XVI à Napoléon* (Paris, 1993).

Crowston, Clare, 'Engendering the Guilds: Seamstresses, Tailors and the Clash of Corporate Identities in Old Regime France', *French Historical Studies*, 23 (2000), pp. 339–71.

—, 'The Queen and her "Minister of Fashion": Gender, Credit and Politics in Pre-Revolutionary France', *Gender and History*, 14 (2002), pp. 92–116.

Darnton, Robert, *Mesmerism and the End of the Enlightenment in France* (Cambridge, Massachusetts, 1968).

—, *The Forbidden Bestsellers of Prerevolutionary France* (New York, 1995).

Darrow, Margaret H., 'Economic Terror in the City: The General Maximum in Montauban', *French Historical Studies*, 17 (1991), pp. 498–525.

Desan, Suzanne, *Reclaiming the Sacred: Lay religion and popular politics in revolutionary France* (Ithaca, 1990).

—, '"War Between Brothers and Sisters": Inheritance Law and Gender Politics in Revolutionary France', *French Historical Studies*, 20 (1997), pp. 597–634.

Devlin, Jonathan D., 'The Army, Politics and Public Order in Directorial Provence, 1795–1800', *Historical Journal* 32 (1989), pp. 87–106.

DiCaprio, Lisa, 'Women Workers, State-Sponsored Work, and the Right to Subsistence during the French Revolution', *Journal of Modern History*, 71 (1999), pp. 519–51.

Doyle, William, *Origins of the French Revolution* (3rd edn, Oxford, 1999).

—, *The Oxford History of the French Revolution* (Oxford, 1989).

— (ed.), *Old Regime France, 1648–1788* (Oxford, 2001).

Edelstein, Melvin, 'Les administrateurs du Haut-Rhin en 1790: aspects sociaux', *Annales historiques de la Révolution française*, 327 (2002), pp. 75–81.

Edmonds, William D., '"Federalism" and Urban Revolt in France in 1793', *Journal of Modern History* 55 (1983), pp. 22–53.

—, *Jacobinism and the Revolt of Lyon, 1789–1793* (Oxford, 1990).

Egret, Jean, *The French Prerevolution, 1787–1788* (Chicago, 1977).

Emsley, Clive, 'La Maréchaussée à la fin de l'ancien régime: note sur la composition du corps', *Revue d'histoire moderne et contemporaine*, 33 (1986), pp. 622–44.

Faguay, Sophie, 'Bourgeois du faubourg Saint-Antoine, 1791–1792', in M. Vovelle (ed.), *Paris et la Révolution: actes du colloque de Paris I, 14–16 avril 1989* (Paris, 1989), pp. 89–95.

Fairchilds, Cissie, *Domestic Enemies: Servants and their Masters in Old Regime France* (Baltimore, 1984).

Farge, Arlette, *Fragile Lives: Violence, Power and Solidarity in Eighteenth-Century Paris* (Cambridge, 1993).

—, *Subversive Words: Public Opinion in Eighteenth-Century France* (Cambridge, 1994).

—, and Jacques Revel, *The Rules of Rebellion: Child Abductions in Paris in 1750* (Cambridge, 1991).

Fitzsimmons, Michael P., *The Remaking of France: The National Assembly and the Constitution of 1791* (Cambridge, 1994).

Forrest, Alan, *Conscripts and Deserters: The Army and French Society during the Revolution and Empire* (Oxford, 1989).

—, 'Federalism', in Colin Lucas (eds), *The French Revolution and the Creation of Modern Political Culture*, ii, *The Political Culture of the French Revolution* (Oxford, 1988), pp. 309–25.

—, *Society and Politics in Revolutionary Bordeaux* (London, 1975).

—, *The French Revolution and the Poor* (Oxford, 1981).

—, *The Soldiers of the French Revolution* (Durham, North Carolina, 1990).

Forster, Robert, and Elborg Forster (ed.), *European Society in the Eighteenth Century* (London, 1969)

Foucault, Michel, *Discipline and Punish: The Birth of the Prison* (Harmondsworth, 1977).

Freeman, Andrew, *The Compromising of Louis XVI: The Armoire de Fer and the French Revolution* (Exeter, 1989).

Furet, François, *The French Revolution, 1770–1814* (Oxford, 1996).

Garrioch, David, *Neighbourhood and Community in Paris, 1740–1790* (Cambridge, 1986).

—, 'The Everyday Lives of Parisian Women and the October Days of 1789', *Social History*, 24 (1999), pp. 231–49.

—, *The Formation of the Parisian Bourgeoisie, 1690–1830* (Cambridge, Massachusetts, 1996).

—, *The Making of Revolutionary Paris* (Berkeley, 2002).

—, and Michael Sonenscher, '*Compagnonnages*, Confraternities and Associations of Journeymen in Eighteenth-Century Paris', *European History Quarterly*, 16 (1986), pp. 25–45.

Gelbart, Nina, *The King's Midwife: A History and Mystery of Madame du Coudray* (Berkeley, 1998).

Genty, Maurice, *Paris, 1789–1795: l'apprentissage de la citoyenneté* (Paris, 1987).

Gérard, Alain, '*Par principe d'humanité': la Terreur et la Vendée* (Paris, 1999).

Godechot, Jacques, *The Counter-Revolution: Doctrine and Action 1789–1804* (Princeton, 1971).

—, *The Taking of the Bastille, July 14th 1789* (London, 1970).

Godineau, Dominique, *The Women of Paris and Their French Revolution* (Berkeley, 1998).

Goujard, Philippe, 'L'homme de masse sans les masses ou le déchristianisateur malheureux', *Annales historiques de la Révolution française*, 58 (1986), pp. 160–80.

Greer, Donald, *The Incidence of the Terror during the French Revolution: A Statistical Interpretation* (Gloucester, Massachusetts, 1966).

Gross, Jean-Pierre, *Fair Shares for All: Jacobin Egalitarianism in Practice* (Cambridge, 1997).

Gueniffey, Patrice, *La politique de la terreur: essai sur la violence révolutionnaire, 1789–1794* (Paris, 2000).

—, *Le nombre et la raison: la Révolution française et les élections* (Paris, 1993).

Guilhaumou, Jacques, *L'avènement des porte-parole de la République (1789–1792): essai de synthèse sur les langages de la Révolution française* (Lille, 1998).

Gutton, Jean-Pierre, *La sociabilité villageoise dans l'ancienne France* (Paris, 1979).

Hafter, Daryl, 'Female Masters in the Ribbonmaking Guild of Eighteenth-Century Rouen', *French Historical Studies*, 20 (1997), pp. 1–14.

Hampson, Norman, *Danton* (London, 1978).

—, *Prelude to Terror; The Constituent Assembly and the Failure of Consensus, 1789–1791* (Oxford, 1988).

Hanson, Paul R., *The Jacobin Republic Under Fire: The Federalist Revolt in the French Revolution* (University Park, Pennsylvania, 2003).

Hardman, John (ed.) *French Revolution Documents* (Oxford, 1973).

—, *The French Revolution Sourcebook* (London, 1999).

Headrick, Daniel R., *When Information Came of Age: Technologies of Knowledge in the Age of the Information Revolution, 1700–1850* (Oxford, 2000).

Hébert, Jacques-René, *Le Père Duchesne* (reprinted in 10 vols, Paris, 1969).

Higonnet, Patrice, *Goodness Beyond Virtue: Jacobins during the French Revolution* (Cambridge, Massachusetts, 1998).

Hollander, Paul d', 'Les Gardes nationales en Limousin (juillet 1789 – juillet 1790)', *Annales historiques de la Révolution française*, 290 (1992), pp. 465–89.

Horn, Jeff, 'The Legacy of 14 July 1789 in the Cultural History of French Industrialisation', unpublished paper presented to the Society for French Historical Studies, 47th Annual Meeting, 8–10 March 2001, Chapel Hill, North Carolina.

Hufton, Olwen H., 'Attitudes towards Authority in Eighteenth-Century Languedoc', *Social History*, 3 (1978), pp. 281–302.

—, *The Poor of Eighteenth-Century France, 1750–1789* (Oxford, 1974).

—, 'The Reconstruction of a Church, 1796–1801', in Lewis and Lucas, *Beyond the Terror*, pp. 21–52.

—, *Women and the Limits of Citizenship in the French Revolution* (Toronto, 1992).

Hunt, Lynn, *Politics, Culture and Class in the French Revolution* (London, 1984).

Jaume, Lucien, *Le discours jacobin et la démocratie* (Paris, 1989).

Johnson, Hubert C., *The Midi in Revolution: A Study of Regional Political Diversity, 1789–1793* (Princeton, 1986).

Jones, Colin, *The Great Nation: France from Louis XV to Napoleon 1715–99* (London, 2002).

—, *The Longman Companion to the French Revolution* (London, 1988).

—, and Rebecca Spang, 'Sans-Culottes, *Sans Café, Sans Tabac*: Shifting Realms of Necessity and Luxury in Eighteenth-Century France', in Maxine Berg and Helen Clifford (ed.), *Consumers and Luxury; Consumer Culture in Europe, 1650–1850* (Manchester, 1999), pp. 37–62.

Jones, Peter M., *Reform and Revolution in France: The Politics of Transition, 1774–1791* (Cambridge, 1995).

—, 'The "Agrarian Law": Schemes for Land Redistribution during the French Revolution', *Past and Present*, 133 (1991), pp. 96–133.

—, *The Peasantry in the French Revolution* (Cambridge, 1988).

Jordan, David P., *The King's Trial: The French Revolution versus Louis XVI* (Berkeley, 1979).

Kaplan, Steven L., *La fin des corporations* (Paris, 2001).

—, 'La lutte pour la contrôle du marché du travail à Paris au XVIIIe siècle', *Revue d'histoire moderne et contemporaine*, 36 (1989), pp. 361–412.

—, 'Social classification and representation in the corporate world of eighteenth-century France: Turgot's "carnival"', in Steven L. Kaplan and Cynthia J. Koepp (eds), *Work in France: Representations, Meaning, Organization and Practice* (Ithaca, New York, 1986), pp. 176–228.

—, 'The character and implications of strife amongst masters in the guilds of eighteenth-century Paris', *Journal of Social History*, 19 (1985–86), pp. 631–47.

—, *The Famine Plot Persuasion in Eighteenth-Century France* (Philadelphia, 1982).

Kaplow, Jeffry, *The Names of Kings: The Parisian Laboring Poor in the Eighteenth Century* (New York, 1972).

Kates, Gary (ed.), *The French Revolution: Recent Debates and New Controversies* (London, 1998).

Kennedy, Michael L., *The Jacobin Clubs in the French Revolution; The First Years* (Princeton, 1981).

Lacroix, Sigismond, *Actes de la Commune de Paris pendant la Révolution*, 1st series, vol. 1 (Paris, 1894).

Ladjouzi, Diane, 'Les journées de 4 et 5 septembre 1793 à Paris: un mouvement d'union entre le peuple, la Commune de Paris et la Convention pour un exécutif révolutionnaire', *Annales historiques de la Révolution française*, 321 (2000), pp. 27–44.

Lefebvre, Georges, *Les paysans du Nord pendant la Révolution française* (originally published 1924; reprinted Paris, 1972).

—, *The Great Fear of 1789* (original publication 1932; translated by Joan White, London, 1973).

Le Goff, T. J. A., and D. M. G. Sutherland, 'The Revolution and the Rural Community in Eighteenth-Century Brittany', *Past and Present* 62 (1974), pp. 96–107.

Leith, James A., *Space and Revolution: Projects for Monuments, Squares and Public Buildings in France, 1789–1799* (Montreal, 1991).

Leroy, Charles, *Paysans normands au XVIIIe siècle: la vie rurale* (original publication 1904; reprinted Brionne, 1978).

Lewis, Gwynne, 'Political Brigandage and Popular Disaffection in the South-east of France, 1795–1804', in Lewis and Lucas, *Beyond the Terror*, pp. 195–231.

—, *The Advent of Modern Capitalism in France, 1770–1840: The Contribution of Pierre-François Tubeuf* (Oxford, 1993).

—, *The Second Vendée: The Continuity of Counter-Revolution in the Department of the Gard, 1789–1815* (Oxford, 1978).

Lewis, Gwynne, and Colin Lucas (eds), *Beyond the Terror: Essays in French Regional and Social History, 1794–1815* (Cambridge, 1983).

Lucas, Colin, Talking About Urban Popular Violence in 1789', in Alan Forrest and Peter Jones (ed.), *Reshaping France: Town Country and Region during the French Revolution* (Manchester, 1991), pp. 122–36.

—, 'Themes in Southern Violence after 9 Thermidor', in Lewis and Lucas, *Beyond the Terror*, pp. 152–94.

—, *The Structure of the Terror: The Example of Javogues and the Loire* (Oxford, 1973).

Lyons, Martin, *France under the Directory* (Cambridge, 1975).

McManners, John, *Church and Society in Eighteenth-Century France* 2 vols (Oxford, 1998).

McPhee, Peter, *A Social History of France, 1780–1880* (London, 1992).

—, *Revolution and Environment in Southern France 1780–1830: Peasants, Lords and Murder in the Corbières* (Oxford, 1999).

—, *The French Revolution, 1789–1799* (Oxford, 2002).

—, '"The Misguided Greed of Peasants"? Popular Attitudes to the Environment in the Revolution of 1789', *French Historical Studies* 24 (2001), pp. 247–69.

Maciak, Jill, 'Of News and Networks: The Communication of Political Information in the Rural Southwest during the French Revolution', *French History*, 15 (2001), pp. 273–306.

Margadant, Ted W., *Urban Rivalries in the French Revolution* (Princeton, 1992).

Markoff, John, *The Abolition of Feudalism: Peasants, Lords and Legislators in the French Revolution* (University Park, Pennsylvania, 1996).

Martin, Jean-Clément, *Guerre et répression; la Vendée et le monde* (Nantes, 1993).

—, 'Histoire et polémique, less massacres de Machecoul', *Annales historiques de la Révolution française*, 291 (1993), pp. 33–60.

—, *La Vendée et la France* (Paris, 1987).

Mason, Laura, and Tracey Rizzo (eds), *The French Revolution: A Document Collection* (Boston, Massachusetts, 1999).

Mathiez, Albert, *La vie chère et le mouvement social sous la terreur* (Paris, 1927).

—, *Le club des Cordeliers pendant la crise de Varennes et la massacre du Champ de Mars* (Paris, 1910 reprinted Geneva, 1975).

Maza, Sarah C., *Servants and Masters in Eighteenth-Century France: The Uses of Loyalty* (Princeton, 1983).

Ménétra, Jacques-Louis, *Journal of My Life* introduction and commentary by Daniel Roche, translated by Arthur Goldhammer (New York, 1986).

Mercier, Louis-Sébastien, *Le tableau de Paris* selected by J. Kaplow (Paris, 1979).

Merrick, Jeffrey, 'Commissioner Foucault, Inspector Noël, and the "Pederasts" of Paris, 1780–83', *Journal of Social History*, 32 (1998), pp. 287–307.

Miller, Stephen S., 'Lords, Peasant Communities and the State in Eighteenth-Century Languedoc', *French Historical Studies*, 26 (2003), pp. 55–86.

Mitchell, C. J., *The French Legislative Assembly of 1791* (Leiden, 1988).

Monnier, Raymonde, *L'espace public démocratique: essai sur l'opinion à Paris de la Révolution au Directoire* (Paris, 1994).

Muller, Christian A., 'Du "peuple égaré" au "peuple enfant": le discours politique révolutionnaire à l'épreuve de la révolte populaire en 1793', *Revue d'histoire moderne et contemporaine*, 47 (2000), pp. 93–112.

Musgrave, Elizabeth C., 'Women in the Male World of Work: The Building Industries of Eighteenth-Century Brittany', *French History*, 7 (1989), pp. 30–52.

Outram, Dorinda, *The Enlightenment* (Cambridge, 1995).

Ozouf, Mona, *Festivals and the French Revolution* (Cambridge, Massachusetts, 1988).

Palmer, R. R., *Twelve Who Ruled: The Year of the Terror in the French Revolution* (original publication 1941; Princeton, 1970).

Parker, Noel, *Portrayals of Revolution: Images, Debates and Patterns of Thought on the French Revolution* (Carbondale, 1990).

Patrick, Alison, *The Men of the First French Republic: Political Alignments in the National Convention of 1792* (Baltimore, 1972).

Petitfrère, Claude, 'La Vendée en l'an II: defaite et répression', *Annales historiques de la Révolution française*, 300 (1995), pp. 173–85.

——, 'The Origins of the Civil War in the Vendée', *French History*, 2 (1988), pp. 187–207.

Phillips, Roderick, 'Women, Neighborhood, and Family in the Late Eighteenth Century', *French Historical Studies*, 18 (1993), pp. 1–12.

Poitrineau, Abel, *La vie rurale en Basse-Auvergne au XVIIIe siècle (1726–1789)* (Marseille, 1979).

Popkin, Jeremy D., *Revolutionary News: The Press in France, 1789–1799* (London, 1990).

Poulet, Jean-François, *La vie quotidienne dans les Pyrénées sous l'ancien régime* (Paris, 1974).

Ramsay, Clay, *The Ideology of the Great Fear: The Soissonnais in 1789* (Baltimore, 1992).

Reinhard, Marcel, *La chute de la royauté* (Paris, 1969).

Reinhardt, Steven G., *Justice in the Sarladais 1770–1790* (Baton Rouge, 1991).

Roche, Daniel, *A History of Everyday Things: The Birth of Consumption in France, 1600–1800* (Cambridge, 2000).

——, *The People of Paris: An Essay in Popular Culture in the Eighteenth Century* (Leamington Spa, 1987).

Root, Hilton, *Peasants and King in Burgundy: Agrarian Foundations of French Absolutism* (Berkeley, 1987).

Rose, R. B., *Gracchus Babeuf: The First Revolutionary Communist* (London, 1978).

—, *The Enragés: Socialists of the French Revolution?* (Sydney, 1965).

—, *The Making of the Sans-culottes: Democratic Ideas and Institutions in Paris, 1789–1792* (Manchester, 1983).

Rudé, George, *The Crowd in the French Revolution* (Oxford, 1959).

Ruff, Julius R., *Crime, Justice and Public Order in Old Regime France: The Sénéchaussées of Libourne and Bazas, 1696–1789* (London, 1984).

Schama, Simon, *Citizens: a Chronicle of the French Revolution* (London, 1989).

Schechter, Ronald (ed.), *The French Revolution: The Essential Readings* (Oxford, 2001).

Schwartz, Robert M., *Policing the Poor in Eighteenth-Century France* (Chapel Hill, North Carolina, 1988).

Scott, James C., *Seeing Like A State: How Certain Schemes to Improve the Human Condition Have Failed* (New Haven, 1998).

Scott, William, *Terror and Repression in Revolutionary Marseille* (London, 1973).

Sewell, William H. Jr, 'Historical Events as Transformations of Structures: Inventing Revolution at the Bastille', *Theory and Society*, 25 (1996), pp. 841–81.

Shapiro, Barry M., *Revolutionary Justice in Paris, 1789–1790* (Cambridge, 1993).

Slavin, Morris, *The Hébertistes to the Guillotine: Anatomy of a 'Conspiracy' in Revolutionary France* (Baton Rouge, 1994).

—, *The Making of an Insurrection: Parisian Sections and the Gironde* (Cambridge, Massachusetts, 1986).

Soboul, Albert, *Les sans-culottes parisians en l'an II: mouvement populaire et gouvernement révolutionnaire* (original publication 1958; Paris, 1968).

—, *The French Revolution* 2 vols (London, 1974).

Sonenscher, Michael, 'Artisans, Sans-culottes and the French Revolution', in Alan Forrest and Peter Jones (ed.), *Reshaping France: Town, Country and Region in the French Revolution* (Manchester, 1991), pp. 105–121.

—, 'Journeymen, the courts and the French trades, 1781–1791', *Past and Present*, 114 (1987), pp. 77–109.

—, *Work and Wages: Natural Law, Politics and the Eighteenth-Century French Trades* (Cambridge, 1989).

Spagnoli, Paul G., 'The Revolution Begins: Lambesc's Charge, 12 July 1789', *French Historical Studies*, 17 (1991), pp. 466–97.

—, 'The Unique Decline of Mortality in Revolutionary France', *Journal of Family History*, 22 (1997), pp. 425–61.

Stephens, H. Morse (ed.) *The Principal Speeches of the Statesmen and Orators of the French Revolution, 1789–1795* (Oxford, 1892).

Stewart, John Hall, *A Documentary Survey of the French Revolution* (New York, 1951).

Stone, Bailey, *Reinterpreting the French Revolution: A Global-Historical Perspective* (Cambridge, 2002).

Sutherland, D. M. G., *France 1789–1815: Revolution and Counterrevolution* (London, 1985).

—, 'Peasants, Lords and Leviathan: Winners and Losers from the Abolition of French Feudalism, 1780–1820', *Journal of Economic History* 62 (2002), pp. 1–24.

—, *The Chouans: The Social Origins of Popular Counter-Revolution in Upper Brittany, 1770–1796* (Oxford, 1982).

—, *The French Revolution and Empire: The Quest for a Civic Order* (Oxford, 2002).

Tackett, Timothy, *Becoming A Revolutionary: The Deputies of the French National Assembly and the Emergence of a Revolutionary Political Culture (1789–1790)* (Princeton, 1996).

—, *Religion, Revolution and Regional Culture in Eighteenth-Century France: the Ecclesiastical Oath of 1791* (Princeton, 1986).

—, 'The West in France in 1789: The Religious Factor in the Origins of the Counterrevolution', *Journal of Modern History*, 54 (1982), pp. 715–45.

Thillay, Alain, *Le Faubourg Saint-Antoine et ses 'faux-ouvriers': la liberté du travail à Paris aux XVIIe et XVIIIe siècles* (Seyssel, 2002).

Thomas, Chantal, *The Wicked Queen: The Origins of the Myth of Marie-Antoinette* (London, 1999).

Tilly, Charles, *The Vendée* (London, 1964).

Tombs, Robert, *France, 1814–1914* (London, 1996).

Tournerie, Jean-André, *Criminels et vagabonds au siècle des lumières* (Paris, 1997).

Upton, Anthony F., *Europe, 1600–1789* (London, 2001).

Vardi, Liana, *The Land and the Loom: Peasants and Profit in Northern France, 1680–1800* (Durham, North Carolina, 1993).

Vovelle, Michel, *The Revolution against the Church: From Reason to the Supreme Being* (Cambridge, 1991).

Whaley, Leigh, 'Political Factions and the Second Revolution: The Insurrection of 10 August 1792', *French History*, 7 (1993)

—, *Radicals: Politics and Republicanism in the French Revolution* (Stroud, 2000).

Williams, Alan, *The Police of Paris, 1718–1789* (Baton Rouge, 1979).

Woloch, Isser, 'From Charity to Welfare in Revolutionary Paris', *Journal of Modern History*, 58 (1986), pp. 779–812.

—, *The New Regime: Transformations of the French Civic Order, 1789–1820s* (New York, 1994).

Woronoff, Denis, *The Thermidorean Regime and the Directory, 1794–1799* (Cambridge, 1984).

Index

Lightning Source UK Ltd.
Milton Keynes UK
UKOW04f1807210814

237336UK00002B/138/P